THE GEOGRAPHY OF DEATH: MORTALITY ATLAS OF BRITISH COLUMBIA, 1985-1989

Western Geographical Series, Volume 26

editorial address

Harold D. Foster, Ph.D.
Department of Geography
University of Victoria
Victoria, British Columbia
Canada

Publication of the Western Geographical Series has been generously supported by the Leon and Thea Koerner Foundation, the Social Science Federation of Canada, the National Centre for Atmospheric Research, the International Geographical Union Congress, the University of Victoria, the Natural Sciences Engineering Research Council of Canada, the Institute of the North American West, and the British Columbia Ministry of Health and Ministry Responsible for Seniors.

The Geography of Death: Mortality Atlas of British Columbia, 1985-1989

(Western geographical series; ISSN 0315-2022; v. 26)
Includes bibliographical references.
ISBN 0-919838-16-2

1. Mortality--British Columbia--Atlases. 2. Mortality--British Columbia--Statistics. I. Foster, Leslie T., II. Edgell, Michael C.R. III. University of Victoria (B.C.). Dept. of Geography. IV. British Columbia. Division of Vital Statistics. V. Series.

HB1360.B7G45 1992   306.6'4'097110223   C92-091309-1

ACKNOWLEDGEMENTS

Throughout the two years that it has taken to bring this atlas into production, many individuals have provided advice, comment, and contributions. In the early stages of development Dr. Bob Evans and Dr. Clyde Hertzman at the University of British Columbia, Dr. Michael Hayes at Simon Fraser University, and Mr. John Spinelli at the British Columbia Cancer Agency provided advice on formats and statistical techniques. Later the Division of Vital Statistics collaborated with the Department of Geography at the University of Victoria in order to produce the atlas. Important data also were supplied by the Planning and Statistics Division of the Ministry of Finance and Corporate Relations. Toward the end of the project statistical advice was provided by Dr. Mike Hunter at the University of Victoria. Dr. Arminée Kazanjian at the University of British Columbia provided advice on Health Human Resource data included in this volume. Mr. Ron Danderfer, Executive Director of the Division of Vital Statistics, ensured that adequate resources were devoted to this project and managed time allocation. This atlas, however, would not have been completed without the financial assistance of the Department of Geography at the University of Victoria and the dedication of staff at the Division of Vital Statistics and the Department of Geography, who undertook statistical, design, narrative, and editorial tasks. These staff rose beyond the normal call of duty in responding to suggestions and changing directions as the atlas evolved. Any errors, omissions, or confusions, however, are the sole responsibility of the editors.

Leslie T. Foster   Michael C.R. Edgell
Assistant Deputy Minister   Chair
Ministry of Health and   Department of Geography
Ministry Responsible for Seniors   University of Victoria

CONTRIBUTORS

This atlas was written and produced collaboratively by individuals from the Ministry of Health and Ministry Responsible for Seniors, and by members of the Geography Department at the University of Victoria.

Dr. Leslie T. Foster; Management Operations, Ministry of Health and Ministry Responsible for Seniors

Dr. Michael C.R. Edgell; Department of Geography, University of Victoria

Dr. Kevin F. Burr; Division of Vital Statistics, Ministry of Health and Ministry Responsible for Seniors

Ms. Dallas Cobb; Division of Vital Statistics, Ministry of Health and Ministry Responsible for Seniors

Mr. Mark Collison; Division of Vital Statistics, Ministry of Health and Ministry Responsible for Seniors

Dr. Harold D. Foster; Department of Geography, University of Victoria

Mr. Weimin Hu; Division of Vital Statistics, Ministry of Health and Ministry Responsible for Seniors

Mr. Ken Josephson; Department of Geography, University of Victoria

Ms. Diane Macdonald; Department of Geography, University of Victoria

Ms. Julie Macdonald; Division of Vital Statistics, Ministry of Health and Ministry Responsible for Seniors

Mr. Jemal Mohamed; Division of Vital Statistics, Ministry of Health and Ministry Responsible for Seniors

Mr. Ron Strohmaier; Division of Vital Statistics, Ministry of Health and Ministry Responsible for Seniors

Mr. Soo-Hong Uh; Division of Vital Statistics, Ministry of Health and Ministry Responsible for Seniors

PREFACE

Maps have been used to visually display spatial variations in mortality and morbidity measures for many years. This is because it is often easier to see patterns on a colour-coded map than it is to sift through numerical tables (Gardner *et al.*, 1979). More recently, advancements in technology have made computerized mapping relatively inexpensive. Recognition of the full potential of such techniques and their incorporation as viable tools in health planning and prevention efforts are just beginning in British Columbia. The demand for vital statistical data to be used in health planning and research has grown considerably over the last several years. This atlas was initiated as part of an overall response to this demand.

One of the principal objectives of the British Columbia Ministry of Health's mortality mapping initiatives is to provide readily understandable community-level information to local health-care practitioners and planners, and to the community at large. This objective is consistent with the goal of empowering communities to take more responsibility for their health. The provision of local information can assist in the development of priorities and solutions specific to the needs of the local community. Pertinent questions can then be identified, which in turn may lead to the generation of hypotheses to be tested through further detailed investigations.

The Peoples' Republic of China has been mapping health correlates for several decades, and has taken the exercise a step further by overlaying environmental and demographic variables in an attempt to shed light on etiological or epidemiological questions. This pursuit has resulted in a number of measures that have helped to reduce the incidence of several diseases and generally promote human longevity (Tan *et al.*, 1990). The recent report of the British Columbia Royal Commission on Health Care and Costs (1991) supports the viewpoint that this is a direction that must be taken by British Columbia.

This atlas presents mortality patterns in British Columbia, for selected and leading causes of death, over the five-year period from 1985 to 1989. The information is taken from Vital Statistics death registrations and is, therefore, subject to the limitations of these data. It is recommended that those unfamiliar with the analysis and mapping of mortality data acquaint themselves with the sections "Materials and Methods" and "Cautions and Caveats" in Chapter 3 before examining the figures and accompanying tables in Chapter 5.

TABLE OF CONTENTS

5 GEOGRAPHICAL VARIATIONS OF MORTALITY
IN BRITISH COLUMBIA 63

Harold D. Foster, Leslie T. Foster, Kevin F. Burr, Jemal Mohamed, and Ken Josephson

LIST OF TABLES
Chapters 1-4

LIST OF FIGURES

Chapters 1-4

1 INTRODUCTION

Leslie T. Foster

BACKGROUND

A recent review of mortality atlases indicates that, between 1976 and 1989, there were approximately 40 mortality atlases produced in more than 20 different countries (Walter & Birnie, 1991). The mapping of mortality, however, is far from a new phenomenon and has a history going back nearly two centuries (Foster *et al.*, in press). Indeed, some authors have gone so far as to suggest that mortality mapping led to the introduction of the scientific approach to epidemiology. Others have indicated that mortality mapping has helped health-services research to be recognized as a legitimate and important area of study (Kemp & Boyle, 1985).

Converting statistical data to map form can often elucidate relationships that are not readily discernible in tabular form. Mapped data also can be used to suggest hypotheses that can be tested through further investigations. Certainly, mapping is the simplest and most informative way to present data that vary over space (Bliss *et al.*, 1990). It is often easier to pick out patterns on a colour-coded or shaded map than it is to interpret tabular data.

The increased use of mortality mapping reflects not only the affordability and simplicity of the use of computer and associated cartographic technology, but also the recognition that mortality and health status vary substantially over time and space. Within Canada, for example, four national mortality atlases have been published related to cancer, general mortality, urban mortality, and general mortality patterns and recent trends (Health and Welfare Canada and Statistics Canada, 1980a; 1980b; 1984; 1991). Provincial atlases of cancer mortality also have been published for Saskatchewan, British Columbia, and Quebec (Saskatchewan Cancer Foundation, 1988; Band *et al.*, 1989; Ghadirian *et al.*, 1989). In all cases, major geographical variations have been noted that suggest the need for further analyses to explain such spatial differences.

There has been an increasing recognition that many factors influence health status. While the quantity and quality of formal health care provided by professionals to individuals and communities is important, other factors are viewed as more significant in determining health status. Aside from genetics, factors such as physical environment, family income, social cohesion, degree of unemployment, diet, lifestyle behaviour, occupation, housing, and education are known to influence health status (Wigle & Mao, 1980; Townsend & Davidson, 1982; Wilkins & Adams, 1983; Wilkinson, 1986; Whitehead, 1987; Research Unit in Health and Behavioural Change, 1989; Rachlis & Kushner, 1989; Evans & Stoddart, 1990; Ontario Premier's Council on Health Strategy, 1990; M. Thomson, 1990; Draper, 1991; Stephens & McCullough, 1991; Sullivan, 1991; Thomson & Philion, 1991; Labonte, 1991a; 1991b). The impact on health of such factors, many of which are interrelated, has become clearer, partly because of the ability to map them by local areas.

OBJECTIVES OF THE BRITISH COLUMBIA MORTALITY ATLAS

There have been several recent major reviews of the Canadian health-services network (Siler-Wells, 1988; Rachlis & Kushner, 1989; Nova Scotia Royal Commission on Health Care, 1988, 1989a, 1989b; Ontario Premier's Council on Health Strategy, 1989a, 1989b; New Brunswick Commission on Selected Health Care Programs, 1989; Ministry of Health and Social Services, 1989; Alberta Premier's Commission on Future Health Care for Albertans, 1989a, 1989b, 1989c; Saskatchewan Commission on Directions in Health Care, 1990; National Council of Welfare, 1990; Barer & Stoddart, 1991; British Columbia Royal Commission on Health Care and Costs, 1991; Porter, 1991). All of these reviews have indicated the need for major changes, especially with respect to measuring and understanding population health status. A recurring theme has been a greater emphasis on health promotion, empowering communities and individuals to address specific health priorities and problems. Providing information and data on health status to communities is one way of assisting them to identify their own local public health needs and priorities (Thunhurst, 1991).

The British Columbia Ministry of Health has started to publish more health statistics on a local geographical basis. The 1988 Annual Report of the Division of Vital Statistics (Danderfer & Foster, 1989) included one map showing preventable, externally caused deaths in all 21 Provincial Health Units. The Ministry of Health Annual Report for 1988/89 (Ministry of Health, 1990) contained three maps of births, all deaths, and deaths related to external causes. Subsequently, the 1989 Annual Report of the Division of Vital Statistics (Danderfer & Foster, 1990) provided many more maps that not only showed differences among Provincial Health Units, but also attached statistical significance levels to those differences. Most recently, the 1990 Annual Report of the Division of Vital Statistics (Danderfer & Foster, 1992) contained six maps showing variations in health-status indicators among the 80 Local Health Areas (LHAs). These health areas make up Provincial Health Units and Regional Hospital Districts which are the main management and administrative subdivisions used by the British Columbia Ministry of Health.

The major objective of this current mortality-mapping initiative is to describe and disseminate relevant community-level health information to the public and to local health-service providers, planners, and educators so that communities can address their own specific health challenges (Foster et al., in press). Such information helps in the identification of important questions concerning the health of a community or area. This information, in turn, may lead to the generation of hypotheses that can be tested through further detailed investigations. These efforts can result in the identification

2

of local health priorities and in more appropriate decision making. Locally based data will assist in the development of locally based solutions. Through this atlas, communities are provided with comparative data about neighbouring and other communities, and with provincial data. Communities, therefore, can compare themselves against others. The atlas, however, does not attempt to explain the geographical patterns that emerge from the mapping of the statistical data. Such explanation is for others to attempt.

ORGANIZATION OF THE ATLAS

In Chapter 2, the general physical and socioeconomic characteristics of British Columbia are described, along with a brief overview of the health-services network in the province. These characteristics, which influence population health status, may help the reader interpret the patterns in the mortality maps. Chapter 3 provides a description of the methods and materials used, particularly with respect to data sources, geographical areas chosen, and time periods analysed. The derivation and significance of the two primary statistical measures - Standardized Mortality Ratio (SMR) and Age Standardized Mortality Rate (ASMR) - are also described. The mortality categories chosen for mapping include the leading causes of death in the province, and others of particular interest. A brief description of the causes of death chosen for presentation is provided, along with some of the more obvious risk or predisposing factors related to the various causes of death. The cautions and caveats that may prevent erroneous conclusions being drawn about the maps and their patterns also are discussed in Chapter 3.

Chapter 4 presents a descriptive summary of the physical, economic, and social milieu of the geographical units which are used for the basis of mapping. Finally, the 49 maps themselves are presented in Chapter 5. Each is accompanied by a brief description of major geographical patterns and data relating to the mortality trend for the period 1985 to 1989. Those areas are identified which show significantly high and low variations from their expected number of deaths, based on the provincial rates. All data used in the mapping are contained in the tables of the Appendix.

2 BRITISH COLUMBIA: THE PHYSICAL, SOCIOECONOMIC, AND HEALTH SERVICES NETWORK SETTING

Ron Strohmaier and Kevin F. Burr

This chapter provides a brief narrative and statistical overview of British Columbia. The physical, social, historical, and economic geography of the province are described, along with a summary of the demographic characteristics of its population. Readers requiring more detailed information are referred to Forward (1987); Ministry of Regional Development, and Ministry of Finance and Corporate Relations (1989); and Ministry of Finance and Corporate Relations (1990a; 1991). In addition, a brief description of the publicly funded health-services network is provided, and may be supplemented by the Ministry of Health Annual Report for 1988/89 (Ministry of Health, 1990). This overview establishes a context in which to place the mortality maps that follow in Chapter 5.

PHYSICAL AND ENVIRONMENTAL CHARACTERISTICS OF BRITISH COLUMBIA

British Columbia is the western-most province of Canada (Figure 1), bordering on the shores of the Pacific Ocean. It has a land area of approximately 950,000 km² and includes a variety of physiographic regions (Figure 2).

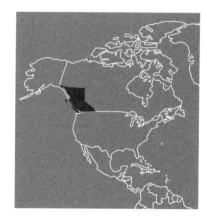

Figure 1 British Columbia in Context

Its major physical features are generally orientated northwest to southeast. The extreme western section of the province consists of the mountains of Vancouver Island and the Queen Charlotte Islands, which are paralleled to the east by a coastal trough and then by the broader coast mountains of the mainland. The fertile alluvial plain of the lower Fraser Valley is located in the extreme southwest of the mainland. This area, along with the southern and eastern parts of Vancouver Island, contains the majority of the province's population.

The interior of British Columbia consists of a central plateau, although there are also some mountainous areas. In the east, the interior is dominated by the Rocky Mountain Trench. The southeast of the province consists of the Rocky Mountains, which extend northward to the Mackenzie Mountain area, while the northeast of the province consists of the Alberta Plateau.

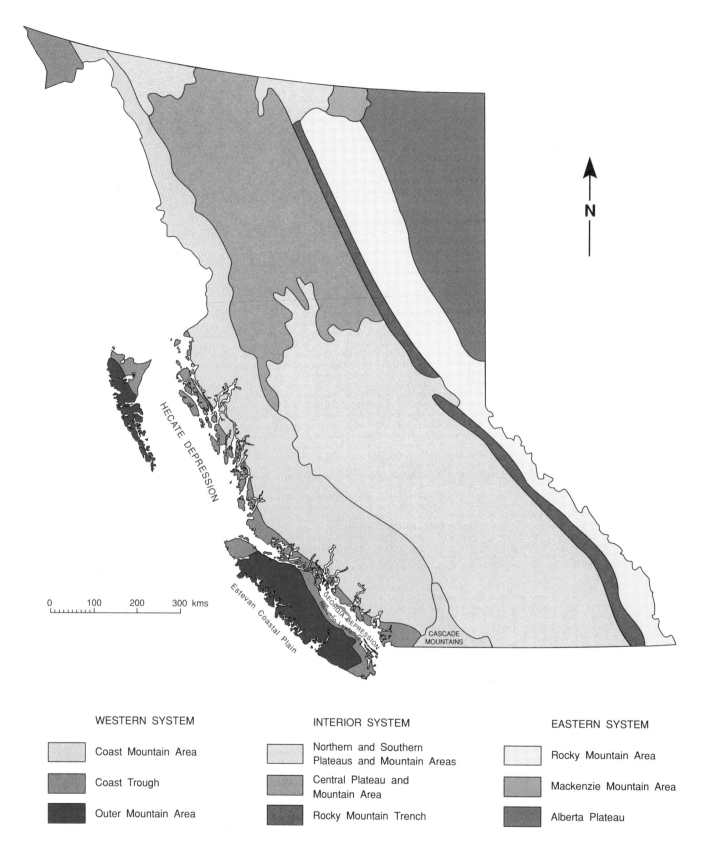

HECATE DEPRESSION

Estevan Coastal Plain

GEORGIA DEPRESSION
Nanaimo Lowlands

CASCADE
MOUNTAINS

N

0   100   200   300 kms

WESTERN SYSTEM

Coast Mountain Area

Coast Trough

Outer Mountain Area

INTERIOR SYSTEM

Northern and Southern
Plateaus and Mountain Areas

Central Plateau and
Mountain Area

Rocky Mountain Trench

EASTERN SYSTEM

Rocky Mountain Area

Mackenzie Mountain Area

Alberta Plateau

Figure 2 Major Physiographic Regions

British Columbia has numerous rivers and lakes; some of the latter are artificial and several are related to hydroelectric projects. In particular, the Fraser and Thompson River and Columbia River systems dominate the southern flow of fresh water, while the Peace River drains to the east. In the northern part of the province the Skeena and Stikine are major rivers flowing to the west. Fresh surface water, which provides the large majority of drinking water in the province, covers approximately 20,000 km^2 (Figure 3).

The precipitation in British Columbia has been described as follows:

> The generally high relief of British Columbia and the westerly atmospheric circulation to which it is subjected result in major variations in precipitation. This ranges from some 25 centimetres (10 inches) in parts of the province's interior to over 500 centimetres (200 inches) along the coast. Interior river basins receive most of their annual precipitation as snow during the winter months. This remains in storage until the late spring or summer when higher temperatures release it to stream flow. Mountain areas also support a multitude of glaciers and ice caps. These are found predominantly in the northwest and southwest of the Coast Mountains,.... (Foster, 1987, p. 45)

Variations in latitude, elevation, land and sea distribution, and relief combine to create a complex climatic mosaic in British Columbia. Climates range from marine temperate on the coast, to continental step and subarctic in the interior and north of the province, respectively.

Approximately 46 percent of the province's area is classified as productive forest land that almost entirely supports coniferous trees, while 4.1 percent is arable or potentially arable, and 16.5 percent has agricultural capability, primarily as grazing land.

TRANSPORTATION AND COMMUNICATIONS

British Columbia has a multifaceted transportation and communication network. The port of Vancouver is the largest dry-cargo port on the North American Pacific seaboard. Additional year-round deep-sea ports are located at Prince Rupert, New Westminster, Victoria, Nanaimo, Port Alberni, Campbell River, and Powell River.

The British Columbia Ferry Corporation, a Crown Corporation owned by the provincial government, operates one of the largest ferry systems in the world that provides transportation between various islands and coastal communities. Land-based transportation routes and population centres generally tend to follow the natural northwest to southeast geography of valleys and waterways (Figure 4).

The province has 6,800 kilometres of mainline railway track operated by British Columbia (BC) Rail, Canadian National (CN) Rail, Canadian Pacific (CP) Rail, and other railways. British Columbia's highway network provides all-weather access to most regions of the province. There are more than 42,000 kilometres of provincial roads and rights-of-way, of which approximately 22,000 kilometres are paved. There are extensive stretches of road in the north and interior of the province along which there is no human settlement at all.

Major domestic and international airline service is provided by Air Canada and Canadian Airlines International. Many other major foreign airlines provide service through Vancouver International Airport. Provincial air facilities include over 200 land-based airports.

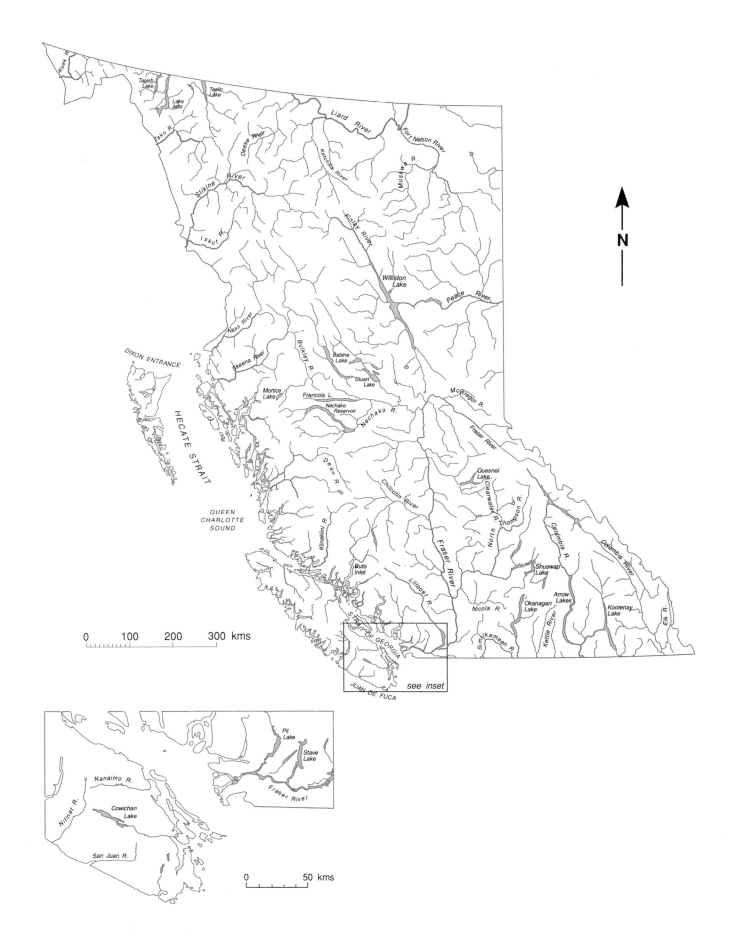

Figure 3 Drainage Systems

8

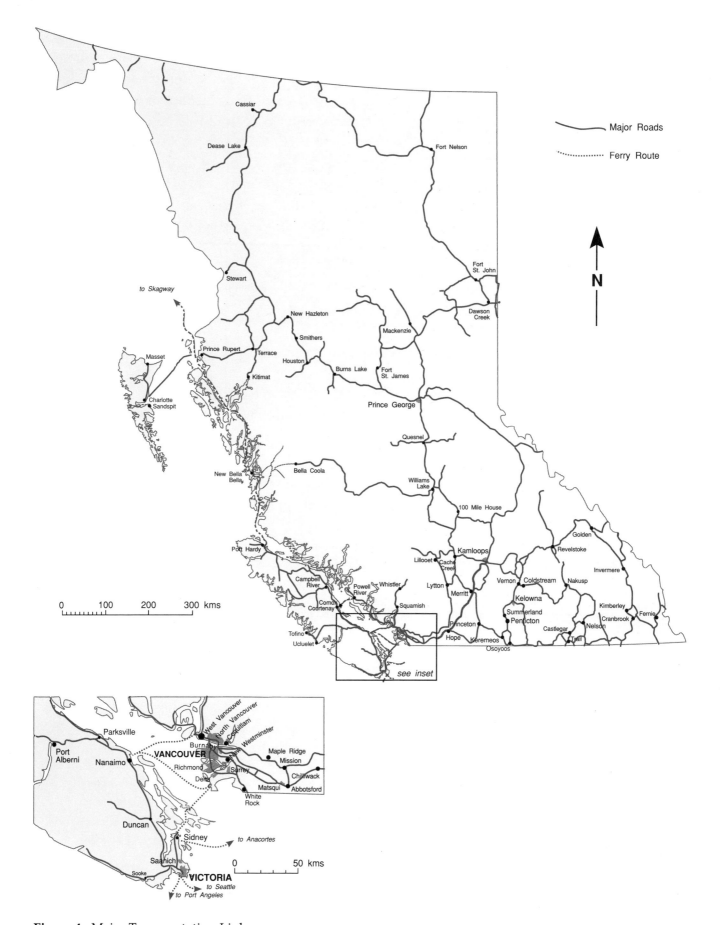

Figure 4 Major Transportation Links

9

In British Columbia, there are more than 70 telecommunication companies that employ 3,000 individuals. These companies provide a variety of products, such as microwave communications, data management systems, high frequency systems, network management systems, data communications, and fibre optics. The advancements in other products, such as mobile satellite communications, radio frequency equipment and paging terminals, satellite communications, mobile data communications, and rural communications, have given British Columbia an international reputation in the field of telecommunications (British Columbia Trade Development Corporation and Industry, Science and Technology Canada, 1991). Modern communication networks link the province's communities with approximately 1.8 million access service lines. Over 98 percent of the province's homes have telephone service and over 80 percent are serviced by cable television (Ministry of the Provincial Secretary, 1990).

HISTORY AND DEMOGRAPHICS OF BRITISH COLUMBIA

British Columbia has been populated by its aboriginal peoples for many millenia. In the late 1700s, however, it was explored by Europeans, primarily the Spanish and British. Much of this exploration was carried out by British fur trading companies. Britain became predominant and established two Crown Colonies, one on the mainland and one covering Vancouver Island. Gold was discovered in 1858, and tens of thousands of prospectors were attracted into what were virtually wilderness areas. The impact of gold prospecting on the development of the province was significant:

> Within a wilderness formerly populated only by a few trading posts and native villages had sprung up a number of permanent white settlements, connected by roads in some cases, agricultural and logging endeavours, and various mining ventures. Much of this growth can be attributed directly or indirectly to gold fever. Although the various gold rushes were individually relatively brief, their consequences were far-reaching and long-lasting. (Gilmartin, 1987, p. 36)

In 1866, the two colonies were merged into the colony of British Columbia, which then joined the Confederation of Canada in 1871, conditional upon a rail link being built to the east. The completion of this railway in the 1880s integrated British Columbia with the rest of Canada, resulting in a boost to economic growth. During this period:

> Railroads were built, mines were sunk, forests cleared, swamps drained and crops planted. However, the optimism of this period was replaced by the doubts and difficulties of World War I and the inter-war period. The late 1940s saw a resurgence as the great housing boom fuelled world demand for construction lumber and minerals, and a period of prosperity ensued. The investment from venture capital of the earlier period was joined by large public expenditure in transportation infrastructure and hydro-electric power. It was an era of road, bridge, railway, port and dam construction, a period inextricably linked with W.A.C. Bennett, the colorful premier. The opportunities for employment attracted many migrants and immigrants. (Wood, 1987, p. 311)

By mid-1989 the province's population had reached approximately 3,050,000. As the data indicate (Figure 5), the increase during the period 1985 to 1989 was largely due to net migration, especially in the last three years, and primarily from other provinces rather than natural increases. As established by the 1986 census, 48 percent of the population were born in the province and 29 percent elsewhere in Canada. The remaining 23 percent were immigrants.

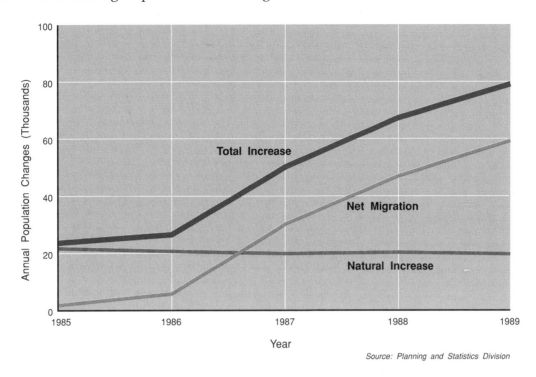

Source: Planning and Statistics Division

Figure 5 Annual Population Changes: 1985-1989

Wood (1987, pp.320-321) has summarized the lifestyle of British Columbians in the following manner:

> The result of a century of European settlement is a mainstream Anglo-Canadian culture based on natural resources extraction and processing tied into the national and world economies. The lifestyle is predominantly urban, salary or wage earning, institutionalized, consumer oriented and heavily influenced by the popular culture of the United States.

Ethnically the province's population is predominantly British. As illustrated in Figure 6, however, census data for 1986 indicate the presence of a wide diversity of ethnic groups. While English was the overwhelming mother tongue, many other languages also were represented. More recently, immigration from Pacific Rim countries has become very important, as British Columbia becomes a more multicultural society.

Demographic characteristics of the population, by age and gender, are shown

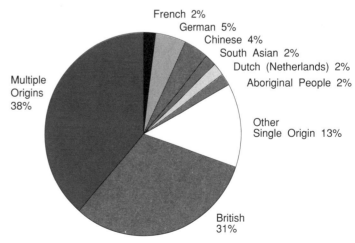

Source: Statistics Canada, 1986 (Census)

Figure 6 Ethnic Distribution: 1986

11

in Figure 7 for the 1986 census year. In the 20 to 39 year age groups, the population shows the characteristic baby-boom bulge of most western societies. In addition, more than 12 percent of the province's population are seniors, the majority of whom are female. This group is the fastest growing section of the population, not only because of aging of the province's own population, but also because British Columbia is a preferred retirement destination for Canadian seniors. The province also has an important aboriginal population, many of whom reside in urban Vancouver and in more remote coastal, interior, and northern communities.

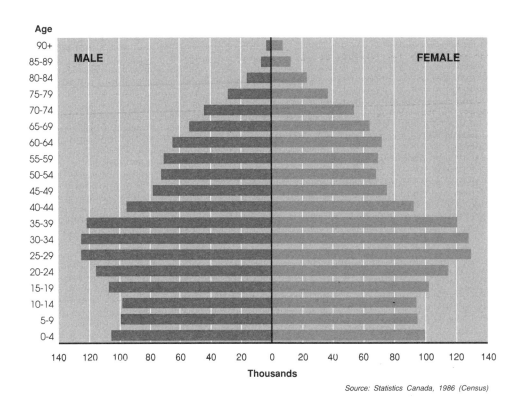

Source: Statistics Canada, 1986 (Census)

Figure 7 Population by Gender and Age Group: 1986

Other demographic characteristics of the population are illustrated in Figure 8, which shows marital status, and Figure 9, which displays household size. Over 50 percent of those aged 15 and over were married. There were relatively few persons per household, and of those families having children at home, slightly in excess of 20 percent were single parent families.

British Columbia has a very uneven population distribution (Figure 10), influenced

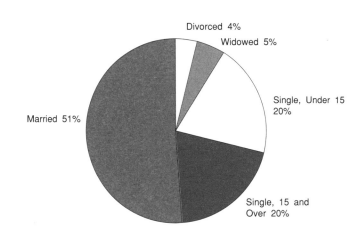

Source: Statistics Canada, 1986 (Census)

Figure 8 Marital Status: 1986

12

in part by the variety of its topography and climate. Settlement is heavily concentrated in the southwestern corner of the province, and the metropolitan areas of Vancouver and Victoria together account for almost 57 percent of the total population. Much of the rest of the province, however, is quite sparsely settled, and the majority of the remaining population is concentrated in several major cities, including Nanaimo, Prince George, Kelowna, and Kamloops, or close to the border with the United States.

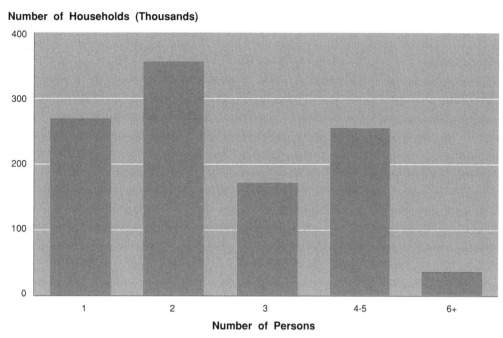

Number of Households (Thousands)

Number of Persons

Source: Statistics Canada, 1986 (Census)

Figure 9 Persons Per Household: 1986

SOCIOECONOMIC PROFILE

The economy of the province is based largely upon natural resource industries, but is becoming more diversified. Historically it has exhibited major swings, based on the "boom-bust" cycle that is characteristic of resource-based, small open economies. In terms of employment, the tertiary, or service sector component of the economy has been the fastest-growing over the last two decades.

Economy

The five largest components of the economy, during the period 1985 to 1989, are briefly described below (Ministry of Regional Development, and Ministry of Finance and Corporate Relations, 1989; Ministry of Finance and Corporate Relations, 1990a; 1991).

> **Forest-based** industries form the most important segment of the provincial economy. Many communities rely to some degree on forestry, which directly employs about seven percent of the labour force. Of all manufacturing industries in British Columbia, wood industries (including sawmills and plywood plants) rank first, followed closely by the paper and allied industries. During 1989, British Columbia shipped $12.5 billion

13

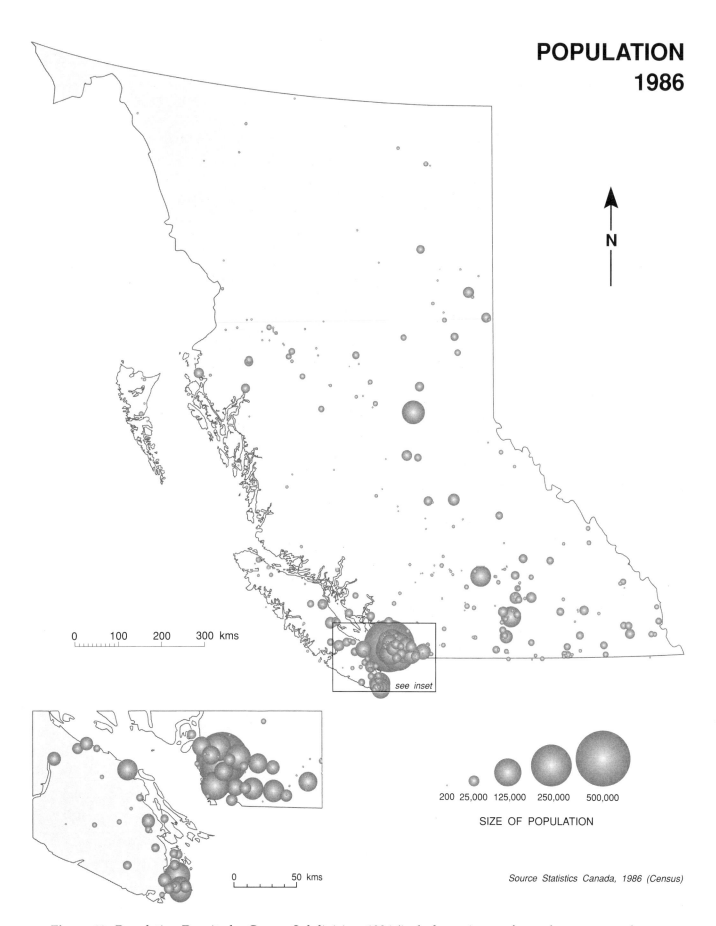

POPULATION
1986

N

0   100   200   300 kms

0   50 kms

200 25,000 125,000 250,000 500,000

SIZE OF POPULATION

Source Statistics Canada, 1986 (Census)

see inset

Figure 10 Population Density by Census Subdivision: 1986 (includes estimates for underenumerated reserve lands). Circles are placed at approximate centroid of census subdivisons.

14

worth of forest products, representing 48 percent of the total manufacturing shipments from thc province. Forestry exports to other countries were worth $10 billion.

Tourism plays an increasingly prominent role in the provincial economy, ranking as the second-largest sector of the economy. British Columbia has many natural and cultural attractions. The value of tourists' expenditures in 1989 was $4 billion. Sharp gains attributable to the success of Expo 86, the 1986 World Exposition on Transportation and Communication in Vancouver, carried over into the following years.

Mineral-based industries form the third-most important segment of the provincial economy. In 1989, the most important mineral products, out of a total of $3.9 billion, were coal ($1 billion), copper ($1 billion), natural gas ($495 million), crude oil ($263 million), gold ($236 million), and silver ($105 million).

Agriculture ranked fourth in the province's industries, and cash receipts from farming operations were $1.2 billion in 1989. Agriculture in British Columbia is extremely diverse, with specialized production in various parts of the province largely being determined by regional climatic conditions. Mixed livestock-crop farming is found throughout the province. Dairying and the production of livestock and related products are the most important components in the agricultural economy. Poultry farming and the growing of tree fruits, grain, vegetables, berries, grapes, bulbs, and ornamental shrubs are some of the other activities carried out in the province.

Marine animals and plants in the Pacific coast waters are valued for commercial fisheries, and mariculture production ranks as the fifth-largest industry. During 1989, the landed value of the catch was $453 million. Processing this catch has generally doubled its value, producing a wholesale value of $946 million in 1989. Salmon was the most valuable component of the industry, with the herring fishcry being the second-most valuable. Other products, such as groundfish varieties and shellfish, ranked considerably lower. In addition to natural harvesting, aquaculture production, an industry of exceptional growth, was valued at $79 million in 1989.

The province's manufacturing industry is largely based on natural resources, and includes products derived from forestry, refined nonferrous metals, fish, agriculture, and petroleum and natural gas. In recent years, the production of chemicals, undersea vessels, commercial vehicles, plastic products, saw-milling and logging equipment, pulp and paper machinery, electronic and electrical products, and specialized metal fabrications have all grown in importance. In 1989, the province's gross domestic product was $67.6 billion. The relative contribution of the various sectors of the economy is illustrated in Figure 11.

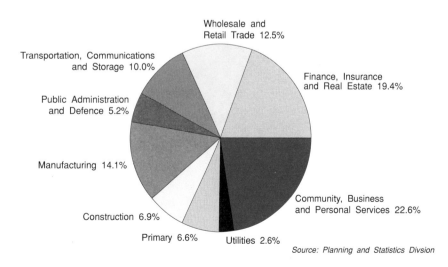

Source: Planning and Statistics Divsion

Figure 11 Gross Domestic Product by Industry: 1989

15

Employment

Employment in British Columbia has tended to parallel the Canadian economy, but has been subject to more extreme variation, due to its dependence on resource-based industries. Recently, increased economic diversification has lessened these extremes. The level of unemployment in the province for the period 1985 to 1989 is illustrated in Figure 12. During these years the average unemployment rate decreased steadily, from a high of 14.1 percent in 1985 to a low of 9.1 percent in 1989. An increasingly strong economy and buoyant job market in British Columbia have caused this steady employment growth. In 1989, with the exception of the agriculture and mining industries and the finance, insurance, and real estate sectors, employment growth was broadly based among all major industries. However, as in most provinces or states in western countries, employment in British Columbia is dominated by the service sector. The distribution of employment by occupational categories for males and females is shown in Table 1. There are marked differences in patterns of occupation between genders, with females dominant in the services, clerical, and sales areas and also in the health field.

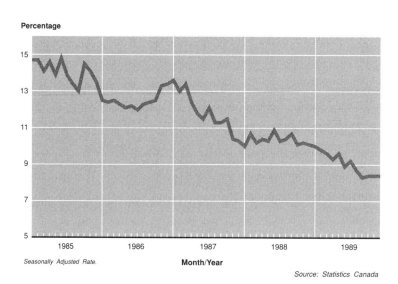

Figure 12 Unemployment Rate: 1985-1989

Table 1   Occupations by Gender: 1986

Occupation	Male	Percent	Female	Percent	Total	Percent
Manager/Admin./etc.	97,455	11.8	45,860	7.5	143,315	10.0
Teaching and Related	21620	2.6	33,990	5.5	55,610	3.9
Medicine and Health	15,505	1.9	54,010	8.8	69,515	4.8
TSR&A	66,440	8.1	35,765	5.8	102,205	7.1
Clerical and Related	47,440	5.8	203,300	33.2	250,740	17.5
Service	94,895	11.5	119,725	19.5	214,620	14.9
Sales	77,710	9.4	66,685	10.9	144,395	10.1
Primary	69,370	8.4	16,975	2.8	86,345	6.0
Processing	43,685	5.3	9,255	1.5	52,940	3.7
MFA&R	94,115	11.4	11,125	1.8	105,240	7.3
Construction	87,105	10.6	1,910	0.3	89,015	6.2
Transport-Operating	55,285	6.7	3,890	0.6	59,175	4.1
Other	52,310	6.4	10,570	1.7	62,880	4.4
TOTAL	**822,935**	**100.0**	**613,060**	**100.0**	**1,435,995**	**100.0**

TSR&A = Technical, Social, Religious, & Artistic   MFA&R = Machining, Fabricating, Assembling, & Repairing

Source: Statistics Canada, 1986 (Census).

In 1986, the median annual household income was $28,770, although the average annual household income was higher at $33,497 (Table 2). Over 25 percent of households, however, had annual incomes of less than $15,000.

Figure 13 indicates the provincial educational levels achieved in 1986 for those aged 15 and over. Approximately 20 percent of the population had some university education, while only 11 percent had received less than a grade 9 education. However, 41 percent of the population had not finished grades 9 to 12 or obtained a certificate.

Table 2 Household Income Level: 1986

Income Level	Households	Percent
Under $5,000	55,235	5.1
$5,000 - 9,999	112,370	10.3
$10,000 - 14,999	111,280	10.2
$15,000 - 19,999	101,830	9.4
$20,000 - 24,999	94,220	8.7
$25,000 - 29,999	90,065	8.3
$30,000 - 34,999	89,815	8.3
$35,000 - 39,999	82,205	7.6
$40,000 - 49,999	134,505	12.4
$50,000 and Over	215,595	19.8

Average : $33,497   Median : $28,770   Source : Statistics Canada, 1986 (Census)

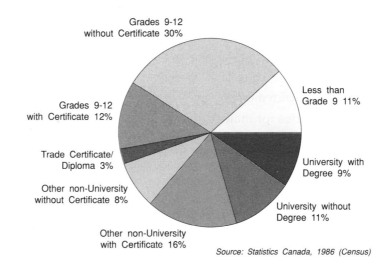

Source: Statistics Canada, 1986 (Census)

Figure 13 Education Level: 1986

OVERVIEW OF HEALTH SERVICES IN BRITISH COLUMBIA

The province has been acknowledged as having one of the best publicly funded health systems in the world (British Columbia Royal Commission on Health Care and Costs, 1991; United States General Accounting Office, 1991). Generally, it is well provided with health-care facilities and workers. In 1989, per 10,000 population, there were 38.9 acute care hospital beds (excluding bassinets), 23.3 physicians, 77.9 registered nurses, and 15.1 licensed practical nurses. Indeed, in 1990, British Columbia had the lowest number of patients per physician of any Canadian province (British Columbia Royal Commission on Health Care and Costs, 1991). There are, of course, many other health-care facilities and health and allied workers in the province.

There were shortages in a small number of selected categories of health-care workers, especially perfusionists and radiation technicians. Nursing shortages appear to fluctuate in a cyclical fashion counter to the economy: when the economy is buoyant, shortages occur. In addition, geographic shortages exist, and tend to impact most adversely on people located in the more remote or isolated areas of the province. Selected statistics for health services in the province are illustrated in Table 3.

Table 3 Selected Statistics - British Columbia Health Services

Health Expenditure Indicators 1989/90

Ministry of Health expenditure as a percentage of GDP: 5.7%
Ministry of Health per capita expenditure: $1,418

Selected Health Care Personnel (June - December 1989)

	Total Number	Rate/ 10,000 Population
Physicians	7,100	23.3
Registered Nurses*	23,800	77.9
Licensed Practical Nurses*	4,600	15.1
Registered Psychiatric Nurses*	2,100	6.9
Dentists	1,900	6.2
Dental Hygienists	800	2.6
Certified Dental Assistants	3,500	11.5
Dieticians and Nutritionists	600	2.0
Medical Lab Techologists	2,600	8.5
Pharmacists	2,300	7.5
Physiotherapists	1600	5.2
Psychologists	700	2.3

*employed in nursing

Hospital (Excluding Mental Institutions) Beds, 1989/90

	Total Beds	Rate/ 10,000 Population	Admissions	Average Stay in Days
Acute/Rehabilitation	11,870	38.9	417,300	7.3
Extended Care	7,760	25.4	6,400	385.7
Newborn	1,220	4.0	45,400	4.2

Leading Causes of Acute/Rehabilitation Hospitalization, 1989/90 (Excluding Mental Institutions)

	Days	%
Circulatory Disease	509,986	15.5
Injury & Poisoning	369,768	11.3
Neoplasms	325,912	9.9
Mental Disorders	312,205	9.5

Continuing Care, 1989/90

Residential Care Beds	16,800

Immunization Percentages (1989/90) at the end of Grade 1

	%
Diphtheria / Pertussis / Tetanus	95
Polio	95
Measles / Mumps / Rubella	96

Emergency Health Services, 1989/90

Patients Transported	303,350
Air Ambulance Trips	5,600

Source: Division of Policy Planning and Legislation, Ministry of Health, from applicable original sources within the Ministry and elsewhere. Division of Hospital Care, Ministry of Health.

Total expenditures by the provincial Ministry of Health during the 1989/90 fiscal year were $4.37 billion (Ministry of Health, 1991), representing $1,418 per capita. The distribution of these expenditures by major program areas is shown in Figure 14, which does not include health-related expenditures operated or funded by other provincial ministries or agencies. Such services include worker's compensation programs, alcohol and drug programs, and federal government services provided to native peoples living on reservations.

Major programs, provided or funded by the Ministry of Health, are described on the following page.

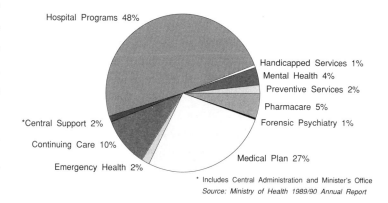

Figure 14 Ministry of Health Expenditures: 1989-1990

18

Medical Services Plan

The Medical Services Plan registers subscribers (approximately 98 percent of the population), collects premiums (amounting to about 50 percent of the costs of the plan), provides premium assistance to those with lower incomes, and pays claims made for all medically required visits to physicians, laboratory and other diagnostic procedures, and dental and oral surgery. In addition, a number of supplementary benefits are covered to varying degrees, including the services of chiropractors, massage therapists, naturopathic physicians, optometrists, orthoptists, podiatrists, and physiotherapists. With the exception of optometrists, a fee of $5 per visit is paid. Those individuals on premium assistance do not pay this fee.

Pharmacare

Pharmacare provides financial assistance for the purchase of prescription medications (above an annual deductible amount of $325 in 1989), and other medically required supplies such as glucose strips for diabetics and designated permanent prosthetic appliances.

Emergency Health Services Commission

The Commission provides ground and air ambulance services throughout the province. User fees cover approximately 16 percent of the service cost.

Hospital Care

Hospital Care oversees the operation of acute care, rehabilitation, and extended-care hospitals, the services of which are paid for by the provincial government. The division operates as a funding agency, leaving responsibility for facility operation with the institutions, which are governed primarily by locally elected hospital boards.

Continuing Care

The Continuing Care Division provides a range of in-home support, residential care, and special support services to assist people whose ability to function independently is affected by long-term, health-related problems. In addition, nursing care is provided to patients who are discharged early from hospital or as an alternative to admission to an acute care hospital. In 1989, residents of long-term care facilities were charged approximately $20 per day to cover overhead costs not related to care.

Preventive Services

Preventive Services staff devise and deliver programs to promote and enable either maintenance or improvement in health status while encouraging the avoidance of health risks. These goals are served through immunization programs, public health inspection, health promotion and education, preventive dentistry, speech and hearing services, health screening, contact tracing and investigations of communicable diseases, and specialized services for high-risk populations.

Services to the Handicapped

Services to the Handicapped develops and funds community-based programs and services for adults and hospitalized children with multiple disabilities.

Forensic Psychiatric Services Commission

The Commission provides court-ordered psychiatric and psychological assessment, diagnosis, and treatment.

Mental Health Services

Mental Health Services provide comprehensive care to British Columbians with mental illness. Services are delivered through community-based outpatient services and hospital-based inpatient settings.

In summary, the province provides a set of health services based on the principles of public administration, comprehensiveness, universality, portability between areas, and accessibility. These principles are laid out in the Canada Health Act (1984).

GEOGRAPHICAL UNITS IN HEALTH SERVICES

Provincial government-operated or funded health-care services have historically evolved within a number of different administrative boundary systems. Health Units have been the basis for the administration of what are generally described as "public-health services" such as public-health nursing, public-health inspection, and epidemiology that have had a long history in the province. Regional Hospital Districts are growing increasingly in administrative importance, as hospitals provide more services in the community outside of the hospital facility setting.

Other administrative boundary systems have been used by various health program areas. These include Emergency Health Services (Royal Canadian Mounted Police regions), Forensic Psychiatric Services (Regional Crown Council Districts), and Medical Services Plan (B.C. Medical Association Electoral Districts). Data analysis has tended, in the past, to be based solely on administrative considerations of the individual program areas.

In 1980, the Ministry of Health designated a set of 80 areas as Local Health Areas (LHAs). LHAs were designed to provide a *common* geographical basis for statistical analysis of data, irrespective of the differing administrative boundary systems of individual programs. LHAs also provided smaller geographical areas for statistical analysis than those of the various program area administrative boundaries. In most instances, LHAs may be aggregated into larger areas whose boundaries are coterminous with the various program administrative boundary systems, in particular, Health Units and Regional Hospital Districts.

3 MORTALITY MAPPING: METHODS, CAVEATS, AND DATA

Jemal Mohamed, Julie Macdonald, Mark Collison, Soo-Hong Uh, and Leslie T. Foster

This chapter contains descriptions of the basic data, and the methods used to calculate the two measures (Standardized Mortality Ratios [SMRs] and Age Standardized Mortality Rates [ASMRs]) used in the development of the mortality maps. An important section on caveats and cautions related to the data, measures, and geographical units is presented to help in the interpretation of the maps displayed in Chapter 5. A fuller discussion of materials and methods, cautions, and caveats is presented in Foster *et al.* (in press). The chapter concludes with a brief description of the disease and age categories used in the maps and some of the important associated risk factors.

MATERIALS AND METHODS

Data Sources

Mortality data have limitations in terms of availability, collection costs, and completeness. However, no other routine system of health-related data collection rivals death records. The death registration system used by British Columbia's Division of Vital Statistics has several characteristics that make it particularly attractive as a data source. All deaths occurring in the province must be reported within a prescribed time period, and the personal particulars of the deceased recorded (Vital Statistics Act, 1979). Among the items included on death records are the underlying cause of death and antecedent causes and/or contributing conditions. In addition, residential address, age, gender, and other particulars related to the death are recorded.

To ensure accuracy in the coding of cause of death information, the Division of Vital Statistics employs trained medical coders to record such information according to the International Classification of Diseases (World Health Organization, 1977). Once coded, this information is stored on computer-readable media. Aside from the relative completeness and accuracy of these data, other benefits include the availability of several years of data to act as a baseline in time-series analyses, and the ability to access original documents for verification purposes in the case of questionable data.

Population and Sample Sizes

When mapping mortality data, population size must be considered, as well as the number of cases used in the calculation of various statistical measures. The areal unit and time period of analysis are important interrelated factors, and their choice is critical.

Areal Units and Time Period of Analysis

The first major consideration, in choosing areal units, is to ensure that they provide a basis for deriving reliable population data for the calculation of various health measures. Therefore, areal units should be based on census-related units such as census tracts and census subdivisions. Census population data, which contain postal codes, may be used to compile population figures for any geographical area in which postal codes aggregate to census areas.

Postal-code data are collected by various units in the Ministry of Health, including the Division of Vital Statistics. Through the use of postal-code translation files, these data may readily be assigned to Local Health Areas (LHAs) or to the aggregates of LHAs that correspond to Health Units and Regional Hospital Districts, the basic health administrative and management units of the province.

The second major consideration, in choosing areal units, is the need for a sufficient number of cases and a population size that will ensure the desired degree of reliability for statistical analysis. The number of cases and population size, however, should not be so large that important anomalies are obscured. In terms of the number of cases, the time period of analysis must be considered in conjunction with the choice of areal units. For example, while there may be a sufficient number of cases (deaths) for statistical analysis using only one year of data for larger Health Units and Regional Hospital Districts, it may be necessary to combine several years of data if LHAs with smaller populations are being used. The number of cases required depends on the nature of the specific analysis.

Maps included in this atlas employ population data for LHAs categorized by gender and five-year age groups, relating to deaths occurring in British Columbia over the five-year period from 1985 to 1989. Any deaths of nonresidents which occurred in the province were excluded. After eliminating mortality records that lacked important data elements, a total of 108,876 cases was compiled, of which 59,656 were male and 49,220 were female.

Statistical Mortality Measures

This atlas uses population-adjusted measures to compare variations in mortality patterns and trends. Adjusted measures, which account for population compositional differences such as age and gender, employ various weighting factors derived from a "standard population". This allows more meaningful mortality-measure comparisons to be made between different areas or time periods. Comparisons of such adjusted measures may be made directly without further manipulation of the data. Measures calculated by one province may be compared with those calculated by others, if the same standard population is utilized.

The choice of the standard population is governed by the purpose of the analysis, the ease with which standard population factors may be obtained, and the "degree of relevancy" to the populations being studied.

It is important to bear in mind that all measures derived from the use of standard population weighting factors are surrogate rather than real measures for the areas chosen. It is the *relative* values of adjusted measures that are important for *comparative* analysis of different time periods or areas, rather than the *absolute* values of the measures. In addition, all such measures are subject to some degree of bias as they cannot totally compensate for population compositional differences. They do, however, lessen the potentially significant biases of unadjusted measures. The two standardized measures used in this atlas are the Age Standardized Mortality Rate and the Standardized Mortality Ratio.

AGE STANDARDIZED MORTALITY RATE (ASMR): This measure utilizes the area's mortality rate and weighting factors based on the proportion of the standard population in various age groups. This method of adjustment is referred to as the "direct method". The general formula for calculating the ASMR per k population is as follows:

$$\text{ASMR} = \frac{\sum\limits_{i=1}^{n} m_i \times \pi_i}{\Pi} \times k$$

Where:
- x = multiply
- Σ = summation of
- p_i = area population in age-group i
- π_i = standard population in age-group i
- Π = $\Sigma\pi_i$ = total standard population
- d_i = deaths in area population in age-group i
- m_i = d_i/p_i = mortality rate in area age-group i
- n = number of age groups
- k = a rate conversion factor, commonly 1,000 or 10,000

All things being equal, the ASMR is the preferred measure for examining time trends in mortality and making comparisons between relatively disparate geographical areas (National Center for Heath Statistics, 1989). Thus, the ASMR is particularly suited for national or interprovincial comparisons. In Canada, the national population from the 1971 Census is generally employed as the standard population. In addition to being standardized for age, ASMR values have been standardized for gender. This atlas, while not mapping ASMRs, provides these measures to show various mortality trends over the five-year period 1985 to 1989.

STANDARDIZED MORTALITY RATIO (SMR): This measure uses the area's population and weighting factors based on age-group mortality rates of the standard population. This method of adjustment is also referred to as the "indirect method" and can be calculated as follows:

$$\text{SMR} = \frac{D}{\sum\limits_{i=1}^{n} \mu_i \times p_i}$$

Where:
- x = multiply
- Σ = summation of
- p_i = area population in age-group i
- π_i = standard population in age-group i
- d_i = deaths in area population in age-group i
- D = Σd_i = total deaths in area
- δ_i = deaths in standard population in age-group i
- μ_i = δ_i/π_i = mortality rate in standard population age-group i
- n = number of age groups

The SMR, like the ASMR, compensates for the differential impact of variations in age composition, although in a somewhat different manner. The SMR is the ratio of observed deaths to the expected deaths for an area, based on the standard population age-specific mortality rates. Because mortality rates vary geographically, it is important to choose a standard population that most closely reflects the mortality experience of the areas under study. As this atlas is concerned with British Columbia mortality, the most appropriate choice of a standard population is the provincial population (estimated except during the census year) for each year considered.

The SMR is the preferred measure when making geographical comparisons that involve a small number of cases, such as areas with relatively small populations (Breslow & Day, 1987). Because many LHAs in British Columbia have sparse populations and small numbers of deaths, the SMR is used as the principal measure for mapping death data in this atlas. In addition to being standardized for age, SMR values in this atlas have been standardized for gender.

Statistical Significance Measures

A Poisson distribution is assumed for observed deaths. The Chi-Square (χ^2) test is employed to determine if the difference of the observed value from the expected value is statistically significant. As some of the data in this atlas involve a small number of deaths, an accurate approximation to the exact Poisson test is employed (Breslow & Day, 1987; Rothman & Boice, 1979). Significance is tested at various levels ($p < 0.05$; $p < 0.01$; $p < 0.001$) and the 95 percent confidence interval is calculated. SMRs testing significant, but involving less than five deaths are not depicted on the maps in Chapter 5 as being statistically significant, although the tables in the Appendix show them as being statistically significant. All non-significant values are included in the Appendix tables.

CAUTIONS AND CAVEATS

Mortality mapping is often undertaken, not to provide definitive answers to issues, but to raise questions and generate hypotheses that require further investigation. For these reasons mapping is frequently carried out at the beginning of a research endeavour. It also can be conducted at the end, to see if some significant factor has been missed (Alderson, 1988). Caution must be used when dealing with data reflecting spatially varying mortality measures. Being forewarned about problems helps to lessen the potential for errors. Many issues are closely interrelated, but for ease of discussion they are grouped into four major categories: data integrity, areal units of analysis, time period of analysis, and interpretation.

Data Integrity

Although mortality data are readily available, their accuracy and consistency should not be assumed. An accurate diagnosis of cause of death is not always possible. This is especially so with older patients, who may suffer from several major concurrent illnesses. Physicians also differ in their skills, and there may be differences in diagnostic practices and preferences among physicians. In addition, there may be variations in death certification and coding practices. The attending physician or coroner may have only a very limited knowledge of the deceased's medical history, having attended only briefly (as during emergency admission to hospital), if at all, prior to death. While autopsies can provide more accurate diagnoses, the Division of Vital Statistics records show that these are performed in only 24 percent of registered deaths in British Columbia.

Another important caveat should be noted. Except for the census year of 1986, *estimates* of population have been used in the calculations. These estimates were provided by the Planning and Statistics Division (PSD) (Ministry of Finance and Corporate Relations, 1990b). The PSD attempts to be consistent in deriving intercensal and postcensal estimates, so that although population figures may not be exact, population-based rate changes, over time, should be minimally affected. It should also be noted that even census data are not comprehensive.

Areal Units of Analysis

The residential mailing address of the deceased is included on the death registration. In some instances, this may not be the place of residence. In analysing the data, the determination of residential location may be difficult, particularly where postal-code translations are employed for rural areas and where post office box addresses are encountered.

Time Period of Analysis

Time periods used in mapping have aggregated data for single years (Danderfer & Foster, 1989; 1990); 10 and 11 years (Pickle *et al.*, 1987); or even 28 years (Band *et al.*, 1989). Short time periods may limit the number of mortality observations, so that reliable statistical measures are difficult to obtain. Long time periods, however, are fraught with problems since they may obscure real trends and are complicated by improvements in diagnoses over time.

Interpretation Issues

It is important to recognize that the absence of statistical significance cannot, in itself, be interpreted to mean that there are no health problems of concern. Conversely, areas recording significantly high or low rates require further investigation to ensure that these rates are indeed "true" and reflective of underlying characteristics of the areas in which they occur.

Interpretation of geographical variations must take into account many factors, particularly migration. Deaths may be related to causal factors experienced in earlier life that are masked or exaggerated by migration patterns. This may be particularly true when selective migration occurs for health reasons. Families with a chronically ill member may change residence to be close to a specific treatment facility. Seniors may move into a long-term care facility, or from rural to urban areas, to enjoy the relative security of knowing that a variety of health services is close at hand (Gardner *et al.*, 1979). In British Columbia these factors may be of particular concern, as certain communities attract retirees, both from within the province and from across the country. This is especially true of southern and eastern Vancouver Island, the lower mainland, the Fraser Valley, and the Okanagan.

ASMR and SMR values for males and females are derived from standard male and female populations. As these populations are different, no direct comparison of the resulting male and female ASMRs and SMRs should be made.

All these factors caution against drawing hasty interpretations and conclusions. The mapping of mortality data is a precursory step to further, detailed epidemiological investigations; it should not be used in isolation as an indicator of health status.

DISEASE DESCRIPTION AND ASSOCIATED RISK FACTORS

All conditions listed on a Registration of Death are assigned codes derived from the *International Classification of Diseases* (ICD-9). A complex set of standard rules is applied to select, from all conditions listed, an underlying cause of death (UCOD). The UCOD categories that are the focus of this atlas were selected first on the basis of major three-digit ICD-9 groupings. Specific conditions that occur most frequently, or are of special contemporary health concern, were selected from within the major groups for detailed consideration and mapping. The major groups and subgroups are now outlined.

Cancer (ICD-9; 140-208)

Cancer includes all malignant neoplasms by primary site, including "systemic" areas affected by lymphosarcoma, Hodgkin's disease, leukaemia, and others.

Lung Cancer (ICD-9; 162)
In recent years, the overall incidence of lung cancer has increased slightly in males, but has almost doubled in females. The British Columbia Cancer Agency and Statistics Canada have indicated that this increase in female lung cancer is due to a rise in cigarette smoking. Another consideration is increased exposure to environmental and occupational hazards, as more women enter new areas of the work force. Lung cancer is more prevalent in urban areas and shows an inverse association with socioeconomic status (Fraumeni & Blot, 1989).

Breast Cancer - Female (ICD-9; 174)
There is still no unifying explanation for the etiology of breast cancer. However, research has substantiated recurrent risk factors. These are higher socioeconomic status, age, early menarche, late menopause, nonpregnancy, late age of first pregnancy, family history in a first degree relative, obesity, high dietary fat consumption, and excess radiation to the chest area (Petrakis *et al.*, 1989).

Endocrine, Nutritional, and Metabolic Diseases and Immunity Disorders (ICD-9; 240-279)

This category includes such conditions as hypothyroidism, diabetes, adrenal insufficiency (metabolic), malnutrition and vitamin deficiencies, gout, obesity, and agammaglobulinaemia.

Diabetes (ICD-9; 250)
Both the more severe Type I Insulin-Dependent Diabetes Mellitus (IDDM), and Type II non-IDDM, are included in this grouping. IDDM is felt to result from an infectious or toxic environmental insult

to the pancreatic B cells of genetically predisposed persons. It occurs most commonly in juveniles (with a peak at 12-14 years) and occasionally in nonobese adults and the elderly (with a peak at 65 years). The vast majority of persons with mild adult onset diabetes are obese. Diabetics form a high risk group because of increased susceptibility to complications of their disease. These include gangrene, nephropathy, neuropathy, and blindness. Diabetics are more likely to suffer hypertension, heart attack, and stroke than the general population (Karam, 1983).

Circulatory System (ICD-9; 390-459)

This category includes all diseases of the heart, veins, arteries, arterioles, capillaries, and lymphatic system. The most common conditions within this group include hypertension, myocardial infarction (heart attack), arteriosclerotic heart disease, and stroke.

Ischaemic Heart Disease (ICD-9; 410-414, 4292)
This term refers to all diseases of the heart that have resulted from a diminished supply of oxygenated blood to the heart muscle. Decreased blood flow to the heart cells (ischaemia) results from coronary blood vessel obstruction caused by arteriosclerosis, vasospasm, thrombosis, and embolism. The most frequent condition in this group is myocardial infarction (heart attack). In about one quarter of these conditions, sudden death is the initial and only clinical manifestation of coronary heart disease. Heart disease is the leading cause of death in British Columbia. Many risk factors are associated with an increased probability of heart attack. These are family history, hypertension, overweight, high fat diet, smoking, inactivity, type 'A' personality, and stress. Heart attacks are most common in males over 30 years of age, but become increasingly frequent in women after menopause (Basta & Coyle, 1980; Sokolow, 1983).

Cerebrovascular Disease/Stroke (ICD-9; 430-434, 436-438)
This category includes conditions that affect the vascular system of the brain. Cerebrovascular Accident (CVA) or stroke is the most frequent cause of death within this category. Three basic processes account for most cerebrovascular accidents: thrombosis, embolism, and haemorrhage of a cerebral blood vessel. CVA is uncommon in persons under age 40. Predisposing illnesses include cerebral arteriosclerosis, syphilis and other infections, dehydration, and trauma (Chusid, 1983).

Diseases of Arteries, Arterioles, and Capillaries (ICD-9; 440-448)
The most common diseases found within this category are arteriosclerosis, aortic aneurysm, and peripheral vascular disease. Arteriosclerosis (or atherosclerosis) is a degenerative process, characterized by lipid deposition in the layer that lines arteries and results in a thickening and loss of elasticity of arterial walls (Friel, 1974). Evidence indicates that this process begins in childhood (earlier and more frequently among males), but does not become apparent until middle or old age. The most important atherogenic risk factors are the metabolic, chemical, physical, biological, and mechanical breakdown of cholesterol and fat. Diseases that predispose to arteriosclerosis include the hyperlipidemic states, diabetes, and hypertension. Smoking also apparently contributes to its development (Erskine, 1983).

Diseases of the Respiratory System (ICD-9; 460-519)

This category includes all diseases of the upper and lower respiratory tract, such as laryngitis, bronchitis, asthma, emphysema, and others.

Pneumonia (ICD-9; 480-486) and Influenza (ICD-9; 487)

All pneumonias and bronchopneumonias (viral and bacterial) are included in this category, except for hypostatic pneumonia or pneumonia that is a manifestation of another infectious disease (such as whooping cough, aspergillosis, and candidiasis). "Influenza" does not include haemophilus influenza infection or meningitis. Mortality from pneumonia and influenza tends to be greatest among the elderly, who are most susceptible due to other chronic debilitating conditions. Where the elderly are concentrated, as in nursing homes and other facilities, risk factors are increased because of the endemic nature of the disease.

Chronic Pulmonary Disease (CPD) (ICD-9; 491, 492, 496)

CPD consists of chronic bronchitis (ICD-9; 491), emphysema (ICD-9; 492), and chronic obstructive pulmonary disease (COPD) (ICD-9; 496). These are the respiratory diseases most associated with smoking. Due to their chronic nature, death tends to occur in individuals over 60 years old (Mao *et al.*, 1988). Because occupations such as farming, mining, and other industries also are factors in prevalence, the mortality rate from CPD is generally higher among males (O'Brien, 1982).

Diseases of the Digestive System (ICD-9; 520-579)

This category includes diseases of the oral cavity, salivary glands, and gastrointestinal tract. Common conditions within this group include appendicitis, hernias, gastric ulcer, and gallbladder disease. Chronic liver disease and cirrhosis are the most frequent causes of digestive system mortality, and except for chronic hepatitis and biliary cirrhosis these are almost exclusively due to chronic alcoholism.

External Causes (ICD-9; E800-E999)

External causes include all environmental events, circumstances, and conditions that have caused injury, poisoning, violence, or other adverse effects. In British Columbia, people of aboriginal descent have a high number of deaths from external causes (Danderfer & Foster, 1991).

Motor Vehicle Traffic Accidents (MVTA) (ICD-9; E810-E819)

In British Columbia in 1985 and 1989, there were 500 and 496 MVTA deaths respectively. In 1987 a peak of 622 mortalities was recorded. Most such fatalities (34.5 percent) were due to head injuries. Deaths from MVTAs in any region may be affected by the age and gender of the population (males in their early 20s are most at risk), weather, road conditions, month of the year (deaths in British Columbia peak in July and September), and the number of vehicles on the roads. This last factor is influenced by the degree of urbanization of a region and seasonal tourist fluctuations. Another factor influencing mortality may be distance from a trauma centre and the emergency response capability in the different areas of the province.

Accidental Falls (ICD-9; E880-E888)

"Small" falls in the home by elderly women, resulting in a fractured hip or femur, are the most common cause of this type of accidental death.

Suicide (ICD-9; E950-E959)

Suicide risk factors include age (25-44), gender (male), accessibility to firearms (105 males, 9 females in 1989), economic and employment factors, degree of isolation, community resources, and alcohol consumption.

Alcohol-Related Deaths

This category includes all events in which alcohol was documented as being directly, or indirectly, related to the cause of death. Alcohol-related deaths include any death in which the underlying cause (direct) or contributing causes (indirect) of death included at least one of the following ICD-9 codes:

291	Alcohol psychoses
303	Alcohol dependence syndrome
305.0	Nondependent abuse of alcohol
357.5	Alcoholic polyneuropathy
425.5	Alcoholic cardiomyopathy
535.3	Alcoholic gastritis
571	Liver disease and cirrhosis (excluding nonalcohol-specific chronic hepatitis [571.4] and billiary cirrhosis [571.6])
577.1	Chronic pancreatitis
648.4	Alcohol and pregnancy
760.7	Fetal Alcohol Syndrome
E860	Accidental alcohol poisoning

In the period 1985 to 1989, 2,009 deaths were due directly to alcohol and in an additional 1,827 deaths, alcohol was indirectly related. Alcohol-related deaths were found to be more common among males than females and infrequent before age 25. Within the indirect cause group, conditions most related to alcohol consumption included heart disease, accidents, respiratory disease, suicide, digestive tract disease, and specific cancer sites such as liver, pancreas, lung, and pharynx (Danderfer & Foster, 1991).

AGE GROUPINGS

Mortality is mapped not only by disease groups and categories, but also by age groups. The seven age groups employed in this atlas were chosen to reflect both standard statistical practices and stages of the life cycle. A descriptive categorization which may be applied to them has been published elsewhere (Foster & Danderfer, 1991) and is shown below:

Under 1 Year	-	Infancy;
1 - 14 Years	-	Childhood;
15 - 24 Years	-	Formative years for work and education;
25 - 44 Years	-	Productive career development and child rearing;
45 - 64 Years	-	Middle years of completed family, career and security;
65 - 84 Years	-	Retirement;
85 Years and over	-	Advanced old age.

LOCAL HEALTH AREA AND HEALTH UNIT DESCRIPTIONS

Kevin F. Burr, Mark Collison, Ron Strohmaier, and Leslie T. Foster

In this chapter, environmental and sociodemographic characteristics of provincial subregions are described at the Health Unit level, so that readers can understand the local community context of the mortality data. As indicated earlier, health status is influenced to varying degrees by the physical environment and by the socioeconomic characteristics of the population. The latter include employment, education, and income. Health status is influenced also by the nature of the health services available to the population in any given area.

Regional Hospital Districts are included in the atlas so that hospitals, which are increasingly providing community-based programs outside of the hospital setting, can appreciate the population-based health status of their "catchment areas". The relationships between Local Health Areas (LHAs) and Health Units (HUs) and between LHAs and Regional Hospital Districts (RHDs) are shown in Tables 4 and 5. The boundaries for these units are shown in Figures 15 to 17.

Overlay transparencies of the Local Health Area, Health Unit, and Regional Hospital District figures are included in a pocket inside the back cover of this atlas. These transparencies can be used to readily identify specific areas on the mortality maps.

POPULATION

The populations of Health Units, Local Health Areas, and Regional Hospital Districts vary substantially in size, density, and average age. In 1986, the populations of Health Units ranged from 435,995 for Vancouver (HU 30) to 50,012 for Coast Garibaldi (HU 11). Local Health Area populations ranged from 435,995 (Vancouver, LHA 39) to 685 (Telegraph Creek, LHA 94), while Regional Hospital Districts' populations varied from 1,336,615 (Greater Vancouver, RHD 16) to 3,167 (Central Coast, RHD 5).

Within most Health Units and Regional Hospital Districts, the variation in the population size of individual Local Health Areas also was quite high. For example, the Capital Regional District (HU 20) had LHAs within it which varied in population from 176,365 to 9,001. In Greater Vancouver Regional Hospital District (RHD 16), Local Health Areas varied in population from 435,995 to 39,972. For the province as a whole, population densities, in 1989, ranged from nearly 3,270 people/km^2 in Vancouver (HU 30) to only 0.3/km^2 in Skeena (HU 16) and Peace River (HU 17).

Table 4   Health Unit/Local Health Area Summary

Health Unit	Local Health Area	1986 * Population	Health Unit	Local Health Area	1986 * Population
01 East Kootenay	01 Fernie	16,767	13 Central Vancouver Island	65 Cowichan	34,972
	02 Cranbrook	21,216		66 Lake Cowichan	5,125
	03 Kimberley	8,652		67 Ladysmith	12,468
	04 Windermere	6,454		68 Nanaimo	60,420
	05 Creston	10,137		69 Qualicum	22,060
	18 Golden	6,652		70 Alberni	30,341
		69,878			**165,386**
02 Central Kootenay	06 Kootenay Lake	3,099	14 Upper Vancouver Island	71 Courtenay	37,553
	07 Nelson	19,809		72 Campbell River	29,596
	09 Castlegar	11,549		84 Vancouver Island West	3,996
	10 Arrow Lakes	4,516		85 Vancouver Island North	14,934
	11 Trail	20,257			**86,079**
	12 Grand Forks	6,984	15 Cariboo	27 Cariboo-Chilcotin	37,036
	13 Kettle Valley	3,094		28 Quesnel	23,437
		69,308		49 Central Coast	3,167
04 North Okanagan	19 Revelstoke	9,011			**63,640**
	20 Salmon Arm	24,436	16 Skeena	50 Queen Charlotte	5,480
	21 Armstrong-Spallumcheen	7,016		52 Prince Rupert	17,581
	22 Vernon	42,802		54 Smithers	14,268
	78 Enderby	5,227		80 Kitimat	12,893
		88,492		87 Stikine	2,022
05 South Okanagan	14 Southern Okanagan	13,676		88 Terrace	24,308
	15 Penticton	29,143		92 Nishga	1,597
	16 Keremeos	3,480		94 Telegraph Creek	685
	17 Princeton	4,704			**78,834**
	23 Central Okanagan	89,730	17 Peace River	59 Peace River South	26,956
	77 Summerland	8,086		60 Peace River North	25,040
		148,819		81 Fort Nelson	5,282
06 South Central	24 Kamloops	76,466			**57,278**
	26 North Thompson	4,730	18 Northern Interior	55 Burns Lake	7,789
	29 Lillooet	4,563		56 Nechako	15,413
	30 South Cariboo	7,603		57 Prince George	89,337
	31 Merritt	9,694			**112,539**
		103,056	20 Capital Regional District	61 Greater Victoria	176,365
07 Upper Fraser Valley	32 Hope	7,185		62 Sooke	39,680
	33 Chilliwack	45,529		63 Saanich	40,339
	34 Abbotsford	66,435		64 Gulf Islands	9,001
	76 Agassiz-Harrison	5,251			**265,385**
		124,400	30 Vancouver	39 Vancouver	**435,995**
08 Central Fraser Valley	35 Langley	70,457	31 Burnaby	41 Burnaby	**145,160**
	42 Maple Ridge	44,200	32 Richmond	38 Richmond	**108,495**
	75 Mission	25,294	33 North Shore	44 North Vancouver	104,306
		139,951		45 West Vancouver-Bowen Island	40,734
09 Boundary	36 Surrey	196,207			**145,040**
	37 Delta	79,789			
		275,996	PROVINCE		**2,889,215**
10 Simon Fraser	40 New Westminster	39,972			
	43 Coquitlam	115,500			
		155,472			
11 Coast-Garibaldi	46 Sechelt	16,758			
	47 Powell River	18,074			
	48 Howe Sound	15,180			
		50,012			

* June 1986 Census Data: provided by Planning and Statistics Division, Ministry of Finance and Corporate Relations

Table 5   Regional Hospital District/Local Health Area Summary

Regional Hospital District	Local Health Area	1986 * Population	Regional Hospital District	Local Health Area	1986 * Population
01 Alberni-Clayoquot	70 Alberni	**30,341**	16 Greater Vancouver	35 Langely	70,457
				36 Surrey	196,207
02 Bulkley-Nechako	54 Smithers	14,268		37 Delta	79,789
	55 Burns Lake	7,789		38 Richmond	108,495
	56 Nechako	15,413		39 Vancouver	435,995
		37,470		40 New Westminster	39,972
				41 Burnaby	145,160
03 Capital	61 Greater Victoria	176,365		43 Coquitlam	115,500
	62 Sooke	39,680		44 North Vancouver	104,306
	63 Saanich	40,339		45 West Vancouver-	
	64 Gulf Islands	9,001		Bowen Island	40,734
		265,385			**1,336,615**
04 Cariboo	27 Cariboo-Chilcotin	37,036	17 Kitimat-Stikine	80 Kitimat	12,893
	28 Quesnel	23,437		88 Terrace***	24,993
		60,473		92 Nishga	1,597
					39,483
05 Central Coast	49 Central Coast	**3,167**			
			18 Kootenay-Boundary	11 Trail	20,257
06 Central Fraser Valley	34 Abbotsford	**66,435**		12 Grand Forks	6,984
				13 Kettle Valley	3,094
07 Central Kootenay	07 Nelson	19,809			**30,335**
	09 Castlegar	11,549			
	10 Arrow Lakes	4,516	19 Mount Waddington	85 Vancouver Island North	**14,934**
	86 Creston-Kaslo**	13,236			
		49,110	20 Nanaimo	68 Nanaimo	60,420
				69 Qualicum	22,060
08 Central Okanagan	23 Central Okanagan	**89,730**			**82,480**
09 Columbia-Shuswap	18 Golden	6,652	21 North Okanagan	21 Armstrong-Spallumcheen	7,016
	19 Revelstoke	9,011		22 Vernon	42,802
	20 Salmon Arm	24,436		78 Enderby	5,227
		40,099			**55,045**
10 Comox-Strathcona	71 Courtenay	37,553	22 Okanagan	14 Southern Okanagan	13,676
	72 Campbell River	29,596	Similkameen	15 Penticton	29,143
	84 Vancouver Island West	3,996		16 Keremeos	3,480
		71,145		17 Princeton	4,704
				77 Summerland	8,086
11 Cowichan Valley	65 Cowichan	34,972			**59,089**
	66 Lake Cowichan	5,125			
	67 Ladysmith	12,468	23 Peace River	59 Peace River South	26,956
		52,565		60 Peace River North	25,040
					51,996
12 Dewdney-Alouette	42 Maple Ridge	44,200			
	75 Mission	25,294	24 Powell River	47 Powell River	**18,074**
		69,494			
			25 Skeena-	50 Queen Charlotte	5,480
13 East Kootenay	01 Fernie	16,767	Queen Charlotte	52 Prince Rupert	17,581
	02 Cranbrook	21,216			**23,061**
	03 Kimberley	8,652			
	04 Windermere	6,454	26 Squamish-Lillooet	29 Lillooet	4,563
		53,089		48 Howe Sound	15,180
					19,743
14 Fraser-Cheam	32 Hope	7,185	27 Stikine	87 Stikine	**2,022**
	33 Chilliwack	45,529			
	76 Agassiz-Harrison	5,251	28 Sunshine Coast	46 Sechelt	**16,758**
		57,965			
			29 Thompson-Nicola	24 Kamloops	76,466
15 Fraser-Fort George	57 Prince George	**89,337**		26 North Thompson	4,730
				30 South Cariboo	7,603
				31 Merritt	9,694
					98,493
			30 Fort Nelson-Liard	81 Fort Nelson	**5,282**
			PROVINCE		**2,889,215**

*   June 1986, Census Data: provided by Planning and Statistics Division, Ministry of Finance and Corporate Relations
** LHAs 5 & 6 Combined   *** LHAs 88 & 94 Combined

33

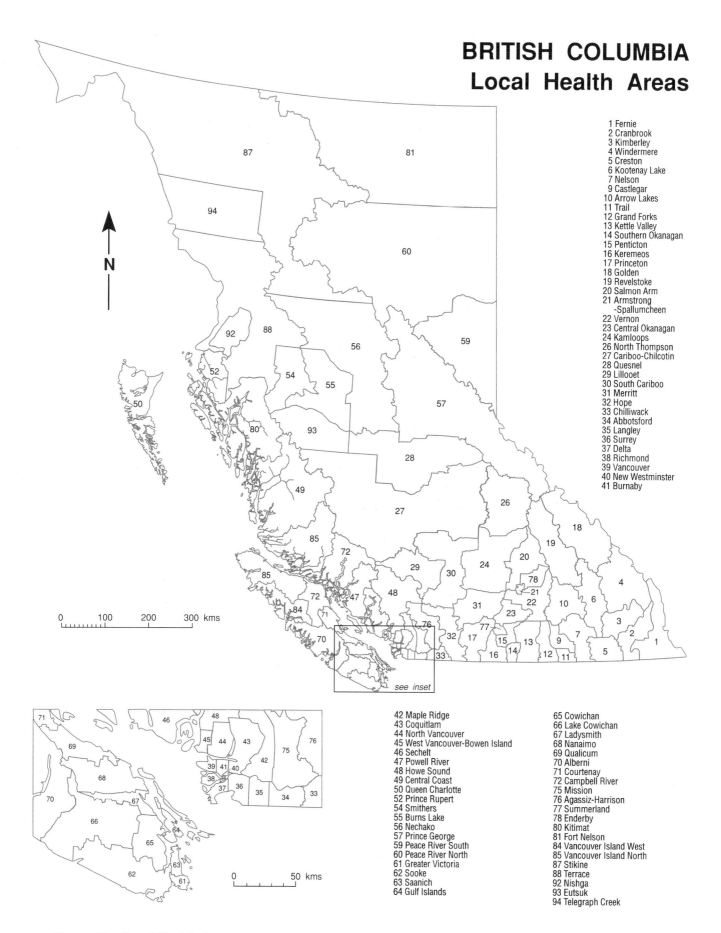

BRITISH COLUMBIA
Local Health Areas

1 Fernie
2 Cranbrook
3 Kimberley
4 Windermere
5 Creston
6 Kootenay Lake
7 Nelson
9 Castlegar
10 Arrow Lakes
11 Trail
12 Grand Forks
13 Kettle Valley
14 Southern Okanagan
15 Penticton
16 Keremeos
17 Princeton
18 Golden
19 Revelstoke
20 Salmon Arm
21 Armstrong
  -Spallumcheen
22 Vernon
23 Central Okanagan
24 Kamloops
26 North Thompson
27 Cariboo-Chilcotin
28 Quesnel
29 Lillooet
30 South Cariboo
31 Merritt
32 Hope
33 Chilliwack
34 Abbotsford
35 Langley
36 Surrey
37 Delta
38 Richmond
39 Vancouver
40 New Westminster
41 Burnaby

42 Maple Ridge
43 Coquitlam
44 North Vancouver
45 West Vancouver-Bowen Island
46 Sechelt
47 Powell River
48 Howe Sound
49 Central Coast
50 Queen Charlotte
52 Prince Rupert
54 Smithers
55 Burns Lake
56 Nechako
57 Prince George
59 Peace River South
60 Peace River North
61 Greater Victoria
62 Sooke
63 Saanich
64 Gulf Islands

65 Cowichan
66 Lake Cowichan
67 Ladysmith
68 Nanaimo
69 Qualicum
70 Alberni
71 Courtenay
72 Campbell River
75 Mission
76 Agassiz-Harrison
77 Summerland
78 Enderby
80 Kitimat
81 Fort Nelson
84 Vancouver Island West
85 Vancouver Island North
87 Stikine
88 Terrace
92 Nishga
93 Eutsuk
94 Telegraph Creek

Figure 15   Local Health Areas

34

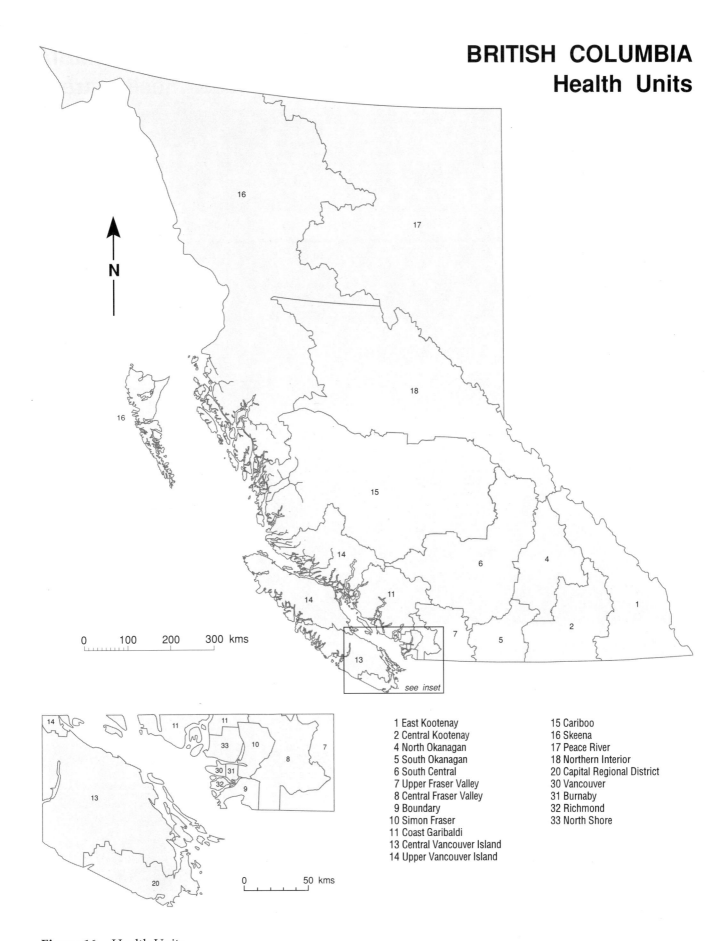

BRITISH COLUMBIA
Health Units

N

0   100   200   300 kms

see inset

1 East Kootenay
2 Central Kootenay
4 North Okanagan
5 South Okanagan
6 South Central
7 Upper Fraser Valley
8 Central Fraser Valley
9 Boundary
10 Simon Fraser
11 Coast Garibaldi
13 Central Vancouver Island
14 Upper Vancouver Island

15 Cariboo
16 Skeena
17 Peace River
18 Northern Interior
20 Capital Regional District
30 Vancouver
31 Burnaby
32 Richmond
33 North Shore

0   50 kms

Figure 16   Health Units

35

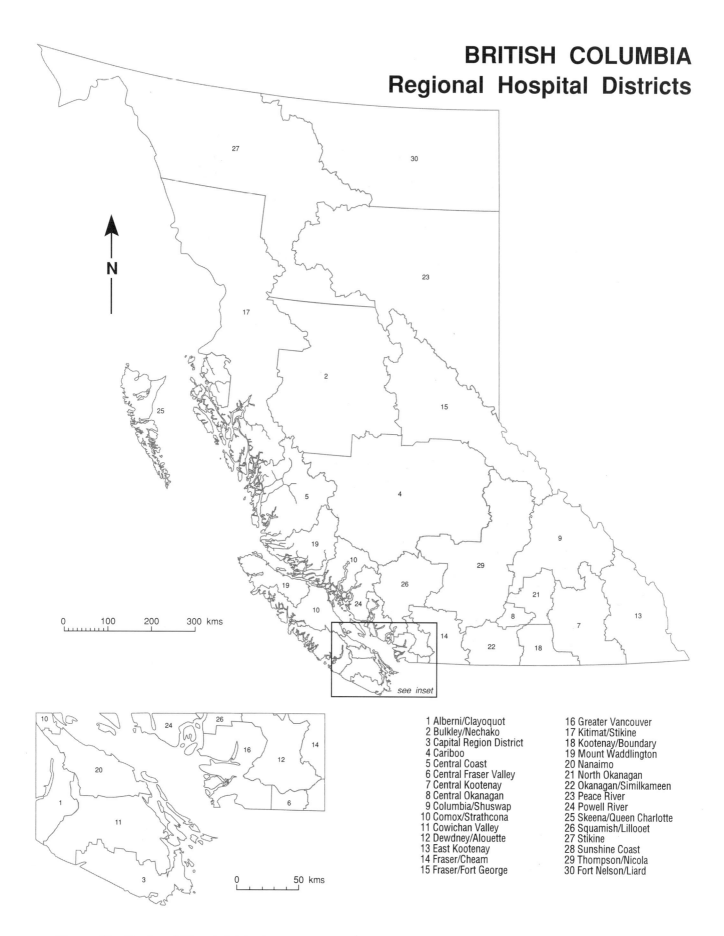

BRITISH COLUMBIA
Regional Hospital Districts

N

| 0   100   200   300 kms | | | |

see inset

0   50 kms

1 Alberni/Clayoquot
2 Bulkley/Nechako
3 Capital Region District
4 Cariboo
5 Central Coast
6 Central Fraser Valley
7 Central Kootenay
8 Central Okanagan
9 Columbia/Shuswap
10 Comox/Strathcona
11 Cowichan Valley
12 Dewdney/Alouette
13 East Kootenay
14 Fraser/Cheam
15 Fraser/Fort George

16 Greater Vancouver
17 Kitimat/Stikine
18 Kootenay/Boundary
19 Mount Waddlington
20 Nanaimo
21 North Okanagan
22 Okanagan/Similkameen
23 Peace River
24 Powell River
25 Skeena/Queen Charlotte
26 Squamish/Lillooet
27 Stikine
28 Sunshine Coast
29 Thompson/Nicola
30 Fort Nelson/Liard

Figure 17   Regional Hospital Districts

ECONOMIC AND EDUCATIONAL FACTORS

The Ministry of Health requires each of its directly administered Health Units to prepare area community profiles that describe population characteristics, health and social statistics, and available services. Some units have also carried out community surveys to determine health problems and issues, as perceived by the community. Most metropolitan Health Departments (Capital Regional District, City of Vancouver, North Shore, and Municipalities of Richmond and Burnaby), which are operated by municipal or regional governments, also have produced similar profiles. The following descriptions of the characteristics of the Health Units have been summarized, in part, from these profiles,[1] some of which are still only in draft form. In addition, information from the *British Columbia Regional Index* (Ministry of Regional Development and Ministry of Finance and Corporate Relations, 1989) has been extensively used.

The descriptions of the Health Unit population characteristics include some indicators of income, education, and employment, which have been linked to health status (Wilkins & Adams, 1983; Evans & Stoddart, 1990). The percentage of the population aged 15 years and over having less than grade 9 education was felt to be the best available single measure of educational attainment, or lack thereof.

HEALTH HUMAN RESOURCE FACTORS

The tables accompanying each of the Health Unit descriptions include data on both registered physicians and registered nurses. Physician numbers include all directory-active physicians (in general practice, specialties, and postgraduate training) who are on the full, special, or temporary registers of the College of Physicians and Surgeons of British Columbia. Total nurse numbers include both registered nurses and licensed practical nurses. Registered nurses are on active registration with the Registered Nurses Association of British Columbia and comprise nurses who are registered, practising, and employed in nursing. Registered psychiatric nurses are not included. Licensed practical nurses are licensed by the British Columbia Council of Licensed Practical Nurses and comprise nurses who are employed on either a regular or casual/seasonal basis.[2] Numbers of physicians and nurses provide an indication of the level of health services available within Local Health Areas. It should be noted, however, that the location of physicians is based on their practice addresses, whereas the location of nurses reflects residential addresses.

Many factors have an impact on the distribution of health-care professionals. These include among others, the health needs of the population they serve, the location of health-care institutions, the accessibility to neighbouring resources, and the differing roles that informal care givers play (Health Manpower Research Unit, 1990). It is to be expected that such health resources will tend to be more available in communities having health-care facilities, particularly in those communities with secondary and tertiary-care hospitals (A.D. Thomson, 1990). Caution should be exercised in deriving conclusions about inequities in health-care provision based on the limited statistics provided on health-care professionals.

---

[1] Those requiring more detailed information on Health Units should contact the Division of Vital Statistics or individual Health Units directly.

[2] Data by LHA were obtained from the Health Human Resources Unit, Centre for Health Services and Policy Research, University of British Columbia, Vancouver.

With the above caveats in mind, it may be noted that the number of physicians per 10,000 population ranged from a low of 10.5 in Peace River (HU 17) to a high of 59.9 in Vancouver (HU 30). Only Vancouver and the Capital Regional District (HU 20) exceeded the provincial rate of 23.3 (Figure 18).

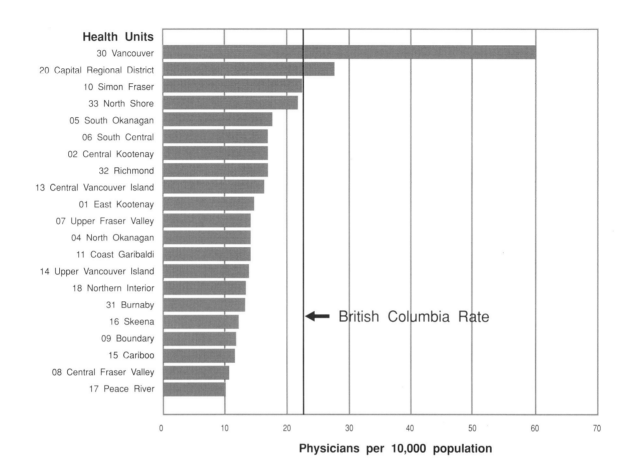

Figure 18 Physicians per 10,000 Population by Health Unit: 1989

This distribution of physicians reflects the concentration of secondary and tertiary health services in these two major urban areas. At the Local Health Area level variation in the rate was even greater, with Nishga (LHA 92) and Telegraph Creek (LHA 94) having no physicians at all, compared with Vancouver (LHA 39), which had the highest rate of physicians in the province (Figure 19).

A similar distribution pattern existed for nurses, with the number per 10,000 population ranging from a low of 60.7 in the Cariboo (HU 15) to a high of 121.6 in the Capital Regional District (HU 20). Figure 20 indicates there were eight Health Units that exceeded the provincial rate of 93.0; the Capital Regional District (HU 20), Central Kootenay (HU 2), North Shore (HU 33), Vancouver (HU 30), South Central (HU 6), Richmond (HU 32), Simon Fraser (HU 10), and South Okanagan (HU 5). This pattern again reflects the concentration of health services in major urban areas. As in the case of physicians, the variations were more pronounced at the LHA level (Figure 21), with nurses per 10,000 population ranging from 16.6 in Sooke (LHA 62) to 162.6 in Trail (LHA 11). The pattern in the major metropolitan areas differed slightly from that for physicians, which may be the result of using residential rather than place-of-practice addresses.

38

Local Health Areas

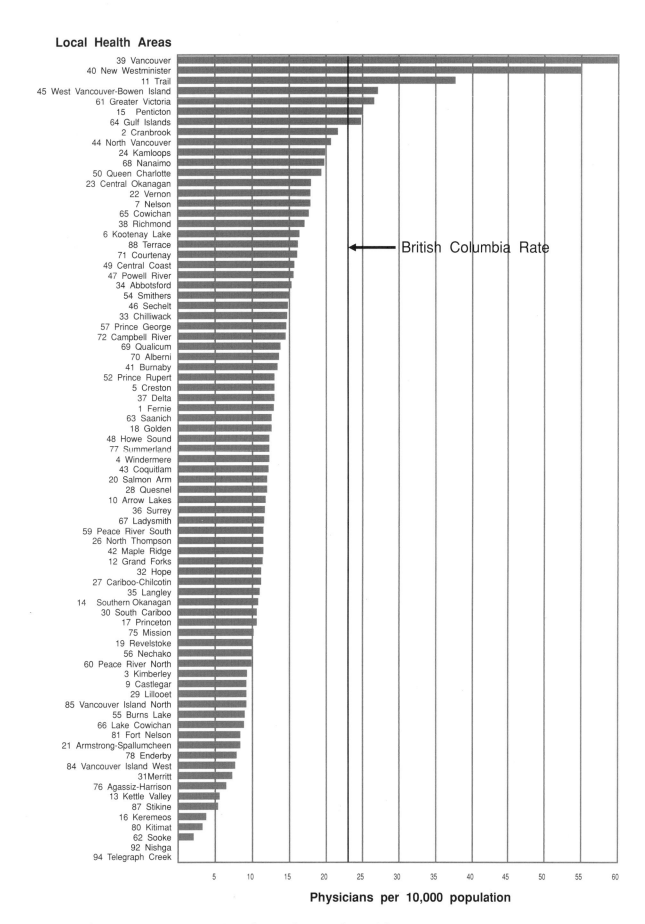

Figure 19 Physicians per 10,000 Population by Local Health Area: 1989

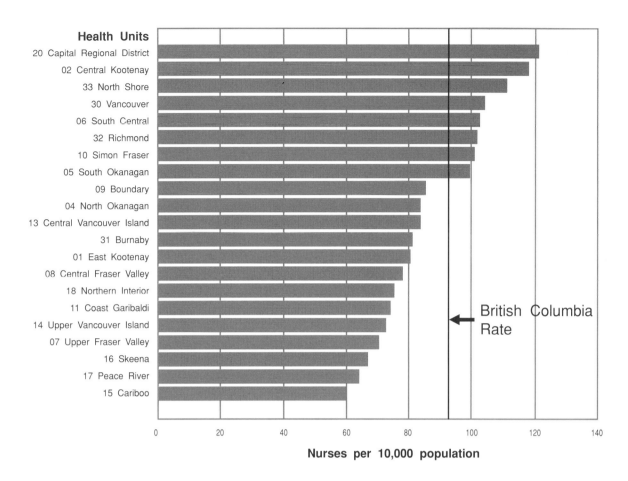

Figure 20 Nurses per 10,000 Population by Health Unit: 1989

HEALTH UNIT DESCRIPTIONS

The remainder of this chapter provides a brief narrative description and tabular summary of provincial Health Units and their constituent Local Health Areas. Although each Health Unit and Local Health Area has a unique number assigned to it, there are gaps in the numbering system due to historical changes, such as the merging of two Health Units into one.

Sources for the data in the tables of Selected Characteristics of Health Units are:

- Planning and Statistics Division, Ministry of Finance and Corporate Relations (Mid-Year Population Estimates)

- Statistics Canada (Incomes and Education)

- Health Human Resources Unit, Centre for Health Services and Policy Research, University of British Columbia (Physicians - September 1989; Registered Nurses - June 1989; Licensed Practical Nurses - September 1989)

Local Health Areas

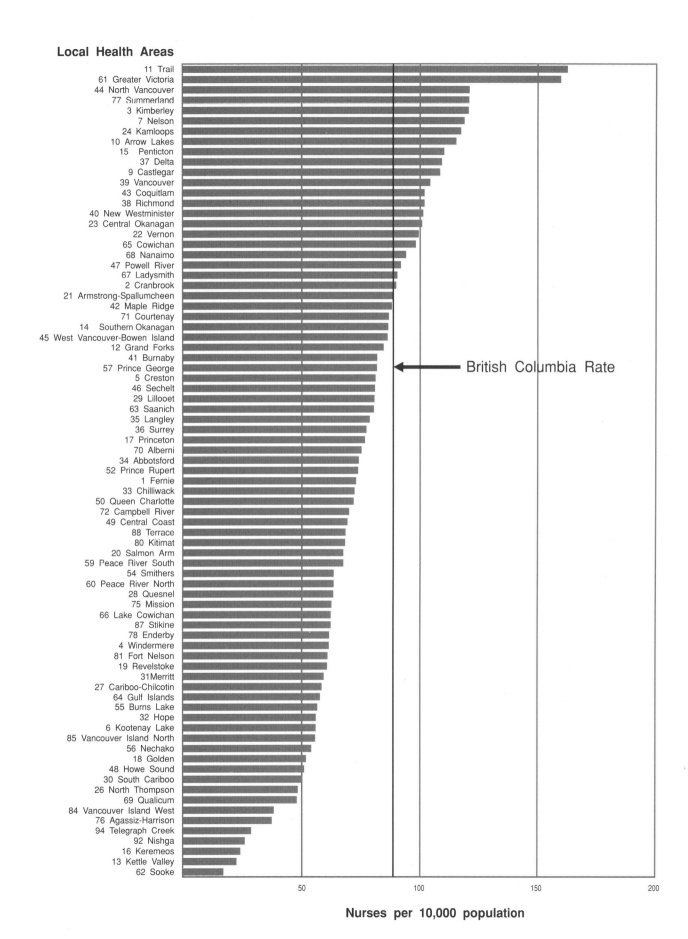

Nurses per 10,000 population

Figure 21   Nurses per 10,000 Population by Local Health Area: 1989

East Kootenay (HU 1) (Table 6)

The East Kootenay Health Unit covers approximately 45,000 km² in the southeast interior of British Columbia. In 1989, the average population density was very low, with about 1.5 persons/km². The topography of the area is dominated by the Purcell and Rocky Mountains and the broad valley of the upper Columbia River. Climatically the region may be described as continental.

The East Kootenay's economy is primarily resource-based. Data from the 1986 census indicate that the retail and wholesale trade segment was the largest employer, accounting for 18.4 percent of the labour force. Mining was the second major source of employment. Manufacturing, which includes forest-related activities, was third, followed by accommodation, which includes food and beverage services. Other sectors of the economy include: transportation, communication, and utilities; community and business services; health and social services; construction; public administration; and financial, insurance, and real estate. Distribution of the labour force by sector varies quite widely among LHAs.

A negative net population growth cycle began in the early 1980s. Golden was the only LHA to show a population increase over the period 1985 to 1989. Average age for the Health Unit was lower than the provincial average, with Kimberley and Creston having a markedly larger proportion of older adults than the other four LHAs.

The 1986 household incomes, which were marginally less than the provincial average, varied substantially within the Health Unit, from a high of $42,564 in Fernie to a low of only $22,854 in Creston. Educational achievement also was lower than the provincial average.

The number of physicians per 10,000 population in the Health Unit, at 15.1 (HU rank 10), was less than the provincial rate of 23.3. This measure varied among LHAs, from a high of 21.7 in Cranbrook (LHA rank 8) to a low of 9.3 in Kimberley (LHA rank 61). The number of nurses per 10,000 population, at 81.2 (HU rank 13), was also below the provincial rate of 93.0. At the LHA level the rate varied from a high of 120.7 in Kimberley (LHA rank 5) to a low of 51.8 in Golden (LHA rank 68).

The three leading causes of death were the same as those for the province as a whole, although chronic lung disease in the Fernie and Cranbrook LHAs and motor vehicle accidents in the Windermere LHA are noteworthy.

Table 6   Selected Characteristics of East Kootenay Health Unit

Local Health Area	Gender	Population 1985	Population 1989	Average Age 1985	Average Age 1989	Top 3 Leading Causes of Death 1985-1989	Household Income (Average) 1986	% 15+ With < Grade 9 1986	Physicians per 10,000 Population	Nurses per 10,000 Population
01 Fernie	Male	9,107	7,651	29.2	30.5	Ischaemic Heart Disease				
	Female	8,239	7,060	28.8	30.6	Cerebrovascular Disease/Stroke			(rank:35)	(rank:41)
	Total	17,346	14,711	29.0	30.5	Chronic Lung Disease	42,564	10.1	12.9	72.7
02 Cranbrook	Male	10,815	9,898	31.0	32.0	Ischaemic Heart Disease				
	Female	10,746	9,939	31.7	33.4	Cerebrovascular Disease/Stroke			(rank:02)	(rank:22)
	Total	21,561	19,837	31.3	32.7	Chronic Lung Disease	32,501	10.9	21.7	89.7
03 Kimberley	Male	4,494	3,739	34.7	36.1	Ischaemic Heart Disease				
	Female	4,495	3,798	35.9	38.2	Lung Cancer			(rank:61)	(rank:05)
	Total	8,989	7,537	35.3	37.1	Cerebrovascular Disease/Stroke	31,838	11.3	9.3	120.7
04 Windermere	Male	3,376	3,355	32.4	33.5	Ischaemic Heart Disease				
	Female	3,172	3,170	32.1	33.0	Cerebrovascular Disease/Stroke			(rank:39)	(rank:57)
	Total	6,548	6,525	32.3	33.3	Motor Vehicle Accidents	31,082	13.0	12.3	61.3
05 Creston	Male	5,025	4,935	39.2	39.8	Ischaemic Heart Disease				
	Female	5,112	5,054	40.6	41.1	Cerebrovascular Disease/Stroke			(rank:33)	(rank:31)
	Total	10,137	9,989	39.9	40.5	Lung Cancer	22,854	20.9	13.0	81.1
18 Golden	Male	3,453	3,711	30.1	31.3	Ischaemic Heart Disease				
	Female	3,169	3,437	29.4	30.5	Cerebrovascular Disease/Stroke			(rank:34)	(rank:68)
	Total	6,622	7,148	29.8	30.9	Lung Cancer	33,312	13.8	12.6	51.8
01 HEALTH UNIT	**Male**	**36,270**	**33,289**	**32.2**	**33.3**	**Ischaemic Heart Disease**				
	Female	**34,933**	**32,458**	**32.7**	**34.2**	**Cerebrovascular Disease/Stroke**			**(rank:10)**	**(rank:13)**
	Total	**71,203**	**65,747**	**32.4**	**33.8**	**Lung Cancer**	**32,358**	**12.8**	**15.1**	**81.2**
PROVINCE	Male	1,422,900	1,506,397	33.9	34.9	Ischaemic Heart Disease				
	Female	1,447,200	1,540,847	35.7	36.7	Cerebrovascular Disease/Stroke				
	Total	2,870,100	3,047,244	34.8	35.8	Lung Cancer	33,497	11.2	23.3	93.0

Central Kootenay (HU 2) (Table 7)

The Central Kootenay area is situated in southern British Columbia, occupying approximately 31,800 km². The area lies mostly within the Selkirk Mountains and its natural features give it great potential for tourism and recreation. The area has a history of extensive mining activity and, more recently, logging. There are also important smelting and sawmill industries. Shifts in economic activity are resulting in more employment in tourism and services.

The average population density in 1989, at approximately 2.1 people/km², was very low, with much of this population living along narrow river valleys in rural areas. The average age was marginally higher than the provincial average, with older populations residing in the Kootenay Lake and Grand Forks LHAs. Populations in all LHAs in the Health Unit declined between 1985 and 1989. While the majority of people are English speaking, there is a large number of people of Russian ethnic origin, particularly in the Grand Forks area, and a large Italian ethnic group residing in Trail.

Average 1986 household income was the second-lowest in the province. The Health Unit also had the largest percentage of the population 15 years and older with less than a grade 9 education.

The number of physicians per 10,000 population in the Health Unit, at 17.3 (HU rank 7), was less than the provincial rate of 23.3. This measure varied considerably among LHAs from a high of 26.6 in Trail (LHA rank 5) to a low of 6.5 in the Kettle Valley (LHA rank 72). The number of nurses per 10,000 population in the Health Unit, at 118.6, was the second-highest in the province. At the LHA level there was considerable variation from a high of 162.6 in Trail (LHA rank 1) to a low of 22.8 in the Kettle Valley (LHA rank 78).

The leading causes of death were the same as those for the province as a whole, although chronic lung disease in the Kootenay Lake and Arrow Lakes LHAs, motor vehicle accidents and suicides in the Kettle Valley LHA, and breast cancer in the Kootenay Lake LHA ranked high in importance.

Table 7   Selected Characteristics of Central Kootenay Health Unit

Local Health Area	Gender	Population 1985	Population 1989	Average Age 1985	Average Age 1989	Top 3 Leading Causes of Death 1985-1989	Household Income (Average) 1986	% 15+ With < Grade 9 1986	Physicians per 10,000 Population	Nurses per 10,000 Population
06 Kootenay Lake	Male	1,595	1,542	38.1	39.9	Ischaemic Heart Disease				
	Female	1,544	1,507	38.1	39.5	Lung Cancer			(rank:18)	(rank:65)
	Total	3,139	3,049	38.1	39.7	Breast Cancer - Chronic Lung Disease	23,155	13.2	16.4	55.8
07 Nelson	Male	10,329	9,757	34.8	35.5	Ischaemic Heart Disease				
	Female	10,363	9,845	36.1	37.2	Cerebrovascular/Stroke			(rank:14)	(rank:06)
	Total	20,692	19,602	35.4	36.4	Lung Cancer	25,465	15.1	17.9	118.9
09 Castlegar	Male	5,958	5,448	33.7	34.4	Ischaemic Heart Disease				
	Female	5,877	5,430	34.5	35.8	Cerebrovascular/Stroke			(rank:63)	(rank:11)
	Total	11,835	10,878	34.1	35.1	Lung Cancer	29,756	17.4	9.2	108.5
10 Arrow Lakes	Male	2,423	2,197	34.3	35.4	Ischaemic Heart Disease				
	Female	2,264	2,051	36.1	37.6	Chronic Lung Disease			(rank:44)	(rank:08)
	Total	4,687	4,248	35.2	36.4	Cerebrovascular/Stroke	28,923	12.1	11.8	115.3
11 Trail	Male	10,482	9,461	34.9	35.9	Ischaemic Heart Disease				
	Female	10,589	9,733	36.7	37.9	Cerebrovascular/Stroke			(rank:05)	(rank:01)
	Total	21,071	19,194	35.8	36.9	Lung Cancer	32,684	13.6	26.6	162.6
12 Grand Forks	Male	3,597	3,506	37.6	38.6	Ischaemic Heart Disease				
	Female	3,542	3,481	39.6	40.6	Cerebrovascular/Stroke			(rank:50)	(rank:28)
	Total	7,139	6,987	38.6	39.6	Lung Cancer	24,344	21.9	11.4	84.4
13 Kettle Valley	Male	1,690	1613	35.0	36.3	Ischaemic Heart Disease				
	Female	1,521	1458	34.1	35.6	Motor Vehichle Accident			(rank:72)	(rank:78)
	Total	3,211	3071	34.6	36.0	Lung Cancer - Suicide	25,563	18.9	6.5	22.8
02 HEALTH UNIT	**Male**	**36,074**	**33,524**	**35.0**	**36.0**	**Ischaemic Heart Disease**				
	Female	**35,700**	**33,505**	**36.3**	**37.6**	**Cerebrovascular/Stroke**			**(rank:07)**	**(rank:02)**
	Total	**71,774**	**67,029**	**35.7**	**36.8**	**Lung Cancer**	**27,127**	**15.6**	**17.3**	**118.6**
PROVINCE	Male	1,422,900	1,506,397	33.9	34.9	Ischaemic Heart Disease				
	Female	1,447,200	1,540,847	35.7	36.7	Cerebrovascular Disease/Stroke				
	Total	2,870,100	3,047,244	34.8	35.8	Lung Cancer	33,497	11.2	23.3	93.0

North Okanagan (HU 4) (Table 8)

The North Okanagan Health Unit, occupying approximately 24,400 km^2, covers the area north of the Okanagan Valley, of which it is a geographical and economic extension. Vernon is the primary commercial centre and contains approximately half of the Health Unit's population. Forestry has played an important role in the area's economy and manufacturing activity continues to be dominated by forest industries, especially sawmills. Traditionally agriculture also has been an important sector of the economy, except in the north around Revelstoke.

The Armstrong-Spallumcheen area marks a transition between climatic zones. Dry-land farming predominates in the southern section where little irrigation water is available at reasonable cost; grain, hay, and field peas and beans are the leading crops. Rainfall is heaviest in the north where dairy farming is the leading activity. Beef cattle are also an important source of income. Tourism makes a significant contribution to the area's economy, with Vernon and Salmon Arm enjoying reputations as vacation destinations. Rail transportation services continue to be the leading source of employment in Revelstoke.

In 1989, population density was approximately 3.6 people/km^2. This has remained quite stable, with the exception of Revelstoke which lost population between 1985 and 1989. Average age was marginally higher than the provincial average, although in Revelstoke it was much lower. With the exception of Revelstoke, all LHAs had average 1986 household income and educational attainment levels substantially below those of the province as a whole.

The number of physicians per 10,000 population in the Health Unit, at 14.3 (HU rank 12), was less than the provincial rate of 23.3. This measure varied between LHAs from a high of 17.9 in Vernon (LHA rank 15) to a low of 7.9 in Enderby (LHA rank 69). The number of nurses per 10,000 population, at 84.1 (HU rank 10), also was less than the provincial rate of 93.0. At the LHA level the rate varied from a high of 99.4 in Vernon (LHA rank 17) to a low of 60.6 in Revelstoke (LHA rank 59).

The leading causes of death were the same as those for the province, although chronic lung disease and motor vehicle accidents ranked high in the Armstrong-Spallumcheen LHA. Deaths due to motor vehicle accidents also were high in the Enderby LHA.

Table 8   Selected Characteristics of North Okanagan Health Unit

Local Health Area	Gender	Population 1985	Population 1989	Average Age 1985	Average Age 1989	Top 3 Leading Causes of Death 1985-1989	Household Income (Average) 1986	% 15+ With < Grade 9 1986	Physicians per 10,000 Population	Nurses per 10,000 Population
19 Revelstoke	Male	4,802	4,110	30.3	31.6	Ischaemic Heart Disease				
	Female	4,423	3,817	30.9	32.4	Lung Cancer			(rank:58)	(rank:59)
	Total	9,225	7,927	30.6	32.0	Cerebrovascular Disease/Stroke	34,319	12.0	10.1	60.6
20 Salmon Arm	Male	12,406	12,080	36.8	37.9	Ischaemic Heart Disease				
	Female	12,343	12,145	37.7	39.0	Cerebrovascular Disease/Stroke			(rank:42)	(rank:49)
	Total	24,749	24,225	37.3	38.5	Lung Cancer	25,553	14.7	12.0	67.3
21 Armstrong-	Male	3,529	3,539	34.5	35.4	Ischaemic Heart Disease				
Spallumcheen	Female	3,567	3,586	34.9	36.2	Chronic Lung Disease			(rank:67)	(rank:23)
	Total	7,096	7,125	34.7	35.8	Motor Vehicle Accident	26,411	16.2	8.4	88.4
22 Vernon	Male	21,397	21,637	34.8	35.8	Ischaemic Heart Disease				
	Female	22,026	22,425	36.3	37.6	Cerebrovascular Disease/Stroke			(rank:15)	(rank:17)
	Total	43,423	44,062	35.6	36.7	Lung Cancer	28,497	15.7	17.9	99.4
78 Enderby	Male	2,697	2,564	35.3	36.4	Ischaemic Heart Disease				
	Female	2,608	2,480	36.9	38.4	Motor Vehicle Accident			(rank:69)	(rank:56)
	Total	5,305	5,044	36.1	37.4	Lung Cancer	22,398	21.0	7.9	61.5
04 HEALTH UNIT	**Male**	**44,831**	**43,930**	**34.9**	**36.0**	**Ischaemic Heart Disease**				
	Female	**44,967**	**44,453**	**36.1**	**37.5**	**Cerebrovascular Disease/Stroke**			**(rank:12)**	**(rank:10)**
	Total	**89,798**	**88,383**	**35.5**	**36.7**	**Lung Cancer**	**27,435**	**15.4**	**14.3**	**84.1**
PROVINCE	Male	1,422,900	1,506,397	33.9	34.9	Ischaemic Heart Disease				
	Female	1,447,200	1,540,847	35.7	36.7	Cerebrovascular Disease/Stroke				
	Total	2,870,100	3,047,244	34.8	35.8	Lung Cancer	33,497	11.2	23.3	93.0

South Okanagan (HU 5) (Table 9)

This Health Unit is located in the south-central interior of British Columbia, occupying approximately 15,700 km². The area is a high mountainous plateau, dissected by Okanagan Lake and many steep-sided river valleys. Only the valley floors and their gentler side slopes are suitable for human habitation (except at ski resorts) and cultivation. These areas experience a mild, dry climate, with hot, sunny summers and cool, cloudy winters.

Most of the labour force in the area is employed in service industries such as retailing, education, health, and business and professional services. Tourism is one of the most important revenue producers in the area. The mountain scenery, relatively consistent warm summer climate, lakes, sandy beaches, and skiing are major attractions. The area is known for its fruit orchards, although profitability of fruit growing often has been marginal, due to distance from markets and world market conditions. There are numerous sawmills and a forest-products plant in the area.

Population increased from less than 40,000 in the early 1940s to about 160,000 in 1989, resulting in a density of approximately 10 people/km². Princeton is the only LHA to have lost population in the period from 1985 to 1989. In 1986, seniors made up 18 percent of the population compared with 12 percent in British Columbia as a whole. In 1989, the Health Unit was tied with the Capital Regional District (HU 20) for the highest average age of 39.7 years. Princeton, again, was anomalous, with an average age close to the provincial average.

This Health Unit had the lowest 1986 average household income in the province. Keremeos had the lowest average household income of any LHA, at only 60 percent of the provincial average. Educational attainment was substantially below the provincial level.

The number of physicians per 10,000 population in the Health Unit, at 17.9 (HU rank 5), was somewhat less than the provincial rate of 23.3. There was considerable variation among LHAs from a high of 25.1 in Penticton (LHA rank 6) to a low of 5.4 in Keremeos (LHA rank 74). The number of nurses per 10,000 population, at 100.1 (HU rank 8), was higher than the provincial rate of 93.0. At the LHA level the rates varied greatly from a high of 120.9 in Summerland (LHA rank 4) to a low of 24.4 in Keremeos (LHA rank 77).

The leading causes of death were the same as those for the province as a whole, although pneumonia and influenza deaths were prominent in the Princeton and Summerland LHAs. Deaths from chronic lung disease were significant in the Keremeos LHA.

Table 9   Selected Characteristics of South Okanagan Health Unit

Local Health Area	Gender	Population 1985	Population 1989	Average Age 1985	Average Age 1989	Top 3 Leading Causes of Death 1985-1989	Household Income (Average) 1986	% 15+ With < Grade 9 1986	Physicians per 10,000 Population	Nurses per 10,000 Population
14 Southern	Male	6,812	6,841	40.9	41.2	Ischaemic Heart Disease				
Okanagan	Female	6,995	7,104	42.3	43.5	Cerebrovascular Disease/Stroke			(rank:54)	(rank:27)
	Total	13,807	13,945	41.6	42.4	Lung Cancer	25,615	18.9	10.8	86.1
15 Penticton	Male	13,811	14,818	38.9	39.4	Ischaemic Heart Disease				
	Female	14,996	16,296	41.0	42.1	Cerebrovascular Disease/Stroke			(rank:06)	(rank:09)
	Total	28,807	31,114	40.0	40.8	Lung Cancer	27,247	14.1	25.1	110.2
16 Keremeos	Male	1,833	1,931	40.1	40.8	Ischaemic Heart Disease				
	Female	1,665	1,751	41.0	41.1	Chronic Lung Disease			(rank:74)	(rank:77)
	Total	3,498	3,682	40.5	40.9	Lung Cancer	20,353	22.7	5.4	24.4
17 Princeton	Male	2,428	2,401	34.8	34.7	Ischaemic Heart Disease				
	Female	2,293	2,297	35.2	35.9	Cerebrovascular Disease/Stroke			(rank:55)	(rank:37)
	Total	4,721	4,698	35.0	35.3	Pneumonia and Influenza	29,912	12.2	10.6	76.6
23 Central	Male	43,201	47,004	37.0	37.9	Ischaemic Heart Disease				
Okanagan	Female	45,410	49,909	38.6	39.9	Cerebrovascular Disease/Stroke			(rank:13)	(rank:16)
	Total	88,611	96,913	37.8	38.9	Lung Cancer	29,494	13.6	18.0	100.9
77 Summerland	Male	3,934	4,348	40.6	40.9	Ischaemic Heart Disease				
	Female	4,118	4,585	42.7	43.5	Cerebrovascular Disease/Stroke			(rank:40)	(rank:04)
	Total	8,052	8,933	41.7	42.2	Pneumonia and Influenza	26,249	14.4	12.3	120.9
05 HEALTH UNIT	**Male**	**72,019**	**77,343**	**37.9**	**38.6**	**Ischaemic Heart Disease**				
	Female	**75,477**	**81,942**	**39.6**	**40.7**	**Cerebrovascular Disease/Stroke**			**(rank:08)**	**(rank:05)**
	Total	**147,496**	**159,285**	**38.8**	**39.7**	**Lung Cancer**	**26,478**	**14.4**	**17.9**	**100.1**
PROVINCE	Male	1,422,900	1,506,397	33.9	34.9	Ischaemic Heart Disease				
	Female	1,447,200	1,540,847	35.7	36.7	Cerebrovascular Disease/Stroke				
	Total	2,870,100	3,047,244	34.8	35.8	Lung Cancer	33,497	11.2	23.3	93.0

South Central (HU 6) (Table 10)

This Health Unit has an area of 52,700 km^2 and also is located in the south-central interior of the province, a region which contains diverse scenery and a wealth of resources. There are two cities and seven villages within its boundaries. The economy of the area is based largely on the primary resource industries of forestry and mining, with service industries, transportation, and agriculture also contributing. The moderate, dry climate and many lakes and mountains draw tourists to the area. Unemployment rates often follow the "boom-bust" cycles of resource-based industries.

In 1989, the average population density of approximately 1.9 people/km^2 was very low, with the majority of the population residing in the city of Kamloops. Much of the remaining population lived in well-defined small communities, located in otherwise virtually unpopulated regions. With the exception of Merritt, all areas lost population during the period from 1985 to 1989. The population included a diversity of ethnic groups, with significant East Indian and Aboriginal components in some locations. The average age was below the provincial average. All LHAs had the unusual characteristic of more males than females.

In 1986, household incomes in all LHAs were less than the provincial average. Educational attainment for the Health Unit also was below the provincial norm, with the Merritt, South Cariboo, and North Thompson LHAs well below and the Kamloops and Lillooet LHAs marginally better.

The number of physicians per 10,000 population in the Health Unit, at 17.3 (HU rank 6), was less than the provincial rate of 23.3. This measure varied considerably between LHAs from a high of 19.9 in Kamloops (LHA rank 10) to a low of 7.3 in Merritt (LHA rank 71). The number of nurses per 10,000 population, at 103.0 (HU rank 5), was greater than the provincial rate of 93.0. At the LHA level the rates varied considerably from a high of 117.4 in Kamloops (LHA rank 7) to a low of 48.4 in North Thompson (LHA rank 71).

The leading causes of death were similar to those for the province as a whole, although their order of significance differed: lung cancer deaths ranked higher than mortality from cerebrovascular disease/stroke. Motor vehicle accidents were prominent causes of death in the North Thompson, Lillooet, and South Cariboo LHAs.

Table 10 Selected Characteristics of South Central Health Unit

Local Health Area	Gender	Population 1985	Population 1989	Average Age 1985	Average Age 1989	Top 3 Leading Causes of Death 1985-1989	Household Income (Average) 1986	% 15+ With < Grade 9 1986	Physicians per 10,000 Population	Nurses per 10,000 Population
24 Kamloops	Male	38,922	38,394	31.6	32.4	Ischaemic Heart Disease				
	Female	38,649	38,376	32.3	33.4	Lung Cancer			(rank:10)	(rank:07)
	Total	77,571	76,770	31.9	32.9	Cerebrovascular Disease/Stroke	32,600	11.1	19.9	117.4
26 North Thompson	Male	2,559	2,265	30.0	30.4	Ischaemic Heart Disease				
	Female	2,351	2,072	29.4	30.0	Lung Cancer*			(rank:47)	(rank:71)
	Total	4,910	4,337	29.7	30.2	Motor Vehicle Accident*	30,675	14.2	11.5	48.4
29 Lillooet	Male	2,391	2,328	31.2	32.4	Ischaemic Heart Disease				
	Female	2,125	2,017	30.6	32.2	Lung Cancer			(rank:62)	(rank:33)
	Total	4,516	4,345	31.0	32.3	Motor Vehicle Accident	29,645	10.6	9.2	80.6
30 South Cariboo	Male	4,127	3,477	31.8	32.3	Ischaemic Heart Disease				
	Female	3,700	3,100	32.1	32.4	Motor Vehicle Accident			(rank:56)	(rank:70)
	Total	7,827	6,577	32.0	32.4	Lung Cancer	29,343	16.6	10.6	50.2
31 Merritt	Male	4,955	5,002	31.1	31.3	Ischaemic Heart Disease				
	Female	4,587	4,621	31.4	31.8	Lung Cancer			(rank:71)	(rank:60)
	Total	9,542	9,623	31.3	31.5	Cerebrovascular Disease/Stroke	28,086	17.3	7.3	59.2
06 HEALTH UNIT	**Male**	**52,954**	**51,466**	**31.5**	**32.2**	**Ischaemic Heart Disease**				
	Female	**51,412**	**50,186**	**32.0**	**33.0**	**Lung Cancer**			**(rank:06)**	**(rank:05)**
	Total	**104,366**	**101,652**	**31.7**	**32.6**	**Cerebrovascular Disease/Stroke**	**30,069**	**12.2**	**17.3**	**103.0**
PROVINCE	Male	1,422,900	1,506,397	33.9	34.9	Ischaemic Heart Disease				
	Female	1,447,200	1,540,847	35.7	36.7	Cerebrovascular Disease/Stroke				
	Total	2,870,100	3,047,244	34.8	35.8	Lung Cancer	33,497	11.2	23.3	93.0

* Tied for second place.

Upper Fraser Valley (HU 7) (Table 11)

The Upper Fraser Valley Health Unit is at the eastern end of the Fraser River delta and extends into the mountainous area of the Fraser Canyon and Manning Park, occupying approximately 11,200 km². In 1989, the average population density was some 12.3 people/km².

The rich soil of the Fraser River valley has encouraged food production. Agricultural products include vegetables and fruits, meat, and dairy products that support several food processing plants. Logging and small business are also major components of the economy. The western part of the region has become a commuter base for the Vancouver area, as well as a retirement area. A large Canadian Forces base in Chilliwack and a concentration of federal and provincial corrections centres are major contributors to the economy. The natural scenery of the area and its accessibility to the lower mainland and the United States border have made it a popular tourist destination.

The population has a diverse cultural, religious, and ethnic mix. It includes a significant aboriginal component residing mainly in the Agassiz-Harrison and Chilliwack areas. These areas were originally settled by British immigrants, and subsequently by German Mennonites and Dutch immigrants. In the Abbotsford area many East Indian immigrants have been part of the cultural mosaic for some time, as is the case in the Fraser Canyon area. Recently, immigrants from Central America and Asian countries have arrived in larger numbers.

With the exception of Hope, all LHAs grew in population between 1985 and 1989. The average age of the population was very similar to that of the province as a whole. In 1986, both household income and educational attainment were below provincial levels for all LHAs in the Health Unit.

The number of physicians per 10,000 population in the Health Unit, at 14.4 (HU rank 11), was less than the provincial rate of 23.3. This measure varied among LHAs from a high of 15.3 in Abbotsford (LHA rank 23) to a low of 3.8 in Agassiz-Harrison (LHA rank 75). The number of nurses per 10,000 population, at 70.9 (HU rank 18), was the fourth-lowest in the province. At the LHA level the number varied from a high of 73.9 in Abbotsford (LHA rank 39) to a low of 37.5 in Agassiz-Harrison (LHA rank 74).

The leading causes of death were the same as those for the province as a whole, although lung cancer deaths were more prominent in the Hope and Agassiz-Harrison LHAs.

Table 11 Selected Characteristics of Upper Fraser Valley Health Unit

Local Health Area	Gender	Population 1985	Population 1989	Average Age 1985	Average Age 1989	Top 3 Leading Causes of Death 1985-1989	Household Income (Average) 1986	% 15+ With < Grade 9 1986	Physicians per 10,000 Population	Nurses per 10,000 Population
32 Hope	Male	3,881	3,678	33.5	34.1	Ischaemic Heart Disease				
	Female	3,641	3,472	33.8	35.1	Lung Cancer			(rank:52)	(rank:64)
	Total	7,522	7,150	33.6	34.6	Cerebrovascular Disease/Stroke	31,134	14.5	11.2	55.9
33 Chilliwack	Male	22,341	24,464	34.4	35.3	Ischaemic Heart Disease				
	Female	22,911	25,215	36.6	37.5	Cerebrovascular Disease/Stroke			(rank:26)	(rank:42)
	Total	45,252	49,679	35.5	36.4	Lung Cancer	28,801	14.7	14.7	72.1
34 Abbotsford	Male	32,094	37,404	33.3	34.7	Ischaemic Heart Disease				
	Female	32,657	38,357	35.1	36.9	Cerebrovascular Disease/Stroke			(rank:23)	(rank:39)
	Total	64,751	75,761	34.2	35.8	Lung Cancer	30,969	15.4	15.3	73.9
76 Agassiz-Harrison	Male	2,866	2,988	34.2	35.6	Ischaemic Heart Disease				
	Female	2,262	2,340	34.7	36.3	Lung Cancer			(rank:75)	(rank:74)
	Total	5,128	5,328	34.4	35.9	Cerebrovascular Disease/Stroke	25,338	14.0	3.8	37.5
07 HEALTH UNIT	**Male**	**61,182**	**68,534**	**33.7**	**34.9**	**Ischaemic Heart Disease**				
	Female	**61,471**	**69,384**	**35.6**	**37.0**	**Cerebrovascular Disease/Stroke**			**(rank:11)**	**(rank:18)**
	Total	**122,653**	**137,918**	**34.7**	**35.9**	**Lung Cancer**	**29,060**	**15.0**	**14.4**	**70.9**
PROVINCE	Male	1,422,900	1,506,397	33.9	34.9	Ischaemic Heart Disease				
	Female	1,447,200	1,540,847	35.7	36.7	Cerebrovascular Disease/Stroke				
	Total	2,870,100	3,047,244	34.8	35.8	Lung Cancer	33,497	11.2	23.3	93.0

Central Fraser Valley (HU 8) (Table 12)

The Central Fraser Valley Health Unit covers approximately 3,200 km² and lies to the east of the Greater Vancouver metropolitan area. As in other areas surrounding metropolitan Vancouver, rapid population growth in recent years is attributable to the development of large tracts of land for residential purposes. In 1989, the average population density was over 50 people/km² and increasing rapidly.

Forestry and agriculture are the leading resource sectors of the economy. In the manufacturing sector, forest-related industries of lumber and shake and shingle mills have been important. Development of industrial sites has attracted numerous manufacturing and warehousing operations to the area, particularly Langley. Dairying is the chief agricultural enterprise. Other agricultural activities of importance include poultry, hogs, beef cattle, sheep, vegetables, greenhouse crops, tree fruit, and berries. A medium-security correctional centre provides a number of jobs in the Mission area.

All LHAs in the Health Unit had a slightly lower average age than the province as a whole. Average 1986 household income and educational attainment levels for the Health Unit were similar to provincial levels. Household incomes were, however, notably higher in the Langley and Maple Ridge LHAs and lower in the Mission LHA. Educational attainment levels also displayed this pattern.

The number of physicians per 10,000 population in the Health Unit, at 11.0 (HU rank 20), was the second-lowest in the province. This measure varied somewhat among LHAs from a high of 11.5 in Maple Ridge (LHA rank 48) to a low of 10.2 in Mission (LHA rank 57). The number of nurses per 10,000 population, at 78.8 (HU rank 14), was less than the provincial rate of 93.0. At the LHA level, the rates varied from a high of 87.9 in Maple Ridge (LHA rank 24) to a low of 62.4 in Mission (LHA rank 53).

The leading causes of death were similar to those for the province as a whole, but lung cancer was more prominent in the Langley and Mission LHAs.

Table 12 Selected Characteristics of Central Fraser Valley Health Unit

Local Health Area	Gender	Population 1985	Population 1989	Average Age 1985	Average Age 1989	Top 3 Leading Causes of Death 1985-1989	Household Income (Average) 1986	% 15+ With < Grade 9 1986	Physicians per 10,000 Population	Nurses per 10,000 Population
35 Langley	Male	34,131	39,520	31.3	33.2	Ischaemic Heart Disease				
	Female	34,281	39,892	32.4	34.2	Lung Cancer			(rank:53)	(rank:35)
	Total	68,412	79,412	31.8	33.7	Cerebrovascular Disease/Stroke	35,016	10.0	11.0	78.6
42 Maple Ridge	Male	21,445	27,084	31.8	32.8	Ischaemic Heart Disease				
	Female	21,213	26,862	33.3	34.1	Cerebrovascular Disease/Stroke			(rank:48)	(rank:24)
	Total	42,658	53,946	32.6	33.4	Lung Cancer	35,170	8.5	11.5	87.9
75 Mission	Male	12,733	14,558	32.3	33.1	Ischaemic Heart Disease				
	Female	12,114	12,812	33.2	33.9	Lung Cancer			(rank:57)	(rank:53)
	Total	24,847	28,370	32.7	33.5	Cerebrovascular Disease/Stroke	30,229	13.6	10.2	62.4
08 HEALTH UNIT	**Male**	**68,309**	**81,162**	**31.7**	**33.1**	**Ischaemic Heart Disease**				
	Female	**67,608**	**80,566**	**32.8**	**34.1**	**Cerebrovascular Disease/Stroke**			**(rank:20)**	**(rank:14)**
	Total	**135,917**	**161,728**	**32.2**	**33.6**	**Lung Cancer**	**33,471**	**10.2**	**11.0**	**78.8**
PROVINCE	Male	1,422,900	1,506,397	33.9	34.9	Ischaemic Heart Disease				
	Female	1,447,200	1,540,847	35.7	36.7	Cerebrovascular Disease/Stroke				
	Total	2,870,100	3,047,244	34.8	35.8	Lung Cancer	33,497	11.2	23.3	93.0

Boundary (HU 9) (Table 13)

The Boundary Health Unit is located in the lower mainland and encompasses approximately 540 km² of prime residential, agricultural, and industrial land. It is bounded by the lower arm of the Fraser River to the north, the Canada-U.S. border to the south, the municipality of Langley to the east, and Boundary Bay to the west. It serves the municipalities of Delta and Surrey, and the city of White Rock (in the Surrey LHA).

Improved rapid transit and road access to Surrey have resulted in the Unit's continued expansion as a major residential suburb of Greater Vancouver. In 1989, average population density was in excess of 570 people/km². Agriculture remains important, particularly on low-lying lands, which cover a large part of the area. Retail trade and services are the leading sources of employment. The continued extension of rapid transit services to the area over the next few years, and the availability of land for continued industrial and residential expansion, promise to encourage growth at above the provincial average. Delta has also continued to expand as both a residential and industrial suburb of Vancouver. The city of White Rock, within the Surrey LHA, is primarily residential, having no agricultural land and very little industry. The coastal location and desirable climate have made White Rock a prime retirement community.

The region has experienced a rapid population increase over the last several years, growing from an estimated 267,883 in 1985 to 310,068 in 1989. The average age was marginally less than the provincial average, with only 10.2 percent of the population aged over 65. In the census year of 1986, however, 35.5 percent of White Rock's population was over 65 years of age.

Household income (1986) and educational attainment were substantially above the provincial average in the Delta LHA, but similar to it in the Surrey LHA.

The number of physicians per 10,000 population in the Health Unit, at 12.1 (HU rank 18), was the fourth-lowest in the province. This low number probably reflects proximity to other Health Units in the lower mainland which have high numbers of physicians. There is little difference between the two LHAs; Delta with 13.0 (LHA rank 32) compares with Surrey's 11.7 (LHA rank 45). The number of nurses per 10,000 population, at 85.8 (HU rank 9), was slightly less than the provincial rate of 93.0. At the LHA level the rates varied from 109.3 in Delta (LHA rank 10) to 77.2 in Surrey (LHA rank 36).

The principal causes of death were the same as those for the province as a whole.

Table 13 Selected Characteristics of Boundary Health Unit

Local Health Area	Gender	Population 1985	Population 1989	Average Age 1985	Average Age 1989	Top 3 Leading Causes of Death 1985-1989	Household Income (Average) 1986	% 15+ With < Grade 9 1986	Physicians per 10,000 Population	Nurses per 10,000 Population
36 Surrey	Male	93,630	112,343	32.5	34.5	Ischaemic Heart Disease				
	Female	95,577	115,112	34.1	36.2	Cerebrovascular Disease/Stroke			(rank:32)	(rank:10)
	Total	189,207	227,455	33.3	35.4	Lung Cancer	33,835	10.5	11.7	77.2
37 Delta	Male	39,275	41,137	31.2	32.3	Ischaemic Heart Disease				
	Female	39,401	41,476	32.2	33.6	Cerebrovascular Disease/Stroke			(rank:32)	(rank:10)
	Total	78,676	82,613	31.7	32.9	Lung Cancer	43,881	6.3	13.0	109.3
09 HEALTH UNIT	**Male**	**132,905**	**153,480**	**32.1**	**33.9**	**Ischaemic Heart Disease**				
	Female	**134,978**	**156,588**	**33.6**	**35.5**	**Cerebrovascular Disease/Stroke**			**(rank:18)**	**(rank:09)**
	Total	**267,883**	**310,068**	**32.9**	**34.7**	**Lung Cancer**	**38,858**	**9.3**	**12.1**	**85.8**
PROVINCE	Male	1,422,900	1,506,397	33.9	34.9	Ischaemic Heart Disease				
	Female	1,447,200	1,540,847	35.7	36.7	Cerebrovascular Disease/Stroke				
	Total	2,870,100	3,047,244	34.8	35.8	Lung Cancer	33,497	11.2	23.3	93.0

Simon Fraser (HU 10) (Table 14)

The Simon Fraser Health Unit covers New Westminster, Coquitlam, and several smaller communities encompassing an area of 230 km². Population density, in 1989, was approximately 750 people/km².

Major employers in the New Westminster LHA are in the trade and service sector. They include the second largest hospital in the lower mainland, a facility for mentally-handicapped children, a college, and major provincial court facilities. New Westminster is also the site of a number of forest-manufacturing plants and a brewery.

The Coquitlam LHA is primarily a "bedroom community". The majority of its residents commute to workplaces in other parts of the lower mainland. The major employers in the area are a sawmill and plywood complex, an oil refinery, a thermal-electric generating plant, a rail-freight terminus, and the province's largest mental health facility.

Population characteristics in the two areas are quite different. The New Westminster LHA is an older, established city with a relatively stable population base. The Coquitlam LHA, on the other hand, is one of the fastest-growing communities in the province, with a relatively young population and low proportion of seniors.

In 1986, household income was well below, and educational attainment was near, the provincial averages in the New Westminster LHA. Household income and educational attainment were substantially better than provincial levels in the Coquitlam LHA.

The number of physicians per 10,000 population in the Health Unit, at 22.7, was the third-highest in the province. This measure varied between the two LHAs; New Westminster with 55.0 (LHA rank 2) compared with Coquitlam's 12.2 (LHA rank 41). The number of nurses per 10,000 population, at 101.7 (HU ranks 7), was greater than the provincial rate of 93.0. At the LHA level the rates varied only marginally between 101.9 in Coquitlam (LHA rank 13) and 101.3 in New Westminster (LHA rank 15).

The principal causes of death were the same as those for the province as a whole.

Table 14 Selected Characteristics of Simon Fraser Health Unit

Local Health Area	Gender	Population 1985	Population 1989	Average Age 1985	Average Age 1989	Top 3 Leading Causes of Death 1985-1989	Household Income (Average) 1986	% 15+ With < Grade 9 1986	Physicians per 10,000 Population	Nurses per 10,000 Population
40 New Westminster	Male	19,149	20,400	37.2	37.5	Ischaemic Heart Disease				
	Female	20,567	21,961	41.4	41.9	Cerebrovascular/Stroke			(rank:02)	(rank:15)
	Total	39,716	42,361	39.4	39.8	Lung Cancer	26,656	12.3	55.0	101.3
43 Coquitlam	Male	56,745	64,457	31.0	32.3	Ischaemic Heart Disease				
	Female	56,847	65,207	32.2	33.5	Cerebrovascular/Stroke			(rank:41)	(rank:13)
	Total	113,592	129,664	31.6	32.9	Lung Cancer	39,385	6.3	12.2	101.9
10 HEALTH UNIT	**Male**	**75,894**	**84,857**	**32.6**	**33.5**	**Ischaemic Heart Disease**				
	Female	**77,414**	**87,168**	**34.6**	**35.6**	**Cerebrovascular/Stroke**			**(rank:03)**	**(rank:07)**
	Total	**153,308**	**172,025**	**33.6**	**34.6**	**Lung Cancer**	**33,020**	**8.0**	**22.7**	**101.7**
PROVINCE	Male	1,422,900	1,506,397	33.9	34.9	Ischaemic Heart Disease				
	Female	1,447,200	1,540,847	35.7	36.7	Cerebrovascular Disease/Stroke				
	Total	2,870,100	3,047,244	34.8	35.8	Lung Cancer	33,497	11.2	23.3	93.0

Coast Garibaldi (HU 11) (Table 15)

The Coast Garibaldi Health Unit covers the coastal region of the mainland immediately north of Greater Vancouver, encompassing an area of 17,900 km².

In the Sechelt area, logging is the leading economic-resource sector, and the largest single source of employment is a pulp mill. A significant number of fishermen are based in small communities along the coast. The mining industry consists of a number of large sand and gravel pits. The area's proximity to Vancouver and frequent ferry service have been instrumental in attracting an increasing number of visitors.

The Powell River economy is based on forest industries, which are by far the largest single source of employment. Forestry is also the leading economic resource sector in the Howe Sound LHA, with logging providing much of the employment. There is a large sawmill at Squamish and a pulp mill at Woodfibre. The British Columbia Railway (BCR) maintenance centre is a large employer at Squamish, where there are also chemical manufacturing and deep-sea port services. Improved road access has allowed development of a major, internationally recognized winter sports complex at Whistler.

People seeking an alternative lifestyle and the newly retired have accounted for most of the Sechelt LHA's population increase, while the Whistler complex has been the source of most of the Howe Sound LHA's growth since the early 1980s. The Powell River LHA experienced rapid growth in the latter part of the 1960s. Since then, the trend has been slowly downward, continuing throughout the 1985 to 1989 period, reflecting mechanization in the pulp and paper industry. The average population density was nearly 3 people/km² in 1989.

The average age of the population in the Howe Sound LHA was less than that for the province, while those of the Sechelt and Powell River LHAs were greater. Average 1986 household income was just below the provincial level for the Howe Sound LHA and even lower in the other two LHAs. Educational attainment levels were higher than the provincial average in the Sechelt and Howe Sound LHAs, but somewhat lower in the Powell River LHA.

The number of physicians per 10,000 population in the Health Unit, at 14.3 (HU rank 13), was less than the provincial rate of 23.3. This measure varied among LHAs from a high of 15.6 in Powell River (LHA rank 22) to a low of 12.3 in Howe Sound (LHA rank 38). The number of nurses per 10,000 population, at 74.9 (HU rank 16), was less than the provincial rate of 93.0. At the LHA level the rates varied from a high of 91.7 in Powell River (LHA rank 20) to a low of 51.0 in Howe Sound (LHA rank 69).

Principal causes of death were the same as those for the province as a whole, although motor vehicle accidents were significant in the Howe Sound LHA.

Table 15 Selected Characteristics of Coast Garibaldi Health Unit

Local Health Area	Gender	Population 1985	Population 1989	Average Age 1985	Average Age 1989	Top 3 Leading Causes of Death 1985-1989	Household Income (Average) 1986	% 15+ With < Grade 9 1986	Physicians per 10,000 Population	Nurses per 10,000 Population
46 Sechelt	Male	8,377	8,727	37.6	38.7	Ischaemic Heart Disease				
	Female	8,417	8,857	38.8	40.1	Cerebrovascular/Stroke			(rank:25)	(rank:32)
	Total	16,794	17,584	38.2	39.4	Lung Cancer	28,427	9.2	14.8	80.8
47 Powell River	Male	9,268	9,072	34.7	34.8	Ischaemic Heart Disease				
	Female	9,036	8,929	35.6	36.1	Cerebrovascular/Stroke			(rank:22)	(rank:20)
	Total	18,304	18,001	35.1	35.4	Lung Cancer	28,812	12.8	15.6	91.7
48 Howe Sound	Male	7,696	8,986	30.0	31.0	Ischaemic Heart Disease				
	Female	6,860	8,059	29.4	30.8	Motor Vehicle Accident			(rank:38)	(rank:69)
	Total	14,556	17,045	29.7	30.9	Lung Cancer	33,112	7.6	12.3	51.0
11 HEALTH UNIT	**Male**	**25,341**	**26,785**	**34.3**	**34.8**	**Ischaemic Heart Disease**				
	Female	**24,313**	**25,845**	**34.9**	**35.8**	**Cerebrovascular/Stroke**			**(rank:13)**	**(rank:16)**
	Total	**49,654**	**52,630**	**34.6**	**35.3**	**Lung Cancer**	**30,117**	**10.1**	**14.3**	**74.9**
PROVINCE	Male	1,422,900	1,506,397	33.9	34.9	Ischaemic Heart Disease				
	Female	1,447,200	1,540,847	35.7	36.7	Cerebrovascular Disease/Stroke				
	Total	2,870,100	3,047,244	34.8	35.8	Lung Cancer	33,497	11.2	23.3	93.0

Central Vancouver Island (HU 13) (Table 16)

The Central Vancouver Island Health Unit includes the southern communities of Vancouver Island, immediately north of the Greater Victoria region, and encompasses approximately 13,100 km². In 1989, average population density was approximately 13 people/km².

The forest industries (including logging, sawmills, pulp and paper, and newsprint) are the foundation of the area's economy. Commercial fishing and agriculture are also important. Nanaimo has a deep-sea port, a major ferry terminus, manufacturing industries, and a postsecondary education facility. Qualicum, and to a lesser extent Ladysmith, have become major retirement communities. Tourism is significant, and Qualicum Beach on the east coast is one of the most popular summer vacation areas on the Island. The West Coast Trail and Long Beach in the Pacific Rim National Park also are major attractions.

Communities such as Lake Cowichan and Alberni, in which economies were heavily dependent upon the forest industries, experienced population declines between the 1981 and 1986 censuses. These have continued through 1989 as a consequence of increased mechanization in the industry, and, in some areas, because of limitations imposed by declining timber resources. Population has increased, however, in LHAs such as Cowichan, Nanaimo, and Qualicum, where service industries and trade are the leading source of employment.

Average 1986 household incomes in all LHAs were lower than the provincial average. Educational attainment levels were near the provincial level, except for the Lake Cowichan, Ladysmith, and Alberni LHAs, which were significantly lower.

The number of physicians per 10,000 population in the Health Unit, at 16.5 (HU rank 9), was less than the provincial rate of 23.3. This measure varied among LHAs from a high of 19.8 in Nanaimo (LHA rank 11) to a low of 8.9 in Lake Cowichan (LHA rank 66). The number of nurses per 10,000 population, at 84.1 (HU rank 11), was less than the provincial rate of 93.0. At the LHA level the rates varied from a high of 98.2 in Cowichan (LHA rank 18) to a low of 48.0 in Qualicum (LHA rank 72).

The principal causes of death are the same as those for the province, although lung cancer was more prominent in the Lake Cowichan and Ladysmith LHAs.

Table 16 Selected Characteristics of Central Vancouver Island Health Unit

Local Health Area	Gender	Population 1985	Population 1989	Average Age 1985	Average Age 1989	Top 3 Leading Causes of Death 1985-1989	Household Income (Average) 1986	% 15+ With < Grade 9 1986	Physicians per 10,000 Population	Nurses per 10,000 Population
65 Cowichan	Male	17,431	18,128	34.1	35.4	Ischaemic Heart Disease				
	Female	17,767	18,623	35.2	36.6	Cerebrovascular Disease/Stroke			(rank:16)	(rank:18)
	Total	35,198	36,751	34.7	36.0	Lung Cancer	30,542	11.1	17.7	98.2
66 Lake Cowichan	Male	2,824	2,312	32.4	34.2	Ischaemic Heart Disease				
	Female	2,682	2,200	32.6	34.8	Lung Cancer			(rank:66)	(rank:55)
	Total	5,506	4,512	32.5	34.5	Cerebrovascular Disease/Stroke	29,174	16.6	8.9	62.1
67 Ladysmith	Male	6,075	6,396	37.0	37.2	Ischaemic Heart Disease				
	Female	6,219	6,570	37.5	38.2	Lung Cancer			(rank:46)	(rank:21)
	Total	12,294	12,966	37.2	37.7	Cerebrovascular Disease/Stroke	27,808	14.3	11.6	90.2
68 Nanaimo	Male	29,683	31,423	34.5	35.8	Ischaemic Heart Disease				
	Female	30,499	32,582	36.0	37.4	Cerebrovascular Disease/Stroke			(rank:11)	(rank:19)
	Total	60,182	64,005	35.3	36.6	Lung Cancer	29,284	10.3	19.8	^93.9
69 Qualicum	Male	10,733	11,728	39.7	41.8	Ischaemic Heart Disease				
	Female	11,023	12,250	41.1	43.1	Cerebrovascular Disease/Stroke			(rank:29)	(rank:72)
	Total	21,756	23,978	40.4	42.5	Lung Cancer	27,522	10.4	13.8	48.0
70 Alberni	Male	15,879	15,000	31.8	32.3	Ischaemic Heart Disease				
	Female	15,144	14,444	32.7	33.8	Cerebrovascular Disease/Stroke			(rank:30)	(rank:38)
	Total	31,023	29,444	32.3	33.0	Lung Cancer	32,352	15.4	13.6	75.1
13 HEALTH UNIT	**Male**	**82,625**	**84,987**	**34.7**	**36.0**	**Ischaemic Heart Disease**				
	Female	**83,334**	**86,669**	**35.9**	**37.4**	**Cerebrovascular Disease/Stroke**			**(rank:09)**	**(rank:11)**
	Total	**165,959**	**171,656**	**35.3**	**36.7**	**Lung Cancer**	**29,447**	**11.9**	**16.5**	**84.1**
PROVINCE	Male	1,422,900	1,506,397	33.9	34.9	Ischaemic Heart Disease				
	Female	1,447,200	1,540,847	35.7	36.7	Cerebrovascular Disease/Stroke				
	Total	2,870,100	3,047,244	34.8	35.8	Lung Cancer	33,497	11.2	23.3	93.0

Upper Vancouver Island (HU 14) (Table 17)

The Upper Island Health Unit includes the northern half of Vancouver Island, numerous islands, and a section of the south-central coast of the mainland. The Unit encompasses 12 municipalities and 32 Indian Reserves, and occupies approximately 45,900 km². In 1989, average population density at nearly 2 people/km² was one of the lowest in the province.

The economy of the area is based on logging, mining, and fishing. In addition, there are pulp and paper mills and agriculture-based industries. However, tourism and recreation have become increasingly important components of the area's economy. Government and commercial services are major employers in the larger centres. There is a Canadian Forces installation at Comox.

The north and west areas of the Health Unit had very young but declining populations in 1985 and 1989. Conversely, the larger communities of Courtenay and Campbell River grew in population during this period. The Unit contains a number of small but distinct cultural and religious groups. These include an East Indian population, a Mennonite settlement, bilingual French Canadians at Comox, a Finnish community, and over 3,200 Aboriginals.

Average household incomes varied substantially among LHAs in the Health Unit. The Vancouver Island West and Vancouver Island North LHAs had 1986 household incomes that were substantially higher than the provincial average. In the Campbell River LHA, average household income was marginally below the provincial level, while in the Courtenay LHA, it was considerably below the provincial average. Educational attainment levels, in all LHAs, were at or slightly better than the provincial levels.

The number of physicians per 10,000 population in the Health Unit, at 14.1 (HU rank 14), was less than the provincial rate of 23.3. This measure varied among LHAs from a high of 16.1 in Courtenay (LHA rank 20) to a low of 7.7 in Vancouver Island West (LHA rank 70). The number of nurses per 10,000 population, at 73.6 (HU rank 17), was less than the provincial rate of 93.0. At the LHA level, rates varied from a high of 86.4 in Courtenay (LHA rank 26) to a low of 38.3 in Vancouver Island West (LHA rank 73).

Lung cancer deaths were more prominent than deaths from cerebrovascular/strokes in all LHAs in the Health Unit. Deaths from motor vehicle traffic accidents were notable in the Vancouver Island West LHA.

Table 17 Selected Characteristics of Upper Vancouver Island Health Unit

Local Health Area	Gender	Population 1985	Population 1989	Average Age 1985	Average Age 1989	Top 3 Leading Causes of Death 1985-1989	Household Income (Average) 1986	% 15+ With < Grade 9 1986	Physicians per 10,000 Population	Nurses per 10,000 Population
71 Courtenay	Male	18,789	20,095	34.3	35.3	Ischaemic Heart Disease				
	Female	18,815	20,283	35.2	36.7	Lung Cancer			(rank:20)	(rank:26)
	Total	37,604	40,378	34.7	36.0	Cerebrovascular Disease/Stroke	28,765	10.0	16.1	86.4
72 Campbell River	Male	14,971	16,208	31.4	32.2	Ischaemic Heart Disease				
	Female	14,381	15,620	31.7	32.7	Lung Cancer			(rank:28)	(rank:44)
	Total	29,352	31,828	31.5	32.4	Cerebrovascular Disease/Stroke	32,843	11.2	14.5	69.7
84 Vancouver Island West	Male	2,247	2,105	27.4	27.7	Ischaemic Heart Disease				
	Female	1,917	1,809	25.4	24.4	Lung Cancer			(rank:70)	(rank:73)
	Total	4,164	3,914	26.5	26.2	Motor Vehicle Accident	41,204	10.7	7.7	38.3
85 Vancouver Island North	Male	8,059	7,495	27.9	29.2	Ischaemic Heart Disease				
	Female	7,168	6,703	26.3	27.7	Lung Cancer			(rank:64)	(rank:66)
	Total	15,227	14,198	27.1	28.5	Cerebrovascular Disease/Stroke	37,806	10.8	9.2	55.6
14 HEALTH UNIT	**Male**	**44,066**	**45,903**	**31.8**	**32.9**	**Ischaemic Heart Disease**				
	Female	**42,281**	**44,415**	**32.0**	**33.4**	**Lung Cancer**			**(rank:14)**	**(rank:17)**
	Total	**86,347**	**90,318**	**31.9**	**33.1**	**Cerebrovascular Disease/Stroke**	**35,154**	**10.6**	**14.1**	**73.6**
PROVINCE	Male	1,422,900	1,506,397	33.9	34.9	Ischaemic Heart Disease				
	Female	1,447,200	1,540,847	35.7	36.7	Cerebrovascular Disease/Stroke				
	Total	2,870,100	3,047,244	34.8	35.8	Lung Cancer	33,497	11.2	23.3	93.0

Cariboo (HU 15) (Table 18)[3]

The Cariboo Health Unit covers the central interior and central coast areas of British Columbia, occupying 104,700 km^2. Landforms vary from rugged mountains to flat and gently rolling plateaus and rangelands dotted with lakes. Vegetation includes forests and extensive natural grasslands.

Except for three municipalities, much of the region is rural and supports only small scattered settlements. In 1989, with an average density of 0.6 people/km^2, Cariboo was the Health Unit with the third-lowest population density in the province. The economy of the region is dominated by the natural resource industries of forestry, mining, and fishing. Cattle ranching and tourism also contribute. Government and commercial services are additional major employers in the three urbanized areas.

A large number of residents in the Central Coast and Chilcotin areas are Native Indians. The cities of Williams Lake and Quesnel also have extensive East Indian populations. The Health Unit population, which fell marginally between 1985 and 1989, was substantially younger than the provincial average. Average 1986 household incomes and education attainment levels were well below provincial levels, especially for the Central Coast LHA.

The number of physicians per 10,000 population in the Health Unit, at 11.8 (HU rank 19), was the third-lowest in the province. This measure varied among LHAs from a high of 15.7 in Central Coast (LHA rank 21) to a low of 11.2 in Cariboo-Chilcotin (LHA rank 51). The number of nurses per 10,000 population, at 60.7 (HU rank 21), was the lowest in the province. At the LHA level, rates varied from a high of 69.1 in Central Coast (LHA rank 45) to a low of 58.3 in Cariboo-Chilcotin (LHA rank 61).

Principal causes of death differed from those of the province as a whole. While ischaemic heart disease was still the leading cause of death, lung cancer ranked second rather than third, while motor vehicle accidents ranked third. For the Cariboo-Chilcotin LHA, motor vehicle accidents were the second leading cause of death.

Table 18 Selected Characteristics of Cariboo Health Unit

Local Health Area	Gender	Population 1985	Population 1989	Average Age 1985	Average Age 1989	Top 3 Leading Causes of Death 1985-1989	Household Income (Average) 1986	% 15+ With < Grade 9 1986	Physicians per 10,000 Population	Nurses per 10,000 Population
27 Cariboo-Chilcotin	Male	19,337	18,209	29.9	31.3	Ischaemic Heart Disease				
	Female	18,359	17,455	29.2	30.8	Motor Vehicle Accident			(rank:51)	(rank:61)
	Total	37,696	35,664	29.5	31.1	Lung Cancer	30,659	13.4	11.2	58.3
28 Quesnel	Male	12,106	11,805	29.2	31.0	Ischaemic Heart Disease				
	Female	11,626	11,452	29.5	30.9	Lung Cancer			(rank:43)	(rank:52)
	Total	23,732	23,257	29.7	30.9	Cerebrovascular/Stroke	30,873	16.1	12.0	63.2
49 Central Coast	Male	1,638	1,657	29.7	31.3	Ischaemic Heart Disease				
	Female	1,501	1,526	29.3	29.8	Cerebrovascular/Stroke			(rank:21)	(rank:45)
	Total	3,139	3,183	29.5	30.6	Lung Cancer	24,501	21.0	15.7	69.1
15 HEALTH UNIT	**Male**	**33,081**	**31,671**	**29.9**	**31.2**	**Ischaemic Heart Disease**				
	Female	**31,486**	**30,433**	**29.3**	**30.8**	**Lung Cancer**			**(rank:19)**	**(rank:21)**
	Total	**64,567**	**62,104**	**29.6**	**31.0**	**Motor Vehicle Accident**	**28,677**	**14.8**	**11.8**	**60.7**
PROVINCE	Male	1,422,900	1,506,397	33.9	34.9	Ischaemic Heart Disease				
	Female	1,447,200	1,540,847	35.7	36.7	Cerebrovascular Disease/Stroke				
	Total	2,870,100	3,047,244	34.8	35.8	Lung Cancer	33,497	11.2	23.3	93.0

[3] Although LHA 93, Eutsuk, is included within the Cariboo Health Unit, no data are shown as this LHA does not have a residential population.

Skeena (HU 16) (Table 19)

The Skeena Health Unit covers the northwest region of the province including the Queen Charlotte Islands. It is the largest Health Unit in the province, covering 257,400 km². With 0.3 people/km² in 1989, it was one of the least populated areas in the province.

The economy of the northwest is resource based. Forestry, mining, and fishing are key industries. A major aluminum smelter is located in Kitimat. Prince Rupert is the second-most significant deep-sea port on Canada's west coast, exporting grain, lumber, coal, and other resources. Farm revenue is derived from the sale of beef cattle, milk, hay, grain, vegetables, and potatoes. The natural beauty of the area and opportunities for outdoor recreation have contributed to the growth of tourism.

Population fell by approximately 2,000 people between 1985 and 1989. The Health Unit had the lowest average age in the province in 1989. Males outnumbered females in all LHAs.

Average 1986 household incomes were above the provincial average for the majority of LHAs, especially in the Kitimat LHA. However, the Nishga and Telegraph Creek LHA incomes were below the provincial average. Educational attainment levels were below the provincial level for most LHAs. In the Telegraph Creek LHA 31.2 percent of those 15 years of age and older had completed less than grade 9, and in the Nishga LHA, 25.4 percent.

The number of physicians per 10,000 population in the Health Unit, at 12.8 (HU rank 17), was less than the provincial rate of 23.3. Queen Charlotte had a rate of 19.4 (LHA rank 12) while Nishga and Telegraph Creek had no resident physicians. The number of nurses per 10,000 population, at 67.4 (HU rank 19), was the third-lowest in the province. LHA rates varied from 73.6 in Prince Rupert (LHA rank 40) to 26.3 in Nishga (LHA rank 76).

Major causes of death differed from those elsewhere in the province. Ischaemic heart disease ranked first, but motor vehicle accidents ranked second, followed by lung cancer. Deaths from suicide in Telegraph Creek, and accidental falls in Nishga, were notable. Deaths due to chronic lung, ischaemic heart, and cerebrovascular diseases were equally important in Telegraph Creek. Deaths due to pneumonia and influenza were important in Terrace.

Table 19 Selected Characteristics of Skeena Health Unit

Local Health Area	Gender	Population 1985	Population 1989	Average Age 1985	Average Age 1989	Top 3 Leading Causes of Death 1985-1989	Household Income (Average) 1986	% 15+ With < Grade 9 1986	Physicians per 10,000 Population	Nurses per 10,000 Population
50 Queen	Male	2,998	2,867	28.7	28.5	Ischaemic Heart Disease				
Charlotte	Female	2,467	2,293	27.3	28.2	Lung Cancer			(rank:12)	(rank:43)
	Total	5,465	5,160	28.1	28.4	Motor Vehicle Accident	35,591	14.4	19.4	71.7
52 Prince Rupert	Male	9,350	9,075	29.3	29.5	Ischaemic Heart Disease				
	Female	8,731	8,596	29.1	29.5	Lung Cancer			(rank:34)	(rank:40)
	Total	18,081	17,671	29.2	29.5	Cerebrovascular Disease/Stroke	38,446	14.9	13.0	73.6
54 Smithers	Male	7,655	7,686	28.1	28.9	Ischaemic Heart Disease				
	Female	6,930	7,004	27.9	29.1	Motor Vehicle Accident			(rank:24)	(rank:50)
	Total	14,585	14,690	28.1	29.0	Cerebrovascular Disease/Stroke	37,100	11.1	15.0	63.3
80 Kitimat	Male	6,992	6,211	28.2	28.6	Ischaemic Heart Disease				
	Female	6,510	5,831	27.1	27.4	Lung Cancer			(rank:76)	(rank:47)
	Total	13,502	12,042	27.7	28.0	Cerebrovascular Disease/Stroke	43,081	12.3	3.3	68.1
87 Stikine	Male	1,109	960	28.3	29.1	Ischaemic Heart Disease				
	Female	936	812	26.9	29.2	Chronic Lung Disease			(rank:73)	(rank:54)
	Total	2,045	1,772	27.7	29.1	Motor Vehicle Accident	37,600	9.8	5.6	62.1
88 Terrace	Male	12,883	13,187	28.5	28.5	Ischaemic Heart Disease				
	Female	11,796	12,159	27.4	27.8	Motor Vehicle Accident			(rank:19)	(rank:46)
	Total	24,679	25,346	28.0	28.1	Pneumonia and Influenza	34,594	16.0	16.2	68.3
92 Nishga	Male	864	816	26.4	24.6	Ischaemic Heart Disease				
	Female	738	704	27.1	23.6	Cerebrovascular Disease/Stroke			(rank:78)	(rank:76)
	Total	1,602	1,520	26.7	24.1	Accidental Falls	24,839	25.4	0.0	26.3
94 Telegraph	Male	364	384	27.3	25.7	Motor Vehicle Accident				
Creek	Female	291	307	26.7	28.1	Suicide			(rank:79)	(rank:75)
	Total	655	691	27.0	26.8	*	22,847	31.2	0.0	28.9
16 HEALTH UNIT	**Male**	**42,215**	**41,186**	**28.5**	**28.7**	**Ischaemic Heart Disease**				
	Female	**38,399**	**37,706**	**27.8**	**28.3**	**Motor Vehicle Accident**			**(rank:17)**	**(rank:19)**
	Total	**80,614**	**78,892**	**28.2**	**28.5**	**Lung Cancer**	**34,262**	**14.3**	**12.8**	**67.4**
PROVINCE	Male	1,422,900	1,506,397	33.9	34.9	Ischaemic Heart Disease				
	Female	1,447,200	1,540,847	35.7	36.7	Cerebrovascular Disease/Stroke				
	Total	2,870,100	3,047,244	34.8	35.8	Lung Cancer	33,497	11.2	23.3	93.0

* Chronic Lung Disease, Cerebrovascular Disease, and Ischaemic Heart Disease tied for third place.

Peace River (HU 17) (Table 20)

The Peace River Health Unit is located in the northeast of British Columbia. It is the second-largest Health Unit in the province, occupying an area of 205,900 km², which is more than 21 percent of the province's land area.

It is composed of two distinct geographic regions. The western section is rolling to mountainous in character and includes a portion of the Rocky Mountain Trench, which trends from northwest to southeast, is flat-bottomed and steep-sided, and varies from 8 to 16 kilometres in width. The eastern section, except for the deep valleys of the larger rivers, is an undulating plain of between 300 and 900 metres elevation. Poorly drained areas of swamp and muskeg dominate hundreds of square kilometres of the plain north of the Peace River. Boreal forest prevails in much of the region, but trees of commercial size are confined primarily to the southern portion and major river valleys in the north.

The economy of the area is primarily resource based. Historically, in the Dawson Creek area, the economy has depended largely on agriculture and forestry. Since 1981, development of coal deposits has made mining the largest resource component of the economy. In the Fort St. John area, services related to oil and gas exploration and development are the leading source of employment. Agriculture and forestry also are important sectors in the Fort St. John area. Hydro-electric projects on the Peace River have had an impact in both areas. The economy of the Fort Nelson area was originally transportation-oriented, then grew rapidly to accommodate the oil and gas industry. More recently, forest resources surrounding Fort Nelson have provided further growth and diversity.

The Health Unit, in 1989, was the least densely populated of any in the province, at less than 0.3 people/km². The population also had one of the lowest average ages in the province and males outnumbered females by about 6 percent. Population fell in all LHAs between 1985 and 1989. English is the predominant mother tongue of 88 percent of the population, followed by German which represents 4 percent of the population. A number of aboriginal languages are also spoken. The population is mainly concentrated in the area's major communities. There is also a substantial rural population, principally in the southern farming portions of the region.

Average 1986 household incomes were near the provincial average, while educational attainment levels were below that of the province, particularly for the Peace River North and Fort Nelson LHAs.

The number of physicians per 10,000 population in the Health Unit, at 10.5 (HU rank 21), was the lowest in the province. This measure varied among LHAs from a high of 11.5 in Peace River South (LHA rank 49) to a low of 8.4 in Fort Nelson (LHA rank 68). The number of nurses per 10,000 population, at 65.0 (HU rank 20), was the second-lowest in the province. At the LHA level, the rates varied little from a high of 67.3 in Peace River South (LHA rank 49) to a low of 60.8 in Fort Nelson (LHA rank 58).

As in the province as a whole, ischaemic heart disease and cerebrovascular disease/stroke were the highest-ranking causes of death. Motor vehicle deaths, however, ranked third and were particularly notable in Peace River North and Fort Nelson.

Table 20 Selected Characteristics of Peace River Health Unit

Local Health Area	Gender	Population 1985	Population 1989	Average Age 1985	Average Age 1989	Top 3 Leading Causes of Death 1985-1989	Household Income (Average) 1986	% 15+ With < Grade 9 1986	Physicians per 10,000 Population	Nurses per 10,000 Population
59 Peace River South	Male	14,108	12,979	29.2	31.5	Ischaemic Heart Disease				
	Female	13,215	12,277	29.0	31.3	Cerebrovascular Disease/Stroke			(rank:49)	(rank:49)
	Total	27,323	25,256	29.1	31.4	Lung Cancer	33,361	13.6	11.5	67.3
60 Peace River North	Male	13,091	11,939	27.9	28.5	Ischaemic Heart Disease				
	Female	12,171	11,296	27.4	28.5	Motor Vehicle Accident			(rank:60)	(rank:51)
	Total	25,262	23,235	27.7	28.5	Cerebrovascular Disease/Stroke	32,184	16.7	9.9	63.3
81 Fort Nelson	Male	2,786	2,509	25.8	26.8	Lung Cancer				
	Female	2,507	2,257	24.1	25.7	Motor Vehicle Accident			(rank:68)	(rank:58)
	Total	5,293	4,766	25.0	26.3	Ischaemic Heart Disease	35,438	15.0	8.4	60.8
17 HEALTH UNIT	**Male**	**29,985**	**27,427**	**28.3**	**29.8**	**Ischaemic Heart Disease**				
	Female	**27,893**	**25,830**	**27.8**	**29.6**	**Cerebrovascular Disease/Stroke**			**(rank:21)**	**(rank:20)**
	Total	**57,878**	**53,257**	**28.1**	**29.7**	**Motor Vehicle Accident**	**33,661**	**15.1**	**10.5**	**65.0**
PROVINCE	Male	1,422,900	1,506,397	33.9	34.9	Ischaemic Heart Disease				
	Female	1,447,200	1,540,847	35.7	36.7	Cerebrovascular Disease/Stroke				
	Total	2,870,100	3,047,244	34.8	35.8	Lung Cancer	33,497	11.2	23.3	93.0

Northern Interior (HU 18) (Table 21)

The Northern Interior Health Unit covers the central-eastern region of the province. This area includes nine municipalities, districts, or villages, and occupies an area of approximately 115,700 km². The average population density in 1989 of almost 1 person/km² was very low. The Rocky Mountains form the northeastern boundary of the region. Part of the area is within the Rocky Mountain Trench, but Prince George is on the eastern edge of the Interior Plateau.

Prince George is the major industrial and transportation centre in the area. The dominant economic activities are associated with forestry, and include sawmilling, logging, and pulp mills. Mining of molybdenum at Fraser Lake, copper at Granisle, and coal at Tumbler Ridge are other sources of employment. Gold mining north of Fort St. James, manufacturing, hydro-electric generation, and the marketing of petroleum products are other secondary industries.

The Health Unit had one of the lowest average ages in the province, with 35 percent of the population being age 19 or younger and only 4 percent being age 65 or over. A significant portion (22 percent) of the population lived outside municipal boundaries in unorganized areas. The population comprises many ethnic groups, with British (26 percent) being the most prominent, followed by German (7 percent), French (4 percent), and Aboriginal (5 percent).

In 1986, the Prince George LHA had an average household income considerably above the provincial level, while those for Burns Lake and Nechako LHAs were marginally below it. Educational attainment was below provincial levels, and substantially so in the Burns Lake and Nechako LHAs.

The number of physicians per 10,000 population in the Health Unit, at 13.6 (HU rank 15), was less than the provincial rate of 23.3. This measure varied among LHAs from a high of 14.6 in Prince George (LHA rank 27) to a low of 9.0 in Burns Lake (LHA rank 65). The number of nurses per 10,000 population, at 76.0 (HU rank 15), was below the provincial rate of 93.0. At the LHA level, rates varied from a high of 81.6 in Prince George (LHA rank 30) to a low of 54.0 in Nechako (LHA rank 67).

The leading causes of death were different from those in the province as a whole. While ischaemic heart disease ranked first, lung cancer was second in importance, followed by motor vehicle traffic accidents.

Table 21 Selected Characteristics of Northern Interior Health Unit

Local Health Area	Gender	Population 1985	Population 1989	Average Age 1985	Average Age 1989	Top 3 Leading Causes of Death 1985-1989	Household Income (Average) 1986	% 15+ With < Grade 9 1986	Physicians per 10,000 Population	Nurses per 10,000 Population
55 Burns Lake	Male	4,035	4,041	28.8	29.4	Ischaemic Heart Disease				
	Female	3,716	3,749	27.3	28.3	Motor Vehicle Accident			(rank:65)	(rank:63)
	Total	7,751	7,790	28.1	28.9	Lung Cancer	32,289	17.4	9.0	56.5
56 Nechako	Male	8,371	7,805	28.1	28.8	Ischaemic Heart Disease				
	Female	7,686	7,187	27.6	28.6	Motor Vehicle Accident			(rank:59)	(rank:67)
	Total	16,057	14,992	27.8	28.7	Lung Cancer	31,892	17.5	10.0	54.0
57 Prince George	Male	46,305	43,925	28.5	29.4	Ischaemic Heart Disease				
	Female	43,968	42,105	28.0	29.1	Lung Cancer			(rank:27)	(rank:30)
	Total	90,273	86,030	28.3	29.2	Motor Vehicle Accident	36,397	12.2	14.6	81.6
18 HEALTH UNIT	**Male**	**58,711**	**55,771**	**28.5**	**29.3**	**Ischaemic Heart Disease**				
	Female	**55,370**	**53,041**	**27.9**	**29.0**	**Lung Cancer**			**(rank:15)**	**(rank:15)**
	Total	**114,081**	**108,812**	**28.2**	**29.1**	**Motor Vehicle Accident**	**33,526**	**13.2**	**13.6**	**76.0**
PROVINCE	Male	1,422,900	1,506,397	33.9	34.9	Ischaemic Heart Disease				
	Female	1,447,200	1,540,847	35.7	36.7	Cerebrovascular Disease/Stroke				
	Total	2,870,100	3,047,244	34.8	35.8	Lung Cancer	33,497	11.2	23.3	93.0

Capital Regional District (HU 20) (Table 22)

The Capital Region District (CRD) is located on the southern end of Vancouver Island and includes several of the Gulf Islands. It has an area of 2,300 km² and comprises 10 municipalities, including Victoria, the legislative capital of British Columbia.

Coastal location and moderate climate have made the CRD one of the most attractive locales in Canada. As a result, population maintains a steady growth, primarily due to in-migration, especially retirees. The average population density was approximately 121 people/km² in 1989. Because of the number of retirees in the CRD Health Unit, the average age in 1989 was 39.7 years. This average age, shared with South Okanagan (HU 5), was the highest in the province. The Gulf Islands LHA had the highest average age of any LHA in the province. Conversely, the Sooke LHA's population was below the provincial average.

Resource-based industries, including agriculture, logging, and fishing were the most significant industries until the mid-1900s. More recently there has been a shift to service industries. The largest employment base is the business and personal service sector followed by public administration, including all levels of government, a university and college, and a federal naval base. There also are a number of small-scale manufacturing companies producing a variety of goods including furniture, boats, robots, and oceanographic products.

Average 1986 household incomes were below the provincial average, with the exception of the Saanich LHA. Educational attainment levels were substantially above the provincial norm.

The number of physicians per 10,000 population in the CRD, at 27.8, was the second-highest in the province. This measure varied greatly among LHAs from a high of 37.7 in Greater Victoria (LHA rank 3) to a low of 2.1 in Sooke (LHA rank 77). The number of nurses per 10,000 population, at 121.6, was the highest in the province. At the LHA level, the rates also varied greatly from a high of 159.8 in Greater Victoria (LHA rank 2) to a low of 16.6 in Sooke (LHA rank 79). This latter LHA had the lowest rate in the province, which probably reflected the concentration of health facilities in neighbouring Greater Victoria.

The leading causes of death were the same as those for the province as a whole, although lung cancer mortalities were more prominent in the Sooke LHA.

Table 22 Selected Characteristics of Capital Regional District Health Unit

Local Health Area	Gender	Population 1985	Population 1989	Average Age 1985	Average Age 1989	Top 3 Leading Causes of Death 1985-1989	Household Income (Average) 1986	% 15+ With < Grade 9 1986	Physicians per 10,000 Population	Nurses per 10,000 Population
61 Greater Victoria	Male	81,978	86,277	37.7	38.3	Ischaemic Heart Disease				
	Female	93,289	97,715	42.2	42.7	Cerebrovascular Disease/Stroke			(rank:03)	(rank:02)
	Total	175,267	183,992	40.1	40.6	Lung Cancer	30,326	7.9	37.7	159.8
62 Sooke	Male	19,621	21,539	31.8	33.5	Ischaemic Heart Disease				
	Female	19,270	21,318	32.5	34.2	Lung Cancer			(rank:77)	(rank:79)
	Total	38,891	42,857	32.1	33.8	Cerebrovascular Disease/Stroke	32,200	7.1	2.1	16.6
63 Saanich	Male	19,190	22,209	37.4	39.8	Ischaemic Heart Disease				
	Female	19,820	23,180	39.0	41.2	Cerebrovascular Disease/Stroke			(rank:36)	(rank:34)
	Total	39,010	45,389	38.2	40.5	Lung Cancer	38,320	5.9	12.6	80.4
64 Gulf Islands	Male	4,347	4,905	42.9	44.3	Ischaemic Heart Disease				
	Female	4,620	5,160	43.8	45.2	Cerebrovascular Disease/Stroke			(rank:07)	(rank:62)
	Total	8,967	10,065	43.4	44.7	Lung Cancer	25,783	7.0	24.8	57.6
20 HEALTH UNIT	**Male**	**125,136**	**134,930**	**36.9**	**38.0**	**Ischaemic Heart Disease**				
	Female	**136,999**	**147,373**	**40.4**	**41.3**	**Cerebrovascular Disease/Stroke**			**(rank:02)**	**(rank:01)**
	Total	**262,135**	**282,303**	**38.7**	**39.7**	**Lung Cancer**	**31,657**	**7.4**	**27.8**	**121.6**
PROVINCE	Male	1,422,900	1,506,397	33.9	34.9	Ischaemic Heart Disease				
	Female	1,447,200	1,540,847	35.7	36.7	Cerebrovascular Disease/Stroke				
	Total	2,870,100	3,047,244	34.8	35.8	Lung Cancer	33,497	11.2	23.3	93.0

Vancouver (HU 30) (Table 23)

The Vancouver Health Unit, encompassing the City of Vancouver, and the University of British Columbia Endowment Lands, has a land area of approximately 140 km^2. It had a population of approximately 460,000 in 1989 and the highest population density in the province at nearly 3,270 people/km^2.

The climate is greatly influenced by the Pacific Ocean which produces rather small ranges of seasonal temperature and moderate to heavy precipitation. The frost-free period generally exceeds 200 days.

Vancouver is the largest city and the economic heart of the province. It is one of North America's busiest ports and the base for a large commercial fishing fleet. The city also is an important railway hub, a financial centre, and the principal manufacturing, trade, and service centre of the province. Most of the major industrial concerns in British Columbia have their head offices in the city.

Although post-secondary educational services are increasingly available in all parts of the province, Vancouver remains the centre of such activity. The city's scenic setting, numerous attractions, and wide range of facilities (including several tertiary treatment hospitals) have made it a significant retirement centre and the major tourist destination in British Columbia. Retail, commercial, and industrial sectors have tended to follow the population shift to the suburbs although the city of Vancouver still retains its central role in these activities.

Vancouver is very much a multicultural city. According to 1986 census data, only 62.4 percent of its population claim English as their mother tongue, while a further 12.9 percent claim Chinese.

A high proportion of those who earn their livelihood in the city are residents of adjacent municipalities. Average household income and educational attainment were both below provincial levels. In recent years single detached dwellings in the urban area have been rapidly replaced by multiple-dwelling units, while the outlying districts have provided space for rapidly developing single-family residences. As a consequence, Vancouver has a significantly smaller portion of its population aged 15 and under compared to the provincial average. In 1989, the average age of inhabitants of the Health Unit was 38.0 years, exceeded only by the Capital Regional District and South Okanagan Health Units.

The number of physicians per 10,000 population in the Health Unit, at 59.9, was by far the highest in the province, reflecting the large number of medical facilities, especially tertiary and teaching hospitals. In addition, many people who live in adjacent Health Units but work in Vancouver, have their family physician in Vancouver (A.D. Thompson, 1990). The number of nurses per 10,000 population, at 104.3 (HU rank 4; LHA rank 12), was also higher than the provincial rate of 93.0.

The leading causes of death were the same as those for the province as a whole.

Table 23 Selected Characteristics of Vancouver Health Unit

Local Health Area	Gender	Population 1985	Population 1989	Average Age 1985	Average Age 1989	Top 3 Leading Causes of Death 1985-1989	Household Income (Average) 1986	% 15+ With < Grade 9 1986	Physicians per 10,000 Population	Nurses per 10,000 Population
39 Vancouver	Male	210,689	223,673	36.7	36.6	Ischaemic Heart Disease				
	Female	221,949	234,010	39.4	39.2	Cerebrovascular Disease/Stroke			(rank:01)	(rank:12)
	Total	432,638	457,683	38.1	38.0	Lung Cancer	32,491	13.4	59.9	104.3
30 HEALTH UNIT	**Male**	**210,689**	**223,673**	**36.7**	**36.6**	**Ischaemic Heart Disease**				
	Female	**221,949**	**234,010**	**39.4**	**39.2**	**Cerebrovascular/Stroke**			**(rank:01)**	**(rank:04)**
	Total	**432,638**	**457,683**	**38.1**	**38.0**	**Lung Cancer**	**32,491**	**13.4**	**59.9**	**104.3**
PROVINCE	Male	1,422,900	1,506,397	33.9	34.9	Ischaemic Heart Disease				
	Female	1,447,200	1,540,847	35.7	36.7	Cerebrovascular Disease/Stroke				
	Total	2,870,100	3,047,244	34.8	35.8	Lung Cancer	33,497	11.2	23.3	93.0

Burnaby (HU 31) (Table 24)

This Health Unit covers the District of Burnaby, a community immediately east of the City of Vancouver. It has an area of approximately 104 km² and in 1989 contained some 153,000 residents. With nearly 1470 people/km², it had the second-highest population density in the province.

Burnaby's economic base is well diversified. Originally a sparsely populated rural district, it soon became a residential community housing workers employed in Vancouver and New Westminster. This stage was followed by major industrial development and the construction of large wholesale and retail outlets. More recently, the area has become increasingly urbanized with the construction of large apartment buildings, post-secondary educational facilities, and office buildings. In terms of manufacturing output, Burnaby ranks second in the lower mainland, after Vancouver. The leading employers are involved in telecommunications equipment, and milk and related products. Urban development is expected to continue, particularly in districts served by the new rapid transit system.

The average age of the population was greater than that of the province as a whole. Average household income and educational attainment also were somewhat higher than the provincial levels.

The number of physicians per 10,000 population in the Health Unit, at 13.4 (HU rank 16; LHA rank 31), was less than the provincial rate of 23.3. The number of nurses per 10,000 population, at 81.7 (HU rank 12; LHA rank 29), was slightly lower than the provincial rate of 93.0.

The principal causes of death were the same as those for the province as a whole.

Table 24 Selected Characteristics of Burnaby Health Unit

Local Health Area	Gender	Population 1985	Population 1989	Average Age 1985	Average Age 1989	Top 3 Leading Causes of Death 1985-1989	Household Income (Average) 1986	% 15+ With < Grade 9 1986	Physicians per 10,000 Population	Nurses per 10,000 Population
41 Burnaby	Male	69,482	74,012	35.7	36.5	Ischaemic Heart Disease				
	Female	73,556	78,698	38.2	38.9	Cerebrovascular Disease/Stroke			(rank:31)	(rank:29)
	Total	143,038	152,710	37.0	36.5	Lung Cancer	35,087	10.2	13.4	81.7
31 HEALTH UNIT	**Male**	**69,482**	**74,012**	**35.7**	**36.5**	**Ischaemic Heart Disease**				
	Female	**73,556**	**78,698**	**38.2**	**38.9**	**Cerebrovascular/Stroke**			**(rank:16)**	**(rank:12)**
	Total	**143,038**	**152,710**	**37.0**	**37.7**	**Lung Cancer**	**35,087**	**10.2**	**13.4**	**81.7**
PROVINCE	Male	1,422,900	1,506,397	33.9	34.9	Ischaemic Heart Disease				
	Female	1,447,200	1,540,847	35.7	36.7	Cerebrovascular Disease/Stroke				
	Total	2,870,100	3,047,244	34.8	35.8	Lung Cancer	33,497	11.2	23.3	93.0

Richmond (HU 32) (Table 25)

Richmond is a large residential suburb, covering approximately 127 km² and in 1989 contained approximately 120,000 people. Its population density of 932 people/km² was third only to Vancouver and Burnaby.

Many of the area's inhabitants are employed in other parts of metropolitan Vancouver. Its function as a "bedroom municipality" is responsible for most of the area's growth over the past quarter century. The economy, however, is becoming increasingly diversified with the development of manufacturing, trade, and service industries. Despite the loss of farmland to alternate uses, agriculture remains an important economic activity. Many fishermen are based here, and the community of Steveston contains a number of canneries and related industries. Service industries provide the majority of jobs. Vancouver International Airport is the largest single source of employment. In terms of industrial diversity and employment, Richmond ranked second in the lower mainland, following Vancouver. In 1987, major industries included wood, food, fabricated metal products, and electrical and electronic products.

The average age of the population was close to that of the province as a whole, while average household income and educational attainment were substantially above provincial levels.

The number of physicians per 10,000 population in the Health Unit, at 17.1 (HU rank 8; LHA rank 17), was lower than the provincial rate of 23.3. The number of nurses per 10,000 population, at 101.9 (HU rank 6; LHA rank 14), was above the provincial rate of 93.0.

In terms of leading causes of death, lung cancer and cerebrovascular diseases/stroke ranked second and third for this Health Unit, compared to third and second, respectively, for the province as a whole.

Table 25 Selected Characteristics of Richmond Health Unit

Local Health Area	Gender	Population 1985	Population 1989	Average Age 1985	Average Age 1989	Top 3 Leading Causes of Death 1985-1989	Household Income (Average) 1986	% 15+ With < Grade 9 1986	Physicians per 10,000 Population	Nurses per 10,000 Population
38 Richmond	Male	51,954	57,823	32.9	34.3	Ischaemic Heart Disease				
	Female	53,900	60,566	34.5	36.1	Lung Cancer			(rank:17)	(rank:14)
	Total	105,854	118,389	33.8	35.2	Cerebrovascular Disease/Stroke	41,494	7.4	17.1	101.9
32 HEALTH UNIT	**Male**	**51,954**	**57,823**	**32.9**	**34.3**	**Ischaemic Heart Disease**				
	Female	**53,900**	**60,566**	**34.5**	**36.1**	**Lung Cancer**			**(rank:08)**	**(rank:06)**
	Total	**105,854**	**118,389**	**33.8**	**35.2**	**Cerebrovascular Disease/Stroke**	**41,494**	**7.4**	**71.1**	**101.9**
PROVINCE	Male	1,422,900	1,506,397	33.9	34.9	Ischaemic Heart Disease				
	Female	1,447,200	1,540,847	35.7	36.7	Cerebrovascular Disease/Stroke				
	Total	2,870,100	3,047,244	34.8	35.8	Lung Cancer	33,497	11.2	23.3	93.0

North Shore (HU 33) (Table 26)

The North Shore Health Unit includes the City of North Vancouver, the District of North Vancouver, the District of West Vancouver, and Bowen Island, and covers a land area of approximately 570 km². It is located primarily on the south-facing lower slopes of the coastal mountains that form the northern edge of the lower mainland region. It contained close to 155,000 people in 1989, and had a population density of over 270 people/km².

The North Shore enjoys a favourable coastal climate characterized by mild, wet winters and warm, moist summers. The area is primarily a residential suburb, with most of its residents employed in other parts of metropolitan Vancouver. The major source of employment within the West Vancouver area is a large shopping centre. The North Shore also contains the terminus for ferries serving Nanaimo, Bowen Island, and the Sunshine Coast. North Vancouver is an important shipping and rail centre and the site of a wide range of manufacturing and service operations. Tourism plays an important role in the economy, offering skiing, sightseeing, picnicking, hiking, boating, fishing, and swimming.

While the average age was higher than the province as a whole, this was primarily related to a large retired population in the West Vancouver-Bowen Island LHA. The North Shore also had the highest 1986 average household income and the smallest percentage of people 15 years of age and older with less than a grade nine education in the province. The West Vancouver-Bowen Island LHA had the highest average household income of any LHA, nearly twice that of the provincial average. It also had the highest level of educational attainment.

The number of physicians per 10,000 population in the Health Unit, at 22.4, was the fourth-highest in the province. This measure varied from 27.1 in West Vancouver-Bowen Island (LHA rank 4) to 20.7 in North Vancouver (LHA rank 9). The number of nurses per 10,000 population, at 111.5, was the third-highest in the province. At the LHA level, rates were 121.1 in North Vancouver (LHA rank 3) and 86.6 in West Vancouver-Bowen Island (LHA rank 25).

Overall, the Health Unit parallels the province in leading causes of death, although deaths from pneumonia and influenza ranked third in the West Vancouver-Bowen Island LHA.

Table 26 Selected Characteristics of North Shore Health Unit

Local Health Area	Gender	Population 1985	Population 1989	Average Age 1985	Average Age 1989	Top 3 Leading Causes of Death 1985-1989	Household Income (Average) 1986	% 15+ With < Grade 9 1986	Physicians per 10,000 Population	Nurses per 10,000 Population
44 North	Male	49,956	54,326	34.2	35.0	Ischaemic Heart Disease				
Vancouver	Female	52,517	57,512	36.4	37.0	Cerebrovascular Disease/Stroke			(rank:09)	(rank:03)
	Total	102,473	111,838	35.3	36.0	Lung Cancer	40,954	4.5	20.7	121.1
45 West	Male	19,221	20,318	39.4	40.2	Ischaemic Heart Disease				
Vancouver-	Female	21,243	22,499	42.9	43.9	Cerebrovascular/Stroke			(rank:04)	(rank:25)
Bowen Island	Total	40,464	42,817	41.3	42.1	Pneumonia and Influenza	59,979	2.3	27.1	86.6
33 HEALTH UNIT	**Male**	**69,177**	**74,644**	**35.7**	**36.4**	**Ischaemic Heart Disease**				
	Female	**73,760**	**80,011**	**38.2**	**39.0**	**Cerebrovascular Disease/Stroke**			**(rank:04)**	**(rank:03)**
	Total	**142,937**	**154,655**	**37.0**	**37.7**	**Lung Cancer**	**50,466**	**3.9**	**22.4**	**111.5**
PROVINCE	Male	1,422,900	1,506,397	33.9	34.9	Ischaemic Heart Disease				
	Female	1,447,200	1,540,847	35.7	36.7	Cerebrovascular Disease/Stroke				
	Total	2,870,100	3,047,244	34.8	35.8	Lung Cancer	33,497	11.2	23.3	93.0

5

GEOGRAPHICAL VARIATIONS OF MORTALITY IN BRITISH COLUMBIA

Harold D. Foster, Leslie T. Foster, Kevin F. Burr,
Jemal Mohamed, and Ken Josephson

This chapter presents the results of the mortality analyses as maps, with supporting tabular information and summary text. Overlay transparencies of the Local Health Area, Health Unit, and Regional Hospital District figures are included in a pocket inside the back cover of this atlas. These transparencies can be used to readily identify specific areas on the mortality maps. A brief guide to aid in the reading of the maps and accompanying tables is also provided.

READING THE MAPS AND TABLES

The mortality measure that is employed in the construction of the maps contained in this atlas is the Standardized Mortality Ratio (SMR). Each SMR value is tested for the degree of statistical significance between observed and expected deaths, based on the provincial rates. Since mapping based on significance levels alone does not give any indication of the magnitude of the SMR, the plotting method used incorporates both significance and size of the measure by utilizing the following four-colour scheme:

Rust indicates that the observed deaths in the LHAs are statistically significantly higher than the expected deaths, and have SMRs that fall within the top decile (10 percent);

Tan indicates that the observed deaths in the LHAs are statistically significantly higher than the expected deaths, but do not have SMRs that fall within the top decile;

Beige indicates that the observed deaths in the LHAs either are not statistically significantly different from the expected deaths, or have fewer than five observed cases;

Green indicates that the observed deaths in the LHAs are statistically significantly lower than the expected deaths.

Additional information pertinent to each statistically significant SMR is contained in the accompanying tables. The colours used in the tables correspond to those used in the maps, facilitating the process of comparing an area of interest on the map to the data in the table. SMRs have been ranked in terms of their relative magnitude. Additionally, the observed and expected deaths used in the calculation of the SMRs are provided, in order to give some perspective of the actual numbers involved.

In the accompanying tables, the column labelled (p) indicates the level at which a particular SMR was statistically significant. One star (*) indicates significance at the $p<0.05$ level; two stars (**) depict significance at the $p<0.01$ level; and three stars (***) indicate significance at the $p<0.001$ level. The last column presents the 95 percent confidence interval, which may be used in conjunction with the statistical significance, or as an independent means of determining significance.

Each map is also accompanied by a bar graph of Age Standardized Mortality Rate (ASMR) trends for the five-year period (single-year ASMRs by LHA are provided for each mortality category in the Appendix). The ASMR is based on a population of 10,000 and this measure is useful when examining the change in mortality rates over the five-year period 1985 to 1989, by individual years.

In the narrative that accompanies each map, reference to the "highest" or "lowest" SMRs refers only to those values that are *statistically significant*. There may indeed be higher or lower SMR values for other Local Health Areas, but only those that are statistically significant and have a minimum of five deaths over the 1985 to 1989 period are referred to in the following text. The SMR values for all Local Health Areas are provided in the Appendix.

All Causes of Death: Both Genders

During the period 1985 to 1989, there was a total of 108,876 deaths in British Columbia. Over this time, ASMRs dropped from a rate of 54.6 to 51.5. In general, mortality tended to be low in the south and east of the province, elevated in central British Columbia and coastal areas, and not statistically significant in the north.

The geographic distribution of all causes of mortality for both genders was similar to the patterns for males and females individually. The significantly lowest mortalities occurred in the southeast and south-central areas, including Kootenay Lake, Windermere, Penticton, Central Okanagan, Salmon Arm, Armstrong-Spallumcheen, and some LHAs on southern Vancouver Island such as Greater Victoria, Saanich, Qualicum, and the Gulf Islands. Five LHAs in the southwest of British Columbia (Surrey, Delta, Richmond, Abbotsford, and West Vancouver-Bowen Island) also reported significantly low mortality for both genders.

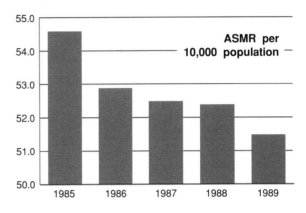

The significantly high mortalities were located in central and coastal British Columbia and a large part of Vancouver Island. These included Central Coast, Lillooet, Prince Rupert, Princeton, Merritt, and Burns Lake, which were all in the top 10 percent. For a large part of northern and southeastern British Columbia, SMRs were not statistically significant.

All Causes of Death: Both Genders

	Local Health Area	Observed Deaths	Expected Deaths	SMR	(p)	95% C.I. Lower	95% C.I. Upper
49	Central Coast	115	69.78	1.65	***	1.36	1.98
29	Lillooet	167	126.75	1.32	***	1.13	1.53
52	Prince Rupert	486	372.40	1.31	***	1.19	1.43
17	Princeton	209	160.67	1.30	***	1.13	1.49
31	Merritt	324	248.82	1.30	***	1.16	1.45
55	Burns Lake	203	158.90	1.28	***	1.11	1.47
85	Vancouver Island North	265	207.59	1.28	***	1.13	1.44
57	Prince George	1812	1479.64	1.22	***	1.17	1.28
28	Quesnel	637	526.51	1.21	***	1.12	1.31
30	South Cariboo	252	208.52	1.21	**	1.06	1.37
54	Smithers	323	266.18	1.21	***	1.08	1.35
27	Cariboo-Chilcotin	928	772.15	1.20	***	1.13	1.28
70	Alberni	998	849.83	1.17	***	1.10	1.25
80	Kitimat	212	181.04	1.17	*	1.02	1.34
88	Terrace	528	449.70	1.17	***	1.08	1.28
67	Ladysmith	617	567.81	1.09	*	1.00	1.18
72	Campbell River	810	741.81	1.09	*	1.02	1.17
24	Kamloops	2246	2084.60	1.08	***	1.03	1.12
42	Maple Ridge	1582	1463.76	1.08	**	1.03	1.14
40	New Westminster	2242	2085.87	1.07	***	1.03	1.12
68	Nanaimo	2492	2326.13	1.07	***	1.03	1.11
65	Cowichan	1439	1363.17	1.06	*	1.00	1.11
39	Vancouver	21111	20022.14	1.05	***	1.04	1.07
43	Coquitlam	3087	2936.78	1.05	**	1.01	1.09
36	Surrey	6764	7071.81	0.96	***	0.93	0.98
37	Delta	1925	2047.26	0.94	**	0.90	0.98
61	Greater Victoria	10111	10793.06	0.94	***	0.92	0.96
69	Qualicum	1137	1222.06	0.93	*	0.88	0.99
38	Richmond	2956	3248.65	0.91	***	0.88	0.94
15	Penticton	1507	1714.87	0.88	***	0.83	0.92
34	Abbotsford	2417	2764.10	0.87	***	0.84	0.91
23	Central Okanagan	3768	4374.54	0.86	***	0.83	0.89
45	West Vancouver-Bowen Is	1924	2246.59	0.86	***	0.82	0.90
64	Gulf Islands	481	561.36	0.86	***	0.78	0.94
20	Salmon Arm	909	1077.58	0.84	***	0.79	0.90
21	Armstrong-Spallumcheen	231	274.30	0.84	**	0.74	0.96
63	Saanich	1577	1893.73	0.83	***	0.79	0.87
4	Windermere	135	179.47	0.75	***	0.63	0.89
6	Kootenay Lake	106	152.28	0.70	***	0.57	0.84

Significantly High and SMR within top 10%
Significantly High and SMR not within top 10%
Significantly Low

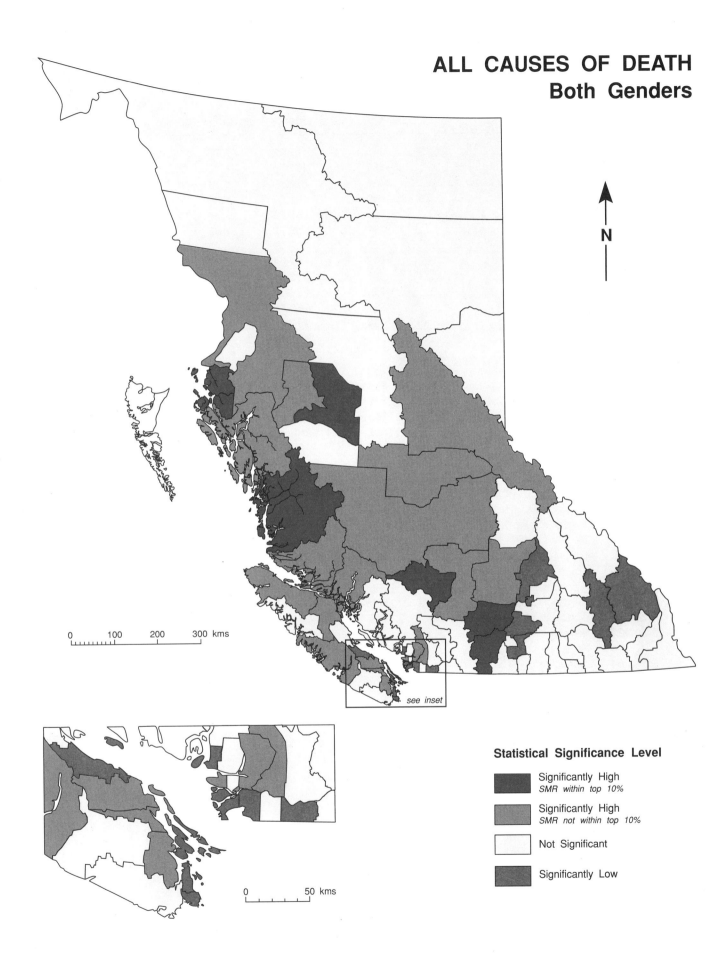

ALL CAUSES OF DEATH
Both Genders

N

0   100   200   300 kms

see inset

0   50 kms

Statistical Significance Level

Significantly High
SMR within top 10%

Significantly High
SMR not within top 10%

Not Significant

Significantly Low

67

All Causes of Death: Male

	Local Health Area	Observed Deaths	Expected Deaths	SMR	(p)	95% C.I. Lower	95% C.I. Upper
49	Central Coast	81	47.32	1.71	***	1.36	2.13
17	Princeton	139	92.35	1.51	***	1.27	1.78
85	Vancouver Island North	190	132.78	1.43	***	1.23	1.65
52	Prince Rupert	303	228.76	1.32	***	1.18	1.48
31	Merritt	198	150.92	1.31	***	1.14	1.51
55	Burns Lake	137	105.69	1.30	**	1.09	1.53
54	Smithers	211	163.16	1.29	***	1.12	1.48
29	Lillooet	103	83.26	1.24	*	1.01	1.50
57	Prince George	1136	929.50	1.22	***	1.15	1.30
30	South Cariboo	163	135.09	1.21	*	1.03	1.41
27	Cariboo-Chilcotin	586	486.71	1.20	***	1.11	1.31
28	Quesnel	404	336.62	1.20	***	1.09	1.32
56	Nechako	234	202.35	1.16	*	1.01	1.31
70	Alberni	573	493.37	1.16	***	1.07	1.26
40	New Westminster	1139	994.53	1.15	***	1.08	1.21
72	Campbell River	496	437.34	1.13	**	1.04	1.24
88	Terrace	341	300.51	1.13	*	1.02	1.26
24	Kamloops	1362	1222.66	1.11	***	1.06	1.17
39	Vancouver	11270	10201.94	1.10	***	1.08	1.13
42	Maple Ridge	878	808.61	1.09	*	1.02	1.16
68	Nanaimo	1402	1316.00	1.07	*	1.01	1.12
36	Surrey	3808	3982.89	0.96	**	0.93	0.99
61	Greater Victoria	4848	5144.26	0.94	***	0.92	0.97
69	Qualicum	656	716.22	0.92	*	0.85	0.99
15	Penticton	849	958.96	0.89	***	0.83	0.95
37	Delta	1012	1134.98	0.89	***	0.84	0.95
77	Summerland	278	313.87	0.89	*	0.78	1.00
34	Abbotsford	1359	1550.88	0.88	***	0.83	0.92
38	Richmond	1565	1781.66	0.88	***	0.84	0.92
23	Central Okanagan	2183	2533.46	0.86	***	0.83	0.90
62	Sooke	560	667.36	0.84	***	0.77	0.91
20	Salmon Arm	537	651.55	0.82	***	0.76	0.90
64	Gulf Islands	266	331.55	0.80	***	0.71	0.90
63	Saanich	846	1075.42	0.79	***	0.73	0.84
45	West Vancouver-Bowen Is	826	1111.49	0.74	***	0.69	0.80
6	Kootenay Lake	62	92.34	0.67	**	0.51	0.86
4	Windermere	78	117.97	0.66	***	0.52	0.83

Significantly High and SMR within top 10%
Significantly High and SMR not within top 10%
Significantly Low

ALL CAUSES OF DEATH
Male

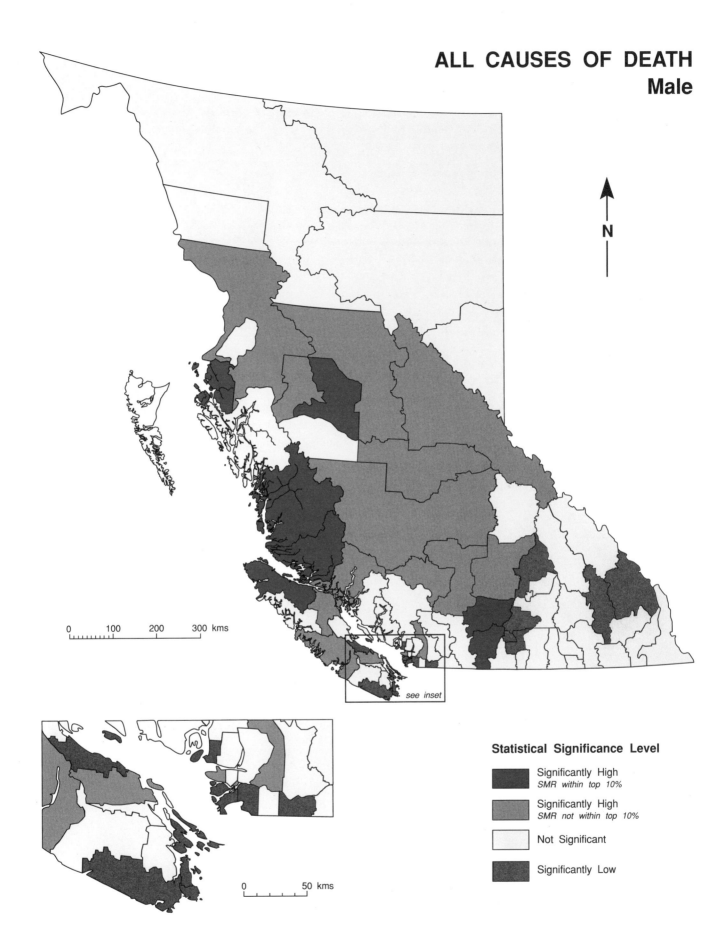

0   100   200   300 kms

see inset

0   50 kms

Statistical Significance Level

Significantly High
SMR within top 10%

Significantly High
SMR not within top 10%

Not Significant

Significantly Low

All Causes of Death: Male

During the period 1985 to 1989, there were 59,656 male deaths in British Columbia. Over this time, ASMRs fell from 63.7 to 59.9. In general, mortality tended to be low in the south of the province, elevated in central British Columbia, and not statistically signicant in the north.

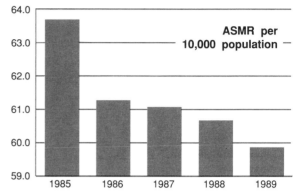

To illustrate, three clear concentrations of low male mortality occurred in the south. The first of these was located in the southwest including several areas on southern Vancouver Island (Greater Victoria, Saanich, Qualicum, and Sooke) and the Gulf Islands. Significantly low mortality was also apparent in some lower mainland areas, including Richmond, Delta, Surrey, Abbotsford, and West Vancouver-Bowen Island. A second cluster of areas experiencing significantly low male mortality can be identified in the Okanagan, consisting of Penticton, Summerland, Central Okanagan, and Salmon Arm. The lowest male mortality occurred in a third concentration in the southeast of British Columbia, in Windermere and Kootenay Lake.

In contrast, most areas with significantly high male mortality were located in the central coast and interior of British Columbia. These included Central Coast, Princeton, Vancouver Island North, Prince Rupert, Merritt, and Burns Lake. Of these LHAs, Central Coast experienced the significantly highest mortality in the province.

Male deaths in northern British Columbia, for example, in Stikine, Telegraph Creek, Fort Nelson, Peace River North, and Peace River South, were not statistically significant.

All Causes of Death: Female

There were 49,220 female deaths in British Columbia during the period 1985 to 1989, nearly 20 percent fewer than those for males. ASMRs dropped during this time from 46.1 to 43.7. This reduction was not consistent, as 1988 showed a higher rate than 1987.

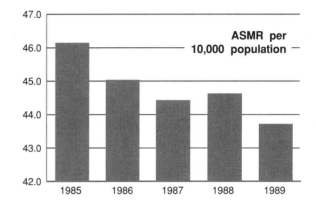

While there were differences between male and female mortality patterns, there were also obvious similarities. There was, for example, a tendency for lower female mortality to occur in the south. To illustrate, mortality was low in Penticton, Central Okanagan, Southern Okanagan, Salmon Arm, and Armstrong-Spallumcheen. As with males, significantly low mortality was also experienced in several areas in the southwest, including Abbotsford, Surrey, Richmond, Greater Victoria, and Saanich. The lowest female SMR, however, occurred in the southeast in Kootenay Lake.

As with males, there was also a tendency among females to experience significantly higher mortality, in the top decile, in central British Columbia, especially Central Coast, Lillooet, and Merritt. Central Coast reported the significantly highest mortality for females in the province, as it did for males.

All Causes of Death: Female

		Local Health Area	Observed Deaths	Expected Deaths	SMR	(p)	95% C.I. Lower	95% C.I. Upper
	49	Central Coast	34	22.46	1.51	*	1.05	2.12
	29	Lillooet	64	43.50	1.47	**	1.13	1.88
	31	Merritt	126	97.90	1.29	**	1.07	1.53
	52	Prince Rupert	183	143.63	1.27	**	1.10	1.47
	88	Terrace	187	149.19	1.25	**	1.08	1.45
	28	Quesnel	233	189.89	1.23	**	1.07	1.40
	57	Prince George	676	550.14	1.23	***	1.14	1.32
	27	Cariboo-Chilcotin	342	285.44	1.20	**	1.07	1.33
	70	Alberni	425	356.46	1.19	***	1.08	1.31
	11	Trail	411	358.62	1.15	**	1.04	1.26
	67	Ladysmith	266	230.90	1.15	*	1.02	1.30
	43	Coquitlam	1424	1270.77	1.12	***	1.06	1.18
	65	Cowichan	650	587.74	1.11	*	1.02	1.19
	62	Sooke	503	458.12	1.10	*	1.00	1.20
	44	North Vancouver	1753	1624.36	1.08	**	1.03	1.13
	68	Nanaimo	1090	1010.13	1.08	*	1.02	1.15
	36	Surrey	2956	3088.92	0.96	*	0.92	0.99
	38	Richmond	1391	1466.99	0.95	*	0.90	1.00
	61	Greater Victoria	5263	5648.80	0.93	***	0.91	0.96
	14	Southern Okanagan	314	352.24	0.89	*	0.80	1.00
	63	Saanich	731	818.32	0.89	**	0.83	0.96
	15	Penticton	658	755.91	0.87	***	0.81	0.94
	20	Salmon Arm	372	426.03	0.87	**	0.79	0.97
	34	Abbotsford	1058	1213.22	0.87	***	0.82	0.93
	23	Central Okanagan	1585	1841.09	0.86	***	0.82	0.90
	21	Armstrong-Spallumcheen	88	108.80	0.81	*	0.65	1.00
	6	Kootenay Lake	44	59.94	0.73	*	0.53	0.99

Significantly High and SMR within top 10%
Significantly High and SMR not within top 10%
Significantly Low

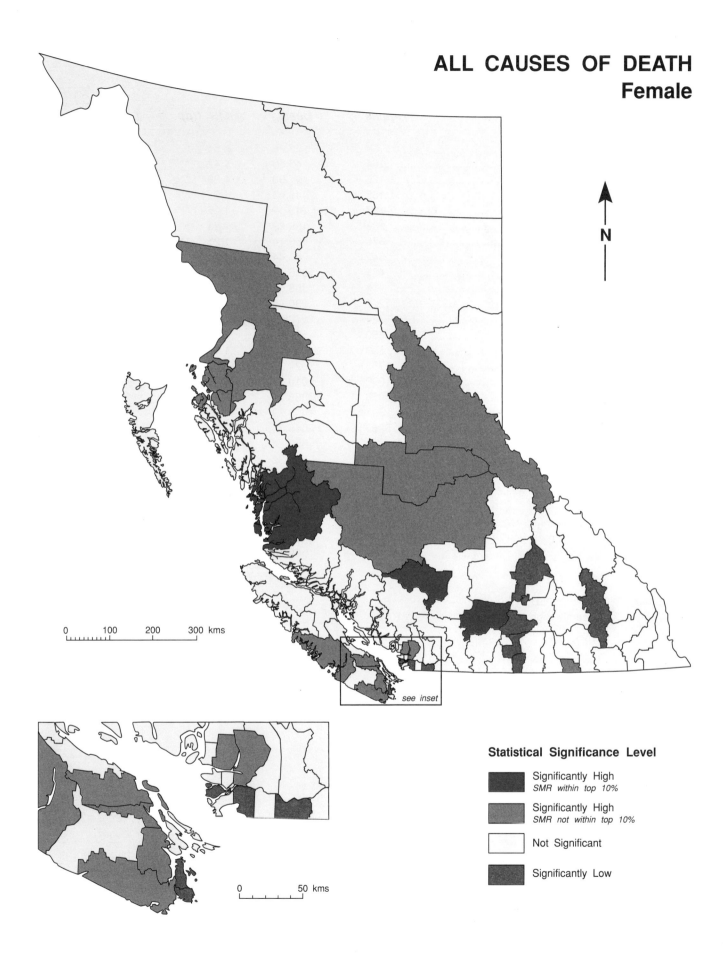

ALL CAUSES OF DEATH
Female

N

0   100   200   300 kms

see inset

Statistical Significance Level

Significantly High
SMR within top 10%

Significantly High
SMR not within top 10%

Not Significant

Significantly Low

0   50 kms

73

All Cancer Sites: Male

	Local Health Area	Observed Deaths	Expected Deaths	SMR	(p)	95% C.I. Lower	Upper
72	Campbell River 140	114.46	1.22	*	1.03	1.44
40	New Westminster 290	253.65	1.14	*	1.02	1.28
39	Vancouver 2802	2583.23	1.08	***	1.04	1.13
22	Vernon 227	271.25	0.84	**	0.73	0.95
34	Abbotsford 329	394.20	0.83	***	0.75	0.93
45	West Vancouver-Bowen Is 248	300.54	0.83	**	0.73	0.93
59	Peace River South 72	90.92	0.79	*	0.62	1.00
2	Cranbrook 63	81.16	0.78	*	0.60	0.99
20	Salmon Arm 139	178.45	0.78	**	0.65	0.92
21	Armstrong-Spallumcheen 26	43.23	0.60	**	0.39	0.88
6	Kootenay Lake 15	25.40	0.59	*	0.33	0.97

Significantly High and SMR within top 10%
Significantly High and SMR not within top 10%
Significantly Low

During the period 1985 to 1989, there were 15,399 male cancer deaths. Over this time, ASMRs fluctuated in the range 15.0 to 15.6. There was little statistically significant variation in mortality from male cancer in northern and central British Columbia, with the exception of Peace River South where it was low.

Statistically significant differences were generally limited to the south of the province. In this region, only Campbell River experienced a death rate that was both significantly high and in the top decile. Mortality was also elevated in New Westminster and Vancouver. The lowest male mortality for cancer occurred in southeastern and south-central British Columbia, with Armstrong-Spallumcheen and Kootenay Lake having the two significantly lowest SMRs in the province.

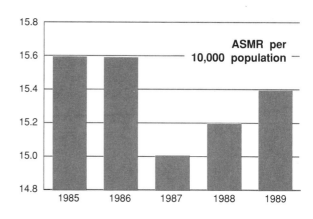

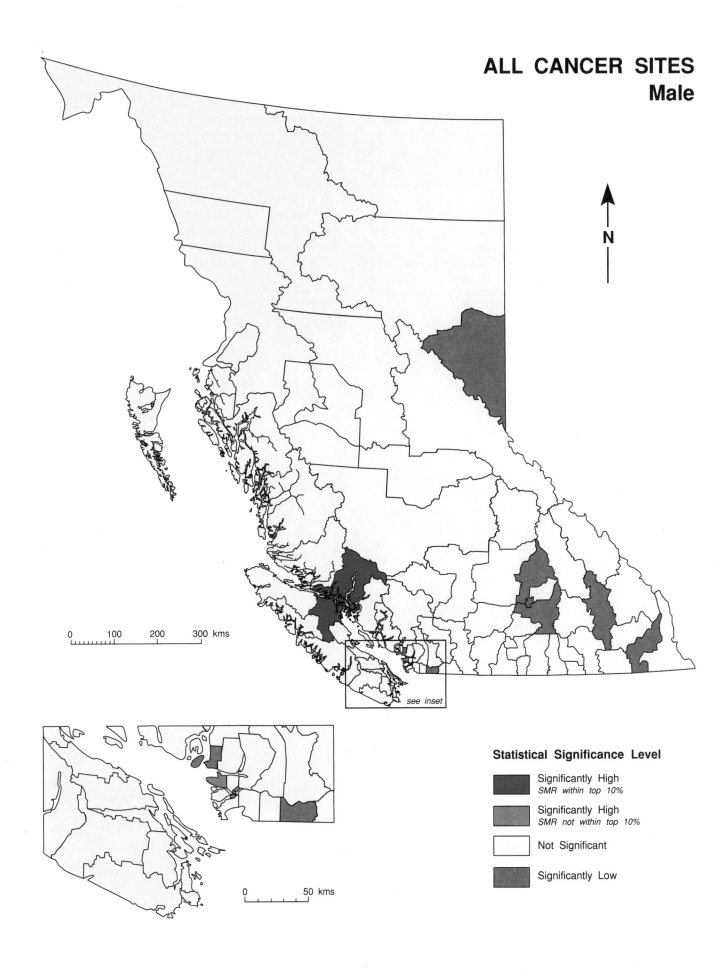

ALL CANCER SITES
Male

N

0   100   200   300 kms

Statistical Significance Level

Significantly High
SMR within top 10%

Significantly High
SMR not within top 10%

Not Significant

Significantly Low

see inset

0   50 kms

75

All Cancer Sites: Female

	Local Health Area	Observed Deaths	Expected Deaths	SMR	(p)	95% C.I. Lower	Upper
66	Lake Cowichan 27	17.53	1.54	*	1.01	2.24
65	Cowichan 210	161.68	1.30	***	1.13	1.49
27	Cariboo-Chilcotin 111	88.48	1.25	*	1.03	1.51
57	Prince George....................................207	168.74	1.23	**	1.07	1.41
43	Coquitlam 417	365.85	1.14	**	1.03	1.25
23	Central Okanagan 464	515.00	0.90	*	0.82	0.99
34	Abbotsford 262	322.61	0.81	***	0.72	0.92
14	Southern Okanagan 63	96.47	0.65	***	0.50	0.84
10	Arrow Lakes 12	21.35	0.56	*	0.29	0.98
76	Agassiz-Harrison 10	20.39	0.49	*	0.23	0.90

Significantly High and SMR within top 10%

Significantly High and SMR not within top 10%

Significantly Low

During the period 1985 to 1989, there were 13,141 female cancer deaths, approximately 15 percent fewer than those for males. Over this time, ASMRs fluctuated in the range 12.4 to 12.9. The geographical pattern of female cancer mortality was generally quite different from that of males, although some similarities, including the lack of statistically significant SMRs, were apparent in the north of the province.

Obvious differences included the elevated mortalities of females in Lake Cowichan and Cowichan. Both of these LHAs reported female cancer mortalities that were statistically significant and in the top decile. Mortality also was high in central British Columbia, especially Cariboo-Chilcotin and Prince George. Coquitlam was the only lower mainland LHA to be significantly high. In contrast, significantly low mortality was restricted to the south and included Agassiz-Harrison, Southern Okanagan, Central Okanagan, Arrow Lakes, and Abbotsford. The latter was particularly noticeable because it was the only LHA recording significantly low cancer mortality for both genders.

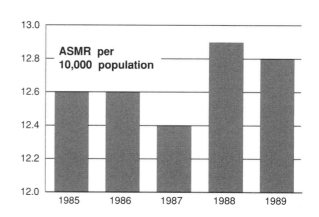

ASMR per 10,000 population

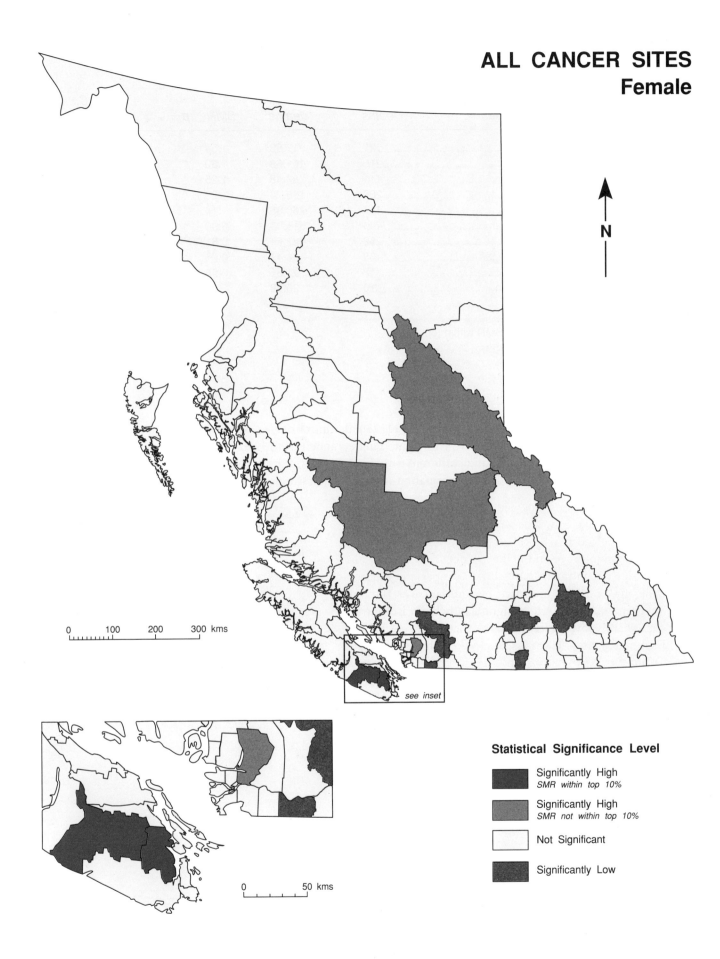

ALL CANCER SITES
Female

0   100   200   300 kms

see inset

N

0   50 kms

Statistical Significance Level

Significantly High
SMR within top 10%

Significantly High
SMR not within top 10%

Not Significant

Significantly Low

77

Lung Cancer: Male

	Local Health Area	Observed Deaths	Expected Deaths	SMR	(p)	95% C.I. Lower	95% C.I. Upper
81	Fort Nelson	10	2.76	3.62	**	1.73	6.66
72	Campbell River	51	36.33	1.40	*	1.05	1.85
11	Trail	54	39.43	1.37	*	1.03	1.79
57	Prince George	95	71.75	1.32	**	1.07	1.62
24	Kamloops	124	98.70	1.26	*	1.04	1.50
39	Vancouver	884	791.15	1.12	**	1.04	1.19
63	Saanich	72	95.01	0.76	*	0.59	0.95
45	West Vancouver-Bowen Is	59	94.51	0.62	***	0.48	0.81
34	Abbotsford	72	120.79	0.60	***	0.47	0.75
64	Gulf Islands	16	29.80	0.54	**	0.31	0.87
77	Summerland	10	24.78	0.40	**	0.19	0.74

Significantly High and SMR within top 10%
Significantly High and SMR not within top 10%
Significantly Low

During the period 1985 to 1989, there were 4,777 male lung cancer deaths. Over this time, ASMRs fluctuated in the range of 4.6 to 5.0. Significantly high male lung cancer mortality did not display any obvious regional pattern. Three isolated LHAs, however, recorded significantly high mortality, in the top decile, namely Fort Nelson, Campbell River, and Trail. In addition, significantly high mortalities also appeared in south-central (Kamloops), central (Prince George), and southwest (Vancouver) British Columbia.

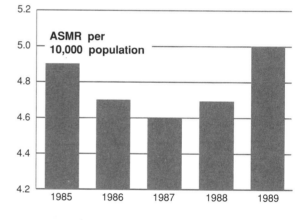

In contrast, significantly low male lung cancer mortality was restricted to the south. Summerland, located in the southern interior, reported the significantly lowest male mortality from lung cancer in British Columbia. This trend was also illustrated in the southwest by the Gulf Islands, Abbotsford, West Vancouver-Bowen Island, and Saanich, although Vancouver with its previously noted significantly high SMR, was a major exception.

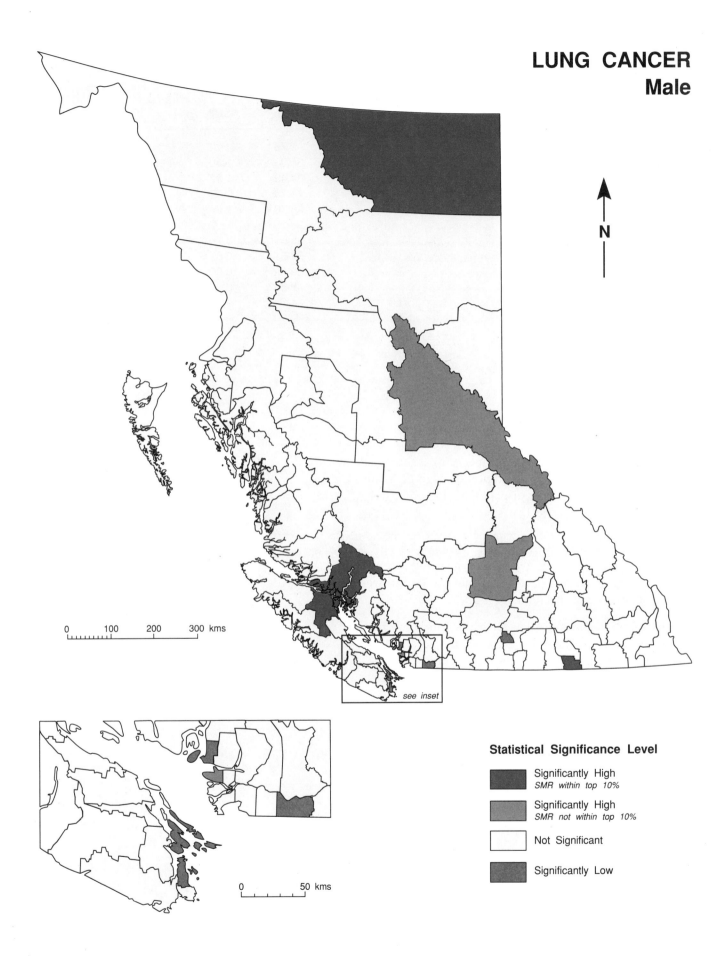

LUNG CANCER
Male

N

0   100   200   300 kms

see inset

0   50 kms

Statistical Significance Level

Significantly High
SMR within top 10%

Significantly High
SMR not within top 10%

Not Significant

Significantly Low

Lung Cancer: Female

	Local Health Area	Observed Deaths	Expected Deaths	SMR	(p)	95% C.I. Lower	Upper
57	Prince George	53	33.67	1.57	**	1.18	2.06
43	Coquitlam	95	72.52	1.31	*	1.06	1.60
61	Greater Victoria	200	244.29	0.82	**	0.71	0.94
45	West Vancouver-Bowen Is	39	55.65	0.70	*	0.50	0.96

Significantly High and SMR within top 10%
Significantly High and SMR not within top 10%
Significantly Low

During the period 1985 to 1989, there were 2,568 female lung cancer deaths, just more than half as many as for males. Over this time, ASMRs showed a steady increase from 2.2 to 2.7. As with males, elevated female lung cancer mortality did not display any clear regional pattern.

Only Prince George reported significantly high female mortality, in the top decile. This area also had a high SMR for males, although not in the top decile. Coquitlam also reported significantly high female mortality, but not in the top decile. Significantly low female mortality occurred only in the southwest of British Columbia, in Greater Victoria and West Vancouver-Bowen Island. The latter also reported significantly low male lung cancer mortality.

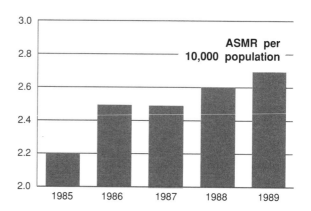

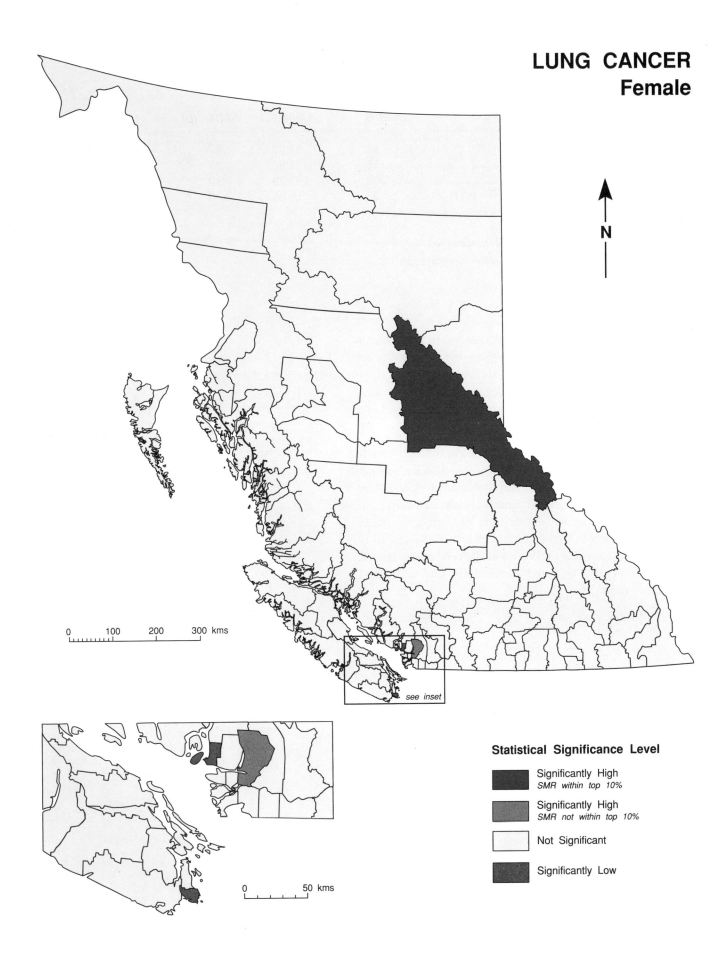

LUNG CANCER
Female

N

0 100 200 300 kms

see inset

0 50 kms

Statistical Significance Level

Significantly High
SMR within top 10%

Significantly High
SMR not within top 10%

Not Significant

Significantly Low

81

Breast Cancer: Female

	Local Health Area	Observed Deaths	Expected Deaths	SMR	(p)	95% C.I. Lower	Upper
47	Powell River 24		14.83	1.62	*	1.04	2.41

Significantly High and SMR within top 10%
Significantly High and SMR not within top 10%
Significantly Low

During the period 1985 to 1989, there were 2,440 female breast cancer deaths. Over this time, ASMRs remained fairly stable, fluctuating in the range of 2.3 to 2.6. Only Powell River recorded significantly high mortality, in the top decile, for this cause of death. No areas reported significantly low mortality.

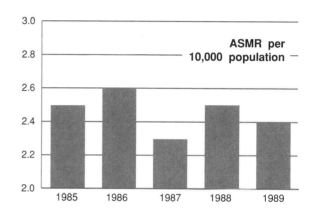

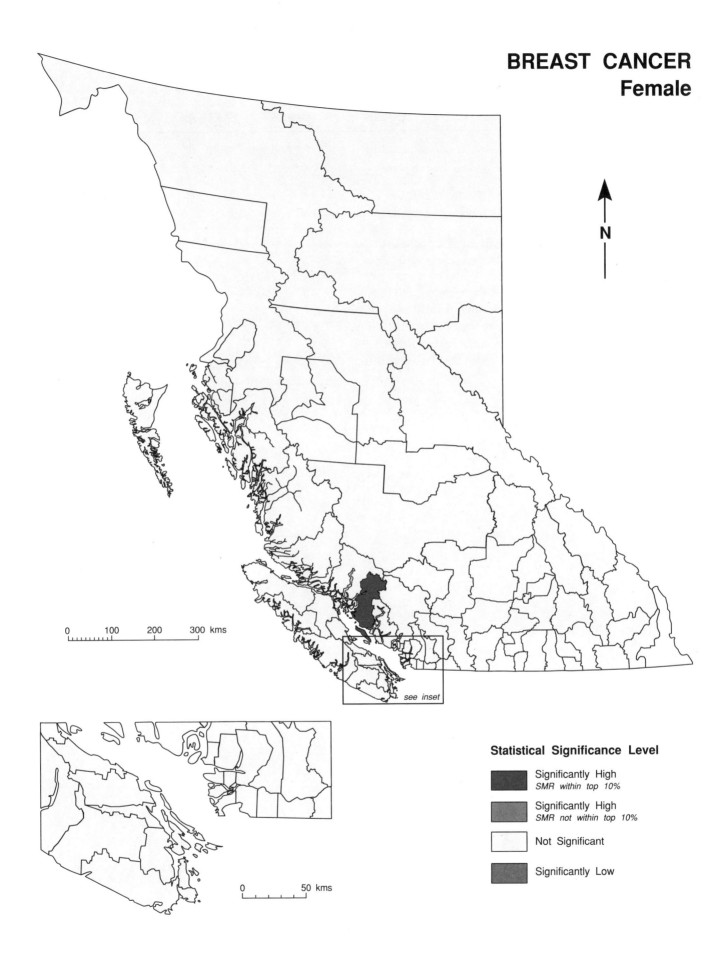

BREAST CANCER
Female

N

0   100   200   300 kms

see inset

0   50 kms

Statistical Significance Level

Significantly High
SMR within top 10%

Significantly High
SMR not within top 10%

Not Significant

Significantly Low

83

Endocrine, Nutritional, and Metabolic Diseases and Immunity Disorders: Male

	Local Health Area	Observed Deaths	Expected Deaths	SMR	(p)	95% C.I. Lower	Upper
14	Southern Okanagan 18		10.17	1.77	*	1.05	2.80
39	Vancouver 262		206.40	1.27	***	1.12	1.43
45	West Vancouver-Bowen Is 13		22.60	0.58	*	0.31	0.98
69	Qualicum 7		14.75	0.47	*	0.19	0.98

Significantly High and SMR within top 10%
Significantly High and SMR not within top 10%
Significantly Low

During the period 1985 to 1989, there were 1,208 male deaths due to endocrine, nutritional, and metabolic diseases and immunity disorders. Over this time, ASMRs remained fairly stable, fluctuating in the range 1.1 to 1.3. There was very little regional variation in mortality. Only Southern Okanagan reported a significantly high SMR value, in the top decile. Mortality was also elevated in Vancouver, but was not in the top 10 percent. West Vancouver-Bowen Island and Qualicum were two LHAs that experienced significantly low mortality.

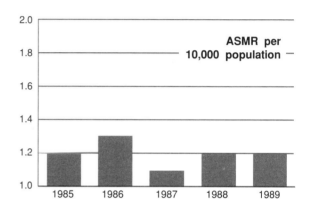

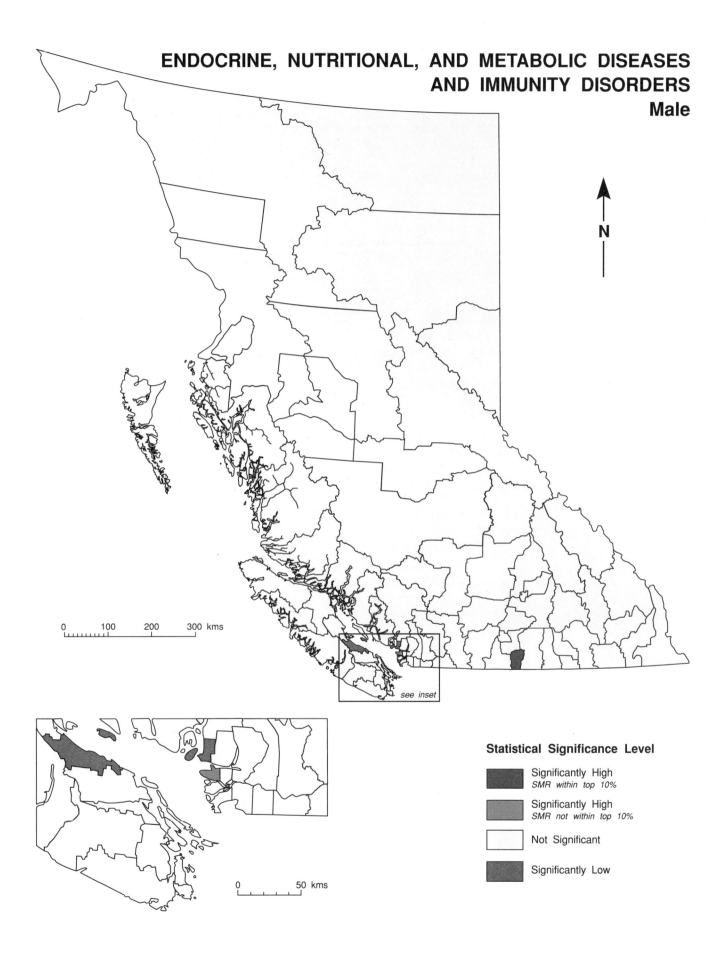

ENDOCRINE, NUTRITIONAL, AND METABOLIC DISEASES AND IMMUNITY DISORDERS
Male

N

0   100   200   300 kms

see inset

0   50 kms

Statistical Significance Level

Significantly High
SMR within top 10%

Significantly High
SMR not within top 10%

Not Significant

Significantly Low

85

Endocrine, Nutritional, and Metabolic Diseases and Immunity Disorders: Female

	Local Health Area	Observed Deaths	Expected Deaths	SMR	(p)	95% C.I. Lower	Upper
54	Smithers 7	2.53	2.77	*	1.11	5.70
1	Fernie 8	3.14	2.55	*	1.10	5.03
52	Prince Rupert 9	3.57	2.52	*	1.15	4.79
59	Peace River South 13	5.66	2.30	*	1.22	3.93
2	Cranbrook 14	6.29	2.23	*	1.22	3.74
57	Prince George 27	13.22	2.04	**	1.35	2.97
24	Kamloops 39	21.95	1.78	**	1.26	2.43
61	Greater Victoria 117	147.74	0.79	*	0.65	0.95
69	Qualicum 5	13.46	0.37	*	0.12	0.87

Significantly High and SMR within top 10%
Significantly High and SMR not within top 10%
Significantly Low

During the period 1985 to 1989, there were 1,276 female deaths due to endocrine, nutritional, and metabolic diseases and immunity disorders, marginally higher than those for males. Over this time, ASMRs showed a slight but steady increase from 1.0 to 1.2.

Five LHAs reported significantly high female mortality, in the top decile. The most elevated SMR was that recorded for Smithers, while SMRs were also high in Fernie, Prince Rupert, Peace River South, and Cranbrook. Another two LHAs in central British Columbia, Prince George and Kamloops, recorded significantly high mortality from these causes. Significantly low mortality was limited to Vancouver Island, specifically Greater Victoria and Qualicum.

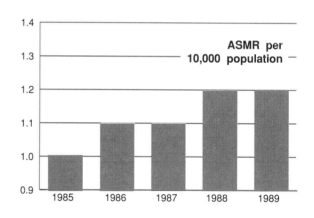

ENDOCRINE, NUTRITIONAL, AND METABOLIC DISEASES AND IMMUNITY DISORDERS
Female

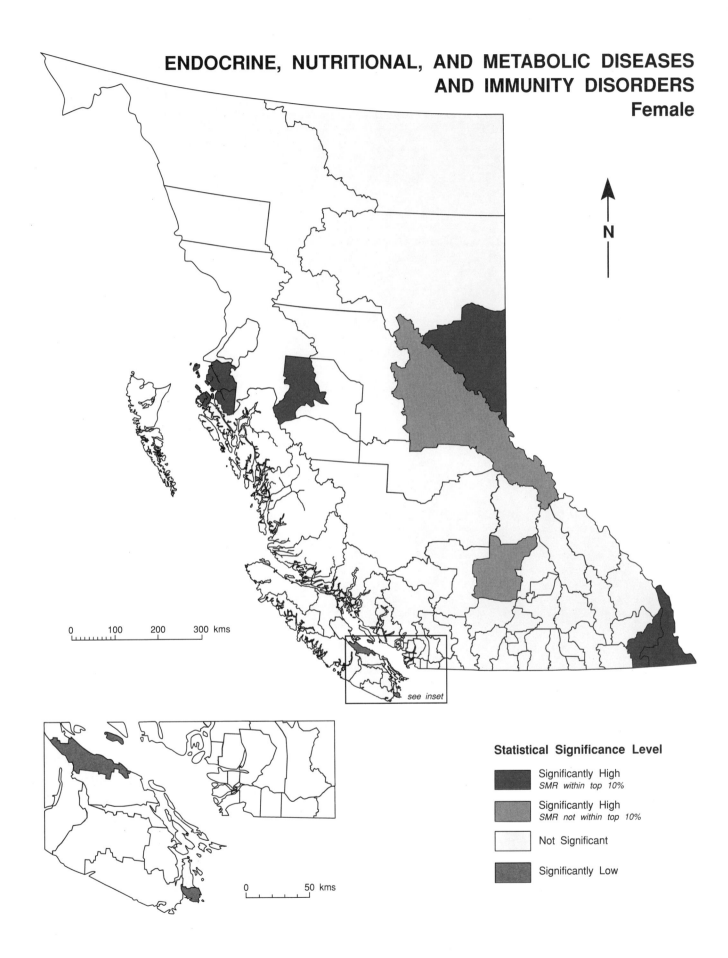

N

0   100   200   300 kms

see inset

0   50 kms

Statistical Significance Level

Significantly High
SMR within top 10%

Significantly High
SMR not within top 10%

Not Significant

Significantly Low

87

Diabetes: Male

	Local Health Area	Observed Deaths	Expected Deaths	SMR	(p)	95% C.I. Lower	Upper
14	Southern Okanagan 15		7.82	1.92	*	1.07	3.16
57	Prince George..20		11.83	1.69	*	1.03	2.61
35	Langley 28		18.52	1.51	*	1.00	2.19
45	West Vancouver-Bowen Is 8		17.09	0.47	*	0.20	0.92

Significantly High and SMR within top 10%
Significantly High and SMR not within top 10%
Significantly Low

During the period 1985 to 1989, there were 881 male diabetes deaths. Over this time, ASMRs remained fairly stable, fluctuating in the range of 0.8 to 1.0. There were no pronounced regional trends. Southern Okanagan was the only LHA to report significantly high mortality, in the top decile. Mortality was also elevated in Prince George and Langley. West Vancouver-Bowen Island was the only LHA displaying significantly low mortality.

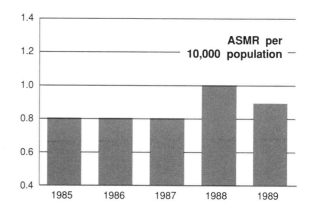

ASMR per 10,000 population

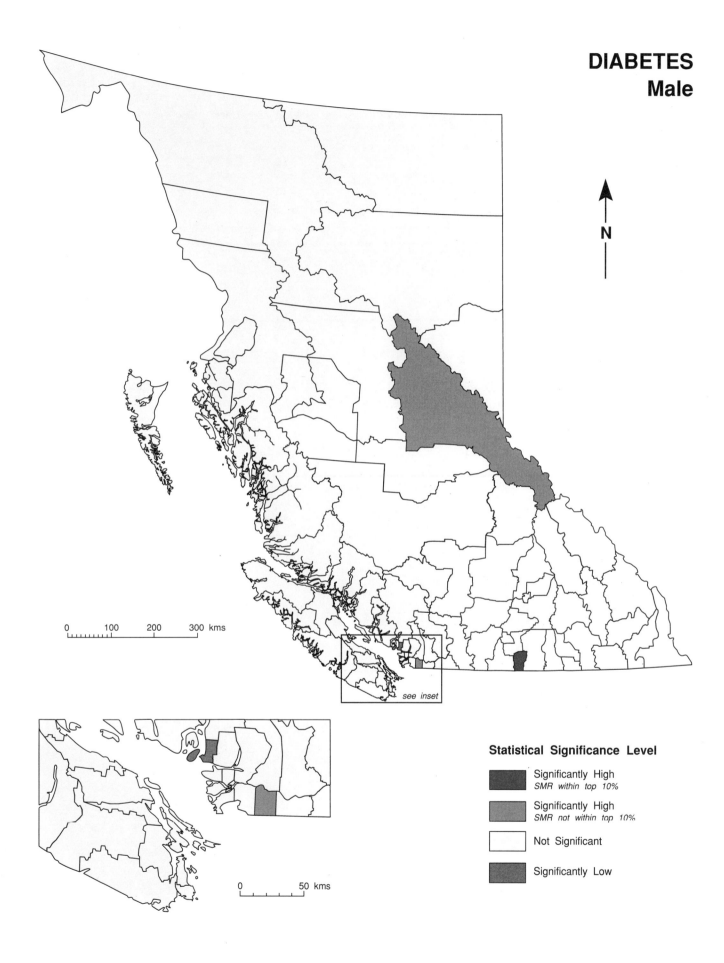

DIABETES
Male

0   100   200   300 kms

N

see inset

Statistical Significance Level

Significantly High
SMR within top 10%

Significantly High
SMR not within top 10%

Not Significant

Significantly Low

0   50 kms

89

Diabetes: Female

	Local Health Area	Observed Deaths	Expected Deaths	SMR	(p)	95% C.I. Lower	Upper
1	Fernie 8		2.25	3.55	**	1.53	7.00
59	Peace River South 11		4.06	2.71	**	1.35	4.85
57	Prince George..20		9.25	2.16	**	1.32	3.34
24	Kamloops 32		16.01	2.00	***	1.37	2.82
61	Greater Victoria 81		109.30	0.74	**	0.59	0.92

Significantly High and SMR within top 10%
Significantly High and SMR not within top 10%
Significantly Low

During the period 1985 to 1989, there were 942 female diabetes deaths, marginally higher than those for males. Over this time, ASMRs showed a steady rise from 0.7 to 0.9. Significant mortality levels for female diabetes had little in common with those for males, with the exception of Prince George which reported high SMRs for both genders. Kamloops also reported significantly high mortality for female diabetes. The most elevated female mortalities for diabetes, in the top decile, were recorded in Fernie and Peace River South. In contrast, only Greater Victoria was significantly low.

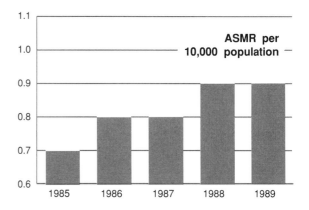

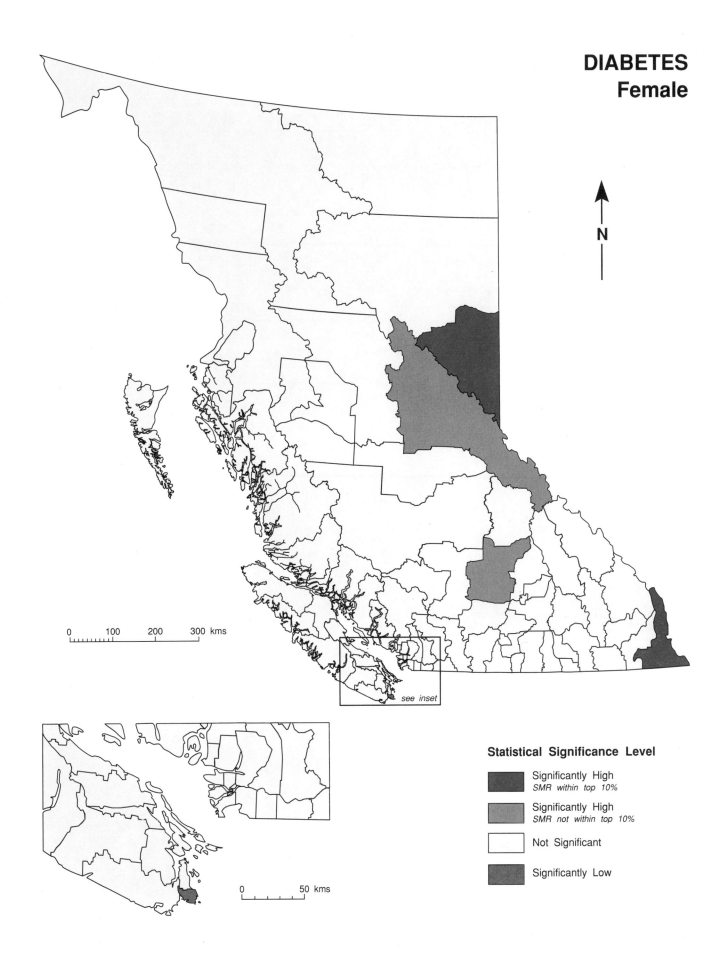

DIABETES
Female

N

0   100   200   300 kms

see inset

0   50 kms

Statistical Significance Level

Significantly High
SMR within top 10%

Significantly High
SMR not within top 10%

Not Significant

Significantly Low

91

Circulatory System: Male

	Local Health Area	Observed Deaths	Expected Deaths	SMR	(p)	95% C.I. Lower	95% C.I. Upper
17	Princeton	59	35.89	1.64	***	1.25	2.12
85	Vancouver Island North	59	38.44	1.54	**	1.17	1.98
31	Merritt	77	55.53	1.39	**	1.09	1.73
54	Smithers	74	54.01	1.37	*	1.08	1.72
12	Grand Forks	108	85.90	1.26	*	1.03	1.52
52	Prince Rupert	101	79.92	1.26	*	1.03	1.54
57	Prince George	371	298.93	1.24	***	1.12	1.37
47	Powell River	190	157.47	1.21	*	1.04	1.39
60	Peace River North	123	101.48	1.21	*	1.01	1.45
59	Peace River South	159	134.46	1.18	*	1.01	1.38
24	Kamloops	522	457.07	1.14	**	1.05	1.24
40	New Westminster	462	404.11	1.14	**	1.04	1.25
68	Nanaimo	576	521.66	1.10	*	1.02	1.20
41	Burnaby	1321	1229.17	1.07	**	1.02	1.13
39	Vancouver	4317	4119.31	1.05	**	1.02	1.08
38	Richmond	609	660.68	0.92	*	0.85	1.00
61	Greater Victoria	1994	2169.23	0.92	***	0.88	0.96
35	Langley	430	486.79	0.88	**	0.80	0.97
15	Penticton	346	407.41	0.85	**	0.76	0.94
20	Salmon Arm	221	266.75	0.83	**	0.72	0.95
23	Central Okanagan	845	1051.72	0.80	***	0.75	0.86
62	Sooke	193	248.18	0.78	***	0.67	0.90
45	West Vancouver-Bowen Is	354	458.57	0.77	***	0.69	0.86
64	Gulf Islands	108	139.76	0.77	**	0.63	0.93
63	Saanich	318	436.37	0.73	***	0.65	0.81
4	Windermere	31	44.44	0.70	*	0.47	0.99
6	Kootenay Lake	19	38.24	0.50	***	0.30	0.78

Significantly High and SMR within top 10%

Significantly High and SMR not within top 10%

Significantly Low

During the period 1985 to 1989, there were 23,481 male circulatory system deaths, with ASMRs showing a steady decline from 25.2 to 21.3. There was a general tendency for significantly low male mortality to be limited to southern British Columbia. This is illustrated by the low mortality experienced in Kootenay Lake and Windermere in the southeast, and Saanich and the Gulf Islands in the southwest. In total, 12 LHAs located in the south of the province reported significantly low mortalities.

In contrast, elevated SMRs, in the top decile, were recorded in central and southern British Columbia. Particularly noteworthy were the significantly high SMRs in Princeton, Vancouver Island North, Merritt, Smithers, Grand Forks, and Prince Rupert. Although not in the top decile, there was a notable cluster of high SMRs in the east-central part of the province. In all, 15 LHAs, including three in the lower mainland, experienced significantly high SMRs.

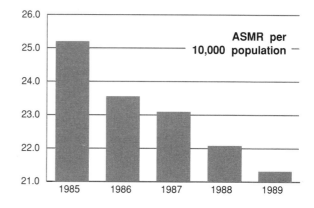

ASMR per 10,000 population

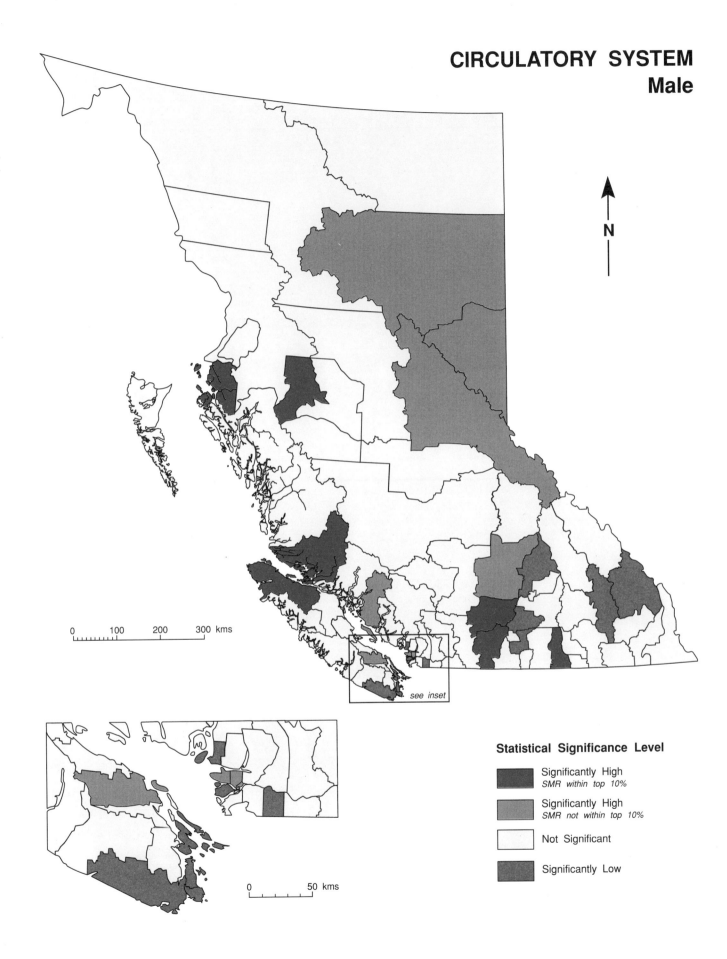

CIRCULATORY SYSTEM
Male

N

0 100 200 300 kms

see inset

0 50 kms

Statistical Significance Level

Significantly High
SMR within top 10%

Significantly High
SMR not within top 10%

Not Significant

Significantly Low

93

Circulatory System: Female

	Local Health Area	Observed Deaths	Expected Deaths	SMR	(p)	95% C.I. Lower	Upper
28	Quesnel	97	66.07	1.47	***	1.19	1.79
12	Grand Forks	82	58.55	1.40	**	1.11	1.74
11	Trail	204	149.62	1.36	***	1.18	1.56
52	Prince Rupert	69	51.77	1.33	*	1.04	1.69
67	Ladysmith	127	95.68	1.33	**	1.11	1.58
70	Alberni	175	137.73	1.27	**	1.09	1.47
59	Peace River South	107	85.10	1.26	*	1.03	1.52
77	Summerland	125	101.05	1.24	*	1.03	1.47
43	Coquitlam	579	485.29	1.19	***	1.10	1.29
7	Nelson	180	154.57	1.16	*	1.00	1.35
57	Prince George	205	176.29	1.16	*	1.01	1.33
44	North Vancouver	751	668.94	1.12	**	1.04	1.21
68	Nanaimo	463	414.40	1.12	*	1.02	1.22
33	Chilliwack	381	343.24	1.11	*	1.00	1.23
41	Burnaby	1376	1279.43	1.08	**	1.02	1.13
61	Greater Victoria	2377	2650.67	0.90	***	0.86	0.93
63	Saanich	299	340.13	0.88	*	0.78	0.98
23	Central Okanagan	634	776.36	0.82	***	0.75	0.88
15	Penticton	247	331.79	0.74	***	0.65	0.84
6	Kootenay Lake	13	25.17	0.52	*	0.27	0.88

Significantly High and SMR within top 10%
Significantly High and SMR not within top 10%
Significantly Low

During the period 1985 to 1989, there were 20,865 female circulatory system deaths, about 10 percent fewer than those for males. Over this time, ASMRs showed a steady decline from 19.0 to 16.0. The geographical pattern of female mortality displayed some similarities to that for males. While there were fewer areas with significantly low female mortality, these were again limited to the south of the province. Several LHAs with low female mortality, including Kootenay Lake, Penticton, Central Okanagan, Saanich, and Greater Victoria, also displayed the same tendency for males.

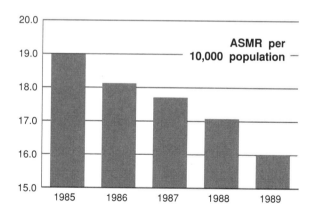

As with males, significantly high female mortality was restricted to LHAs in central and southern British Columbia. Two of these, namely Grand Forks and Prince Rupert, also reported significantly elevated SMRs, in the top decile, for males. The highest SMR in the province for females, however, occurred in Quesnel, an LHA in which male mortality was not statistically significant.

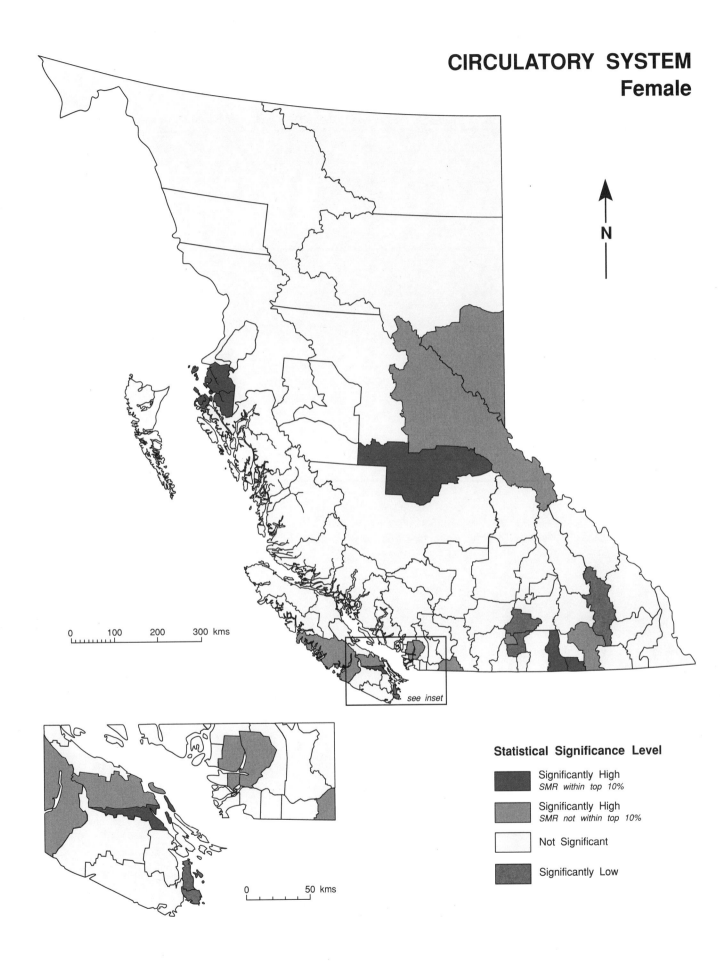

CIRCULATORY SYSTEM
Female

N

0   100   200   300 kms

see inset

0   50 kms

Statistical Significance Level

Significantly High
SMR within top 10%

Significantly High
SMR not within top 10%

Not Significant

Significantly Low

95

Ischaemic Heart Disease: Male

	Local Health Area	Observed Deaths	Expected Deaths	SMR	(p)	95% C.I. Lower	Upper
85	Vancouver Island North	46	25.38	1.81	***	1.33	2.42
17	Princeton	40	23.38	1.71	**	1.22	2.33
52	Prince Rupert	75	51.48	1.46	**	1.15	1.83
31	Merritt	49	36.18	1.35	*	1.00	1.79
12	Grand Forks	72	54.96	1.31	*	1.03	1.65
28	Quesnel	100	78.53	1.27	*	1.04	1.55
40	New Westminster	321	256.58	1.25	***	1.12	1.40
47	Powell River	125	100.82	1.24	*	1.03	1.48
59	Peace River South	107	86.26	1.24	*	1.02	1.50
57	Prince George	230	196.92	1.17	*	1.02	1.33
24	Kamloops	336	295.77	1.14	*	1.02	1.26
41	Burnaby	894	787.81	1.13	***	1.06	1.21
36	Surrey	1081	988.56	1.09	**	1.03	1.16
61	Greater Victoria	1182	1362.33	0.87	***	0.82	0.92
15	Penticton	211	257.82	0.82	**	0.71	0.94
20	Salmon Arm	138	172.39	0.80	**	0.67	0.95
23	Central Okanagan	504	669.38	0.75	***	0.69	0.82
62	Sooke	121	161.73	0.75	***	0.62	0.89
64	Gulf Islands	66	90.28	0.73	**	0.57	0.93
45	West Vancouver-Bowen Is	213	294.70	0.72	***	0.63	0.83
63	Saanich	187	282.49	0.66	***	0.57	0.76
6	Kootenay Lake	12	24.68	0.49	**	0.25	0.85

Significantly High and SMR within top 10%
Significantly High and SMR not within top 10%
Significantly Low

During the period 1985 to 1989, there were 15,036 male ischaemic heart disease deaths. Over this time, ASMRs showed a steady decline from 16.7 to 13.0. Significantly low mortality was limited to the south of the province. This was evident in the southern coastal areas of Saanich, the Gulf Islands, Sooke, Greater Victoria, and West Vancouver-Bowen Island. A second cluster of low male mortality occurred in the Okanagan, notably in Central Okanagan, Salmon Arm, and Penticton. In the southeast, Kootenay Lake also experienced low mortality.

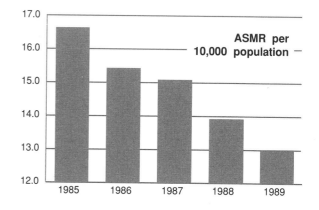

As with diseases of the whole circulatory system for both males and females, elevated ischaemic heart disease mortality in males was recorded in both south and central British Columbia. Examples of significantly elevated mortality, in the top decile, include those of Vancouver Island North, Princeton, Prince Rupert, Merritt, and Grand Forks. Eight other LHAs also reported significantly high mortality, but not in the top decile. The most notable cluster was in east-central British Columbia.

ISCHAEMIC HEART DISEASE
Male

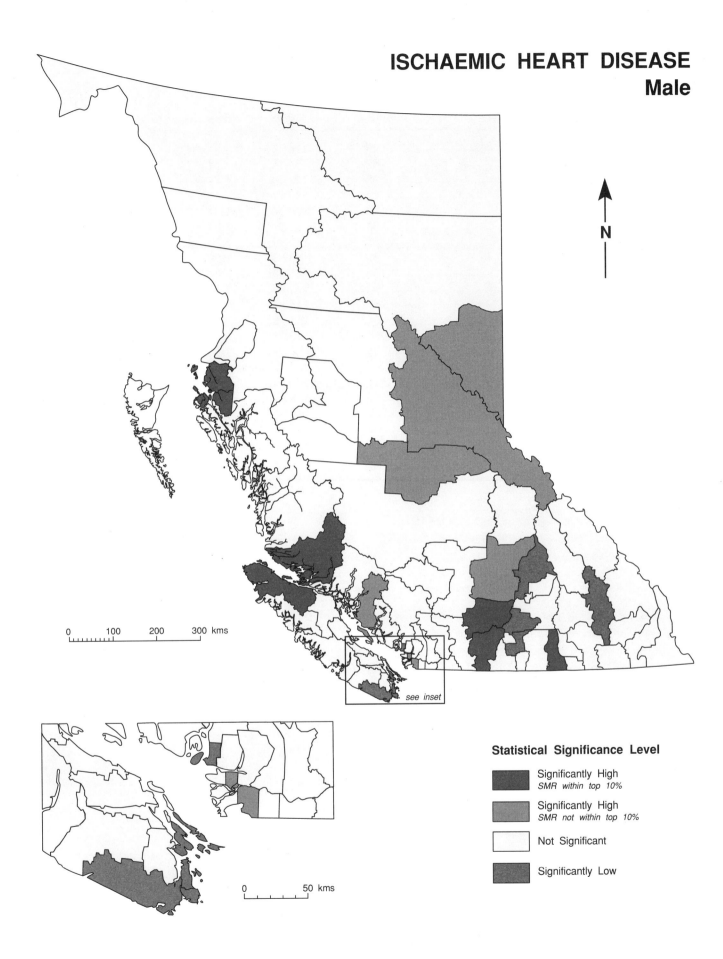

N

0   100   200   300 kms

see inset

0   50 kms

Statistical Significance Level

Significantly High
SMR within top 10%

Significantly High
SMR not within top 10%

Not Significant

Significantly Low

97

Ischaemic Heart Disease: Female

	Local Health Area	Observed Deaths	Expected Deaths	SMR	(p)	95% C.I. Lower	95% C.I. Upper
1	Fernie	39	24.30	1.61	**	1.14	2.19
12	Grand Forks	47	31.17	1.51	**	1.11	2.00
52	Prince Rupert	39	27.00	1.44	*	1.03	1.97
43	Coquitlam	360	253.04	1.42	***	1.28	1.58
28	Quesnel	48	34.64	1.39	*	1.02	1.84
11	Trail	108	79.27	1.36	**	1.12	1.64
67	Ladysmith	66	50.90	1.30	*	1.00	1.65
77	Summerland	69	53.50	1.29	*	1.00	1.63
33	Chilliwack	229	181.90	1.26	***	1.10	1.43
7	Nelson	100	81.24	1.23	*	1.00	1.50
68	Nanaimo	253	218.90	1.16	*	1.02	1.31
40	New Westminster	298	261.39	1.14	*	1.01	1.28
44	North Vancouver	398	349.89	1.14	*	1.03	1.25
41	Burnaby	753	669.01	1.13	**	1.05	1.21
36	Surrey	720	663.78	1.08	*	1.01	1.17
61	Greater Victoria	1157	1383.96	0.84	***	0.79	0.89
63	Saanich	141	179.48	0.79	**	0.66	0.93
23	Central Okanagan	322	410.51	0.78	***	0.70	0.87
69	Qualicum	83	111.78	0.74	**	0.59	0.92
15	Penticton	128	175.26	0.73	***	0.61	0.87
27	Cariboo-Chilcotin	35	50.90	0.69	*	0.48	0.96
54	Smithers	8	18.84	0.42	**	0.18	0.84

Significantly High and SMR within top 10%
Significantly High and SMR not within top 10%
Significantly Low

During the period 1985 to 1989, there were 10,944 female ischaemic heart disease deaths, less than 75 percent of the number of male deaths. Over this time, ASMRs showed a steady decline from 10.3 to 8.1. The geographical pattern of female mortality differed markedly from that of males in that significantly low mortality was not limited to the south. While Greater Victoria, Saanich, Central Okanagan, and Penticton did report significantly low mortalities for both genders, female mortality was also low in Smithers, Qualicum, and Cariboo-Chilcotin.

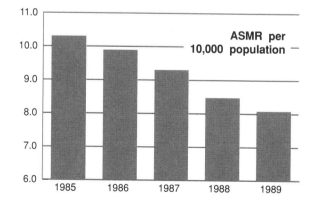

High female mortality was evident in both central and southern British Columbia, as it was for males. Only Prince Rupert and Grand Forks, however, recorded significantly high mortality, in the top decile, for both genders. Fernie experienced the highest significant female SMR in the province. Other areas having high female mortality, in the top decile, were Coquitlam, Quesnel, and Trail. Several areas in the lower mainland and central part of Vancouver Island had high SMRs, but they were not in the top decile.

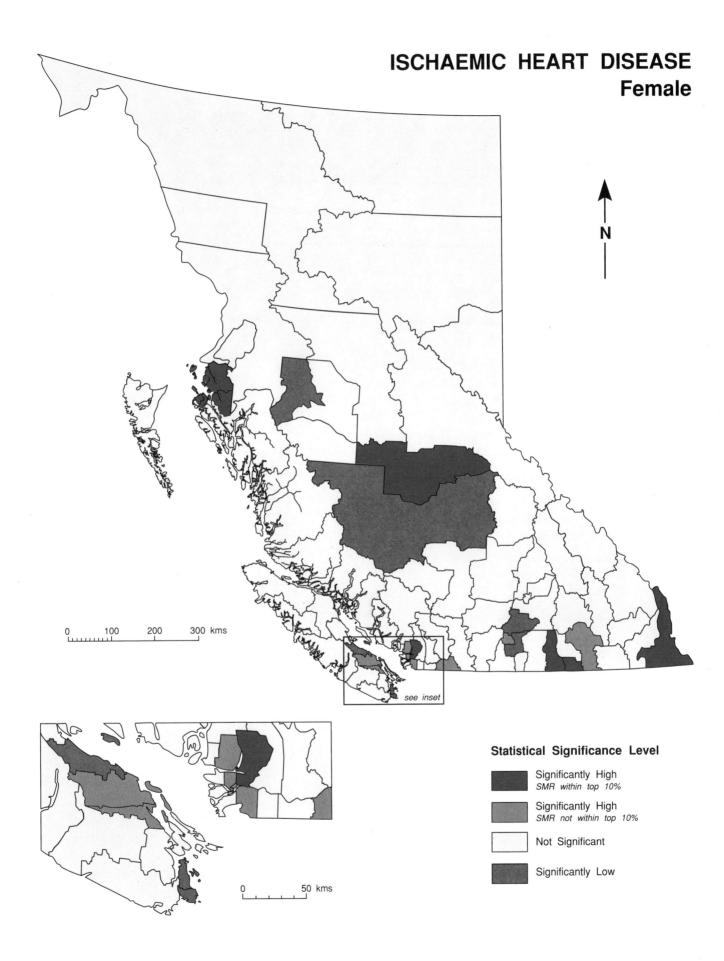

ISCHAEMIC HEART DISEASE
Female

N

0 100 200 300 kms

see inset

0 50 kms

Statistical Significance Level

Significantly High
SMR within top 10%

Significantly High
SMR not within top 10%

Not Significant

Significantly Low

99

Cerebrovascular Disease/Stroke: Male

	Local Health Area	Observed Deaths	Expected Deaths	SMR	(p)	95% C.I. Lower	Upper
17	Princeton	12	5.51	2.18	*	1.12	3.80
2	Cranbrook	32	18.27	1.75	**	1.20	2.47
60	Peace River North	26	15.82	1.64	*	1.07	2.41
7	Nelson	50	31.62	1.58	**	1.17	2.08
11	Trail	47	32.28	1.46	*	1.07	1.94
68	Nanaimo	102	82.67	1.23	*	1.01	1.50
39	Vancouver	750	680.54	1.10	**	1.02	1.18
23	Central Okanagan	144	172.85	0.83	*	0.70	0.98
35	Langley	55	77.86	0.71	**	0.53	0.92

Significantly High and SMR within top 10%
Significantly High and SMR not within top 10%
Significantly Low

During the period 1985 to 1989, there were 3,788 male cerebrovascular disease/stroke deaths. Over this period, ASMRs remained stable at 3.6, with the exception of 3.9 recorded in 1985. Significantly high, in the top decile, variations in male mortality were limited to southern British Columbia (except for Peace River North). In the south, several LHAs displayed statistically significantly high or low mortalities. LHAs with elevated SMRs, in the top decile, included Princeton, Cranbrook, and Nelson. In contrast, significantly low SMRs occurred in Central Okanagan and Langley.

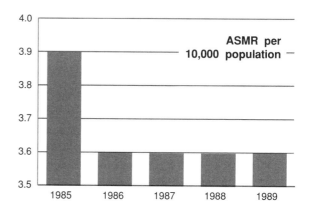

CEREBROVASCULAR DISEASE / STROKE
Male

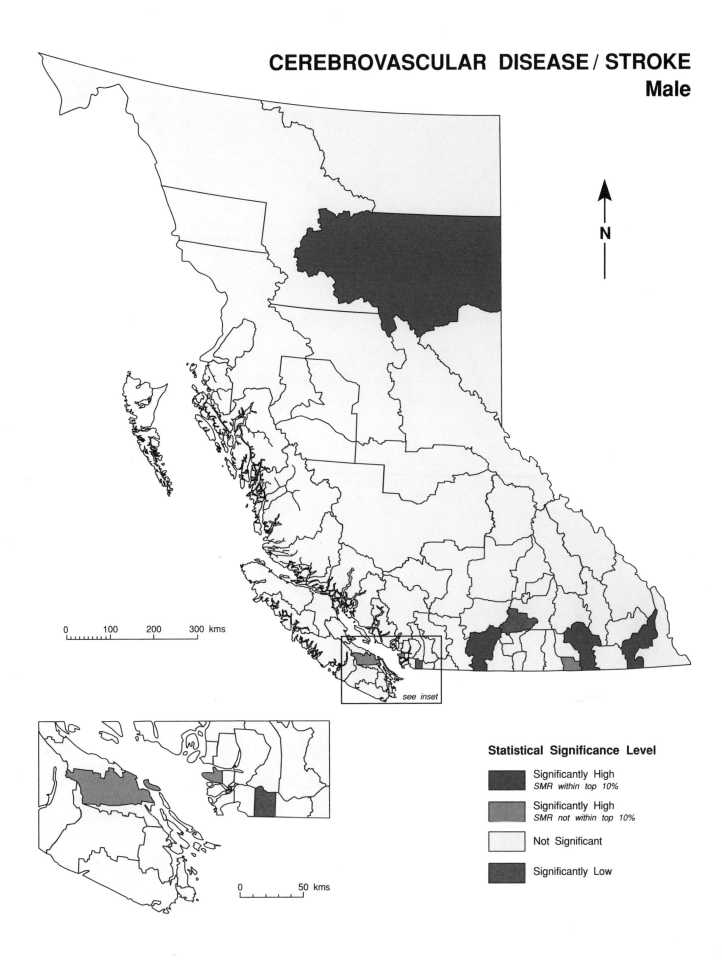

N

0   100   200   300 kms

see inset

0   50 kms

Statistical Significance Level

Significantly High
SMR within top 10%

Significantly High
SMR not within top 10%

Not Significant

Significantly Low

101

Cerebrovascular Disease/Stroke: Female

		Observed Deaths	Expected Deaths	SMR	(p)	95% C.I. Lower	Upper
28	Quesnel 33		15.85	2.08	***	1.43	2.92
70	Alberni 47		32.81	1.43	*	1.05	1.91
44	North Vancouver 199		161.28	1.23	**	1.07	1.42
61	Greater Victoria 554		641.24	0.86	***	0.79	0.94
15	Penticton 61		79.15	0.77	*	0.59	0.99

Significantly High and SMR within top 10%
Significantly High and SMR not within top 10%
Significantly Low

During the period 1985 to 1989, there were 5,016 female cerebrovascular disease/stroke deaths, nearly a third higher than those for males. Over this period, with the exception of 1988, ASMRs declined from 4.5 to 3.9.

With the exception of Quesnel, which had the significantly highest SMR in the province, all significant variation in mortality was limited to southern British Columbia. SMRs were elevated in Alberni and North Vancouver, with the former being in the top decile. In contrast, significantly low mortality was recorded in Greater Victoria and Penticton.

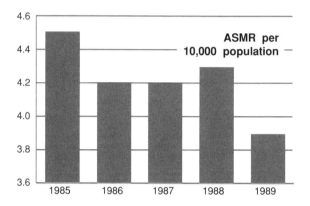

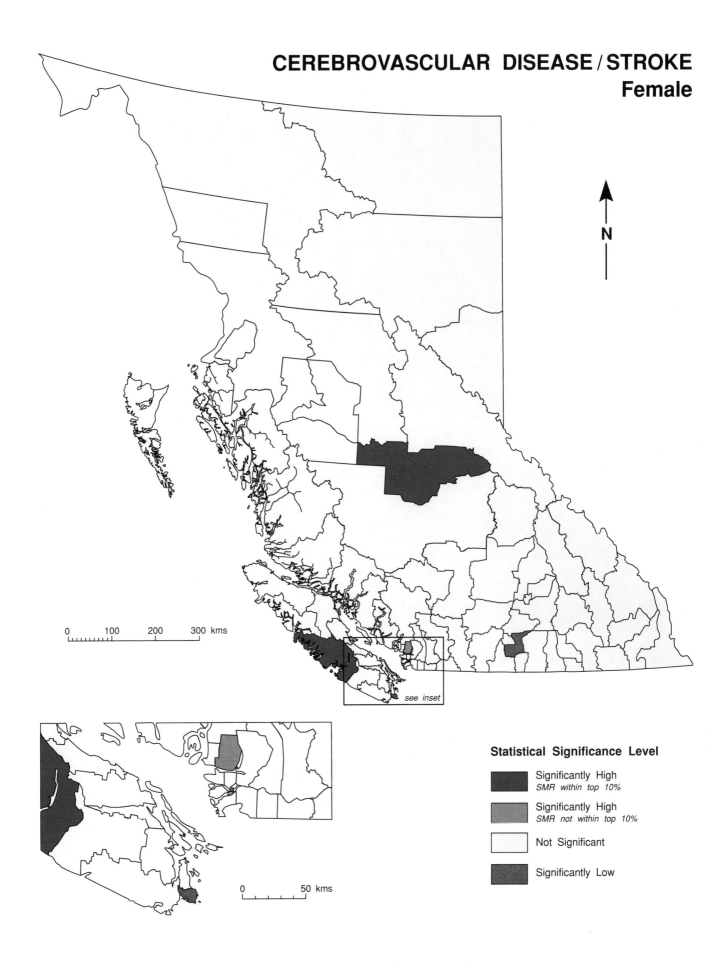

CEREBROVASCULAR DISEASE / STROKE
Female

N

0   100   200   300 kms

see inset

0   50 kms

Statistical Significance Level

Significantly High
SMR within top 10%

Significantly High
SMR not within top 10%

Not Significant

Significantly Low

103

Diseases of Arteries, Arterioles, and Capillaries: Male

	Local Health Area	Observed Deaths	Expected Deaths	SMR	(p)	95% C.I. Lower	Upper
72	Campbell River	18	9.95	1.81	*	1.07	2.86
42	Maple Ridge	31	20.50	1.51	*	1.03	2.15
71	Courtenay	31	20.73	1.50	*	1.02	2.12
68	Nanaimo	49	35.43	1.38	*	1.02	1.83
23	Central Okanagan	54	73.62	0.73	*	0.55	0.96
34	Abbotsford	27	43.39	0.62	*	0.41	0.91
35	Langley	19	32.81	0.58	*	0.35	0.90
38	Richmond	25	42.83	0.58	**	0.38	0.86

Significantly High and SMR within top 10%
Significantly High and SMR not within top 10%
Significantly Low

During the period 1985 to 1989, there were 1,600 male deaths from diseases of arteries, arterioles, and capillaries, and ASMRs declined steadily from 1.7 to 1.3. With the exception of significantly low mortality in the Central Okanagan, all statistically significant variations in male SMRs occurred in southwestern British Columbia. The lower mainland, for example, experienced SMRs that were both significantly high and low. To illustrate, the mortality in Maple Ridge was significantly high, while Richmond, Langley, and Abbotsford recorded low mortalities. Significantly high mortality also was displayed by three LHAs on eastern Vancouver Island, namely Campbell River (which had the significantly highest SMR in the province), Courtenay, and Nanaimo.

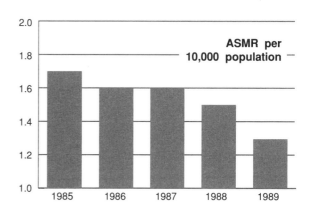

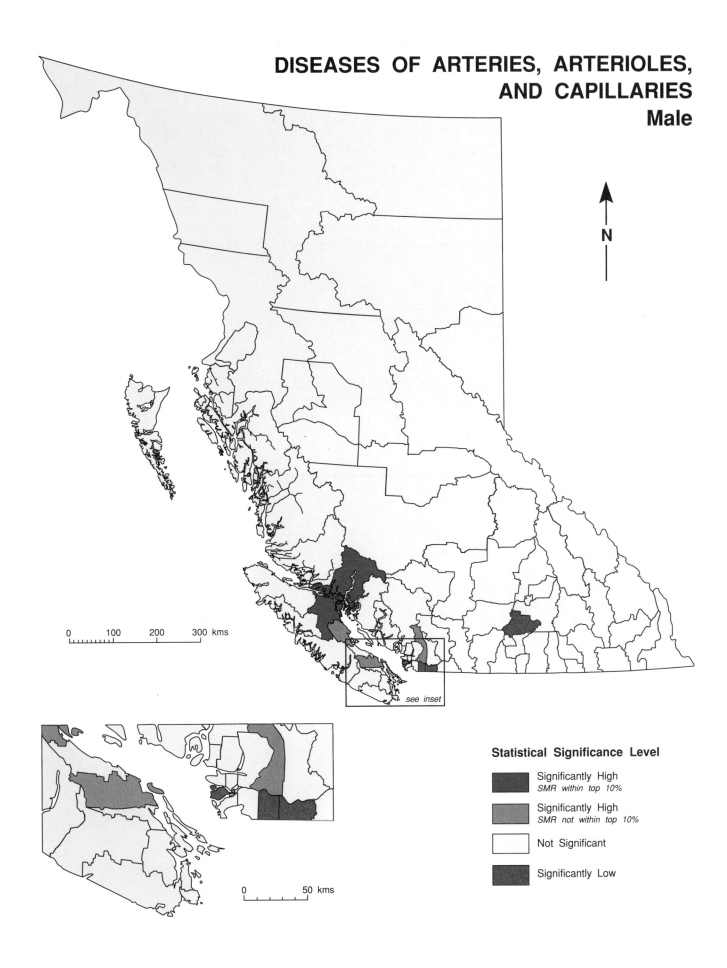

DISEASES OF ARTERIES, ARTERIOLES, AND CAPILLARIES
Male

N

0   100   200   300 kms

see inset

0   50 kms

Statistical Significance Level

Significantly High
SMR within top 10%

Significantly High
SMR not within top 10%

Not Significant

Significantly Low

Diseases of Arteries, Arterioles, and Capillaries: Female

	Local Health Area	Observed Deaths	Expected Deaths	SMR	(p)	95% C.I. Lower	Upper
11	Trail 27		9.95	2.71	***	1.79	3.95
67	Ladysmith 16		6.29	2.54	**	1.45	4.13
69	Qualicum 24		13.99	1.72	*	1.10	2.55
71	Courtenay 25		15.44	1.62	*	1.05	2.39
36	Surrey 63		84.34	0.75	*	0.57	0.96
15	Penticton 12		22.33	0.54	*	0.28	0.94
23	Central Okanagan 25		51.78	0.48	***	0.31	0.71

Significantly High and SMR within top 10%
Significantly High and SMR not within top 10%
Significantly Low

During the period 1985 to 1989, there were 1,414 female deaths from diseases of arteries, arterioles, and capillaries, more than 10 percent fewer than male deaths. Over this period, ASMRs fluctuated in the range of 1.0 to 1.3. As in males, significant geographical variations in female mortality were limited to southern British Columbia. Parallels with male mortality, however, were limited to significantly low mortality for females in Central Okanagan and significantly high mortality in Courtenay. In addition, female mortality was significantly low in Penticton and Surrey, but significantly high, in the top decile, in Trail, Ladysmith, and Qualicum.

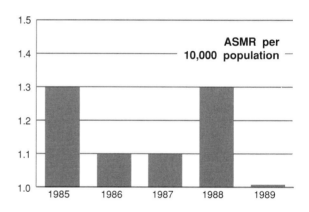

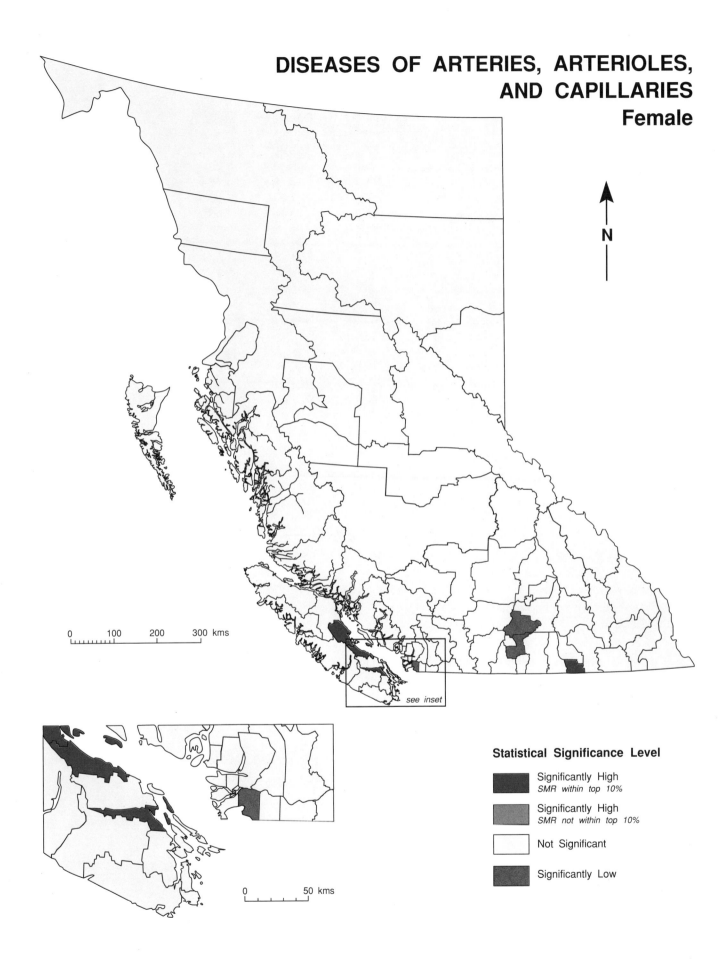

DISEASES OF ARTERIES, ARTERIOLES, AND CAPILLARIES
Female

N

0   100   200   300 kms

see inset

0   50 kms

Statistical Significance Level

Significantly High
SMR within top 10%

Significantly High
SMR not within top 10%

Not Significant

Significantly Low

107

Respiratory System: Male

	Local Health Area	Observed Deaths	Expected Deaths	SMR	(p)	95% C.I. Lower	95% C.I. Upper
2	Cranbrook	52	26.30	1.98	***	1.48	2.59
17	Princeton	15	8.06	1.86	*	1.04	3.07
48	Howe Sound	23	13.09	1.76	*	1.11	2.64
10	Arrow Lakes	19	11.30	1.68	*	1.01	2.63
88	Terrace	37	23.17	1.60	**	1.12	2.20
43	Coquitlam	190	131.60	1.44	***	1.25	1.66
28	Quesnel	39	27.30	1.43	*	1.02	1.95
42	Maple Ridge	100	71.51	1.40	**	1.14	1.70
39	Vancouver	1112	1001.92	1.11	***	1.05	1.18
23	Central Okanagan	217	256.28	0.85	*	0.74	0.97
15	Penticton	80	101.57	0.79	*	0.62	0.98
34	Abbotsford	119	152.13	0.78	**	0.65	0.94
63	Saanich	78	100.10	0.78	*	0.62	0.97
71	Courtenay	53	71.15	0.74	*	0.56	0.97
62	Sooke	37	54.82	0.67	*	0.48	0.93
45	West Vancouver-Bowen Is	70	108.16	0.65	***	0.50	0.82
5	Creston	24	37.81	0.63	*	0.41	0.94
12	Grand Forks	11	20.65	0.53	*	0.27	0.95

Significantly High and SMR within top 10%
Significantly High and SMR not within top 10%
Significantly Low

During the period 1985 to 1989, there were 5,550 male respiratory system deaths. Over this time, ASMRs fluctuated, with a high of 5.7 in 1985 and a low of 5.1 in 1986. With the exception of the significantly high SMR (in the top decile) experienced by Terrace, all other significantly elevated SMRs were limited to southern British Columbia. This included Cranbrook (which had the highest mortality in the province), Princeton, Howe Sound, Arrow Lakes, and Coquitlam.

Significantly low mortality was also limited to the south, where it occurred in nine LHAs. Significantly low SMRs were recorded in Grand Forks, Creston, West Vancouver-Bowen Island, Abbotsford, Penticton, and Central Okanagan. SMRs in Saanich, Sooke, and Courtenay on Vancouver Island were also significantly low.

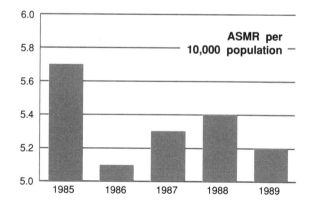

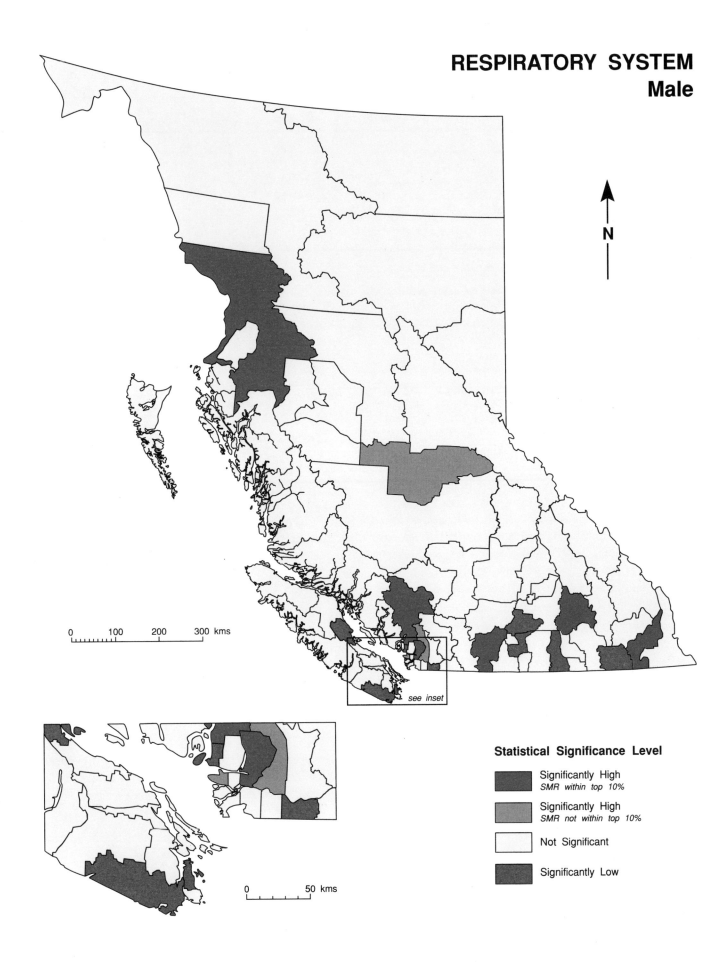

RESPIRATORY SYSTEM
Male

N

0   100   200   300 kms

see inset

0   50 kms

Statistical Significance Level

Significantly High
SMR within top 10%

Significantly High
SMR not within top 10%

Not Significant

Significantly Low

109

Respiratory System: Female

	Local Health Area	Observed Deaths	Expected Deaths	SMR	(p)	95% C.I. Lower	Upper
30	South Cariboo 12		5.87	2.04	*	1.05	3.57
57	Prince George 53		38.27	1.38	*	1.04	1.81
43	Coquitlam 131		102.79	1.27	**	1.07	1.51
44	North Vancouver 167		140.54	1.19	*	1.01	1.38
23	Central Okanagan 132		162.55	0.81	*	0.68	0.96
65	Cowichan 37		51.34	0.72	*	0.51	0.99

Significantly High and SMR within top 10%

Significantly High and SMR not within top 10%

Significantly Low

During the period 1985 to 1989, there were 4,369 female respiratory system deaths, approximately 20 percent fewer than those for males. Over this time, ASMRs fluctuated in the range of 3.5 to 3.8.

Only Central Okanagan and Cowichan experienced significantly low female mortality. Male mortality from this cause was also significantly low in Central Okanagan. Elevated mortality, in the top decile, was reported for South Cariboo. Prince George, Coquitlam, and North Vancouver reported significantly high mortality, but not in the top decile. The rest of the province experienced SMRs that were not statistically significant.

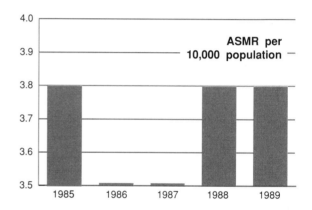

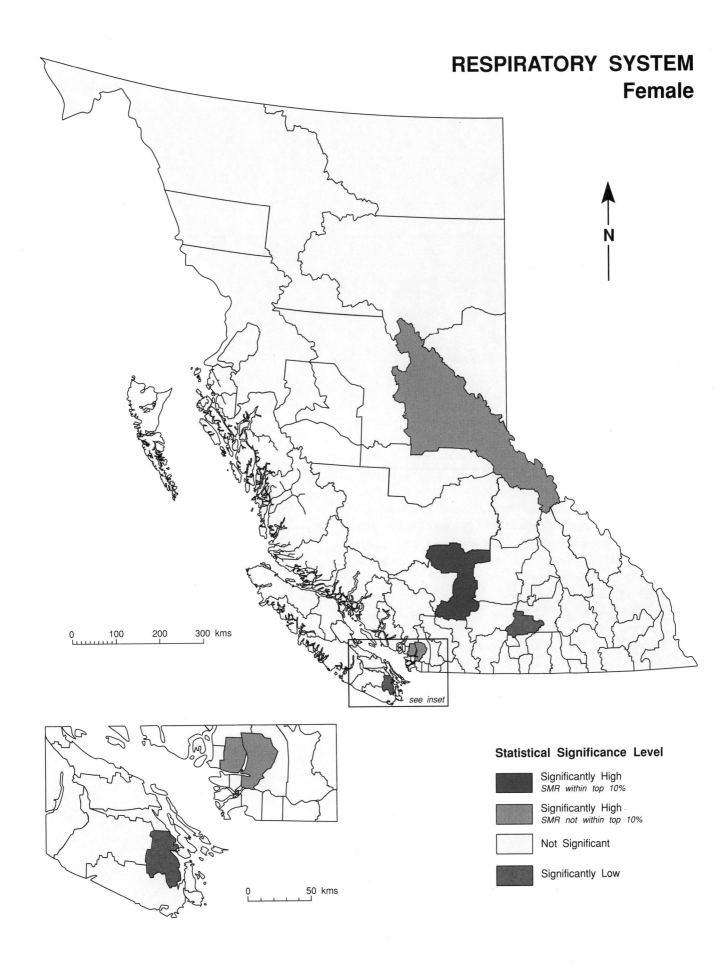

RESPIRATORY SYSTEM
Female

N

0 100 200 300 kms

see inset

0 50 kms

Statistical Significance Level

Significantly High
SMR within top 10%

Significantly High
SMR not within top 10%

Not Significant

Significantly Low

Pneumonia and Influenza: Male

	Local Health Area	Observed Deaths	Expected Deaths	SMR	(p)	95% C.I. Lower	Upper
80	Kitimat 7	2.13	3.28	*	1.32	6.76
88	Terrace 22	9.45	2.33	***	1.46	3.52
43	Coquitlam 92	51.72	1.78	***	1.43	2.18
42	Maple Ridge 46	28.19	1.63	**	1.19	2.18
39	Vancouver 489	407.69	1.20	***	1.10	1.31
36	Surrey 110	143.37	0.77	**	0.63	0.92
15	Penticton 24	40.55	0.59	**	0.38	0.88
7	Nelson 10	18.42	0.54	*	0.26	1.00
11	Trail 10	18.61	0.54	*	0.26	0.99
62	Sooke 11	20.28	0.54	*	0.27	0.97
71	Courtenay 12	27.47	0.44	**	0.23	0.76

Significantly High and SMR within top 10%
Significantly High and SMR not within top 10%
Significantly Low

During the period 1985 to 1989, there were 2,185 male deaths from pneumonia and influenza, with ASMRs showing a downward trend from 2.3 to 2.0. There was a general tendency for both significantly high and low male mortalities to be limited to coastal regions, although in the interior, Penticton, Trail, and Nelson also experienced significantly low mortalities. Coastal LHAs with statistically significant low mortality ratios were represented by Courtenay, Sooke, and Surrey. In contrast, mortality was significantly high, in the top decile, in Kitimat and Terrace on the northwest coast, and Coquitlam and Maple Ridge in the south. Vancouver was the only area with a significantly high SMR, which was not in the top decile.

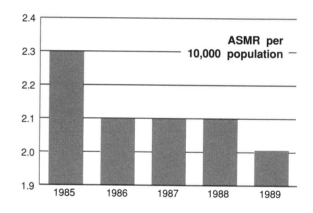

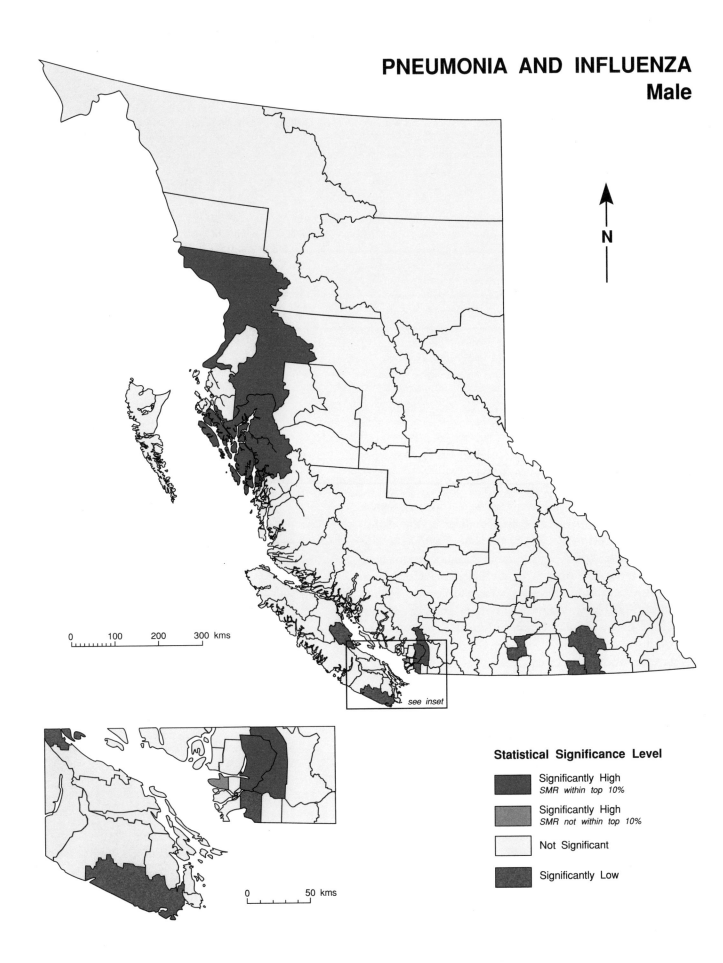

PNEUMONIA AND INFLUENZA
Male

N

0   100   200   300 kms

see inset

0   50 kms

Statistical Significance Level

Significantly High
SMR within top 10%

Significantly High
SMR not within top 10%

Not Significant

Significantly Low

113

Pneumonia and Influenza: Female

	Local Health Area	Observed Deaths	Expected Deaths	SMR	(p)	95% C.I. Lower	Upper
30	South Cariboo	8	2.98	2.69	*	1.16	5.29
17	Princeton	8	3.30	2.42	*	1.04	4.77
43	Coquitlam	83	55.11	1.51	***	1.20	1.87
22	Vernon	50	36.57	1.37	*	1.01	1.80
44	North Vancouver	100	77.23	1.29	*	1.05	1.57
61	Greater Victoria	361	323.36	1.12	*	1.00	1.24
40	New Westminster	38	58.25	0.65	**	0.46	0.90
37	Delta	26	41.11	0.63	*	0.41	0.93
65	Cowichan	15	27.81	0.54	*	0.30	0.89
47	Powell River	6	14.10	0.43	*	0.16	0.93

Significantly High and SMR within top 10%
Significantly High and SMR not within top 10%
Significantly Low

During the period 1985 to 1989, there were 2,410 female deaths from pneumonia and influenza, 10 percent higher than the number of male deaths. Over this period, ASMRs fluctuated between 1.8 and 2.1. Elevated and low female mortalities were limited to southern British Columbia. In the southwest significantly low SMRs were recorded by Powell River, Cowichan, Delta, and New Westminster. Two LHAs in the southern interior, namely South Cariboo with the highest female SMR in the province, and Princeton, also experienced significantly high SMRs that were in the top decile. Areas with SMRs that were significantly high, but not in the top decile, were Coquitlam, Vernon, North Vancouver, and Greater Victoria.

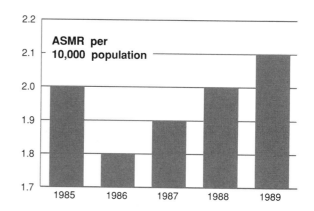

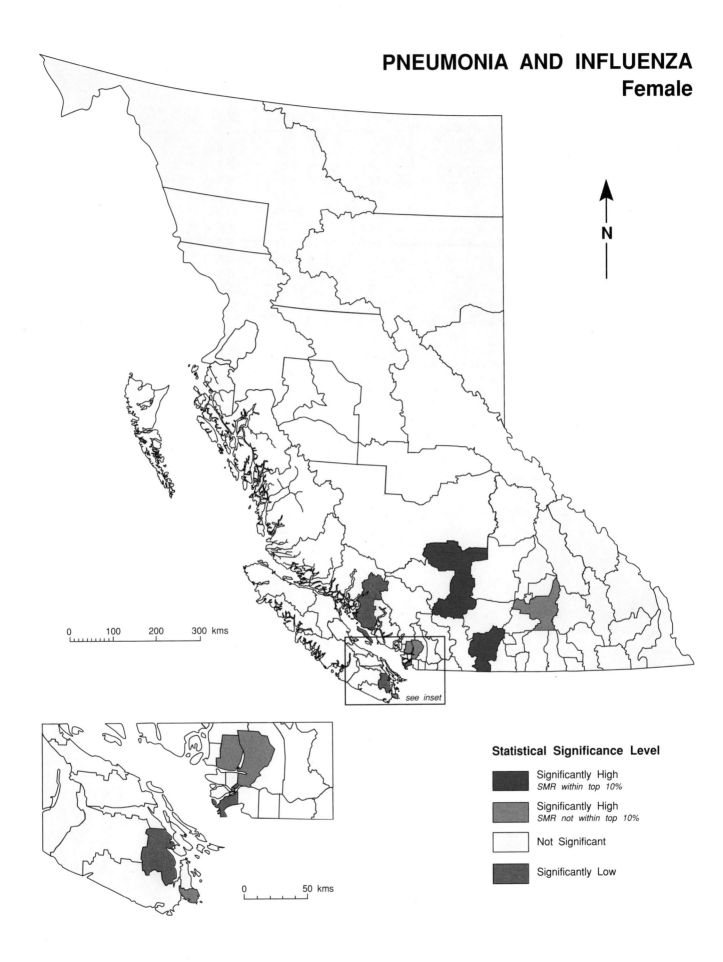

PNEUMONIA AND INFLUENZA
Female

N

0   100   200   300 kms

see inset

0   50 kms

Statistical Significance Level

Significantly High
SMR within top 10%

Significantly High
SMR not within top 10%

Not Significant

Significantly Low

115

Chronic Lung Disease: Male

	Local Health Area	Observed Deaths	Expected Deaths	SMR	(p)	95% C.I. Lower	Upper
2	Cranbrook	32	12.58	2.54	***	1.74	3.59
17	Princeton	9	3.89	2.31	*	1.06	4.39
10	Arrow Lakes	12	5.35	2.24	*	1.16	3.92
28	Quesnel	24	12.70	1.89	**	1.21	2.81
43	Coquitlam	84	60.97	1.38	**	1.10	1.71
24	Kamloops	67	48.89	1.37	*	1.06	1.74
23	Central Okanagan	94	122.25	0.77	**	0.62	0.94
34	Abbotsford	48	71.77	0.67	**	0.49	0.89
63	Saanich	31	49.42	0.63	**	0.43	0.89
47	Powell River	9	17.69	0.51	*	0.23	0.97
45	West Vancouver-Bowen Is	25	52.04	0.48	***	0.31	0.71

Significantly High and SMR within top 10%
Significantly High and SMR not within top 10%
Significantly Low

During the period 1985 to 1989, there were 2,625 male chronic lung disease deaths. Over this period, ASMRs fluctuated between 2.4 and 2.6. Statistically significant variations in male mortality were limited to south and central British Columbia. With the exception of Quesnel, the areas with significantly high mortality, in the top decile, were located in southern British Columbia. Other LHAs with significantly high mortality, in the top decile, were Cranbrook, Princeton, and Arrow Lakes. Four of the five LHAs reporting significantly low mortality were located in the southwest, with the fifth, Central Okanagan, being in the southern interior. The lowest SMR occurred in West Vancouver-Bowen Island. Other LHAs reporting low mortality included Powell River, Saanich, and Abbotsford.

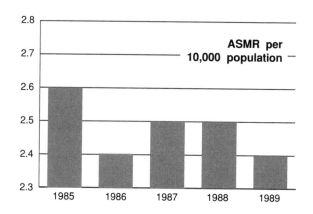

116

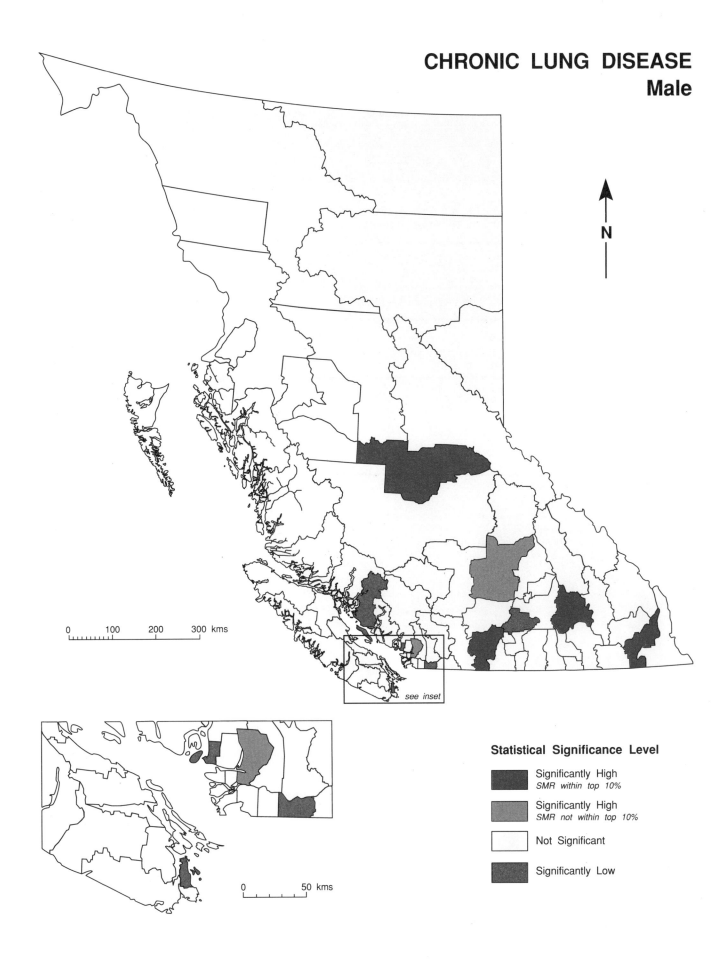

CHRONIC LUNG DISEASE
Male

N

0   100   200   300 kms

see inset

Statistical Significance Level

Significantly High
SMR within top 10%

Significantly High
SMR not within top 10%

Not Significant

Significantly Low

0   50 kms

117

Chronic Lung Disease: Female

		Local Health Area	Observed Deaths	Expected Deaths	SMR	(p)	95% C.I. Lower	Upper
	16	Keremeos 6		2.04	2.94	*	1.07	6.39
	3	Kimberley 10		4.01	2.49	*	1.19	4.58

Significantly High and SMR within top 10%
Significantly High and SMR not within top 10%
Significantly Low

During the period 1985 to 1989, there were 1,322 female chronic lung disease deaths, only half the total for males. Over this period, ASMRs fluctuated between 1.0 and 1.2. Female deaths showed little statistically significant geographical variation. Keremeos and Kimberley recorded significantly high mortality, both in the top decile. There were no LHAs with significantly low SMRs.

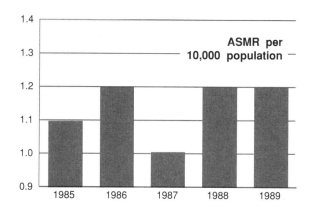

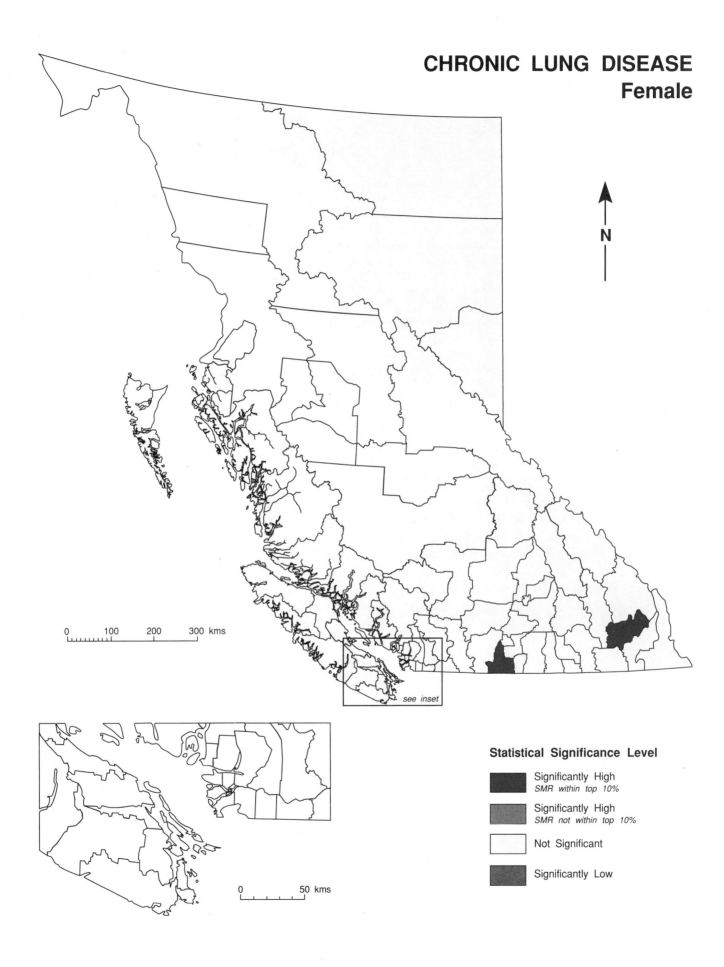

CHRONIC LUNG DISEASE
Female

N

0   100   200   300 kms

see inset

0   50 kms

Statistical Significance Level

Significantly High
SMR within top 10%

Significantly High
SMR not within top 10%

Not Significant

Significantly Low

119

Digestive System: Male

	Local Health Area	Observed Deaths	Expected Deaths	SMR	(p)	95% C.I. Lower	Upper
52	Prince Rupert	16	8.14	1.97	*	1.12	3.19
40	New Westminster	58	34.96	1.66	***	1.26	2.15
57	Prince George	46	33.63	1.37	*	1.00	1.82
39	Vancouver	465	363.72	1.28	***	1.16	1.40
23	Central Okanagan	65	90.42	0.72	**	0.55	0.92
35	Langley	32	45.36	0.71	*	0.48	1.00
34	Abbotsford	38	54.12	0.70	*	0.50	0.96
45	West Vancouver-Bowen Is	26	40.85	0.64	*	0.42	0.93
63	Saanich	25	39.43	0.63	*	0.41	0.94
71	Courtenay	18	28.65	0.63	*	0.37	0.99
37	Delta	22	41.86	0.53	**	0.33	0.80

Significantly High and SMR within top 10%
Significantly High and SMR not within top 10%
Significantly Low

During the period 1985 to 1989, there were 2,138 male digestive system deaths, and ASMRs showed a steady decline from 2.5 to 2.0. Significantly low male mortality was limited to southern British Columbia. It was centred in the southwestern LHAs of Delta, Courtenay, Saanich, West Vancouver-Bowen Island, Abbotsford, and Langley. The only exception to this was Central Okanagan, located in south-central British Columbia. In contrast, elevated mortalities, within the top decile, were reported in both southern and central British Columbia. In these regions, the significantly highest SMRs were those in Prince Rupert and New Westminster. Prince George and Vancouver were also significantly high, but not in the top decile.

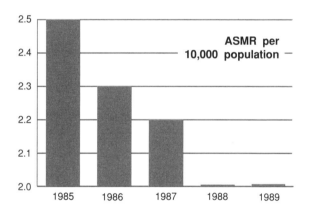

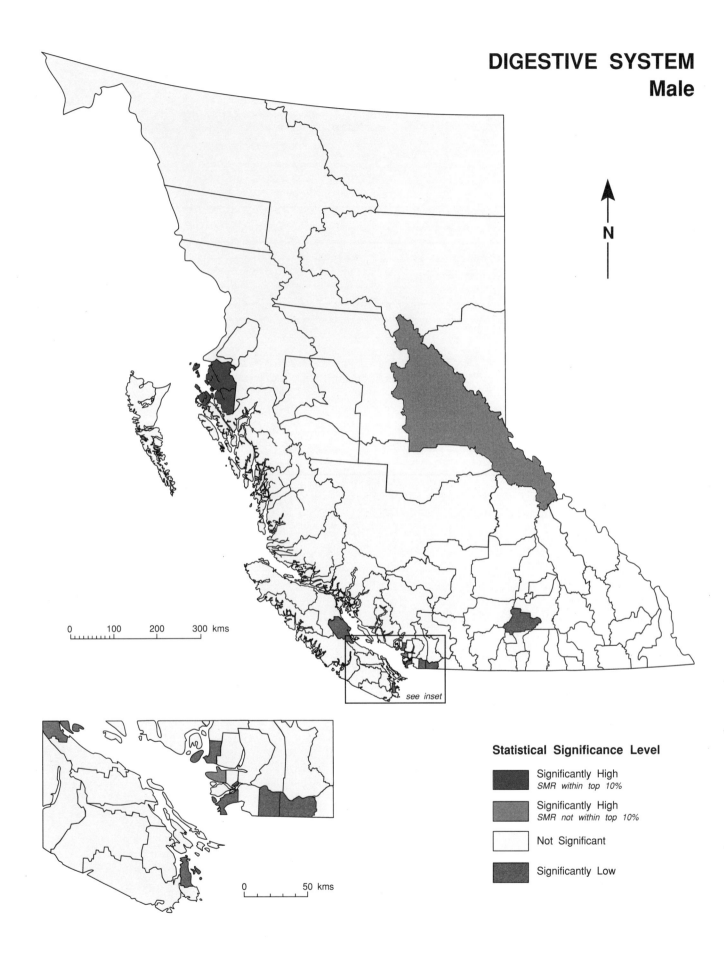

DIGESTIVE SYSTEM
Male

N

0   100   200   300 kms

see inset

0   50 kms

Statistical Significance Level

Significantly High
SMR within top 10%

Significantly High
SMR not within top 10%

Not Significant

Significantly Low

121

Digestive System: Female

	Local Health Area	Observed Deaths	Expected Deaths	SMR	(p)	95% C.I. Lower	Upper
29	Lillooet 7		1.77	3.96	**	1.59	8.17
30	South Cariboo 8		3.02	2.64	*	1.14	5.21
5	Creston 18		9.75	1.85	*	1.09	2.92
23	Central Okanagan 55		76.67	0.72	*	0.54	0.93
45	West Vancouver-Bowen Is 31		47.76	0.65	*	0.44	0.92

Significantly High and SMR within top 10%
Significantly High and SMR not within top 10%
Significantly Low

During the period 1985 to 1989, there were 2,040 female digestive system deaths, marginally fewer than the total for males. Over this time, ASMRs showed a steady decline from 2.0 to 1.7. Statistically significant geographical variations in female mortality were limited to southern British Columbia. Lillooet, South Cariboo, and Creston recorded elevated mortalities which were in the top decile. In contrast, Central Okanagan and West Vancouver-Bowen Island experienced significantly low female mortalities, reflecting a pattern similar to that for males.

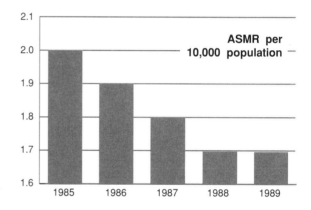

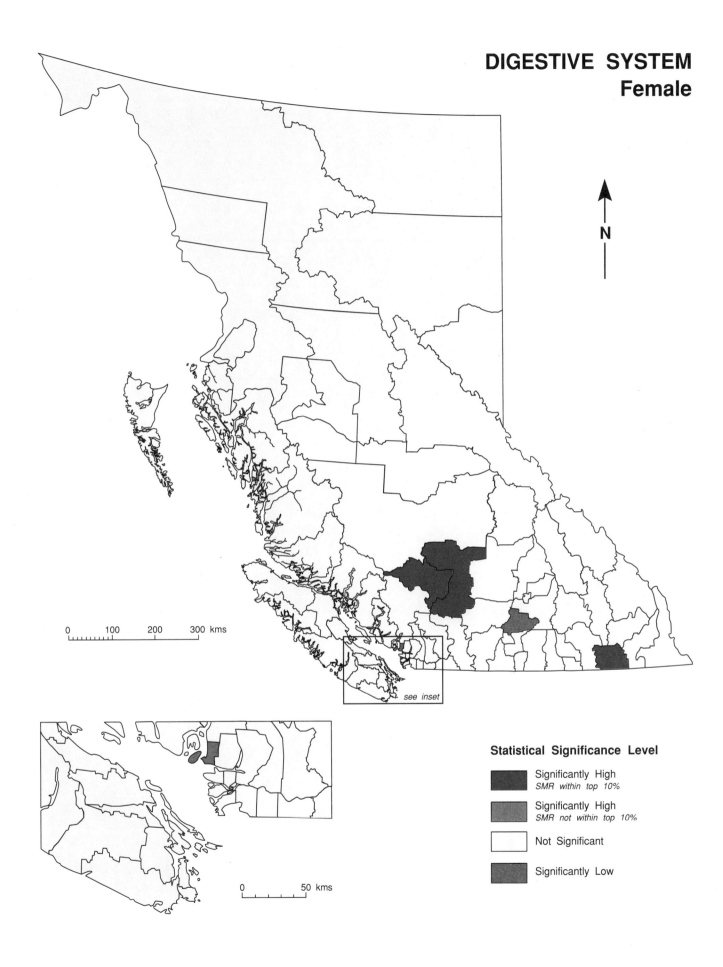

DIGESTIVE SYSTEM
Female

N

0   100   200   300 kms

see inset

0   50 kms

Statistical Significance Level

Significantly High
SMR within top 10%

Significantly High
SMR not within top 10%

Not Significant

Significantly Low

123

Motor Vehicle Traffic Accidents: Male

	Local Health Area	Observed Deaths	Expected Deaths	SMR	(p)	95% C.I. Lower	Upper
78	Enderby	16	3.08	5.20	***	2.97	8.45
30	South Cariboo	20	4.45	4.49	***	2.74	6.94
16	Keremeos	9	2.20	4.09	**	1.87	7.76
17	Princeton	10	2.86	3.49	**	1.67	6.43
13	Kettle Valley	6	1.87	3.22	*	1.17	7.00
56	Nechako	24	9.33	2.57	***	1.65	3.83
27	Cariboo-Chilcotin	55	21.84	2.52	***	1.90	3.28
54	Smithers	22	8.87	2.48	***	1.55	3.76
55	Burns Lake	11	4.75	2.32	*	1.15	4.14
20	Salmon Arm	27	14.10	1.91	**	1.26	2.79
88	Terrace	28	15.29	1.83	**	1.22	2.65
59	Peace River South	30	16.74	1.79	**	1.21	2.56
60	Peace River North	26	14.73	1.77	*	1.15	2.59
57	Prince George	92	53.37	1.72	***	1.39	2.11
75	Mission	26	15.66	1.66	*	1.08	2.43
28	Quesnel	23	14.06	1.64	*	1.04	2.45
22	Vernon	38	25.33	1.50	*	1.06	2.06
24	Kamloops	65	45.85	1.42	**	1.09	1.81
23	Central Okanagan	75	54.14	1.39	**	1.09	1.74
35	Langley	60	43.14	1.39	*	1.06	1.79
41	Burnaby	59	92.72	0.64	***	0.48	0.82
39	Vancouver	177	284.05	0.62	***	0.53	0.72
44	North Vancouver	36	64.79	0.56	***	0.39	0.77
43	Coquitlam	40	74.05	0.54	***	0.39	0.74
63	Saanich	11	23.81	0.46	**	0.23	0.83
38	Richmond	30	66.63	0.45	***	0.30	0.64
45	West Vancouver-Bowen Is	10	23.85	0.42	**	0.20	0.77
61	Greater Victoria	39	111.22	0.35	***	0.25	0.48

Significantly High and SMR within top 10%
Significantly High and SMR not within top 10%
Significantly Low

During the period 1985 to 1989, there were 1,787 male motor vehicle traffic accident deaths, with ASMRs fluctuating in the range 2.1 to 2.7. Significantly low male mortality was limited to the urban areas in the southwest of the province. To illustrate, significantly low SMRs were recorded for Greater Victoria and Saanich on Vancouver Island and six lower mainland LHAs, including West Vancouver-Bowen Island, Richmond, Coquitlam, North Vancouver, Vancouver, and Burnaby.

In contrast, this cause of death was particularly common in the province's interior, where the highest mortality occurred for residents of the Enderby LHA. Other

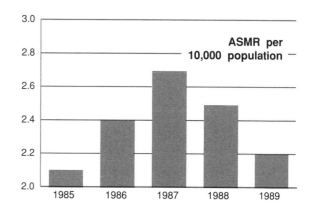

LHAs in the interior with significantly high SMRs, in the top decile, included South Cariboo, Keremeos, Princeton, Kettle Valley, Nechako, and Cariboo-Chilcotin. Elevated mortality also occurred in numerous other low population density interior and north-central LHAs.

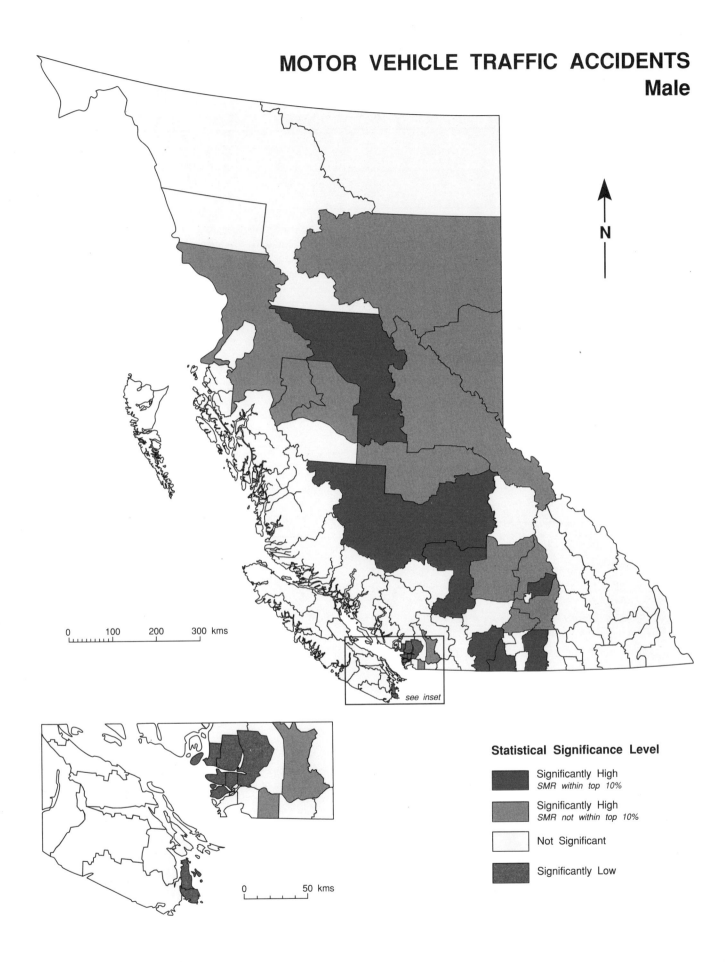

MOTOR VEHICLE TRAFFIC ACCIDENTS
Male

0   100   200   300 kms

N

see inset

0   50 kms

Statistical Significance Level

Significantly High
SMR within top 10%

Significantly High
SMR not within top 10%

Not Significant

Significantly Low

125

Motor Vehicle Traffic Accidents: Female

	Local Health Area	Observed Deaths	Expected Deaths	SMR	(p)	95% C.I. Lower	Upper
29	Lillooet	7	0.99	7.11	***	2.85	14.64
26	North Thompson	7	1.02	6.88	***	2.76	14.18
81	Fort Nelson	6	1.08	5.58	**	2.04	12.14
30	South Cariboo	8	1.62	4.95	***	2.13	9.76
56	Nechako	16	3.33	4.81	***	2.75	7.81
55	Burns Lake	8	1.67	4.79	***	2.06	9.45
10	Arrow Lakes	5	1.07	4.69	*	1.51	10.94
21	Armstrong-Spallumcheen	6	1.75	3.42	*	1.25	7.45
31	Merritt	7	2.19	3.20	*	1.28	6.59
27	Cariboo-Chilcotin	26	8.26	3.15	***	2.05	4.61
5	Creston	7	2.71	2.59	*	1.04	5.33
88	Terrace	14	5.42	2.58	**	1.41	4.33
75	Mission	12	6.19	1.94	*	1.00	3.39
33	Chilliwack	21	12.29	1.71	*	1.06	2.61
39	Vancouver	86	123.01	0.70	***	0.56	0.86
61	Greater Victoria	35	53.87	0.65	**	0.45	0.90
44	North Vancouver	15	27.61	0.54	*	0.30	0.90
38	Richmond	10	28.05	0.36	***	0.17	0.66

Significantly High and SMR within top 10%
Significantly High and SMR not within top 10%
Significantly Low

During the period 1985 to 1989, there were 754 female motor vehicle traffic accident deaths, nearly 60 percent fewer than male deaths from this cause. Over this period, ASMRs fluctuated between 0.7 and 1.2. The geographical variation of female mortality was similar to that for males. To illustrate, significantly low female mortality was again limited to southwestern British Columbia. As with males, low female mortalities were recorded in Greater Victoria, Richmond, North Vancouver, and Vancouver.

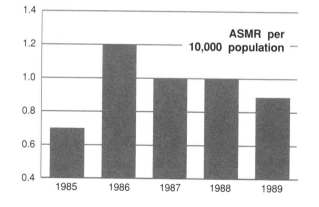

Significantly high female SMRs, in the top decile, also occurred in several interior areas. The most elevated mortality was recorded by Lillooet. Other areas reporting SMRs that were significantly high and in the top decile included North Thompson, Fort Nelson, Burns Lake, and Arrow Lakes. Only South Cariboo and Nechako had such SMRs for both genders.

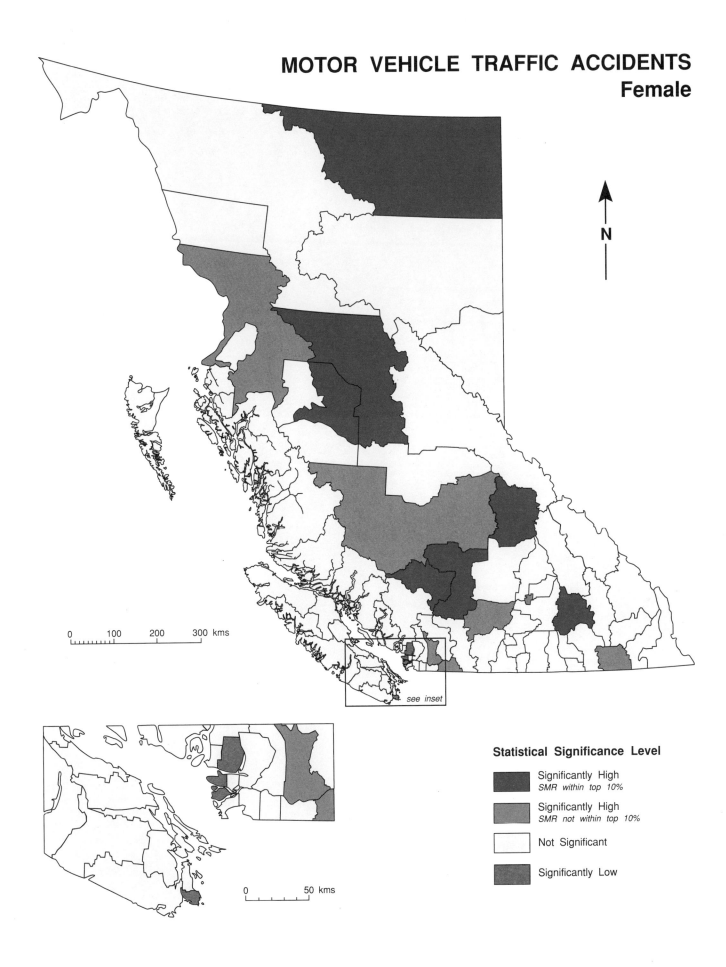

MOTOR VEHICLE TRAFFIC ACCIDENTS
Female

N

0   100   200   300 kms

see inset

0   50 kms

Statistical Significance Level

Significantly High
SMR within top 10%

Significantly High
SMR not within top 10%

Not Significant

Significantly Low

127

Accidental Falls: Male

	Local Health Area	Observed Deaths	Expected Deaths	SMR	(p)	95% C.I. Lower	Upper
39	Vancouver 177		122.84	1.44	***	1.24	1.67

Significantly High and SMR within top 10%
Significantly High and SMR not within top 10%
Significantly Low

During the period 1985 to 1989, there were 690 male deaths from accidental falls, and ASMRs fluctuated between 0.6 and 0.8. Little geographical variation was apparent in male mortality. Only Vancouver experienced significantly high mortality from this cause of death, but not in the top decile. No areas recorded significantly low SMRs during this time period.

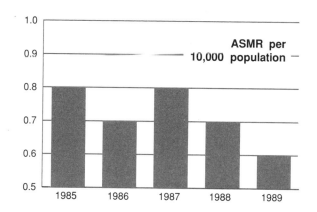

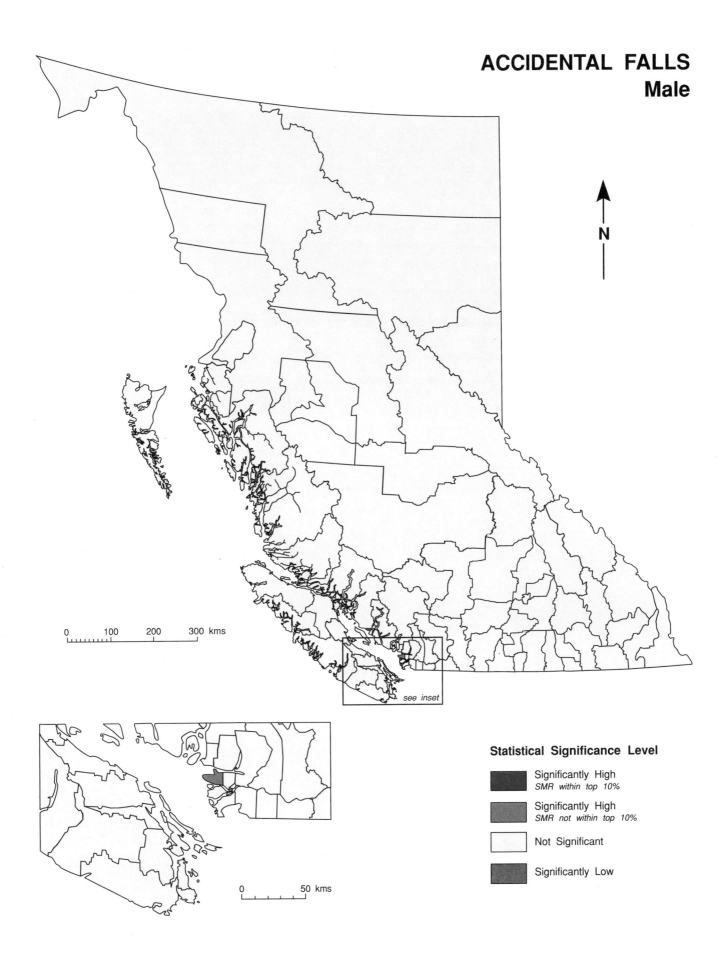

ACCIDENTAL FALLS
Male

N

0   100   200   300 kms

see inset

Statistical Significance Level

Significantly High
SMR within top 10%

Significantly High
SMR not within top 10%

Not Significant

Significantly Low

0   50 kms

129

Accidental Falls: Female

	Local Health Area	Observed Deaths	Expected Deaths	SMR	(p)	95% C.I. Lower	95% C.I. Upper
88	Terrace	7	1.55	4.52	**	1.81	9.32
39	Vancouver	172	143.15	1.20	*	1.03	1.40
36	Surrey	23	38.72	0.59	**	0.38	0.89

Significantly High and SMR within top 10%
Significantly High and SMR not within top 10%
Significantly Low

During the period 1985 to 1989, there were 659 female deaths from accidental falls, marginally fewer than those for males. During this time, ASMRs showed a steady decline from 0.7 to 0.5. Female mortality was significantly high and in the top decile only in Terrace. As with males, death from this cause also was significantly high in Vancouver, but not in the top decile. In contrast, significantly low mortality occurred in Surrey.

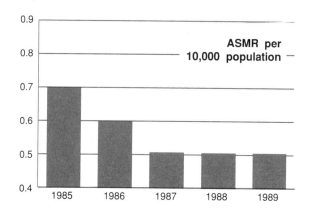

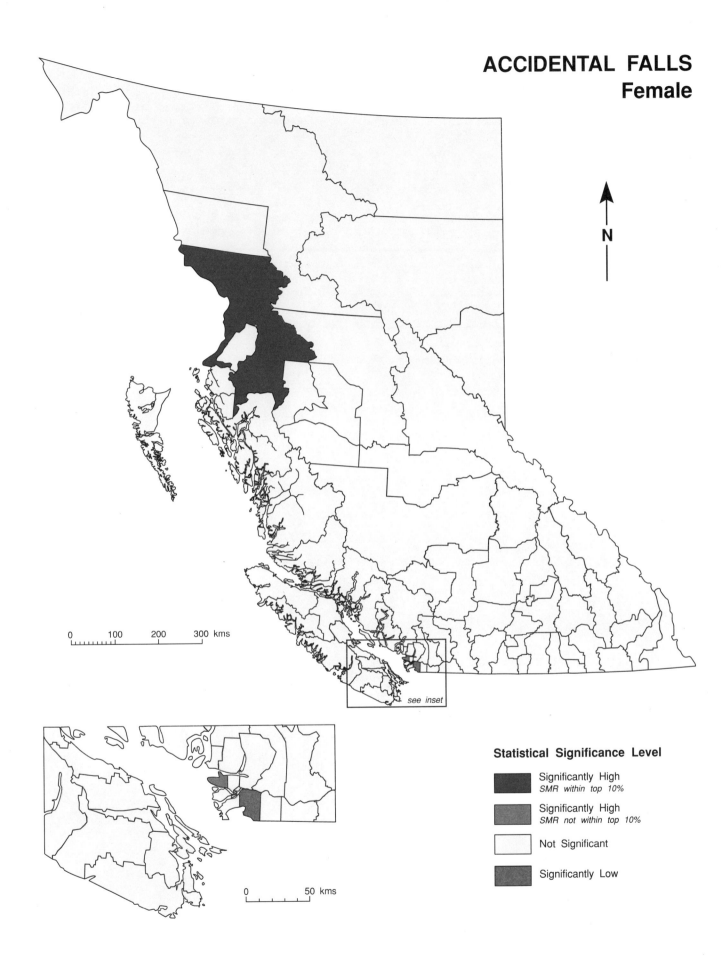

ACCIDENTAL FALLS
Female

N

0   100   200   300 kms

see inset

0   50 kms

Statistical Significance Level

Significantly High
SMR within top 10%

Significantly High
SMR not within top 10%

Not Significant

Significantly Low

131

Suicide: Male

	Local Health Area	Observed Deaths	Expected Deaths	SMR	(p)	95% C.I. Lower	95% C.I. Upper
49	Central Coast 10		1.74	5.74	***	2.75	10.55
17	Princeton 7		2.67	2.62	*	1.05	5.40
85	Vancouver Island North 21		8.15	2.58	***	1.59	3.94
31	Merritt...13		5.21	2.50	**	1.33	4.27
30	South Cariboo 9		4.01	2.25	*	1.03	4.27
80	Kitimat 13		6.56	1.98	*	1.05	3.39
27	Cariboo-Chilcotin 36		19.43	1.85	**	1.30	2.57
71	Courtenay 35		21.43	1.63	**	1.14	2.27
65	Cowichan 31		19.39	1.60	*	1.09	2.27
57	Prince George 63		46.56	1.35	*	1.04	1.73
41	Burnaby 60		87.27	0.69	**	0.52	0.88
61	Greater Victoria 71		102.93	0.69	**	0.54	0.87
38	Richmond 40		62.12	0.64	**	0.46	0.88
45	West Vancouver-Bowen Is 14		23.65	0.59	*	0.32	0.99
37	Delta...24		42.23	0.57	**	0.36	0.85

Significantly High and SMR within top 10%
Significantly High and SMR not within top 10%
Significantly Low

During the period 1985 to 1989, there were 1,655 male suicides. Over this period, ASMRs showed a decline from 2.2 in 1985 and 1986 to 1.9 over the next three years. Significantly low male mortality occurred only in Greater Victoria and the lower mainland. In the latter region, examples of significantly low mortality were provided by Delta, Richmond, Burnaby, and West Vancouver-Bowen Island.

In contrast, significantly high SMRs for suicide, in the top decile, were reported in the southern interior and the central coast regions of the province. In the former, elevated mortalities were recorded in Princeton, Merritt, and South Cariboo. In the latter, significantly high mortalities occurred in Vancouver Island North, Central Coast, and Kitimat.

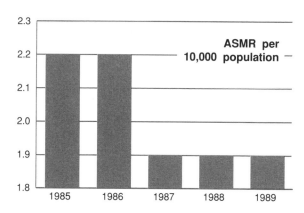

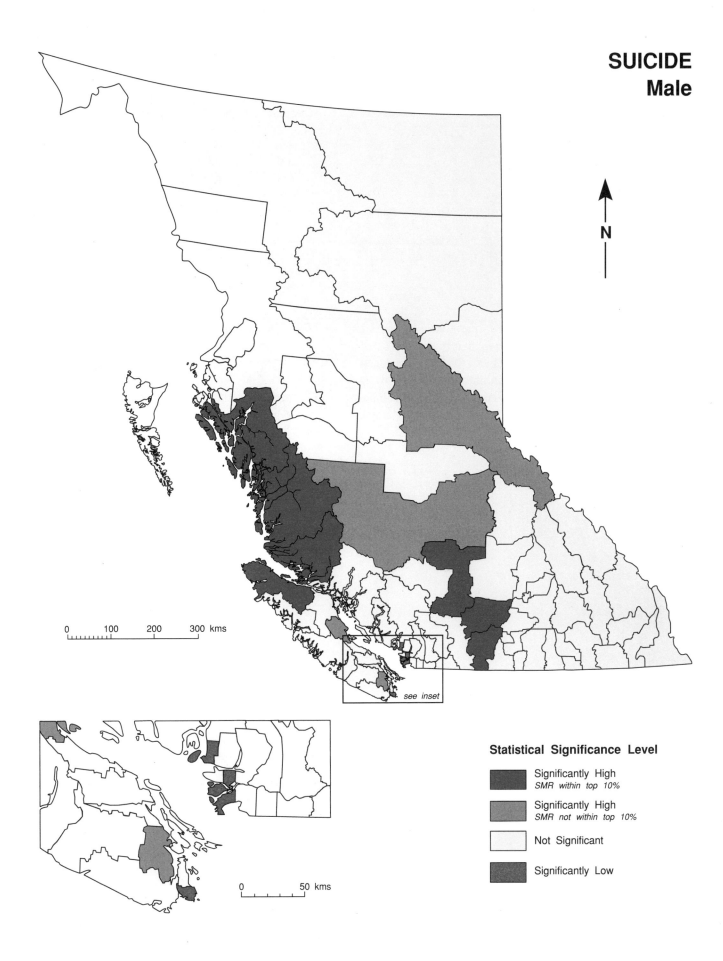

SUICIDE
Male

N

0   100   200   300 kms

see inset

0   50 kms

Statistical Significance Level

Significantly High
SMR within top 10%

Significantly High
SMR not within top 10%

Not Significant

Significantly Low

133

Suicide: Female

	Local Health Area	Observed Deaths	Expected Deaths	SMR	(p)	95% C.I. Lower	95% C.I. Upper
56	Nechako 6		1.97	3.04	*	1.11	6.62
28	Quesnel 10		3.37	2.97	**	1.42	5.46
40	New Westminster 20		7.95	2.51	***	1.54	3.88
39	Vancouver 105		82.81	1.27	*	1.04	1.53

Significantly High and SMR within top 10%
Significantly High and SMR not within top 10%
Significantly Low

During the period 1985 to 1989, there were 500 female suicide deaths, 70 percent fewer than for males. Over this period, ASMRs fluctuated in the 0.5 to 0.7 range. No areas reported significantly low mortality. In contrast, elevated mortality, in the top decile, occurred in Nechako, Quesnel, and New Westminster. Vancouver was also significantly high, but not in the top decile.

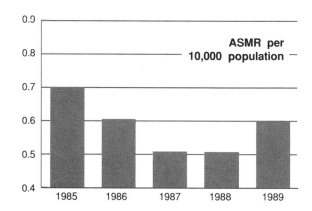

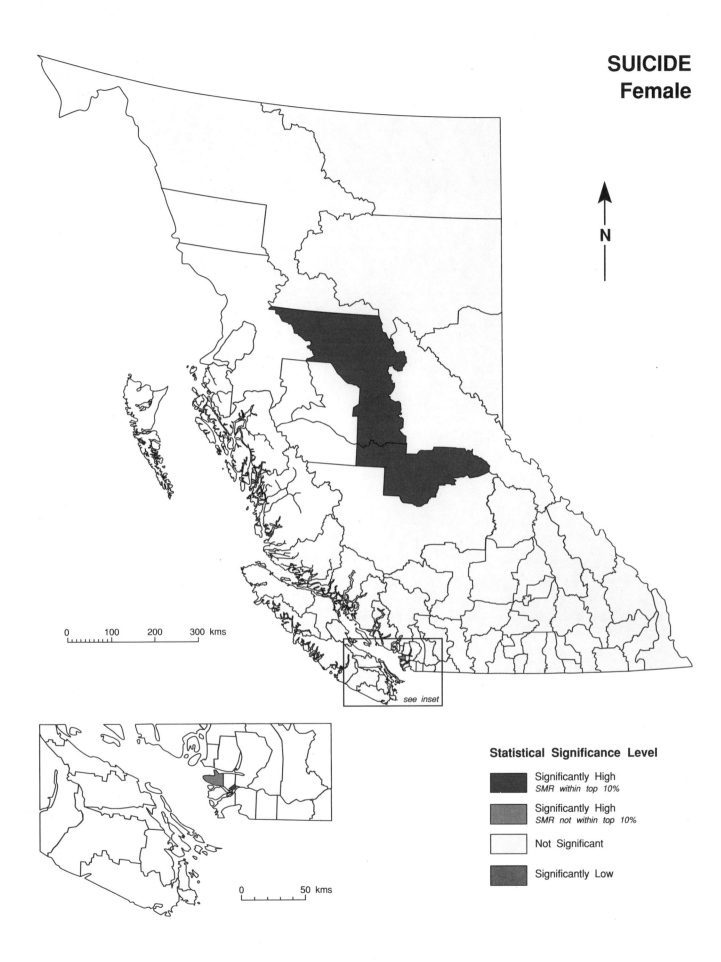

SUICIDE
Female

N

0   100   200   300 kms

see inset

0   50 kms

Statistical Significance Level

Significantly High
SMR within top 10%

Significantly High
SMR not within top 10%

Not Significant

Significantly Low

135

Alcohol-Related Deaths: Male

	Local Health Area	Observed Deaths	Expected Deaths	SMR	(p)	95% C.I. Lower	Upper
49	Central Coast	9	2.51	3.59	**	1.64	6.81
31	Merritt	22	8.18	2.69	***	1.68	4.07
85	Vancouver Island North	19	9.06	2.10	**	1.26	3.28
52	Prince Rupert	25	12.47	2.01	**	1.30	2.96
30	South Cariboo	13	6.63	1.96	*	1.04	3.35
27	Cariboo-Chilcotin	52	28.48	1.83	***	1.36	2.39
39	Vancouver	713	452.74	1.57	***	1.46	1.69
22	Vernon	32	45.26	0.71	*	0.48	1.00
38	Richmond	68	97.27	0.70	**	0.54	0.89
23	Central Okanagan	73	106.68	0.68	***	0.54	0.86
44	North Vancouver	63	96.38	0.65	***	0.50	0.84
20	Salmon Arm	18	29.75	0.60	*	0.36	0.96
35	Langley	36	62.54	0.58	***	0.40	0.80
34	Abbotsford	37	66.64	0.56	***	0.39	0.77
63	Saanich	29	51.46	0.56	***	0.38	0.81
69	Qualicum	18	32.18	0.56	**	0.33	0.88
7	Nelson	10	20.58	0.49	*	0.23	0.89
37	Delta	28	63.87	0.44	***	0.29	0.63

Significantly High and SMR within top 10%
Significantly High and SMR not within top 10%
Significantly Low

During the period 1985 to 1989, there were 2,808 male alcohol-related deaths, and ASMRs fluctuated from 2.8 to 3.4. Significant geographic variations in mortality were concentrated in south-central and southern parts of British Columbia. The only exception to this was Prince Rupert, which had significantly high mortality, in the top decile. Other areas with significantly high mortality were located mostly in south-central, central, and coastal British Columbia. These included Central Coast, Merritt, Vancouver Island North, South Cariboo, and Cariboo-Chilcotin.

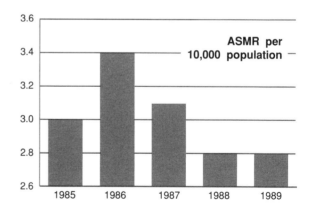

In contrast, significantly low mortality occurred mainly in southwest British Columbia (Saanich, Delta, Richmond, Abbotsford, Langley, and North Vancouver) and in south-central areas (Nelson, Salmon Arm, Vernon, and Central Okanagan).

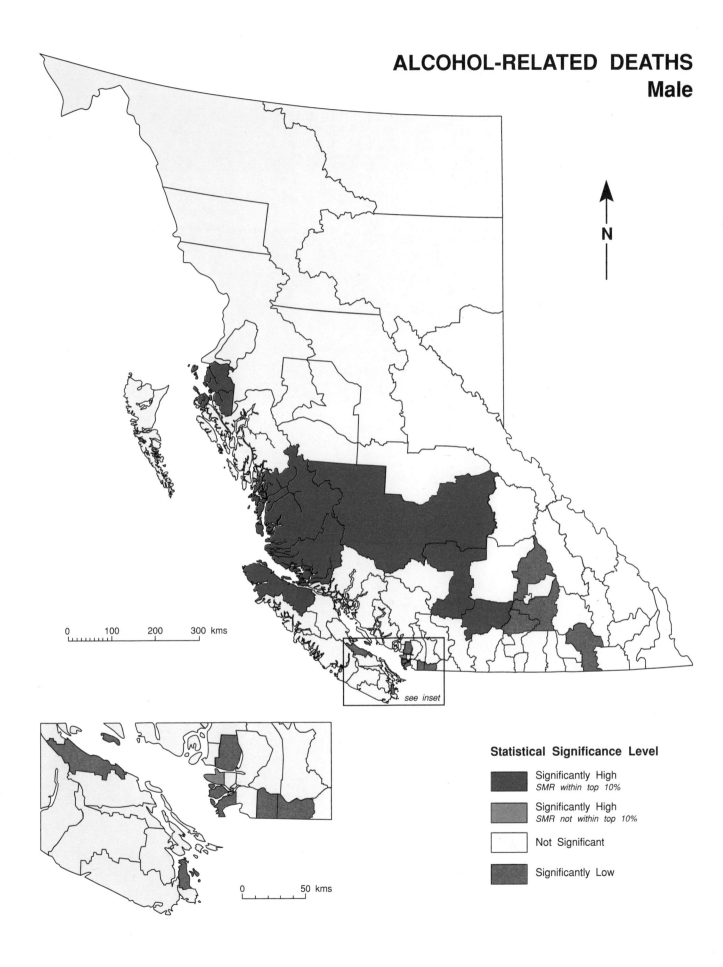

ALCOHOL-RELATED DEATHS
Male

N

0   100   200   300 kms

see inset

0   50 kms

Statistical Significance Level

Significantly High
SMR within top 10%

Significantly High
SMR not within top 10%

Not Significant

Significantly Low

137

Alcohol-Related Deaths: Female

	Local Health Area	Observed Deaths	Expected Deaths	SMR	(p)	95% C.I. Lower	Upper
29	Lillooet	11	1.11	9.94	***	4.96	17.79
81	Fort Nelson	6	0.70	8.57	***	3.13	18.64
30	South Cariboo	7	1.92	3.64	**	1.46	7.50
31	Merritt	7	2.49	2.81	*	1.13	5.79
60	Peace River North	12	4.81	2.50	**	1.29	4.36
88	Terrace	10	4.63	2.16	*	1.03	3.97
40	New Westminster	28	18.46	1.52	*	1.01	2.19
39	Vancouver	244	176.25	1.38	***	1.22	1.57
41	Burnaby	38	57.48	0.66	**	0.47	0.91
43	Coquitlam	18	33.02	0.55	**	0.32	0.86
23	Central Okanagan	21	39.33	0.53	**	0.33	0.82
38	Richmond	19	36.56	0.52	**	0.31	0.81
62	Sooke	5	12.01	0.42	*	0.13	0.97

Significantly High and SMR within top 10%
Significantly High and SMR not within top 10%
Significantly Low

During the period 1985 to 1989, there were 1,028 female alcohol-related deaths (60 percent fewer than for males). Over this time, ASMRs fluctuated between 1.0 and 1.2. The geographical distribution of female alcohol-related mortality was slightly different from that of males. Significantly high mortalities, in the top decile, occurred in northeast (Fort Nelson and Peace River North), northwest (Terrace), and south-central (Lillooet, South Cariboo, and Merritt) British Columbia. South Cariboo and Merritt also displayed significantly high mortality for males. Significantly low mortality occurred in Burnaby, Coquitlam, Sooke, Richmond, and Central Okanagan. The latter two also recorded low male mortality.

In Vancouver, both females and males showed significantly high mortality, but not in the top decile. New Westminster was the other LHA which was significantly high, but not in the top decile, for female deaths related to alcohol.

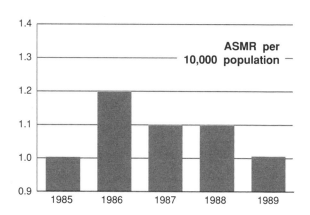

ALCOHOL-RELATED DEATHS
Female

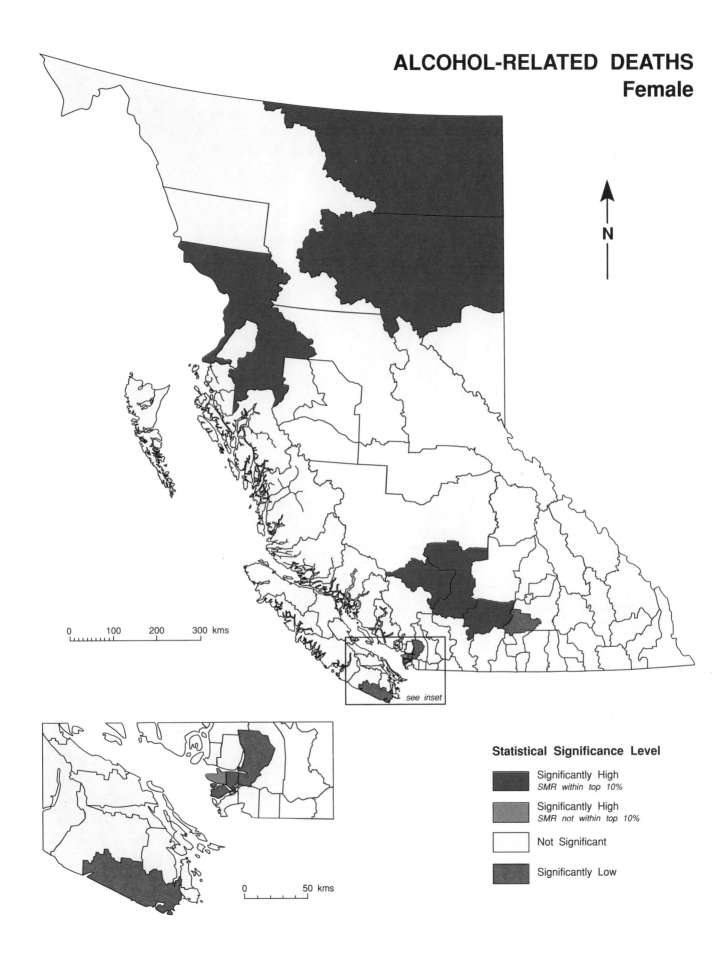

0   100   200   300 kms

see inset

N

Statistical Significance Level

Significantly High
SMR within top 10%

Significantly High
SMR not within top 10%

Not Significant

Significantly Low

0   50 kms

139

Age Under 1 Year: Male

	Local Health Area	Observed Deaths	Expected Deaths	SMR	(p)	95% C.I. Lower	Upper
54	Smithers	16	6.73	2.38	**	1.36	3.86
56	Nechako	15	7.52	1.99	*	1.12	3.29
70	Alberni	22	11.51	1.91	**	1.20	2.89
39	Vancouver	158	116.56	1.36	***	1.15	1.58
41	Burnaby	29	42.59	0.68	*	0.46	0.98

Significantly High and SMR within top 10%
Significantly High and SMR not within top 10%
Significantly Low

During the period 1985 to 1989, there were 999 male deaths among children under one year of age. Over this period, ASMRs fluctuated in the range of 1.5 to 1.7.

There was relatively little statistically significant geographical variation in mortality for males under one year of age. Only Smithers and Nechako had significantly high, in the top decile, male deaths. Although not within the top 10 percent, male deaths were also high in Alberni and Vancouver. The only LHA to report significantly low male mortality was Burnaby.

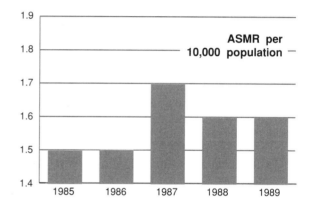

Age Under 1 Year: Female

During the period 1985 to 1989, there were 732 female deaths among children under one year of age. ASMRs fluctuated in the range of 1.1 to 1.3. There was no statistically significant geographic variation in mortality. Because of this, a mortality map for females is not presented.

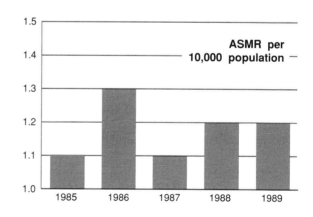

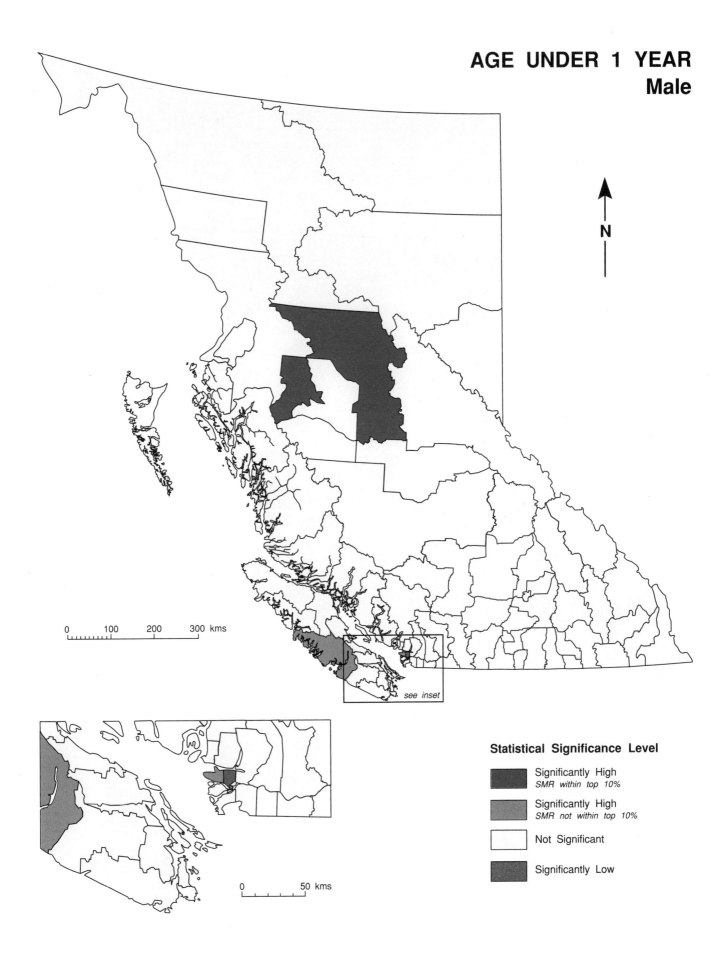

AGE UNDER 1 YEAR
Male

N

0   100   200   300 kms

see inset

Statistical Significance Level

Significantly High
SMR within top 10%

Significantly High
SMR not within top 10%

Not Significant

Significantly Low

0   50 kms

141

Age 1-14 Years: Male

	Local Health Area	Observed Deaths	Expected Deaths	SMR	(p)	95% C.I. Lower	Upper
56	Nechako 11		3.63	3.03	**	1.51	5.42
28	Quesnel 13		4.72	2.76	**	1.47	4.71
36	Surrey 21		32.59	0.64	*	0.40	0.99
38	Richmond 8		16.46	0.49	*	0.21	0.96
37	Delta 7		14.60	0.48	*	0.19	0.99

Significantly High and SMR within top 10%
Significantly High and SMR not within top 10%
Significantly Low

During the period 1985 to 1989, there were 444 male deaths in the 1 to 14 years age group. Over this period, ASMRs remained fairly stable at 0.8, except for 1988 when it reached 0.9. Significantly low mortality was restricted to three LHAs in the lower mainland, namely Delta, Richmond, and Surrey. Quesnel and Nechako in the central interior recorded significantly high mortalities, although only that of the latter area was in the top decile.

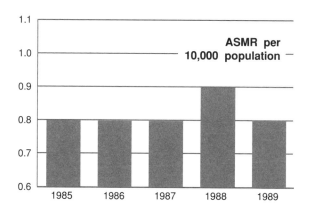

AGE 1-14 YEARS
Male

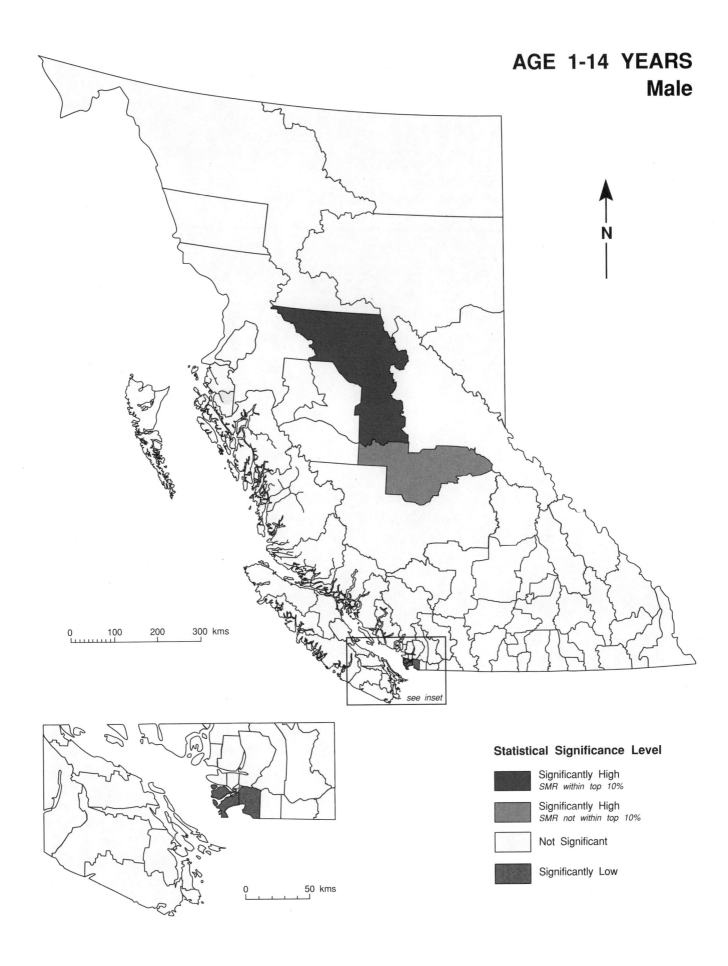

N

0   100   200   300 kms

see inset

0   50 kms

Statistical Significance Level

Significantly High
SMR within top 10%

Significantly High
SMR not within top 10%

Not Significant

Significantly Low

143

Age 1-14 Years: Female

	Local Health Area	Observed Deaths	Expected Deaths	SMR	(p)	95% C.I. Lower	Upper
88	Terrace 9		3.61	2.49	*	1.14	4.74

Significantly High and SMR within top 10%
Significantly High and SMR not within top 10%
Significantly Low

During the period 1985 to 1989, there were 286 female deaths (approximately 65 percent of the number of male deaths) in the 1 to 14 years age group. ASMRs showed a slight but steady decline from 0.6 to 0.4 through the period. Only one LHA, Terrace, had a statistically significant SMR that was high and in the top decile.

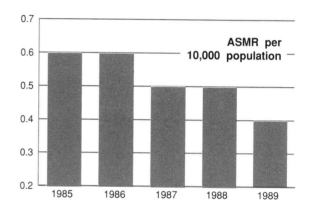

144

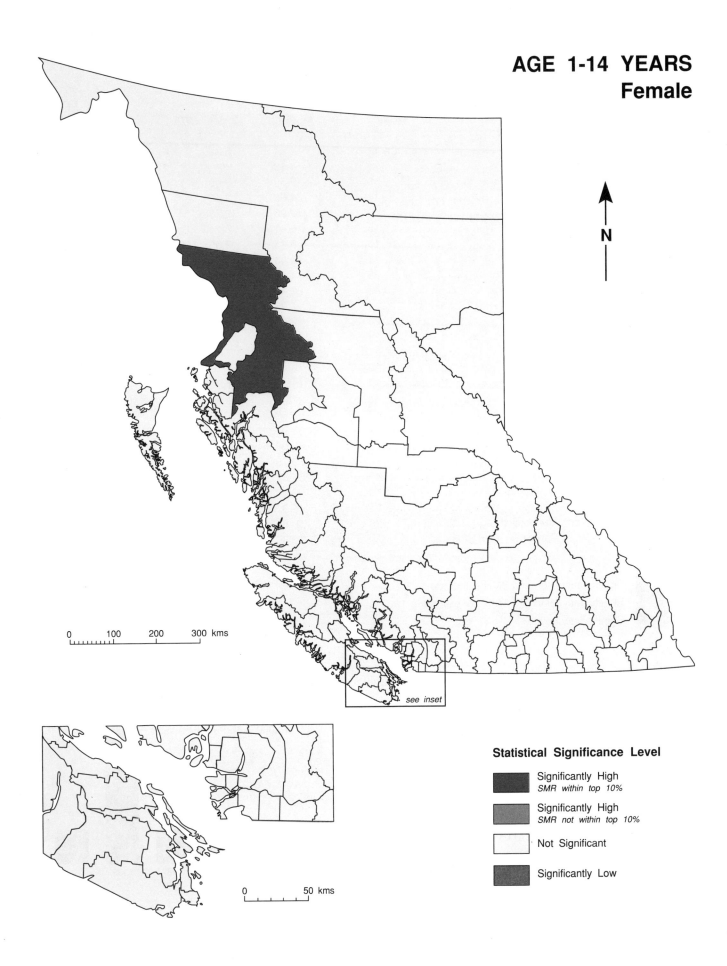

AGE 1-14 YEARS
Female

N

0 100 200 300 kms

see inset

Statistical Significance Level

Significantly High
SMR within top 10%

Significantly High
SMR not within top 10%

Not Significant

Significantly Low

0   50 kms

145

Age 15-24 Years: Male

	Local Health Area	Observed Deaths	Expected Deaths	SMR	(p)	95% C.I. Lower	Upper
49	Central Coast	11	1.64	6.72	***	3.35	12.02
30	South Cariboo	14	4.10	3.41	***	1.87	5.73
78	Enderby	8	2.59	3.09	*	1.33	6.08
55	Burns Lake	11	4.55	2.42	*	1.21	4.33
18	Golden	9	3.96	2.28	*	1.04	4.32
85	Vancouver Island North	18	8.41	2.14	**	1.27	3.38
56	Nechako	19	9.28	2.05	**	1.23	3.20
31	Merritt	11	5.43	2.02	*	1.01	3.62
60	Peace River North	29	14.50	2.00	**	1.34	2.87
27	Cariboo-Chilcotin	40	20.47	1.95	***	1.40	2.66
80	Kitimat	14	7.25	1.93	*	1.05	3.24
75	Mission	24	12.67	1.89	**	1.21	2.82
88	Terrace	28	15.12	1.85	**	1.23	2.68
65	Cowichan	31	17.26	1.80	**	1.22	2.55
70	Alberni	29	16.45	1.76	**	1.18	2.53
28	Quesnel	22	13.14	1.67	*	1.05	2.53
22	Vernon	33	21.34	1.55	*	1.06	2.17
57	Prince George	77	50.69	1.52	***	1.20	1.90
43	Coquitlam	48	68.91	0.70	*	0.51	0.92
38	Richmond	39	58.06	0.67	*	0.48	0.92
41	Burnaby	53	79.59	0.67	**	0.50	0.87
39	Vancouver	149	237.87	0.63	***	0.53	0.74
61	Greater Victoria	60	99.00	0.61	***	0.46	0.78
37	Delta	25	45.32	0.55	**	0.36	0.81
44	North Vancouver	28	56.95	0.49	***	0.33	0.71
45	West Vancouver-Bowen Is	9	19.86	0.45	*	0.21	0.86

Significantly High and SMR within top 10%
Significantly High and SMR not within top 10%
Significantly Low

During the period 1985 to 1989, there were 1,541 male deaths in the 15 to 24 years age group. Over this period, ASMRs remained fairly stable at 2.5, except for 1988 when it reached 2.8. There was an obvious tendency for male mortality to be low in the urban areas of the southwest of the province and elevated in central and northern parts of British Columbia. For example, significantly low mortalities were recorded by seven LHAs in the lower mainland, and by Greater Victoria on Vancouver Island. In contrast, 18 LHAs, many in central British Columbia, reported significantly high SMRs. Five of these were within the top decile: namely Central Coast, South Cariboo, Enderby, Burns Lake, and Golden.

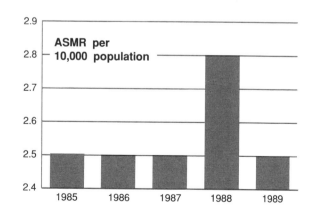

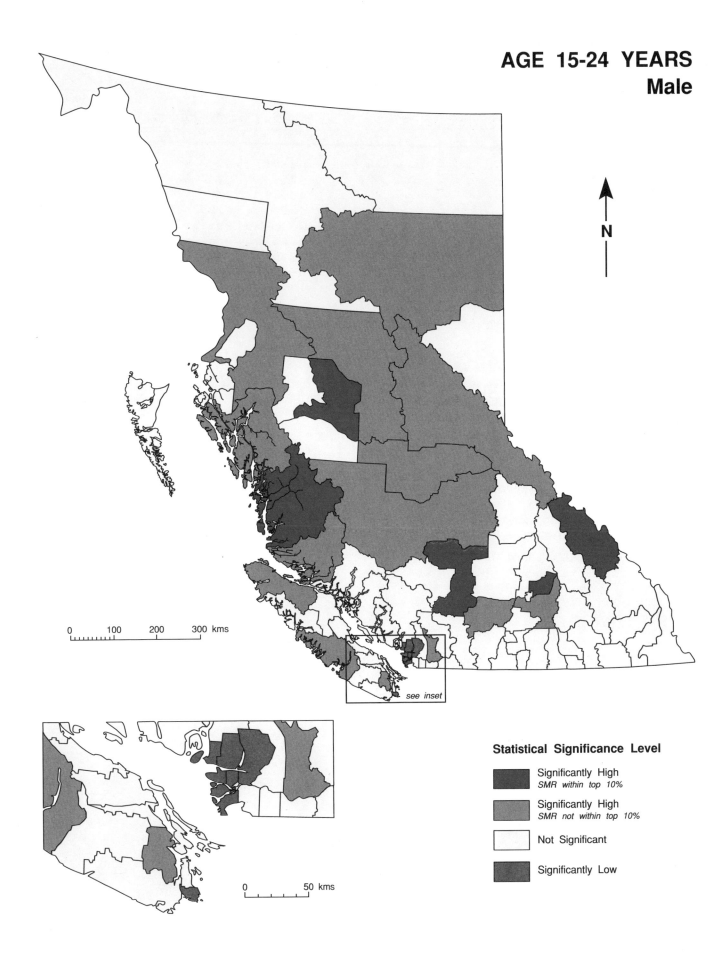

AGE 15-24 YEARS
Male

N

0   100   200   300 kms

see inset

0   50 kms

Statistical Significance Level

Significantly High
SMR within top 10%

Significantly High
SMR not within top 10%

Not Significant

Significantly Low

147

Age 15-24 Years: Female

		Local Health Area	Observed Deaths	Expected Deaths	SMR	(p)	95% C.I. Lower	Upper
	14	Southern Okanagan 7	1.74	4.02	**	1.61	8.29
	27	Cariboo-Chilcotin 19	6.88	2.76	***	1.66	4.31
	88	Terrace 13	4.87	2.67	**	1.42	4.57
	41	Burnaby 16	26.57	0.60	*	0.34	0.98
	43	Coquitlam 11	22.02	0.50	*	0.25	0.89
	37	Delta..6	14.76	0.41	*	0.15	0.88
	38	Richmond 5	19.05	0.26	***	0.08	0.61

Significantly High and SMR within top 10%
Significantly High and SMR not within top 10%
Significantly Low

During the period 1985 to 1989, there were 502 female deaths in the 15 to 24 years age group, or about one third of the number of male deaths. Over this time, ASMRs remained fairly stable, fluctuating between 0.8 and 0.9. There was far less geographical variation in female mortality for this age group than in male mortality. Some similarities are apparent, however, particularly the low SMRs experienced in the lower mainland LHAs, as illustrated by Richmond, Delta, Coquitlam, and Burnaby. Only Southern Okanagan reported significantly high mortality, in the top decile. Cariboo-Chilcotin and Terrace also displayed elevated SMRs, but not in the top decile, for both genders.

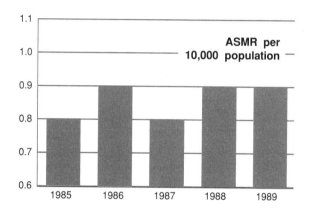

148

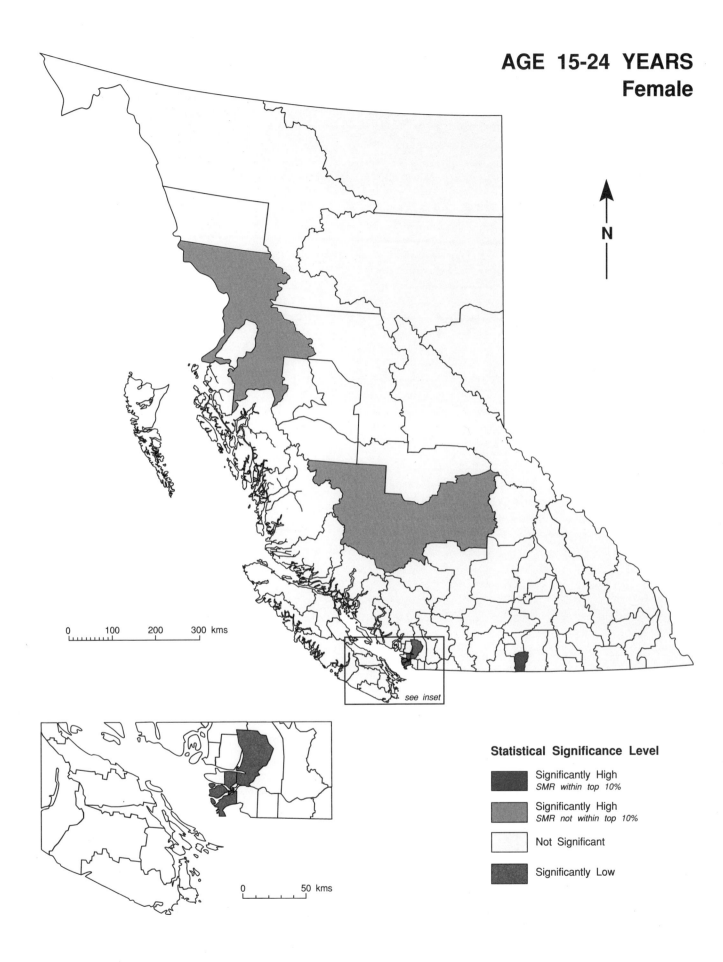

AGE 15-24 YEARS
Female

0   100   200   300 kms

see inset

0   50 kms

Statistical Significance Level

Significantly High
SMR within top 10%

Significantly High
SMR not within top 10%

Not Significant

Significantly Low

149

Age 25-44 Years: Male

	Local Health Area	Observed Deaths	Expected Deaths	SMR	(p)	95% C.I. Lower	Upper
49	Central Coast	17	4.98	3.41	***	1.99	5.47
29	Lillooet	16	6.26	2.56	**	1.46	4.15
47	Powell River	39	23.11	1.69	**	1.20	2.31
52	Prince Rupert	46	27.27	1.69	**	1.23	2.25
85	Vancouver Island North	44	26.52	1.66	**	1.21	2.23
28	Quesnel	52	33.78	1.54	**	1.15	2.02
56	Nechako	31	21.04	1.47	*	1.00	2.09
27	Cariboo-Chilcotin	73	52.69	1.39	**	1.09	1.74
88	Terrace	51	36.80	1.39	*	1.03	1.82
39	Vancouver	942	692.10	1.36	***	1.28	1.45
36	Surrey	269	312.68	0.86	*	0.76	0.97
61	Greater Victoria	195	229.88	0.85	*	0.73	0.98
35	Langley	77	109.48	0.70	**	0.56	0.88
37	Delta	78	111.31	0.70	**	0.55	0.87
41	Burnaby	147	215.86	0.68	***	0.58	0.80
43	Coquitlam	126	187.28	0.67	***	0.56	0.80
38	Richmond	104	167.82	0.62	***	0.51	0.75
44	North Vancouver	100	160.67	0.62	***	0.51	0.76
1	Fernie	16	27.03	0.59	*	0.34	0.96
62	Sooke	35	62.10	0.56	***	0.39	0.78
45	West Vancouver-Bowen Is	24	45.95	0.52	***	0.33	0.78

Significantly High and SMR within top 10%
Significantly High and SMR not within top 10%
Significantly Low

During the period 1985 to 1989, there were 4,207 male deaths in the 25 to 44 years age group. Over this period, ASMRs fluctuated between 4.3 and 4.7. With the exception of Fernie, located in the extreme southeast, low male mortality in this age group was restricted to the southwest of the province. In this region, 10 LHAs, including West Vancouver-Bowen Island, Sooke, and North Vancouver experienced notably low SMRs.

There was a general tendency for elevated mortality to be common in coastal areas and in the central interior of the province. In total, 10 LHAs reported significantly high mortalities, four of which were in the top decile. Of these, the highest SMRs in British Columbia occurred in Central Coast, Powell River, and Prince Rupert, all on the coast, and Lillooet in the interior.

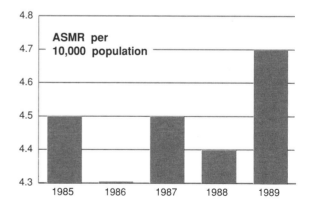

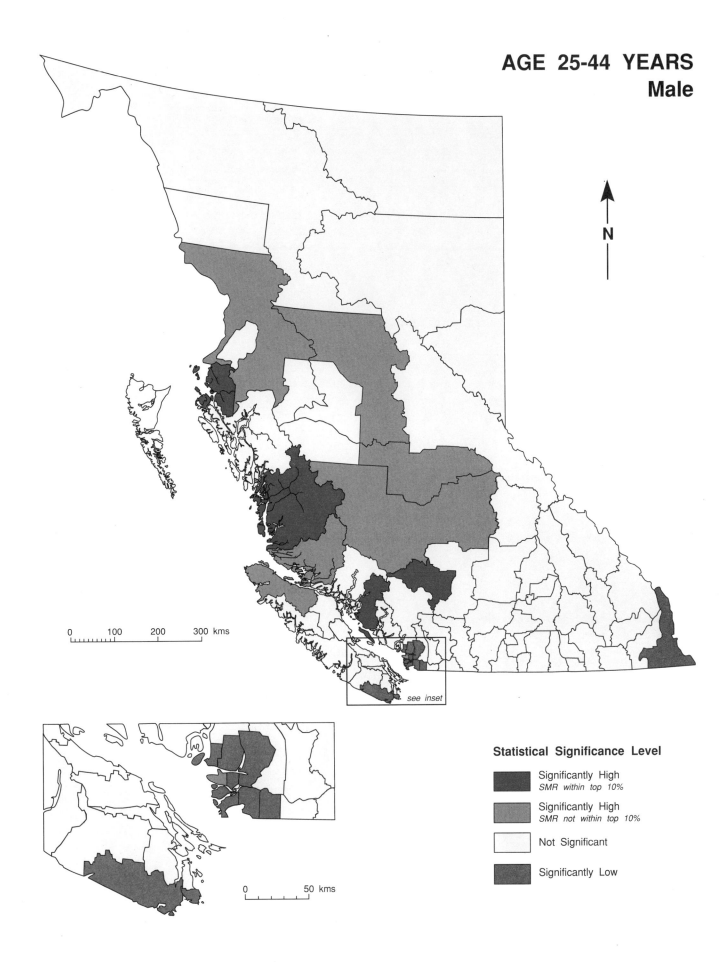

AGE 25-44 YEARS
Male

N

0   100   200   300 kms

see inset

0   50 kms

Statistical Significance Level

Significantly High
SMR within top 10%

Significantly High
SMR not within top 10%

Not Significant

Significantly Low

151

Age 25-44 Years: Female

	Local Health Area	Observed Deaths	Expected Deaths	SMR	(p)	95% C.I. Lower	95% C.I. Upper
26	North Thompson	7	2.80	2.50	*	1.00	5.16
31	Merritt	14	5.66	2.47	**	1.35	4.15
30	South Cariboo	9	3.97	2.27	*	1.03	4.30
52	Prince Rupert	22	10.95	2.01	**	1.26	3.04
40	New Westminster	46	25.29	1.82	***	1.33	2.43
27	Cariboo-Chilcotin	36	22.61	1.59	*	1.12	2.20
65	Cowichan	33	21.27	1.55	*	1.07	2.18
39	Vancouver	329	294.40	1.12	*	1.00	1.25
43	Coquitlam	63	85.95	0.73	*	0.56	0.94
35	Langley	36	51.04	0.71	*	0.49	0.98
38	Richmond	57	80.52	0.71	**	0.54	0.92
37	Delta	40	56.86	0.70	*	0.50	0.96
34	Abbotsford	28	41.83	0.67	*	0.44	0.97

Significantly High and SMR within top 10%
Significantly High and SMR not within top 10%
Significantly Low

During the period 1985 to 1989, there were 1,875 female deaths in the 25 to 44 years age group, less than half the number of deaths for males. Over this time, ASMRs remained fairly stable, fluctuating between 1.9 and 2.0. The two geographical trends in mortality noted in males in this age group were also apparent in females, but were less pronounced. Low SMRs were again limited to the lower mainland, where five LHAs, Abbotsford, Delta, Richmond, Langley, and Coquitlam, reported significantly low mortality.

As in males, elevated female death rates tended to be more common in the coastal areas and central interior of the province. These peaked in North Thompson, Merritt, and South Cariboo in the interior, and Prince Rupert on the coast. All these LHAs had significantly high SMRs, in the top decile.

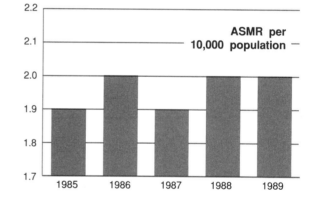

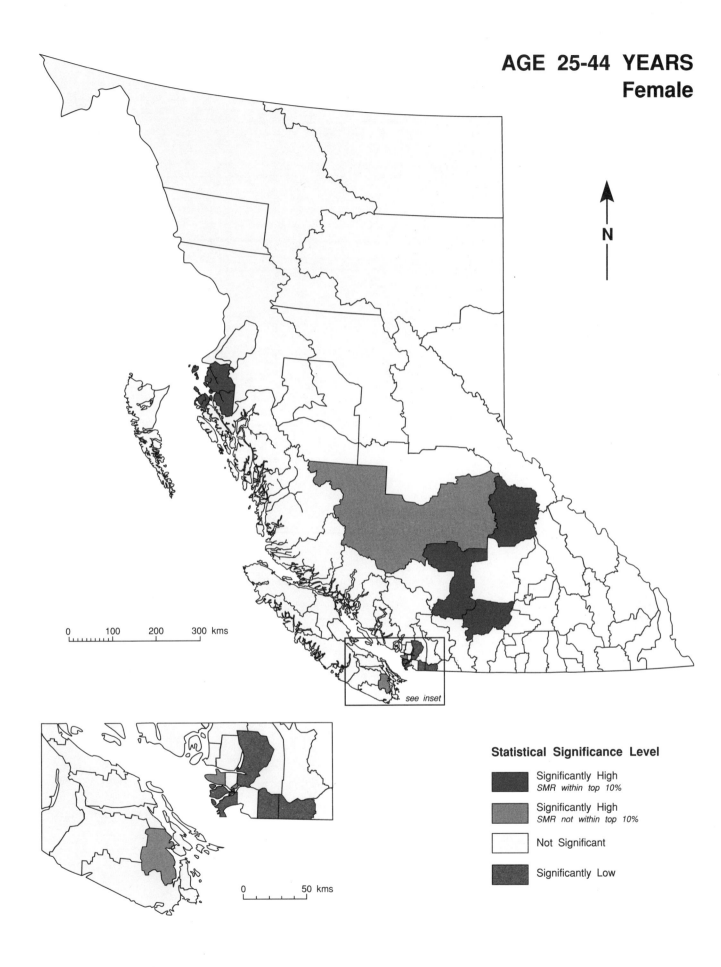

AGE 25-44 YEARS
Female

N

0   100   200   300 kms

see inset

0   50 kms

Statistical Significance Level

Significantly High
SMR within top 10%

Significantly High
SMR not within top 10%

Not Significant

Significantly Low

153

Age 45-64 Years: Male

	Local Health Area	Observed Deaths	Expected Deaths	SMR	(p)	95% C.I. Lower	Upper
55	Burns Lake	40	24.91	1.61	**	1.15	2.19
19	Revelstoke	42	30.08	1.40	*	1.01	1.89
30	South Cariboo	42	30.00	1.40	*	1.01	1.89
85	Vancouver Island North	60	43.03	1.39	*	1.06	1.80
52	Prince Rupert	78	57.32	1.36	*	1.08	1.70
31	Merritt	51	37.83	1.35	*	1.00	1.77
56	Nechako	63	48.38	1.30	*	1.00	1.67
88	Terrace	95	75.49	1.26	*	1.02	1.54
39	Vancouver	2250	1820.46	1.24	***	1.19	1.29
42	Maple Ridge	205	168.85	1.21	**	1.05	1.39
57	Prince George	326	279.55	1.17	**	1.04	1.30
44	North Vancouver	384	453.12	0.85	***	0.76	0.94
43	Coquitlam	361	434.41	0.83	***	0.75	0.92
34	Abbotsford	196	241.98	0.81	**	0.70	0.93
37	Delta	230	292.54	0.79	***	0.69	0.89
38	Richmond	350	441.39	0.79	***	0.71	0.88
23	Central Okanagan	307	401.55	0.76	***	0.68	0.86
64	Gulf Islands	37	52.20	0.71	*	0.50	0.98
63	Saanich	146	207.60	0.70	***	0.59	0.83
69	Qualicum	74	115.59	0.64	***	0.50	0.80
45	West Vancouver-Bowen Is	135	220.73	0.61	***	0.51	0.72

Significantly High and SMR within top 10%
Significantly High and SMR not within top 10%
Significantly Low

During the period 1985 to 1989, there were 11,574 male deaths in the 45 to 64 years age group, and ASMRs showed a steady decline from 14.6 to 13.5. With the exception of Central Okanagan, significantly low male mortality was limited to southwestern British Columbia. In this region, the lowest SMRs were recorded by West Vancouver-Bowen Island, Qualicum, and Saanich, the latter two being on Vancouver Island. Although six other LHAs in the southwest reported significantly low mortalities, those in Vancouver and Maple Ridge were high, but not in the top decile.

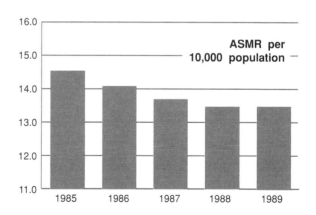

In total, 11 LHAs recorded significantly high SMRs, four of which were within the top decile. The highest occurred in Burns Lake, Revelstoke, South Cariboo, and Vancouver Island North.

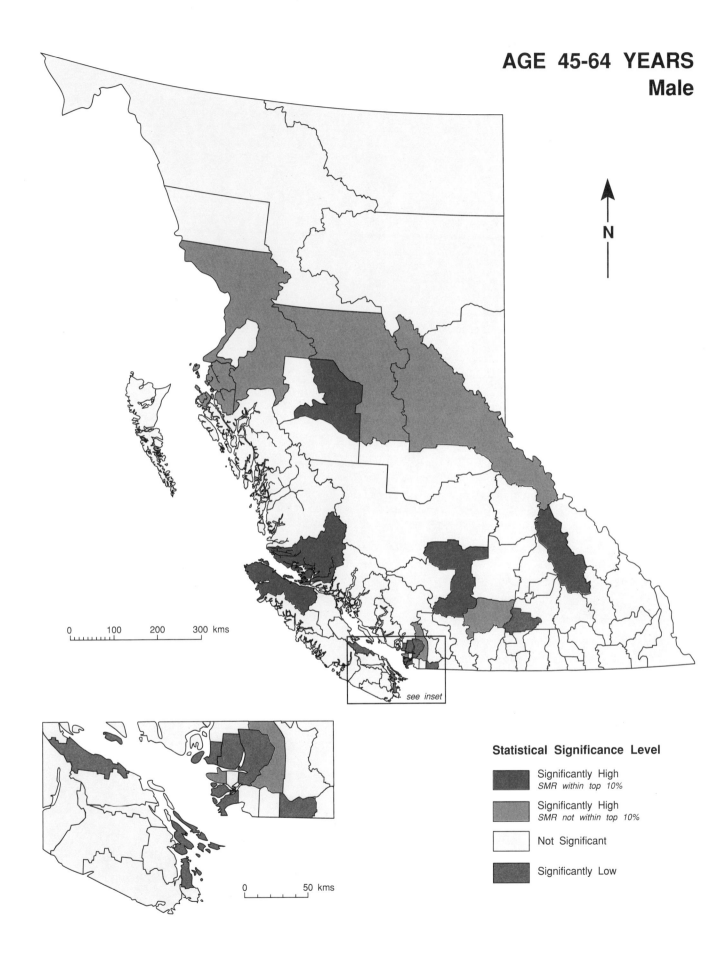

AGE 45-64 YEARS
Male

0   100   200   300 kms

see inset

Statistical Significance Level

Significantly High
SMR within top 10%

Significantly High
SMR not within top 10%

Not Significant

Significantly Low

0   50 kms

155

Age 45-64 Years: Female

	Local Health Area	Observed Deaths	Expected Deaths	SMR	(p)	95% C.I. Lower	Upper
66	Lake Cowichan	23	11.75	1.96	**	1.24	2.94
31	Merritt	28	18.48	1.52	*	1.01	2.19
59	Peace River South	59	43.21	1.37	*	1.04	1.76
40	New Westminster	125	99.64	1.25	*	1.04	1.49
57	Prince George	160	130.07	1.23	*	1.05	1.44
35	Langley	168	139.97	1.20	*	1.03	1.40
63	Saanich	105	128.45	0.82	*	0.67	0.99
23	Central Okanagan	211	259.10	0.81	**	0.71	0.93
38	Richmond	206	263.82	0.78	***	0.68	0.90
45	West Vancouver-Bowen Is	103	137.39	0.75	**	0.61	0.91

Significantly High and SMR within top 10%

Significantly High and SMR not within top 10%

Significantly Low

During the period 1985 to 1989, there were 6,745 female deaths, approximately 60 percent of the number for males, in the 45 to 64 years age group. ASMRs showed a steady decline from 8.6 to 7.9 through the period. Female mortality in this age group displayed less variability than that of males. As a consequence, the resulting geographical pattern is not as complex. There was, however, some evidence of a concentration of significantly low mortality in the southwest, exemplified by West Vancouver-Bowen Island, Richmond, and Saanich. Central Okanagan also showed significantly low mortality for females.

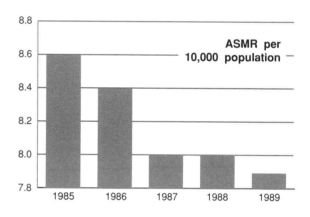

Areas reporting elevated SMRs were widely dispersed, and displayed no obvious geographical pattern. These included Lake Cowichan, Merritt, and Peace River South, which were all in the top decile. New Westminster and Langley in the south, and Prince George in the central interior, also had high mortalities, but these were not in the top decile.

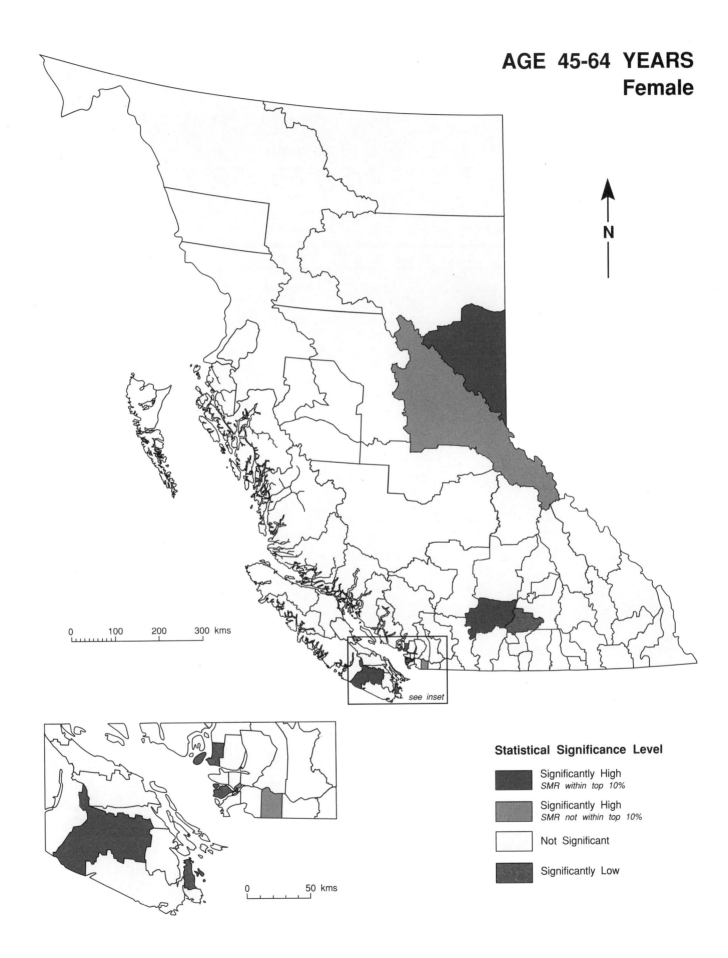

AGE 45-64 YEARS
Female

N

0   100   200   300 kms

see inset

Statistical Significance Level

Significantly High
SMR within top 10%

Significantly High
SMR not within top 10%

Not Significant

Significantly Low

0   50 kms

157

Age 65-84 Years: Male

	Local Health Area	Observed Deaths	Expected Deaths	SMR	(p)	95% C.I. Lower	Upper
17	Princeton	73	48.48	1.51	**	1.18	1.89
85	Vancouver Island North	52	36.61	1.42	*	1.06	1.86
54	Smithers	86	64.23	1.34	*	1.07	1.65
57	Prince George	450	338.68	1.33	***	1.21	1.46
31	Merritt	92	70.38	1.31	*	1.05	1.60
28	Quesnel	187	148.92	1.26	**	1.08	1.45
52	Prince Rupert	111	90.28	1.23	*	1.01	1.48
43	Coquitlam	843	701.50	1.20	***	1.12	1.29
40	New Westminster	672	569.35	1.18	***	1.09	1.27
2	Cranbrook	184	158.06	1.16	*	1.00	1.35
27	Cariboo-Chilcotin	246	211.52	1.16	*	1.02	1.32
72	Campbell River	240	208.19	1.15	*	1.01	1.31
42	Maple Ridge	447	402.91	1.11	*	1.01	1.22
24	Kamloops	653	592.06	1.10	*	1.02	1.19
39	Vancouver	5870	5392.72	1.09	***	1.06	1.12
68	Nanaimo	830	760.03	1.09	*	1.02	1.17
44	North Vancouver	906	843.45	1.07	*	1.01	1.15
22	Vernon	542	590.53	0.92	*	0.84	1.00
61	Greater Victoria	2698	2952.58	0.91	***	0.88	0.95
15	Penticton	516	591.99	0.87	**	0.80	0.95
23	Central Okanagan	1305	1507.72	0.87	***	0.82	0.91
34	Abbotsford	749	871.47	0.86	***	0.80	0.92
77	Summerland	159	191.84	0.83	*	0.70	0.97
62	Sooke	285	346.31	0.82	***	0.73	0.92
20	Salmon Arm	310	400.61	0.77	***	0.69	0.86
45	West Vancouver-Bowen Is	489	642.32	0.76	***	0.70	0.83
63	Saanich	499	653.49	0.76	***	0.70	0.83
64	Gulf Islands	167	221.56	0.75	***	0.64	0.88
4	Windermere	40	59.73	0.67	**	0.48	0.91
6	Kootenay Lake	29	60.18	0.48	***	0.32	0.69

■ Significantly High and SMR within top 10%
■ Significantly High and SMR not within top 10%
■ Significantly Low

During the period 1985 to 1989, there were 31,801 male deaths in the 65 to 84 years age group. ASMRs showed a steady decline from 29.8 to 27.7. Significantly low mortality was restricted to 13 LHAs in the south, notably Vancouver Island (Greater Victoria, Saanich, and Sooke), the Gulf Islands, and the southern interior (Salmon Arm, Summerland, Central Okanagan, Penticton, and Vernon). West Vancouver-Bowen Island and Abbotsford also had significantly low male mortality, but the lowest mortalities were reported for Kootenay Lake and neighbouring Windermere.

Elevated mortality tended to occur in central British Columbia. In total, 17 LHAs recorded significantly high SMRs, with six of these being in the top decile. This latter group included Princeton, Vancouver Island North, Smithers, Prince George, Merritt, and Quesnel.

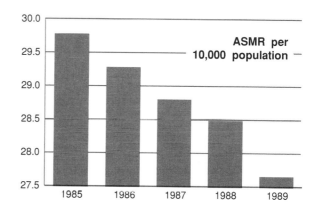

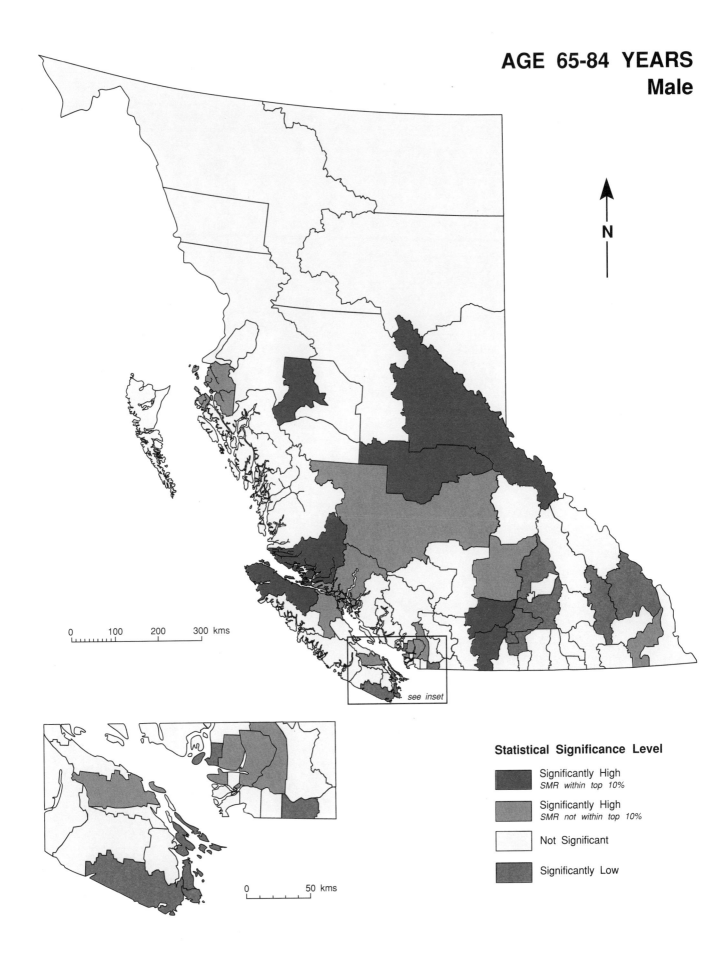

AGE 65-84 YEARS
Male

N

0   100   200   300 kms

see inset

0   50 kms

Statistical Significance Level

Significantly High
SMR within top 10%

Significantly High
SMR not within top 10%

Not Significant

Significantly Low

159

Age 65-84 Years: Female

	Local Health Area	Observed Deaths	Expected Deaths	SMR	(p)	95% C.I. Lower	Upper
80	Kitimat	32	18.23	1.76	**	1.20	2.48
31	Merritt	65	41.43	1.57	***	1.21	2.00
57	Prince George	295	209.19	1.41	***	1.25	1.58
52	Prince Rupert	80	60.14	1.33	*	1.05	1.66
43	Coquitlam	702	554.63	1.27	***	1.17	1.36
70	Alberni	222	179.53	1.24	**	1.08	1.41
27	Cariboo-Chilcotin	140	115.46	1.21	*	1.02	1.43
42	Maple Ridge	343	294.20	1.17	**	1.05	1.30
11	Trail	221	192.70	1.15	*	1.00	1.31
44	North Vancouver	818	744.56	1.10	**	1.02	1.18
41	Burnaby	1463	1364.17	1.07	**	1.02	1.13
61	Greater Victoria	2452	2720.95	0.90	***	0.87	0.94
69	Qualicum	239	276.27	0.87	*	0.76	0.98
34	Abbotsford	520	611.57	0.85	***	0.78	0.93
15	Penticton	348	415.38	0.84	***	0.75	0.93
63	Saanich	349	413.29	0.84	**	0.76	0.94
23	Central Okanagan	803	986.96	0.81	***	0.76	0.87
21	Armstrong-Spallumcheen	41	55.68	0.74	*	0.53	1.00

Significantly High and SMR within top 10%
Significantly High and SMR not within top 10%
Significantly Low

During the period 1985 to 1989, there were 23,969 female deaths in the 65 to 84 years age group, only 75 percent of the number of male deaths. Over this time period, ASMRs showed a generally downward trend from 21.9 to 20.5. While there was less variation in mortality for this age group in females than in males, geographical similarities were still apparent.

Significantly low mortality was again limited to the south of the province, where it was recorded in seven LHAs. These included Central Okanagan, Armstrong-Spallumcheen, and Penticton in the southern interior, and Saanich, Qualicum, and Greater Victoria on Vancouver Island. Abbotsford, located in southwestern British Columbia, also experienced significantly low mortality for females. There was a tendency, also noted in males, for mortality to be elevated in central British Columbia. This was illustrated by the significantly high SMRs, within the top decile, which were reported for Kitimat, Merritt, Prince George, and Prince Rupert.

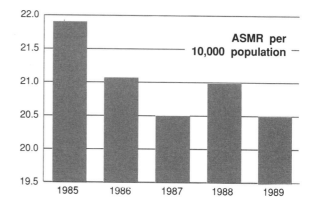

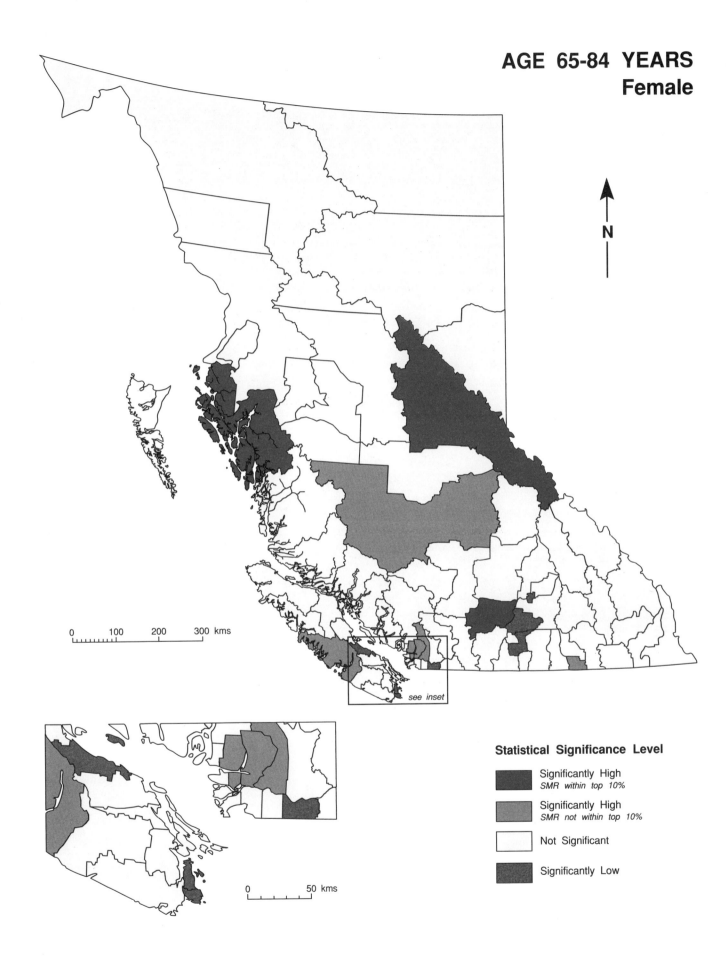

AGE 65-84 YEARS
Female

N

0 100 200 300 kms

see inset

0 50 kms

Statistical Significance Level

Significantly High
SMR within top 10%

Significantly High
SMR not within top 10%

Not Significant

Significantly Low

161

Age 85 Years and Over: Male

	Local Health Area	Observed Deaths	Expected Deaths	SMR	(p)	95% C.I. Lower	Upper
80	Kitimat	7	2.69	2.61	*	1.04	5.37
17	Princeton	21	12.01	1.75	*	1.08	2.67
3	Kimberley	28	16.33	1.71	*	1.14	2.48
2	Cranbrook	47	33.79	1.39	*	1.02	1.85
70	Alberni	58	43.83	1.32	*	1.00	1.71
44	North Vancouver	239	196.67	1.22	**	1.07	1.38
24	Kamloops	180	149.08	1.21	*	1.04	1.40
23	Central Okanagan	372	431.50	0.86	**	0.78	0.95
88	Terrace	29	42.71	0.68	*	0.45	0.98
9	Castlegar	16	27.53	0.58	*	0.33	0.94
28	Quesnel	24	42.97	0.56	**	0.36	0.83

Significantly High and SMR within top 10%
Significantly High and SMR not within top 10%
Significantly Low

During the period 1985 to 1989, there were 9,090 deaths for men aged 85 years and over, and ASMRs showed a generally downward trend from 9.9 to 8.9. Although there was considerable variation in mortality in this age group, areas with significantly high and low SMRs were widely dispersed and it is difficult to identify any clear geographical patterns. For example, elevated mortalities were recorded in seven areas, of which four were in the top decile, namely Kitimat, Princeton, Kimberley, and Cranbrook. In contrast, significantly low mortalities were recorded in Quesnel, Castlegar, Terrace, and Central Okanagan.

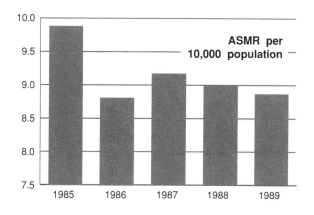

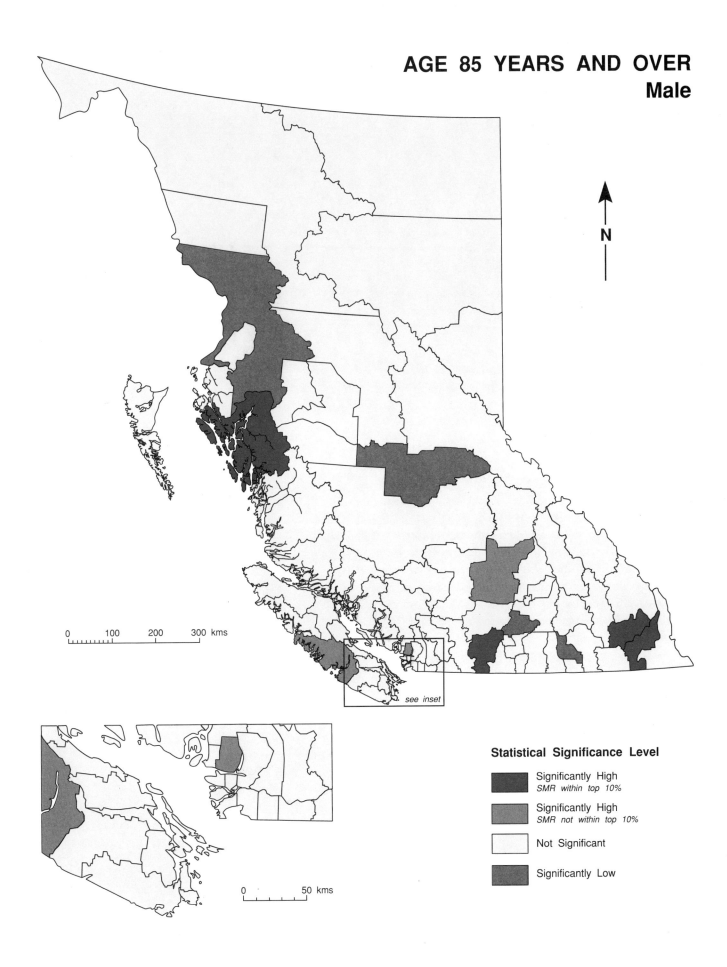

AGE 85 YEARS AND OVER
Male

0   100   200   300 kms

see inset

N

Statistical Significance Level

Significantly High
SMR within top 10%

Significantly High
SMR not within top 10%

Not Significant

Significantly Low

0   50 kms

163

Age 85 Years and Over: Female

	Local Health Area	Observed Deaths	Expected Deaths	SMR	(p)	95% C.I. Lower	95% C.I. Upper
28	Quesnel	54	35.13	1.54	**	1.15	2.01
77	Summerland	104	69.31	1.50	***	1.23	1.82
62	Sooke	143	110.13	1.30	**	1.09	1.53
33	Chilliwack	249	205.91	1.21	**	1.06	1.37
44	North Vancouver	567	485.54	1.17	***	1.07	1.27
37	Delta	284	249.95	1.14	*	1.01	1.28
61	Greater Victoria	2177	2277.67	0.96	*	0.92	1.00
15	Penticton	193	223.89	0.86	*	0.74	0.99
31	Merritt	16	26.52	0.60	*	0.34	0.98
80	Kitimat	6	13.36	0.45	*	0.16	0.98
85	Vancouver Island North	6	13.20	0.45	*	0.17	0.99
6	Kootenay Lake	5	15.84	0.32	**	0.10	0.74

Significantly High and SMR within top 10%
Significantly High and SMR not within top 10%
Significantly Low

During the period 1985 to 1989, there were 15,111 deaths in females who were 85 years and over. This number was 65 percent higher than that for male deaths. Over this period, ASMRs fluctuated in the range 10.7 to 11.5. As with males, areas with significantly high and low SMRs were widely dispersed, making it difficult to identify any clear geographic patterns. Elevated mortality, in the top decile, occurred in Quesnel, Summerland, Sooke, and Chilliwack. In contrast, six LHAs, Penticton, Merritt, Kitimat, Kootenay Lake, Greater Victoria, and Vancouver Island North, reported significantly low female mortality for this age group.

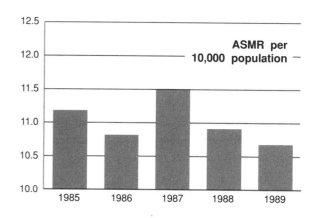

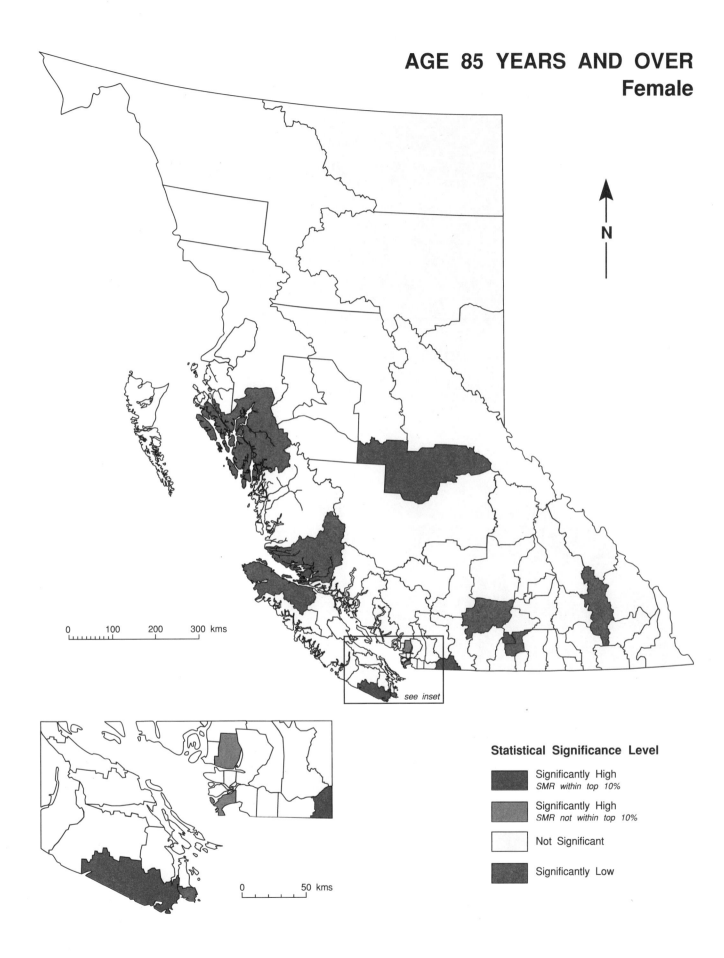

AGE 85 YEARS AND OVER
Female

N

0   100   200   300 kms

see inset

0   50 kms

Statistical Significance Level

Significantly High
SMR within top 10%

Significantly High
SMR not within top 10%

Not Significant

Significantly Low

165

 # REFERENCES

Alberta Premier's Commission on Future Health Care for Albertans (1989a). *The rainbow report: Volume one - Our vision for health.* Edmonton: The Commission.

Alberta Premier's Commission on Future Health Care for Albertans (1989b). *The rainbow report: Volume two - Directions for change.* Edmonton: The Commission.

Alberta Premier's Commission on Future Health Care for Albertans (1989c). *The rainbow report: Volume three - Supplemental information.* Edmonton: The Commission.

Alderson, M.R. (1988). *Mortality, morbidity and health statistics.* Basingstoke: MacMillan.

Band, P.R., Spinelli, J.J., Gallagher, R.P., Threlfall, W.J., Ng, V.T.Y., McBride, M.L., Hislop, T.G., & Coldman, A.J. (1989). *Atlas of cancer mortality in British Columbia 1956-1983.* Ottawa: Statistics Canada.

Barer, M.L., & Stoddart, G.L. (1991). *Toward integrated medical resource policies for Canada* (2 Vols). Vancouver: University of British Columbia, Health Policy Research Unit Centre for Health Services and Policy Research.

Basta, L.L., & Coyle, J.F. (1980). Ischemic heart disease. In H.F. Conn & R.B. Conn (Eds.), *Current diagnosis* (6th ed.), (pp. 345-354). Philadelphia: W.B. Saunders.

Bliss, G., Ho, K., & Foster, L. (1990). Mapping community health information. In J. H. Coward (Ed.), *Proceedings of the third national and the first international conference on information technology in community health* (pp. 38-42). Victoria: University of Victoria Conference Services.

Breslow, N.E., & Day, N.E. (1987). *Statistical methods in cancer research: Vol. II - The design and analysis of cohort studies.* Lyon: International Agency for Research on Cancer.

British Columbia Trade Development Corporation and Industry, Science and Technology Canada (1991). *British Columbia telecommunications 1991: Directory of telecommunication equipment and service suppliers.* Vancouver: British Columbia Trade Development Corporation.

British Columbia Royal Commission on Health Care and Costs (1991). *Closer to home: The report of the British Columbia Royal Commission on health care and costs* (Vols. 1-3). Victoria: Crown Publication Inc.

Canada Health Act (1984). Statutes of Canada, c.6.

Chusid, J. (1983). Vascular diseases of the central nervous system. In M.A. Krupp & M.J. Chatton (Eds.), *Current medical diagnosis & treatment* (pp. 580-582). Los Altos, CA: Lange Medical Publications.

Danderfer, R.J., & Foster, L.T. (Eds.). (1989). *Vital statistics of the Province of British Columbia - 117th annual report (1988)*. Victoria: Ministry of Health, Division of Vital Statistics.

Danderfer, R.J., & Foster, L.T. (Eds.). (1990). *Vital statistics of the Province of British Columbia - 118th annual report (1989)*. Victoria: Ministry of Health, Division of Vital Statistics.

Danderfer, R.J., & Foster, L.T. (Eds.). (1991). *British Columbia vital statistics quarterly digest*. Vol. 1(1 & 2). Victoria: Ministry of Health, Division of Vital Statistics.

Danderfer, R.J., and Foster, L.T. (Eds.). (1992). *Vital statistics of the Province of British Columbia - 119th annual report (1990)*. Victoria: Ministry of Health, Division of Vital Statistics.

Draper, P. (Ed.). (1991). *Health through public policy: The greening of public health*. London: Merlin Press.

Erskine, J.M. (1983). Blood vessels and lymphatics. In M.A. Krupp & M.J. Chatton (Eds.), *Current medical diagnosis & treatment* (pp. 258-288). Los Altos, CA: Lange Medical Publications.

Evans, R.G., & Stoddart, G.L. (1990). Producing health, consuming health care. *Social Science in Medicine*, 31(12), 1347-1363.

Forward, C.N. (Ed.). (1987). *British Columbia: Its resources and people*. Western Geographical Series: Vol. 22. Victoria: University of Victoria, Department of Geography.

Foster, H.D. (1987). Landform and natural hazards. In C.N. Forward (Ed.), *British Columbia: Its resources and people* (pp. 43-63). Western Geographical Series: Vol. 22. Victoria: University of Victoria, Department of Geography.

Foster, L.T., & Danderfer, R.J. (Eds.). (1991). *Mortality in British Columbia: Selected statistical indicators by local health area 1985-1989*. Victoria: Ministry of Health, Division of Vital Statistics.

Foster, L.T., Uh, S.H., & Collison, M.A. (in press). Death in paradise: Considerations and caveats in mapping mortality in British Columbia 1985-1989. In M. Hayes, L.T. Foster, & H.D. Foster (Eds.), *Community, environment, and health: Geographic perspectives*. Western Geographical Series: Vol. 27. Victoria: University of Victoria, Department of Geography.

Fraumeni, J.F., Jr., & Blot, W.J. (1989). Lungs and pleura. In D. Schottenfeld & J.F. Fraumeni (Eds.), *Cancer epidemiology and prevention* (pp. 564-582). Philadelphia: W.B. Saunders.

Friel, J.P. (Ed.) (1974). *Dorland's illustrated medical dictionary* (25th ed.). Philadelphia: W.B. Saunders.

Gardner, M.J., Winter, P.D., Taylor, C.P., & Acheson, E.D. (1979). *Atlas of cancer mortality in England and Wales 1968-1978*. Chichester: Wiley.

Ghadirian, P., Thouez, J.P., PetitClerc, C., Rannou, A., & Beaudoin, Y. (1989). *Cancer incidence: Atlas of the Province of Quebec 1982-1983*. Montreal: Hôpital Hôtel-Dieu de Montréal, Epidemiology Research Unit.

Gilmartin, P.P. (1987). Landmark maps in British Columbia's past. In C.N. Forward (Ed.), *British Columbia: Its resources and people* (pp. 25-42). Western Geographical Series: Vol. 22. Victoria: University of Victoria, Department of Geography.

Health Manpower Research Unit (1990). *Rollcall 89 - A status report of health personnel in the Province of British Columbia* (HMRU 90:30). Vancouver: University of British Columbia.

Health and Welfare Canada and Statistics Canada (1980a). *Mortality atlas of Canada: Vol. 1. Cancer.* Hull: Supply and Services Canada.

Health and Welfare Canada and Statistics Canada (1980b). *Mortality atlas of Canada: Vol. 2. General mortality 1980.* Hull: Supply and Services Canada.

Health and Welfare Canada and Statistics Canada (1984). *Mortality atlas of Canada: Vol. 3. Urban mortality.* Hull: Supply and Services Canada.

Health and Welfare Canada and Statistics Canada (1991). *Mortality atlas of Canada: Vol. 4. General mortality patterns and recent trends.* Hull: Supply and Services Canada.

Karam, J.H. (1983). Diabetes mellitus, hypoglycaemia & lipoprotein disorders. In M.A. Krupp & M.J. Chatton (Eds.), *Current medical diagnosis & treatment* (pp. 743-772). Los Altos, CA: Lange Medical Publications.

Kemp, I., & Boyle, P. (Eds.). (1985). *Atlas of cancer in Scotland (1975-1980): Incidence and epidemiological perspective.* Lyon: IARC Scientific Publications.

Labonte, R. (1991a). Econology: Integrating health and sustainable development. Part one: Theory and background. *Health Promotion International,* 6(1), 49-65.

Labonte, R. (1991b). Econology: Integrating health and sustainable development. Part two: Principles for decision making. *Health Promotion International,* 6(2), 147-156.

Mao, Y., Morrison, H., Nichol, R.D., Pipe, A., & Wigle, D. (1988). The health consequences of smoking among smokers in Canada. *Canadian Journal of Public Health,* 79, 390-391.

Ministry of Finance and Corporate Relations (1990a). *1990 British Columbia economic & statistical review* (50th ed.). Victoria, British Columbia.

Ministry of Finance and Corporate Relations (1990b). *Historical local health area population report.* Unpublished report. Victoria, British Columbia.

Ministry of Finance and Corporate Relations (1991). *1991 British Columbia economic & statistical review,* (51st ed.). Victoria, British Columbia.

Ministry of Health and Social Services (1989). *Improving health and well-being in Quebec.* Montreal, Quebec.

Ministry of Health (1990). *Ministry of Health - 1988/89 annual report.* Victoria, British Columbia.

Ministry of Health (1991). *Ministry of Health - 1989/90 annual report.* Victoria, British Columbia.

Ministry of Regional Development, and Ministry of Finance and Corporate Relations (1989). *British Columbia Regional index.* Victoria, British Columbia.

Ministry of the Provincial Secretary (1990). *Quick facts about British Columbia.* Public Affairs Bureau, Victoria, British Columbia.

National Centre for Health Statistics (NCHS) (1989). *Advance report of final mortality statistics, 1987* 38(5, Supp.). Washington, DC: DHHS Publication, US Government Printing Office.

National Council of Welfare (1990). *Health, health care and medicare* (Autumn, 1990). Ottawa: The Council.

New Brunswick Commission on Selected Health Care Programs (1989). *Report of the Commission on selected health care programs.* Regina: The Commission.

Nova Scotia Royal Commission on Health Care (1988). *Issues and concerns.* Halifax: The Commission.

Nova Scotia Royal Commission on Health Care (1989a). *The report of the Nova Scotia Royal Commission on health care.* Halifax: The Commission.

Nova Scotia Royal Commission on Health Care (1989b). *Research studies of the Nova Scotia Royal Commission on health care.* Halifax: The Commission.

O'Brien, V. (1982). Occupational lung disease. *Your Health*, 11-13, British Columbia Lung Association.

Ontario Premier's Council on Health Strategy (1989a). *A vision of health - Health goals for Ontario (by the Health Goals Committee).* Toronto: The Council.

Ontario Premier's Council on Health Strategy (1989b). *From vision to action (by the Health Care System Committee).* Toronto: The Council.

Ontario Premier's Council on Health Strategy (1990). *Nurturing health - A framework on the determinants of health (A report by the Healthy Public Policy Committee).* Toronto: The Council.

Petrakis, N.L., Ernster, V.L., & King, M.C. (1989). Breast. In D. Schottenfeld & J.F. Fraumeni (Eds.), *Cancer epidemiology and prevention* (pp. 855-870). Philadelphia: W.B. Saunders.

Pickle, L.W., Mason, T.J., Howard, N., Hoover, R., & Fraumeni, J.F. (1987). *Atlas of U.S. cancer mortality among whites 1950-1980.* Washington, DC: DHHS Publication (NIH) 87-2900, US Government Printing Office.

Porter, B. (1991). *The health care system in Canada and its funding: No easy solutions.* The first report of the Standing Committee on health and welfare, social affairs, seniors and the status of women (Reconstituted Committee). Victoria, British Columbia.

Rachlis, M., & Kushner, C. (1989). *Second opinion - What's wrong with Canada's health care system and how to fix it.* Toronto: Collins.

Research Unit in Health and Behavioural Change (1989). *Changing the public health.* Chichester: Wiley.

Rothman, K.J., & Boice, J.D., Jr. (1979). *Epidemiologic analysis with a programmable calculator* (NIH Publication 79-1649). Washington DC: US Government Printing Office.

Saskatchewan Cancer Foundation (1988). *Saskatchewan cancer atlas 1970-1987.* Cancer Registry Report, Regina.

Saskatchewan Commission on Directions in Health Care (1990). *Future directions for health care in Saskatchewan.* Regina: The Commission.

Siler-Wells, G.L. (1988). *Directing change and changing direction: A new health policy agenda for Canada.* Ottawa: Canadian Public Health Association.

Sokolow, M. (1983). Heart and great vessels. In M.A. Krupp & M.J. Chatton (Eds.), *Current medical diagnosis & treatment* (pp. 198-199). Los Altos, CA: Lange Medical Publications.

Stephens, T., & McCullough, R.S. (Eds.) (1991). *Measuring the health of Canadians using population surveys*. Ottawa: National Health Information Council.

Sullivan, T. (1991). Strategic planning for health - How to stay on top of the game. *Health Promotion International*, 30(1), 2-13.

Tan, J., Li, R., & Zhu, W. (1990). Medical geography. In Geographical Society of China, *Recent development of geographical science in China* (pp. 259-279). Beijing: Science Press.

Thomson, A.D. (1990). At home and away: Choices for consumers, providers and managers. *Proceedings of the Pacific Health Forum on New Rules and New Roles: Managing the Evolving Health System* (pp. 177-191). Vancouver: University of British Columbia, Health Care and Epidemiology Alumni Association.

Thomson, M. (1990). Association between mortality and poverty. *British Columbia Medical Journal*, 32(8), 337-338.

Thomson, M., & Philion, J. (1991). Childrens' respiratory hospitalizations and air pollution. *Canadian Journal of Public Health*, 82(3), 203-204.

Thunhurst, C. (1991) Information and public health. In P. Draper (Ed.), *Health through public policy: The greening of public health* (pp. 118-126). London: Merlin Press.

Townsend, P., & Davidson, N. (Eds.) (1982). *Inequalities in health: The Black report*. London: Penguin.

United States General Accounting Office (1991). *Canadian health insurance - Lessons for the United States*. Report to the Chairman, Committee on Government Operations, House of Representatives. Washington, D.C.

Vital Statistics Act (1979). Revised Statues, c. 425, Province of British Columbia, Canada.

Walter, S.D., & Birnie, S.E. (1991). Mapping mortality and morbidity patterns: An international comparison. *International Journal of Epidemiology*, 20(3), 678-689.

Whitehead, M. (1987). *The health divide: Inequalities in health in the 1980s*. London: Health Education Council.

Wigle, D.C., & Mao, Y. (1980). *Mortality by income level in urban Canada*. Ottawa: Ministry of National Health and Welfare, Health Protection Branch.

Wilkins, R., & Adams, O.B. (1983). Health expectancy in Canada, late 1970s: Demographic, regional, and social dimensions. *American Journal of Public Health*, 73(9), 1073 - 1080.

Wilkinson, R.G. (Ed.) (1986). *Class and health: Research and longitudinal data*. London: Tavistock Press.

Wood, C.J.B. (1987). Population and ethnic groups. In C.N. Forward (Ed.), *British Columbia: Its resources and people* (pp. 309-332). Western Geographical Series: Vol. 22. Victoria: University of Victoria, Department of Geography.

World Health Organization (1977). *International classification of diseases, 1975 revision*, (Vol. 1). Geneva: World Health Organization.

APPENDIX

STANDARDIZED MORTALITY RATIOS AND
AGE STANDARDIZED MORTALITY RATES BY LOCAL HEALTH AREA
AND GENDER FOR DISEASE AND AGE CATEGORIES

Soo-Hong Uh and Jemal Mohamed

The Appendix contains tables of the data used in the mapping, and includes the following information for all geographical areas: the observed and expected deaths; the Standardized Mortality Ratio (standardized for age and gender) for the 1985 to 1989 period; the level of significance and confidence interval; and the Age Standardized Mortality Rate (standardized for age and gender) per 10,000 population for each year in the 1985 to 1989 period. Eutsuk, LHA 93, is not included because it has no residential population.

Note that in these tables:

* = p<0.05; ** = p<0.01; *** = p<0.001 significance levels;
C.I. denotes confidence intervals;
+ denotes statistical significance based on less than five deaths;
– denotes SMR or ASMR is 0; and
♦ not applicable or not enough information to make conclusion.

All Causes of Death: Both Genders

	Local Health Area	Observed Deaths	Expected Deaths	SMR	(p)	95% C.I. Lower	Upper	ASMR 1985	1986	1987	1988	1989
1	Fernie	337	338.00	1.00		0.89	1.11	50.1	63.0	54.2	57.8	55.6
2	Cranbrook	586	560.91	1.04		0.96	1.13	72.1	53.4	49.7	51.7	52.3
3	Kimberley	345	322.48	1.07		0.96	1.19	58.6	68.9	53.1	55.2	53.6
4	Windermere	135	179.47	0.75	***	0.63	0.89	51.9	31.3	45.6	41.0	29.4
5	Creston	548	585.46	0.94		0.86	1.02	54.2	45.4	52.9	48.1	51.5
6	Kootenay Lake	106	152.28	0.70	***	0.57	0.84	47.6	37.7	33.7	37.5	54.1
7	Nelson	818	830.99	0.98		0.92	1.05	55.4	58.5	46.5	49.7	53.0
9	Castlegar	383	398.27	0.96		0.87	1.06	58.0	43.0	54.2	44.0	55.5
10	Arrow Lakes	184	196.22	0.94		0.81	1.08	48.7	57.7	57.3	39.2	46.9
11	Trail	898	844.02	1.06		1.00	1.14	57.2	46.1	59.8	55.3	57.3
12	Grand Forks	382	345.83	1.10		1.00	1.22	63.2	57.3	60.8	50.0	59.2
13	Kettle Valley	104	115.05	0.90		0.74	1.10	55.8	48.8	56.8	39.4	66.0
14	Southern Okanagan	817	849.19	0.96		0.90	1.03	50.4	56.5	48.6	53.0	57.3
15	Penticton	1507	1714.87	0.88	***	0.83	0.92	50.6	42.6	49.1	50.8	42.7
16	Keremeos	184	201.31	0.91		0.79	1.06	57.9	58.4	53.2	41.4	52.0
17	Princeton	209	160.67	1.30	***	1.13	1.49	94.7	58.9	62.6	56.2	81.7
18	Golden	135	148.29	0.91		0.76	1.08	50.7	54.4	60.3	45.1	49.2
19	Revelstoke	241	216.79	1.11		0.98	1.26	65.2	51.5	62.7	54.0	67.7
20	Salmon Arm	909	1077.58	0.84	***	0.79	0.90	47.9	48.0	47.3	42.6	43.1
21	Armstrong Spallumcheen	231	274.30	0.84	**	0.74	0.96	48.6	41.7	43.9	49.5	50.9
22	Vernon	1737	1819.97	0.95		0.91	1.00	52.6	55.1	53.9	50.8	45.9
23	Central Okanagan	3768	4374.54	0.86	***	0.83	0.89	44.6	44.1	48.1	47.7	46.7
24	Kamloops	2246	2084.60	1.08	***	1.03	1.12	65.5	53.6	56.7	52.9	58.9
26	North Thompson	117	99.42	1.18		0.97	1.41	79.5	46.5	75.6	56.7	50.6
27	Cariboo-Chilcotin	928	772.15	1.20	***	1.13	1.28	63.4	64.0	49.4	70.1	69.6
28	Quesnel	637	526.51	1.21	***	1.12	1.31	73.5	63.8	63.0	61.6	64.3
29	Lillooet	167	126.75	1.32	***	1.13	1.53	83.8	93.2	76.9	60.0	63.0
30	South Cariboo	252	208.52	1.21	**	1.06	1.37	56.7	58.6	75.2	78.7	66.3
31	Merritt	324	248.82	1.30	***	1.16	1.45	77.9	81.1	68.0	62.3	65.2
32	Hope	255	231.71	1.10		0.97	1.24	60.3	60.4	61.1	66.0	56.3
33	Chilliwack	1981	1938.25	1.02		0.98	1.07	55.5	57.4	50.7	53.1	53.6
34	Abbotsford	2417	2764.10	0.87	***	0.84	0.91	51.1	46.6	47.8	45.5	41.7
35	Langley	2161	2210.74	0.98		0.94	1.02	49.5	57.8	49.7	52.6	51.0
36	Surrey	6764	7071.81	0.96	***	0.93	0.98	53.6	52.5	50.9	48.1	47.1
37	Delta	1925	2047.26	0.94	**	0.90	0.98	53.1	49.2	52.6	44.6	50.8
38	Richmond	2956	3248.65	0.91	***	0.88	0.94	50.8	53.2	46.2	46.6	42.9
39	Vancouver	21111	20022.14	1.05	***	1.04	1.07	57.2	54.6	55.8	56.3	55.3
40	New Westminster	2242	2085.87	1.07	***	1.03	1.12	60.8	54.3	54.8	58.1	59.4
41	Burnaby	6015	6038.26	1.00		0.97	1.02	51.4	52.0	51.7	50.3	49.1
42	Maple Ridge	1582	1463.76	1.08	**	1.03	1.14	65.0	60.8	54.0	56.0	52.5
43	Coquitlam	3087	2936.78	1.05	**	1.01	1.09	61.1	56.8	56.4	54.5	54.4
44	North Vancouver	3451	3380.36	1.02		0.99	1.06	57.1	51.9	52.9	52.8	49.3
45	West Vancouver-Bowen Is	1924	2246.59	0.86	***	0.82	0.90	41.7	42.0	42.0	43.4	41.9
46	Sechelt	796	788.23	1.01		0.94	1.08	53.3	60.3	53.3	49.4	56.7
47	Powell River	709	687.81	1.03		0.96	1.11	55.1	67.7	56.6	50.9	49.3
48	Howe Sound	325	309.96	1.05		0.94	1.17	64.6	62.4	64.5	63.4	34.6
49	Central Coast	115	69.78	1.65	***	1.36	1.98	68.1	102.3	101.6	59.7	72.6
50	Queen Charlotte	120	99.86	1.20		1.00	1.44	78.6	48.9	71.9	80.5	49.3
52	Prince Rupert	486	372.40	1.31	***	1.19	1.43	68.4	69.7	70.9	71.6	61.4
54	Smithers	323	266.18	1.21	***	1.08	1.35	69.9	61.9	57.9	71.7	60.6
55	Burns Lake	203	158.90	1.28	***	1.11	1.47	77.5	79.5	65.1	60.3	61.9
56	Nechako	350	316.73	1.11		0.99	1.23	57.4	54.8	53.0	62.2	58.8
57	Prince George	1812	1479.64	1.22	***	1.17	1.28	70.9	70.1	68.7	59.0	67.1
59	Peace River South	651	602.25	1.08		1.00	1.17	58.4	65.5	57.5	52.2	60.4
60	Peace River North	501	464.76	1.08		0.99	1.18	51.6	57.2	56.1	59.5	64.7
61	Greater Victoria	10111	10793.06	0.94	***	0.92	0.96	49.0	46.7	48.2	49.2	48.6
62	Sooke	1063	1125.48	0.94		0.89	1.00	57.9	55.0	49.8	50.5	43.8
63	Saanich	1577	1893.73	0.83	***	0.79	0.87	43.3	41.5	48.0	42.7	42.9
64	Gulf Islands	481	561.36	0.86	***	0.78	0.94	45.2	45.1	51.7	47.5	48.8
65	Cowichan	1439	1363.17	1.06	*	1.00	1.11	59.2	55.0	54.8	52.9	57.9
66	Lake Cowichan	144	149.46	0.96		0.81	1.13	55.2	27.9	49.6	50.7	69.6
67	Ladysmith	617	567.81	1.09	*	1.00	1.18	58.4	59.5	56.4	58.7	64.2
68	Nanaimo	2492	2326.13	1.07	***	1.03	1.11	56.0	56.6	56.2	56.4	58.5
69	Qualicum	1137	1222.06	0.93	*	0.88	0.99	50.4	53.6	49.3	47.4	51.5
70	Alberni	998	849.83	1.17	***	1.10	1.25	64.5	53.9	67.0	71.5	56.0
71	Courtenay	1367	1357.16	1.01		0.95	1.06	56.5	55.7	51.8	53.5	51.5
72	Campbell River	810	741.81	1.09	*	1.02	1.17	67.5	63.6	54.9	57.9	50.1
75	Mission	891	866.51	1.03		0.96	1.10	60.7	45.8	58.7	58.1	56.4
76	Agassiz-Harrison	178	183.99	0.97		0.83	1.12	38.4	47.3	43.8	59.7	67.7
77	Summerland	530	542.30	0.98		0.90	1.06	46.6	64.6	59.1	47.4	39.1
78	Enderby	256	235.84	1.09		0.96	1.23	68.5	55.4	53.0	65.4	70.1
80	Kitimat	212	181.04	1.17	*	1.02	1.34	58.3	87.2	54.7	57.7	72.4
81	Fort Nelson	68	61.15	1.11		0.86	1.41	22.5	40.0	68.7	73.7	102.8
84	Vancouver Island West	48	44.68	1.07		0.79	1.42	54.7	76.8	93.0	86.4	39.0
85	Vancouver Island North	265	207.59	1.28	***	1.13	1.44	51.1	72.0	67.6	50.6	78.3
87	Stikine	34	26.98	1.26		0.87	1.76	67.0	80.1	45.6	50.7	2.8
88	Terrace	528	449.70	1.17	***	1.08	1.28	57.4	63.4	72.9	61.4	58.2
92	Nishga	39	28.41	1.37		0.98	1.88	23.3	79.8	96.7	126.6	49.2
94	Telegraph Creek	17	11.41	1.49		0.87	2.39	81.7	23.7	53.9	57.1	75.7
	Provincial Total	108,876	◆	1.00		◆	◆	54.6	52.9	52.5	52.4	51.5

All Causes of Death: Male

	Local Health Area	Observed Deaths	Expected Deaths	SMR	(p)	95% C.I. Lower	95% C.I. Upper	ASMR 1985	1986	1987	1988	1989
1	Fernie	197	210.76	0.93		0.81	1.07	53.6	57.9	54.7	70.0	61.5
2	Cranbrook	340	315.79	1.08		0.97	1.20	81.5	65.2	62.3	66.5	61.1
3	Kimberley	184	180.10	1.02		0.88	1.18	73.4	79.9	72.7	45.5	74.0
4	Windermere	78	117.97	0.66	***	0.52	0.83	47.9	38.2	40.2	35.6	39.5
5	Creston	317	351.86	0.90		0.80	1.01	52.7	53.9	57.5	49.4	65.1
6	Kootenay Lake	62	92.34	0.67	**	0.51	0.86	58.1	50.2	44.7	41.5	62.0
7	Nelson	463	472.06	0.98		0.89	1.07	59.9	64.3	57.5	56.8	63.4
9	Castlegar	224	231.59	0.97		0.84	1.10	58.2	63.1	65.5	48.0	62.1
10	Arrow Lakes	110	112.33	0.98		0.80	1.18	63.5	50.1	61.4	61.0	60.8
11	Trail	487	485.40	1.00		0.92	1.10	67.9	64.4	73.5	59.7	79.7
12	Grand Forks	233	206.25	1.13		0.99	1.28	65.1	54.8	71.3	42.5	76.0
13	Kettle Valley	73	79.84	0.91		0.72	1.15	63.4	66.1	64.3	62.8	65.5
14	Southern Okanagan	503	496.96	1.01		0.93	1.10	52.6	46.8	59.6	63.2	50.4
15	Penticton	849	958.96	0.89	***	0.83	0.95	62.1	76.3	69.1	39.9	55.9
16	Keremeos	119	130.43	0.91		0.76	1.09	140.8	79.5	78.8	69.5	101.9
17	Princeton	139	92.35	1.51	***	1.27	1.78	45.6	75.5	53.8	59.0	50.0
18	Golden	82	96.51	0.85		0.68	1.05	89.0	53.9	79.3	50.4	69.5
19	Revelstoke	134	123.71	1.08		0.91	1.28	51.0	49.7	60.1	51.1	46.0
20	Salmon Arm	537	651.55	0.82	***	0.76	0.90	64.2	49.5	52.3	59.8	59.7
21	Armstrong-Spallumcheen	143	165.50	0.86		0.73	1.02	58.7	64.9	65.0	57.8	50.4
22	Vernon	989	1046.60	0.94		0.89	1.01	50.4	52.9	55.9	53.9	52.4
23	Central Okanagan	2183	2533.46	0.86	***	0.83	0.90	85.3	61.7	68.3	61.0	67.2
24	Kamloops	1362	1222.66	1.11	***	1.06	1.17	86.9	40.9	78.2	62.2	55.2
26	North Thompson	69	63.43	1.09		0.85	1.38	74.1	68.9	62.5	80.4	73.9
27	Cariboo-Chilcotin	586	486.71	1.20	***	1.11	1.31	87.2	69.3	62.6	69.2	75.2
28	Quesnel	404	336.62	1.20	***	1.09	1.32	137.5	90.0	70.0	53.4	63.3
29	Lillooet	103	83.26	1.24	*	1.01	1.50	77.0	61.6	75.3	95.2	76.0
30	South Cariboo	163	135.09	1.21	*	1.03	1.41	96.4	102.8	77.4	55.3	83.0
31	Merritt	198	150.92	1.31	***	1.14	1.51	70.7	80.9	64.5	83.7	65.6
32	Hope	164	144.71	1.13		0.97	1.32	67.6	65.9	55.1	60.6	63.3
33	Chilliwack	1128	1110.93	1.02		0.96	1.08	60.3	52.0	55.1	53.7	47.9
34	Abbotsford	1359	1550.88	0.88	***	0.83	0.92	52.8	63.9	56.9	61.0	59.6
35	Langley	1216	1274.09	0.95		0.90	1.01	62.2	59.3	58.9	56.0	55.4
36	Surrey	3808	3982.89	0.96	**	0.93	0.99	59.8	54.9	58.9	49.5	58.6
37	Delta	1012	1134.98	0.89	***	0.84	0.95	57.8	60.7	55.9	52.4	46.9
38	Richmond	1565	1781.66	0.88	***	0.84	0.92	71.3	65.2	67.6	68.5	69.1
39	Vancouver	11270	10201.94	1.10	***	1.08	1.13	77.4	63.6	67.4	73.6	72.0
40	New Westminster	1139	994.53	1.15	***	1.08	1.21	56.4	61.9	59.8	59.1	56.5
41	Burnaby	3034	3109.58	0.98		0.94	1.01	76.6	70.4	61.8	66.8	61.2
42	Maple Ridge	878	808.61	1.09	*	1.02	1.16	67.1	64.3	64.3	61.3	59.8
43	Coquitlam	1663	1666.01	1.00		0.95	1.05	63.8	61.0	61.3	60.7	56.0
44	North Vancouver	1698	1756.00	0.97		0.92	1.01	46.5	42.1	43.3	43.7	44.8
45	West Vancouver-Bowen Is	826	1111.49	0.74	***	0.69	0.80	61.2	62.0	57.3	60.2	63.8
46	Sechelt	453	463.92	0.98		0.89	1.07	67.1	85.9	62.0	61.5	56.8
47	Powell River	422	393.31	1.07		0.97	1.18	80.9	69.0	84.3	77.0	37.6
48	Howe Sound	213	194.17	1.10		0.95	1.25	87.6	104.5	128.7	89.3	75.3
49	Central Coast	81	47.32	1.71	***	1.36	2.13	84.1	56.7	67.2	81.6	51.6
50	Queen Charlotte	76	66.09	1.15		0.91	1.44	71.6	86.1	74.4	86.4	75.4
52	Prince Rupert	303	228.76	1.32	***	1.18	1.48	80.6	69.1	73.8	102.4	71.2
54	Smithers	211	163.16	1.29	***	1.12	1.48	81.1	83.3	78.6	73.5	71.1
55	Burns Lake	137	105.69	1.30	**	1.09	1.53	74.1	64.1	67.1	65.2	66.3
56	Nechako	234	202.35	1.16	*	1.01	1.31	78.6	79.5	76.5	73.9	77.0
57	Prince George	1136	929.50	1.22	***	1.15	1.30	64.8	77.1	57.7	58.0	74.1
59	Peace River South	403	373.69	1.08		0.98	1.19	62.5	60.6	67.8	69.3	71.7
60	Peace River North	327	297.17	1.10		0.98	1.23	58.0	56.2	58.0	57.1	58.2
61	Greater Victoria	4848	5144.26	0.94	***	0.92	0.97	54.6	50.6	47.3	57.2	46.4
62	Sooke	560	667.36	0.84	***	0.77	0.91	50.8	49.9	51.5	47.0	44.8
63	Saanich	846	1075.42	0.79	***	0.73	0.84	50.9	44.0	66.2	47.2	56.2
64	Gulf Islands	266	331.55	0.80	***	0.71	0.90	66.9	64.2	55.6	65.4	66.0
65	Cowichan	789	775.43	1.02		0.95	1.09	55.1	25.0	51.6	56.6	68.6
66	Lake Cowichan	78	93.21	0.84		0.66	1.04	61.6	69.1	55.8	62.5	78.0
67	Ladysmith	351	336.92	1.04		0.94	1.16	59.3	58.1	66.6	65.0	64.9
68	Nanaimo	1402	1316.00	1.07	*	1.01	1.12	57.2	60.9	51.1	53.4	58.8
69	Qualicum	656	716.22	0.92	*	0.85	0.99	77.9	68.5	77.2	82.5	58.0
70	Alberni	573	493.37	1.16	***	1.07	1.26	62.6	67.8	59.8	61.4	55.1
71	Courtenay	784	785.36	1.00		0.93	1.07	88.9	80.1	64.3	69.5	57.1
72	Campbell River	496	437.34	1.13	**	1.04	1.24	67.8	53.7	65.7	71.0	63.4
75	Mission	525	511.58	1.03		0.94	1.12	37.9	68.1	53.2	52.0	77.4
76	Agassiz-Harrison	111	115.06	0.96		0.79	1.16	47.7	75.0	70.3	42.7	39.0
77	Summerland	278	313.87	0.89	*	0.78	1.00	90.8	62.2	66.4	66.2	82.6
78	Enderby	157	142.94	1.10		0.93	1.28	39.3	70.4	59.0	56.9	98.8
80	Kitimat	130	113.73	1.14		0.96	1.36	20.0	40.6	109.6	63.6	97.6
81	Fort Nelson	40	42.30	0.95		0.68	1.29	68.1	70.0	65.4	87.9	48.2
84	Vancouver Island West	29	29.14	1.00		0.67	1.43	57.1	111.4	88.2	56.2	96.6
85	Vancouver Island North	190	132.78	1.43	***	1.23	1.65	77.4	56.9	63.8	64.5	4.9
87	Stikine	25	18.55	1.35		0.87	1.99	55.0	70.6	84.7	68.7	61.1
88	Terrace	341	300.51	1.13	*	1.02	1.26	40.0	66.3	140.4	195.5	50.8
92	Nishga	27	19.22	1.40		0.93	2.04	59.2	-	35.5	52.9	79.8
94	Telegraph Creek	8	7.22	1.11		0.48	2.18					
	Provincial Total	**59,656**	◆	**1.00**		◆	◆	**63.7**	**61.3**	**61.1**	**60.7**	**59.9**

175

All Causes of Death: Female

	Local Health Area	Observed Deaths	Expected Deaths	SMR	(p)	95% C.I. Lower	95% C.I. Upper	ASMR 1985	1986	1987	1988	1989
1	Fernie	140	127.24	1.10		0.93	1.30	45.5	68.2	54.2	42.7	47.4
2	Cranbrook	246	245.12	1.00		0.88	1.14	61.8	43.5	37.7	42.7	45.2
3	Kimberley	161	142.38	1.13		0.96	1.32	43.4	67.5	38.8	64.8	39.8
4	Windermere	57	61.50	0.93		0.70	1.20	55.7	17.0	52.1	49.6	16.1
5	Creston	231	233.60	0.99		0.87	1.12	54.4	33.9	48.0	47.0	37.3
6	Kootenay Lake	44	59.94	0.73	*	0.53	0.99	37.0	22.7	23.5	34.6	48.5
7	Nelson	355	358.93	0.99		0.89	1.10	50.1	51.1	34.8	42.3	41.8
9	Castlegar	159	166.68	0.95		0.81	1.11	49.4	40.6	38.5	44.9	39.9
10	Arrow Lakes	74	83.89	0.88		0.69	1.11	36.4	54.4	49.0	29.5	27.5
11	Trail	411	358.62	1.15	**	1.04	1.26	50.0	42.4	57.6	49.6	53.5
12	Grand Forks	149	139.59	1.07		0.90	1.25	56.6	49.5	47.7	39.1	36.9
13	Kettle Valley	31	35.21	0.88		0.60	1.25	42.4	22.9	36.0	25.9	51.6
14	Southern Okanagan	314	352.24	0.89	*	0.80	1.00	34.8	47.2	32.2	42.5	48.7
15	Penticton	658	755.91	0.87	***	0.81	0.94	48.9	38.4	38.4	39.2	35.9
16	Keremeos	65	70.87	0.92		0.71	1.17	50.1	34.9	37.6	38.9	50.3
17	Princeton	70	68.32	1.02		0.80	1.29	43.1	47.9	46.0	38.0	61.4
18	Golden	53	51.78	1.02		0.77	1.34	86.1	34.4	76.7	32.5	52.4
19	Revelstoke	107	93.08	1.15		0.94	1.39	55.2	47.7	44.7	59.2	67.2
20	Salmon Arm	372	426.03	0.87	**	0.79	0.97	43.8	45.0	34.0	33.9	39.6
21	Armstrong-Spallumcheen	88	108.80	0.81	*	0.65	1.00	33.7	33.3	34.3	37.7	41.5
22	Vernon	748	773.37	0.97		0.90	1.04	46.5	44.7	42.8	43.5	41.1
23	Central Okanagan	1585	1841.09	0.86	***	0.82	0.90	38.5	34.8	39.7	41.0	40.7
24	Kamloops	884	861.95	1.03		0.96	1.10	45.0	44.9	44.8	44.4	50.2
26	North Thompson	48	36.00	1.33		0.98	1.77	73.8	57.2	68.3	42.9	41.5
27	Cariboo-Chilcotin	342	285.44	1.20	**	1.07	1.33	49.5	55.3	33.4	57.1	64.2
28	Quesnel	233	189.89	1.23	**	1.07	1.40	56.0	57.1	64.7	52.9	52.5
29	Lillooet	64	43.50	1.47	**	1.13	1.88	30.5	86.8	88.8	64.3	71.8
30	South Cariboo	89	73.43	1.21		0.97	1.49	30.8	46.1	76.8	56.6	53.5
31	Merritt	126	97.90	1.29	**	1.07	1.53	59.3	56.1	59.7	71.9	46.3
32	Hope	91	87.01	1.05		0.84	1.28	45.8	36.7	54.2	47.9	46.0
33	Chilliwack	853	827.32	1.03		0.96	1.10	43.6	48.9	46.2	45.6	44.5
34	Abbotsford	1058	1213.22	0.87	***	0.82	0.93	41.7	40.8	40.6	37.2	35.8
35	Langley	945	936.65	1.01		0.95	1.08	46.4	51.7	42.1	44.2	43.0
36	Surrey	2956	3088.92	0.96	*	0.92	0.99	45.4	46.0	43.2	40.5	39.4
37	Delta	913	912.28	1.00		0.94	1.07	48.2	45.8	46.3	39.4	43.9
38	Richmond	1391	1466.99	0.95	*	0.90	1.00	45.0	47.7	38.7	42.0	39.6
39	Vancouver	9841	9820.20	1.00		0.98	1.02	45.2	45.6	45.7	45.9	43.3
40	New Westminster	1103	1091.34	1.01		0.95	1.07	49.2	47.9	46.4	46.5	50.9
41	Burnaby	2981	2928.68	1.02		0.98	1.06	47.9	43.9	45.6	43.1	43.5
42	Maple Ridge	704	655.15	1.07		1.00	1.16	54.3	52.8	45.9	45.7	44.2
43	Coquitlam	1424	1270.77	1.12	***	1.06	1.18	56.1	50.7	49.4	48.7	49.8
44	North Vancouver	1753	1624.36	1.08	**	1.03	1.13	53.4	45.6	47.4	48.0	44.6
45	West Vancouver-Bowen Is	1098	1135.10	0.97		0.91	1.03	38.5	42.0	41.6	43.9	40.7
46	Sechelt	343	324.30	1.06		0.95	1.18	44.3	58.4	49.0	38.4	48.3
47	Powell River	287	294.50	0.97		0.87	1.09	41.4	48.9	51.3	40.1	41.8
48	Howe Sound	112	115.80	0.97		0.80	1.16	46.4	52.8	45.6	47.7	30.2
49	Central Coast	34	22.46	1.51	*	1.05	2.12	45.3	110.4	73.2	20.0	76.8
50	Queen Charlotte	44	33.76	1.30		0.95	1.75	72.6	45.5	76.2	78.7	43.2
52	Prince Rupert	183	143.63	1.27	**	1.10	1.47	64.3	50.1	65.4	54.6	44.7
54	Smithers	112	103.02	1.09		0.90	1.31	56.8	57.2	41.4	40.0	50.3
55	Burns Lake	66	53.21	1.24		0.96	1.58	47.9	80.8	41.3	53.9	44.5
56	Nechako	116	114.38	1.01		0.84	1.22	40.0	42.6	34.3	60.6	49.8
57	Prince George	676	550.14	1.23	***	1.14	1.32	62.7	58.4	59.2	42.1	56.2
59	Peace River South	248	228.56	1.09		0.95	1.23	49.8	49.6	57.3	45.5	44.1
60	Peace River North	174	167.60	1.04		0.89	1.20	37.2	49.8	38.8	47.6	56.4
61	Greater Victoria	5263	5648.80	0.93	***	0.91	0.96	43.0	40.1	40.9	43.6	41.4
62	Sooke	503	458.12	1.10	*	1.00	1.20	60.7	57.5	52.2	44.0	39.6
63	Saanich	731	818.32	0.89	**	0.83	0.96	35.6	33.3	44.7	37.7	41.3
64	Gulf Islands	215	229.82	0.94		0.81	1.07	38.2	47.7	36.5	46.8	41.9
65	Cowichan	650	587.74	1.11	*	1.02	1.19	51.4	45.3	53.7	50.5	49.4
66	Lake Cowichan	66	56.25	1.17		0.91	1.49	60.2	28.5	44.3	42.5	74.2
67	Ladysmith	266	230.90	1.15	*	1.02	1.30	54.4	50.3	56.9	53.9	48.6
68	Nanaimo	1090	1010.13	1.08	*	1.02	1.15	53.0	44.4	45.6	48.4	52.7
69	Qualicum	481	505.84	0.95		0.87	1.04	42.0	43.8	45.9	40.6	43.9
70	Alberni	425	356.46	1.19	***	1.08	1.31	50.8	39.2	58.2	61.6	53.8
71	Courtenay	583	571.80	1.02		0.94	1.11	49.4	43.1	43.4	45.3	48.1
72	Campbell River	314	304.47	1.03		0.92	1.15	49.7	49.9	45.5	45.8	42.2
75	Mission	366	354.93	1.03		0.93	1.14	53.5	36.9	49.4	43.9	48.4
76	Agassiz-Harrison	67	68.92	0.97		0.75	1.23	38.3	26.8	33.7	68.3	52.7
77	Summerland	252	228.43	1.10		0.97	1.25	46.4	52.5	47.2	52.6	39.0
78	Enderby	99	92.90	1.07		0.87	1.30	42.4	50.1	38.2	67.4	55.7
80	Kitimat	82	67.31	1.22		0.97	1.51	77.8	52.6	51.0	63.8	47.3
81	Fort Nelson	28	18.85	1.49		0.99	2.15	24.5	28.2	23.1	90.3	82.1
84	Vancouver Island West	19	15.54	1.22		0.74	1.91	55.2	23.8	80.2	45.9	10.4
85	Vancouver Island North	75	74.80	1.00		0.79	1.26	22.5	42.2	44.7	45.1	53.8
87	Stikine	9	8.42	1.07		0.49	2.03	10.7	01.3	61.2	17.0	-
88	Terrace	187	149.19	1.25	**	1.08	1.45	60.4	50.3	57.7	53.1	49.5
92	Nishga	12	9.19	1.31		0.67	2.28	à	50.9	67.8	44.1	47.0
94	Telegraph Creek	9	4.18	2.15		0.98	4.08	123.2	58.4	38.4	57.7	52.8
	Provincial Total	**49,220**	♦	1.00		♦	♦	46.1	45.0	44.4	44.6	43.7

All Cancer Sites: Male

	Local Health Area	Observed Deaths	Expected Deaths	SMR (p)	95% C.I. Lower	Upper	ASMR 1985	1986	1987	1988	1989
1	Fernie	46	51.58	0.89	0.65	1.19	14.3	11.7	19.6	21.0	9.9
2	Cranbrook	63	81.16	0.78 *	0.60	0.99	15.1	12.3	10.7	13.2	8.5
3	Kimberley	47	49.19	0.96	0.70	1.27	19.4	19.9	12.2	11.4	10.2
4	Windermere	21	30.96	0.68	0.42	1.04	13.2	7.2	13.9	11.1	4.5
5	Creston	87	91.44	0.95	0.76	1.17	9.2	11.3	19.3	16.3	22.1
6	Kootenay Lake	15	25.40	0.59 *	0.33	0.97	13.1	4.0	3.0	3.7	15.6
7	Nelson	126	122.32	1.03	0.86	1.23	19.2	15.5	18.7	13.4	14.4
9	Castlegar	70	61.45	1.14	0.89	1.44	18.5	11.8	19.3	13.3	25.9
10	Arrow Lakes	20	29.02	0.69	0.42	1.06	4.2	7.2	6.8	19.5	17.7
11	Trail	139	127.23	1.09	0.92	1.29	17.0	10.9	20.6	20.1	15.9
12	Grand Forks	57	55.26	1.03	0.78	1.34	17.2	14.3	13.9	12.8	16.9
13	Kettle Valley	20	21.09	0.95	0.58	1.46	11.3	15.8	17.8	7.4	20.4
14	Southern Okanagan	132	132.73	0.99	0.83	1.18	15.0	15.3	19.7	16.7	17.8
15	Penticton	228	249.67	0.91	0.80	1.04	11.4	13.3	13.8	16.9	14.5
16	Keremeos	31	35.54	0.87	0.59	1.24	5.7	19.9	26.2	4.6	17.2
17	Princeton	34	24.93	1.36	0.94	1.91	38.3	13.5	32.6	13.9	13.8
18	Golden	21	23.58	0.89	0.55	1.36	18.2	7.2	7.5	21.7	19.6
19	Revelstoke	38	30.82	1.23	0.87	1.69	26.7	17.1	28.2	13.1	9.6
20	Salmon Arm	139	178.45	0.78 **	0.65	0.92	8.8	12.7	15.5	9.9	12.8
21	Armstrong-Spallumcheen	26	43.23	0.60 **	0.39	0.88	17.1	12.9	8.3	3.2	8.9
22	Vernon	227	271.25	0.84 **	0.73	0.95	13.4	17.5	10.3	11.4	11.8
23	Central Okanagan	617	666.10	0.93	0.85	1.00	12.6	13.9	14.5	15.1	14.6
24	Kamloops	350	315.35	1.11	1.00	1.23	21.4	15.7	15.3	15.0	18.0
26	North Thompson	19	16.35	1.16	0.70	1.81	15.3	5.3	28.9	25.7	16.8
27	Cariboo-Chilcotin	140	126.42	1.11	0.93	1.31	15.8	16.3	19.7	18.9	14.2
28	Quesnel	83	84.64	0.98	0.78	1.22	23.3	11.0	13.6	14.7	13.4
29	Lillooet	16	21.15	0.76	0.43	1.23	19.5	33.4	6.6	-	3.0
30	South Cariboo	36	34.76	1.04	0.73	1.43	18.2	8.6	11.2	25.1	17.8
31	Merritt	47	39.43	1.19	0.88	1.59	31.1	16.2	22.4	3.5	24.4
32	Hope	38	39.68	0.96	0.68	1.31	22.5	22.7	9.4	11.4	10.0
33	Chilliwack	288	290.61	0.99	0.88	1.11	12.5	17.9	14.7	14.6	16.1
34	Abbotsford	329	394.20	0.83 ***	0.75	0.93	12.9	12.4	10.7	15.1	12.7
35	Langley	340	325.75	1.04	0.94	1.16	14.8	15.7	17.2	15.3	17.5
36	Surrey	982	1021.22	0.96	0.90	1.02	15.5	15.1	14.6	13.2	15.5
37	Delta	299	295.39	1.01	0.90	1.13	15.4	16.6	12.5	15.6	18.6
38	Richmond	445	468.89	0.95	0.86	1.04	16.7	17.0	11.8	14.7	12.9
39	Vancouver	2802	2583.23	1.08 ***	1.04	1.13	18.5	15.9	16.5	16.9	16.9
40	New Westminster	290	253.65	1.14 *	1.02	1.28	15.2	16.8	18.4	19.7	16.8
41	Burnaby	756	807.43	0.94	0.87	1.01	14.8	14.9	14.1	14.1	13.9
42	Maple Ridge	228	203.73	1.12	0.90	1.27	17.6	15.0	15.7	16.8	17.8
43	Coquitlam	447	417.84	1.07	0.97	1.17	17.6	15.0	15.7	16.8	17.8
44	North Vancouver	470	464.04	1.01	0.92	1.11	16.2	15.6	15.2	15.7	16.4
45	West Vancouver-Bowen Is	248	300.54	0.83 **	0.73	0.93	12.5	13.1	10.1	13.6	13.3
46	Sechelt	136	126.80	1.07	0.90	1.27	13.5	20.9	14.8	16.2	16.2
47	Powell River	108	102.58	1.05	0.86	1.27	15.1	23.3	10.9	14.6	17.7
48	Howe Sound	42	49.86	0.84	0.61	1.14	20.2	18.8	11.7	11.5	6.5
49	Central Coast	10	12.24	0.82	0.39	1.50	18.3	13.1	5.8	16.2	6.9
50	Queen Charlotte	18	14.85	1.21	0.72	1.92	32.5	23.4	26.1	15.2	-
52	Prince Rupert	62	55.14	1.12	0.86	1.44	10.8	18.1	20.0	16.8	19.2
54	Smithers	41	39.56	1.04	0.74	1.41	12.8	6.9	15.9	16.9	27.1
55	Burns Lake	29	26.04	1.11	0.75	1.60	24.5	20.6	20.8	11.7	8.2
56	Nechako	47	49.80	0.94	0.69	1.25	8.2	13.8	16.8	10.4	21.5
57	Prince George	254	228.32	1.11	0.98	1.26	21.6	20.0	14.4	18.6	14.7
59	Peace River South	72	90.92	0.79 *	0.62	1.00	9.1	14.3	10.2	13.4	13.2
60	Peace River North	55	71.20	0.77	0.58	1.01	13.0	9.5	13.9	9.5	11.8
61	Greater Victoria	1282	1290.99	0.99	0.94	1.05	15.8	16.2	15.2	15.5	16.1
62	Sooke	180	177.21	1.02	0.87	1.18	14.6	14.9	14.2	20.3	13.0
63	Saanich	281	298.40	0.94	0.83	1.06	10.7	18.3	13.5	14.3	14.0
64	Gulf Islands	75	93.56	0.80	0.63	1.00	10.0	13.4	19.8	7.2	14.2
65	Cowichan	215	204.15	1.05	0.92	1.20	13.5	19.2	13.7	16.1	17.1
66	Lake Cowichan	20	25.08	0.80	0.49	1.23	7.9	8.1	12.5	13.7	21.2
67	Ladysmith	88	89.98	0.98	0.78	1.20	10.6	15.0	11.8	18.7	16.9
68	Nanaimo	389	351.70	1.11	1.00	1.22	12.9	19.8	15.1	18.6	17.2
69	Qualicum	186	201.46	0.92	0.80	1.07	16.0	15.8	15.7	10.4	13.0
70	Alberni	147	130.73	1.12	0.95	1.32	21.2	14.3	21.2	21.2	15.2
71	Courtenay	220	207.99	1.06	0.92	1.21	14.1	16.2	18.0	15.4	17.6
72	Campbell River	140	114.46	1.22 *	1.03	1.44	21.5	18.9	16.0	15.7	21.1
75	Mission	145	131.91	1.10	0.93	1.29	17.3	16.2	22.0	12.4	17.2
76	Agassiz-Harrison	32	30.27	1.06	0.72	1.49	18.4	12.4	12.3	11.0	25.8
77	Summerland	67	81.33	0.82	0.64	1.05	10.7	10.3	21.3	8.2	14.3
78	Enderby	32	36.98	0.87	0.59	1.22	11.2	10.5	18.9	5.5	21.7
80	Kitimat	35	28.54	1.23	0.85	1.71	17.4	18.1	24.8	8.0	36.8
81	Fort Nelson	14	9.11	1.54	0.84	2.58	14.4	36.0	-	33.0	31.1
84	Vancouver Island West	11	6.47	1.70	0.85	3.04	12.2	10.4	33.2	69.2	22.9
85	Vancouver Island North	38	30.83	1.23	0.87	1.69	13.3	26.6	22.5	20.7	28.2
87	Stikine	1	4.35	0.23	0.00	1.28	-	-	-	♦	-
88	Terrace	65	71.47	0.91	0.70	1.16	11.4	18.2	21.0	15.6	5.1
92	Nishga	3	4.39	0.68	0.14	1.99	-	-	-	64.1	-
94	Telegraph Creek	0	1.80	-	-	-	-	-	-	-	-
	Provincial Total	**15,399**	♦	**1.00**	♦	♦	15.6	15.6	15.0	15.2	15.4

177

All Cancer Sites: Female

	Local Health Area	Observed Deaths	Expected Deaths	SMR (p)	95% C.I. Lower	95% C.I. Upper	ASMR 1985	1986	1987	1988	1989
1	Fernie	36	36.54	0.99	0.69	1.36	8.9	12.8	14.2	11.1	15.7
2	Cranbrook	54	68.16	0.79	0.60	1.03	8.2	7.2	13.9	7.2	14.1
3	Kimberley	52	39.85	1.30	0.97	1.71	9.0	17.9	13.7	23.2	17.1
4	Windermere	20	19.88	1.01	0.61	1.55	15.9	3.2	17.1	21.7	5.6
5	Creston	64	64.06	1.00	0.77	1.28	14.4	5.8	18.7	11.1	14.2
6	Kootenay Lake	17	16.76	1.01	0.59	1.62	11.5	2.7	20.9	10.2	24.2
7	Nelson	89	95.19	0.93	0.75	1.15	13.8	13.7	8.7	12.2	10.0
9	Castlegar	50	47.13	1.06	0.79	1.40	17.8	16.6	10.1	10.3	15.0
10	Arrow Lakes	12	21.35	0.56 *	0.29	0.98	4.7	10.6	11.2	5.8	-
11	Trail	94	100.41	0.94	0.76	1.15	12.7	12.9	13.5	9.0	11.2
12	Grand Forks	35	39.76	0.88	0.61	1.22	13.5	5.5	10.3	10.2	15.6
13	Kettle Valley	11	11.54	0.95	0.48	1.71	38.1	4.6	4.4	8.0	3.8
14	Southern Okanagan	63	96.47	0.65 ***	0.50	0.84	4.5	10.3	4.6	11.1	8.7
15	Penticton	204	201.47	1.01	0.88	1.16	12.2	14.0	12.7	12.8	12.8
16	Keremeos	20	20.36	0.98	0.60	1.52	7.9	13.3	7.9	6.7	21.4
17	Princeton	16	18.79	0.85	0.49	1.38	8.3	4.4	9.7	5.0	24.8
18	Golden	13	15.49	0.84	0.45	1.44	38.5	-	18.7	-	10.6
19	Revelstoke	35	24.98	1.40	0.98	1.95	14.1	16.2	17.4	21.9	23.5
20	Salmon Arm	108	124.81	0.87	0.71	1.04	11.7	11.5	9.2	10.4	12.7
21	Armstrong-Spallumcheen	24	30.85	0.78	0.50	1.16	10.9	14.2	10.1	5.3	8.9
22	Vernon	208	212.47	0.98	0.85	1.12	14.3	12.7	8.2	14.2	12.5
23	Central Okanagan	464	515.00	0.90 *	0.82	0.99	10.2	9.5	11.0	12.0	14.3
24	Kamloops	238	249.53	0.95	0.84	1.08	11.5	11.6	11.7	11.2	14.6
26	North Thompson	17	11.20	1.52	0.88	2.43	31.6	15.9	22.4	5.4	23.8
27	Cariboo-Chilcotin	111	88.48	1.25 *	1.03	1.51	18.1	19.4	10.2	14.4	16.7
28	Quesnel	57	58.19	0.98	0.74	1.27	9.9	18.1	10.7	12.2	15.5
29	Lillooet	8	12.48	0.64	0.28	1.26	7.1	18.1	-	9.1	8.8
30	South Cariboo	24	21.88	1.10	0.70	1.63	11.1	8.0	21.4	17.2	9.1
31	Merritt	34	28.01	1.21	0.84	1.70	16.5	10.1	17.6	18.3	12.3
32	Hope	30	27.20	1.10	0.74	1.57	11.1	15.4	8.4	17.4	15.4
33	Chilliwack	238	233.26	1.02	0.89	1.16	8.8	15.2	10.6	17.4	13.2
34	Abbotsford	262	322.61	0.81 ***	0.72	0.92	9.5	10.1	9.4	10.2	12.2
35	Langley	264	261.57	1.01	0.89	1.14	12.1	15.5	12.4	11.1	13.2
36	Surrey	857	859.42	1.00	0.93	1.07	13.2	13.8	12.6	11.6	12.3
37	Delta	281	258.17	1.09	0.96	1.22	16.9	16.1	13.6	11.8	11.8
38	Richmond	442	425.26	1.04	0.94	1.14	14.9	14.8	11.0	13.4	12.3
39	Vancouver	2467	2429.20	1.02	0.98	1.06	12.8	12.6	13.3	13.4	11.6
40	New Westminster	262	268.62	0.98	0.86	1.10	9.8	11.3	12.3	14.8	17.8
41	Burnaby	760	756.23	1.00	0.93	1.08	13.3	12.2	12.4	12.5	13.1
42	Maple Ridge	162	172.38	0.94	0.80	1.10	16.2	11.5	13.7	9.0	10.4
43	Coquitlam	417	365.85	1.14 **	1.03	1.25	15.9	14.6	12.3	17.8	12.8
44	North Vancouver	462	448.78	1.03	0.94	1.13	13.9	13.1	12.6	14.1	11.6
45	West Vancouver-Bowen Is	272	288.54	0.94	0.83	1.06	10.6	13.8	10.5	12.6	10.8
46	Sechelt	92	94.30	0.98	0.79	1.20	10.7	13.7	10.8	10.8	16.5
47	Powell River	95	79.87	1.19	0.96	1.45	13.8	10.5	18.3	17.4	16.7
48	Howe Sound	30	35.90	0.84	0.56	1.19	14.5	6.1	17.9	6.0	10.3
49	Central Coast	9	7.19	1.25	0.57	2.38	13.2	15.1	14.4	5.9	24.6
50	Queen Charlotte	13	9.31	1.40	0.74	2.39	19.2	7.1	36.8	37.8	7.6
52	Prince Rupert	43	41.32	1.04	0.75	1.40	12.9	12.0	16.8	10.1	13.7
54	Smithers	29	29.57	0.98	0.66	1.41	10.9	22.7	7.0	8.9	13.5
55	Burns Lake	14	15.59	0.90	0.49	1.51	8.4	14.4	16.5	8.9	6.4
56	Nechako	24	33.22	0.72	0.46	1.07	7.2	4.5	8.6	13.3	14.9
57	Prince George	207	168.74	1.23 **	1.07	1.41	18.0	15.8	14.1	11.0	19.9
59	Peace River South	55	64.52	0.85	0.64	1.11	8.7	14.4	12.3	11.5	8.7
60	Peace River North	43	49.00	0.88	0.64	1.18	7.5	15.1	12.7	11.1	10.7
61	Greater Victoria	1260	1317.25	0.96	0.90	1.01	12.7	11.1	11.6	12.6	13.2
62	Sooke	151	136.28	1.11	0.94	1.30	16.1	17.8	15.4	14.0	9.6
63	Saanich	224	234.86	0.95	0.83	1.09	10.7	9.4	12.5	12.8	13.7
64	Gulf Islands	63	68.21	0.92	0.71	1.18	13.6	16.0	9.3	10.0	10.2
65	Cowichan	210	161.68	1.30 ***	1.13	1.49	16.6	15.7	17.8	16.6	16.4
66	Lake Cowichan	27	17.53	1.54 *	1.01	2.24	26.5	7.7	31.2	26.6	7.3
67	Ladysmith	73	66.20	1.10	0.86	1.39	18.3	12.4	16.0	12.5	13.9
68	Nanaimo	299	286.48	1.04	0.93	1.17	13.6	11.9	11.2	14.9	15.6
69	Qualicum	153	147.95	1.03	0.88	1.21	9.5	14.1	12.6	15.5	13.5
70	Alberni	125	105.21	1.19	0.99	1.42	8.1	10.1	17.2	20.8	16.9
71	Courtenay	157	163.65	0.96	0.82	1.12	10.5	12.5	13.6	12.5	11.9
72	Campbell River	92	90.27	1.02	0.82	1.25	18.3	13.8	10.7	13.9	9.9
75	Mission	103	96.99	1.06	0.87	1.29	12.8	11.4	13.9	15.0	14.1
76	Agassiz-Harrison	10	20.39	0.49 *	0.23	0.90	3.3	11.0	5.3	7.7	2.3
77	Summerland	50	60.82	0.82	0.61	1.08	7.9	12.4	17.3	3.9	11.5
78	Enderby	28	26.52	1.06	0.70	1.53	11.9	16.4	13.4	19.8	15.6
80	Kitimat	22	20.58	1.07	0.67	1.62	15.2	17.5	10.6	10.1	8.1
81	Fort Nelson	9	5.58	1.61	0.74	3.06	6.6	28.2	20.0	-	60.6
84	Vancouver Island West	5	4.25	1.18	0.38	2.74	22.4	-	16.7	-	-
85	Vancouver Island North	21	21.98	0.96	0.59	1.46	11.9	21.2	5.1	11.5	15.9
87	Stikine	1	2.82	0.35	0.00	1.97	-	-	◆	-	-
88	Terrace	44	45.03	0.98	0.71	1.31	18.4	6.6	16.2	7.9	16.3
92	Nishga	5	2.74	1.82	0.59	4.25	-	17.9	67.8	-	19.5
94	Telegraph Creek	1	1.18	0.85	0.01	4.73	-	-	-	◆	-
	Provincial Total	**13,141**	◆	**1.00**	◆	◆	**12.6**	**12.6**	**12.4**	**12.9**	**12.8**

Lung Cancer: Male

	Local Health Area	Observed Deaths	Expected Deaths	SMR (p)	95% C.I. Lower	95% C.I. Upper	ASMR 1985	1986	1987	1988	1989
1	Fernie	12	15.86	0.76	0.39	1.32	5.8	1.5	7.7	3.1	1.6
2	Cranbrook	18	25.35	0.71	0.42	1.12	1.9	2.9	4.7	5.1	2.5
3	Kimberley	21	15.57	1.35	0.83	2.06	9.5	9.1	2.6	4.4	3.6
4	Windermere	5	9.79	0.51	0.16	1.19	3.0	2.2	4.9	2.6	-
5	Creston	26	28.01	0.93	0.61	1.36	2.5	3.1	7.2	3.9	8.9
6	Kootenay Lake	6	8.02	0.75	0.27	1.63	1.6	1.7	3.0	3.7	1.8
7	Nelson	27	37.62	0.72	0.47	1.04	2.8	4.0	3.5	3.6	3.3
9	Castlegar	20	19.24	1.04	0.63	1.61	3.2	4.1	3.7	4.0	9.2
10	Arrow Lakes	4	8.91	0.45	0.12	1.15	-	2.5	-	1.8	8.2
11	Trail	54	39.43	1.37 *	1.03	1.79	8.6	4.0	5.3	8.0	6.6
12	Grand Forks	14	17.17	0.82	0.45	1.37	2.8	1.8	3.3	8.2	4.9
13	Kettle Valley	3	6.56	0.46	0.09	1.34	3.3	3.4	3.2	-	-
14	Southern Okanagan	46	41.16	1.12	0.82	1.49	3.4	7.1	6.9	5.0	6.1
15	Penticton	66	76.48	0.86	0.67	1.10	4.2	4.6	3.4	4.3	4.9
16	Keremeos	7	11.12	0.63	0.25	1.30	-	13.0	7.9	-	-
17	Princeton	9	7.93	1.13	0.52	2.15	12.2	-	13.8	2.4	2.8
18	Golden	8	7.28	1.10	0.47	2.16	10.4	-	3.8	12.0	2.6
19	Revelstoke	16	9.53	1.68	0.96	2.73	7.6	8.7	10.3	13.1	-
20	Salmon Arm	42	56.52	0.74	0.54	1.00	2.2	2.4	6.1	3.0	3.7
21	Armstrong-Spallumcheen	4	13.38	0.30 +	0.08	0.77	1.5	2.7	-	-	2.8
22	Vernon	76	83.55	0.91	0.72	1.14	3.0	7.3	4.1	3.0	3.3
23	Central Okanagan	182	206.01	0.88	0.76	1.02	4.7	3.3	4.6	4.4	4.1
24	Kamloops	124	98.70	1.26 *	1.04	1.50	6.2	5.4	6.1	6.3	6.1
26	North Thompson	7	5.14	1.36	0.55	2.81	5.3	5.3	15.9	9.0	-
27	Cariboo-Chilcotin	48	40.26	1.19	0.88	1.58	7.9	3.8	6.1	5.8	4.8
28	Quesnel	35	26.36	1.33	0.92	1.85	9.2	3.2	6.1	8.4	5.2
29	Lillooet	12	6.54	1.83	0.95	3.20	11.1	25.2	6.6	-	3.0
30	South Cariboo	11	10.81	1.02	0.51	1.82	9.9	-	8.8	5.4	2.6
31	Merritt	18	12.46	1.44	0.86	2.28	12.9	8.8	5.8	1.7	10.6
32	Hope	13	12.73	1.02	0.54	1.75	1.6	5.1	1.7	6.4	5.7
33	Chilliwack	106	90.40	1.17	0.96	1.42	5.6	4.3	4.5	6.5	7.3
34	Abbotsford	72	120.79	0.60 ***	0.47	0.75	2.0	3.0	3.2	3.0	3.1
35	Langley	114	101.00	1.13	0.93	1.36	6.0	4.7	5.5	4.9	6.3
36	Surrey	328	316.59	1.04	0.93	1.15	4.8	4.7	4.5	4.9	5.7
37	Delta	93	92.90	1.00	0.81	1.23	5.0	3.4	3.8	5.0	6.5
38	Richmond	133	148.19	0.90	0.75	1.06	4.2	4.7	3.7	4.1	4.3
39	Vancouver	884	791.15	1.12 **	1.04	1.19	5.9	4.9	5.4	5.2	5.8
40	New Westminster	89	77.70	1.15	0.92	1.41	5.0	5.7	4.5	6.8	6.0
41	Burnaby	245	251.49	0.97	0.86	1.10	5.1	4.0	4.5	4.8	4.9
42	Maple Ridge	78	62.89	1.24	0.98	1.55	7.3	6.4	5.9	6.8	3.7
43	Coquitlam	128	130.39	0.98	0.82	1.17	6.8	3.8	4.3	4.0	5.4
44	North Vancouver	139	147.12	0.94	0.79	1.12	5.1	4.6	4.4	4.6	4.1
45	West Vancouver-Bowen Is	59	94.51	0.62 ***	0.48	0.81	3.1	3.7	2.3	3.8	1.3
46	Sechelt	42	40.01	1.05	0.76	1.42	4.9	6.6	4.9	4.5	3.8
47	Powell River	41	31.84	1.29	0.92	1.75	6.8	6.8	4.3	6.2	6.9
48	Howe Sound	9	15.95	0.56	0.26	1.07	6.6	5.7	1.2	3.2	1.3
49	Central Coast	2	3.82	0.52	0.06	1.89	6.1	-	-	-	6.9
50	Queen Charlotte	7	4.40	1.59	0.64	3.28	16.8	12.8	-	11.5	-
52	Prince Rupert	24	16.97	1.41	0.91	2.10	2.9	4.3	6.7	7.3	12.2
54	Smithers	13	12.29	1.06	0.56	1.81	5.7	1.9	1.7	6.1	9.0
55	Burns Lake	10	8.09	1.24	0.59	2.27	7.1	8.9	9.3	2.6	2.6
56	Nechako	20	15.44	1.30	0.79	2.00	2.9	4.3	4.6	4.4	13.0
57	Prince George	95	71.75	1.32 **	1.07	1.62	6.0	9.7	4.4	6.5	5.6
59	Peace River South	21	27.86	0.75	0.47	1.15	2.8	5.9	2.7	3.6	2.8
60	Peace River North	15	21.97	0.68	0.38	1.13	1.3	4.1	3.9	2.7	3.0
61	Greater Victoria	360	389.42	0.92	0.83	1.03	4.3	4.4	4.3	4.2	5.1
62	Sooke	68	56.28	1.21	0.94	1.53	6.2	6.1	5.6	5.1	5.5
63	Saanich	72	95.01	0.76 *	0.59	0.95	3.3	5.7	2.7	3.6	3.4
64	Gulf Islands	16	29.80	0.54 **	0.31	0.87	0.6	1.8	3.4	0.6	3.9
65	Cowichan	57	63.75	0.89 -	0.68	1.16	3.9	6.1	2.1	3.8	4.7
66	Lake Cowichan	7	8.01	0.87	0.35	1.80	2.9	-	8.7	5.2	6.4
67	Ladysmith	31	28.09	1.10	0.75	1.57	4.1	6.0	2.4	6.6	6.5
68	Nanaimo	109	110.57	0.99	0.81	1.19	3.1	5.4	3.8	5.7	4.8
69	Qualicum	64	64.33	0.99	0.77	1.27	5.9	6.4	5.6	4.0	2.9
70	Alberni	40	41.42	0.97	0.69	1.32	4.1	4.6	6.1	5.0	5.5
71	Courtenay	74	65.39	1.13	0.89	1.42	5.7	4.8	6.8	5.1	5.1
72	Campbell River	51	36.33	1.40 *	1.05	1.85	6.5	7.9	4.8	4.0	10.0
75	Mission	47	40.99	1.15	0.84	1.52	4.4	4.8	6.8	4.1	7.3
76	Agassiz-Harrison	10	9.47	1.06	0.51	1.94	7.5	4.6	5.8	2.5	5.5
77	Summerland	10	24.78	0.40 **	0.19	0.74	2.3	2.5	1.3	1.3	2.6
78	Enderby	10	11.39	0.88	0.42	1.61	3.6	5.5	2.3	1.9	5.1
80	Kitimat	11	9.15	1.20	0.60	2.15	4.8	6.5	-	3.0	18.4
81	Fort Nelson	10	2.76	3.62 **	1.73	6.66	11.2	30.6	-	20.3	25.9
84	Vancouver Island West	2	2.01	1.00	0.11	3.59	4.7	-	-	-	22.9
85	Vancouver Island North	13	9.53	1.36	0.73	2.33	1.4	9.0	8.0	9.0	3.8
87	Stikine	0	1.32	-	-	-	-	-	-	-	-
88	Terrace	13	21.91	0.59	0.32	1.01	1.0	3.2	6.1	2.8	2.0
92	Nishga	1	1.33	0.75	0.01	4.19	-	-	-	◆	-
94	Telegraph Creek	0	0.58	-	-	-	-	-	-	-	-
	Provincial Total	4,777	◆	1.00	◆	◆	4.9	4.7	4.6	4.7	5.0

179

Lung Cancer: Female

	Local Health Area	Observed Deaths	Expected Deaths	SMR (p)	95% C.I. Lower	Upper	1985	1986	ASMR 1987	1988	1989
1	Fernie	5	7.18	0.70	0.22	1.63	2.1	3.1	-	1.6	1.8
2	Cranbrook	7	13.42	0.52	0.21	1.07	1.0	-	2.9	-	3.2
3	Kimberley	7	7.98	0.88	0.35	1.81	1.9	1.4	1.5	3.7	1.6
4	Windermere	6	4.10	1.46	0.53	3.18	6.2	-	6.7	3.4	2.5
5	Creston	14	12.73	1.10	0.60	1.85	1.6	1.5	3.4	1.6	6.5
6	Kootenay Lake	3	3.35	0.90	0.18	2.62	-	2.7	-	2.6	3.9
7	Nelson	13	18.48	0.70	0.37	1.20	2.4	2.0	2.0	0.6	1.4
9	Castlegar	7	9.36	0.75	0.30	1.54	5.0	1.4	-	1.4	2.0
10	Arrow Lakes	0	4.08	-	-	-	-	-	-	-	-
11	Trail	17	20.13	0.84	0.49	1.35	0.5	3.0	4.2	1.9	2.1
12	Grand Forks	4	7.93	0.50	0.14	1.29	-	-	2.1	1.5	2.3
13	Kettle Valley	1	2.42	0.41	0.01	2.30	-	-	-	-	♦
14	Southern Okanagan	14	19.39	0.72	0.39	1.21	1.2	1.9	0.5	3.9	3.0
15	Penticton	38	39.66	0.96	0.68	1.32	1.9	2.9	2.6	3.0	1.9
16	Keremeos	5	4.16	1.20	0.39	2.81	-	5.8	-	2.2	8.2
17	Princeton	2	3.75	0.53	0.06	1.93	-	-	-	2.5	2.7
18	Golden	1	3.12	0.32	0.00	1.78	-	-	-	-	♦
19	Revelstoke	7	4.82	1.45	0.58	3.00	-	5.8	8.5	-	4.2
20	Salmon Arm	17	25.63	0.66	0.39	1.06	0.6	1.8	1.7	2.7	2.2
21	Armstrong Spallumcheen	5	6.19	0.81	0.26	1.88	3.0	5.3	-	-	1.5
22	Vernon	35	42.14	0.83	0.58	1.16	2.5	2.0	0.8	2.3	2.3
23	Central Okanagan	88	103.15	0.85	0.68	1.05	1.4	2.5	2.4	2.4	1.8
24	Kamloops	54	49.93	1.08	0.81	1.41	1.6	2.2	2.4	3.1	4.0
26	North Thompson	6	2.25	2.66	0.97	5.80	10.7	10.5	-	-	11.5
27	Cariboo-Chilcotin	26	18.07	1.44	0.94	2.11	5.5	3.4	3.1	2.4	2.3
28	Quesnel	19	11.79	1.61	0.97	2.52	2.4	5.2	2.8	3.5	6.5
29	Lillooet	1	2.50	0.40	0.01	2.22	♦	-	-	-	-
30	South Cariboo	3	4.40	0.68	0.14	1.99	-	2.6	-	5.8	-
31	Merritt	8	5.60	1.43	0.61	2.81	-	-	6.9	6.8	3.9
32	Hope	11	5.69	1.93	0.96	3.46	2.3	4.2	4.8	4.7	8.4
33	Chilliwack	54	46.75	1.15	0.87	1.51	2.7	2.8	1.5	4.3	3.8
34	Abbotsford	48	63.25	0.76	0.56	1.01	1.4	2.3	1.7	2.3	2.0
35	Langley	48	51.65	0.93	0.69	1.23	2.0	3.6	2.1	1.2	3.0
36	Surrey	165	170.61	0.97	0.83	1.13	2.0	2.5	2.4	3.0	2.3
37	Delta	52	50.89	1.02	0.76	1.34	3.4	2.4	2.1	2.5	2.4
38	Richmond	98	85.17	1.15	0.93	1.40	3.4	2.9	2.5	1.9	3.8
39	Vancouver	456	459.05	0.99	0.90	1.09	2.3	2.1	2.6	2.5	2.6
40	New Westminster	58	50.72	1.14	0.87	1.48	1.1	3.4	3.6	4.3	2.8
41	Burnaby	157	146.45	1.07	0.91	1.25	2.3	2.5	3.2	2.5	2.8
42	Maple Ridge	36	33.21	1.08	0.76	1.50	4.1	2.4	2.8	2.2	2.6
43	Coquitlam	95	72.52	1.31 *	1.06	1.60	3.4	2.9	2.9	5.1	2.5
44	North Vancouver	95	88.61	1.07	0.87	1.31	2.6	2.5	2.6	3.1	2.5
45	West Vancouver-Bowen Is	39	55.65	0.70 *	0.50	0.96	1.1	3.1	1.7	1.9	0.6
46	Sechelt	23	19.19	1.20	0.76	1.80	2.7	4.6	2.5	2.1	2.6
47	Powell River	19	15.69	1.21	0.73	1.89	3.5	1.6	0.9	1.8	7.9
48	Howe Sound	7	7.29	0.96	0.38	1.98	-	1.6	3.6	3.0	4.5
49	Central Coast	2	1.46	1.37	0.15	4.93	-	9.3	7.8	-	-
50	Queen Charlotte	2	1.76	1.14	0.13	4.10	-	-	14.7	-	-
52	Prince Rupert	11	8.20	1.34	0.67	2.40	4.2	2.9	2.7	4.1	2.5
54	Smithers	5	5.81	0.86	0.28	2.01	2.0	3.1	2.0	-	3.6
55	Burns Lake	3	3.14	0.95	0.19	2.79	-	3.2	-	8.9	-
56	Nechako	5	6.62	0.75	0.24	1.76	-	1.6	1.6	4.8	1.9
57	Prince George	53	33.67	1.57 **	1.18	2.06	3.0	3.8	2.7	2.9	7.3
59	Peace River South	18	12.67	1.42	0.84	2.25	2.2	6.3	5.3	2.8	1.9
60	Peace River North	2	9.72	0.21 +	0.02	0.74	-	-	-	1.1	1.2
61	Greater Victoria	200	244.29	0.82 **	0.71	0.94	2.1	1.9	2.0	2.1	2.5
62	Sooke	32	27.61	1.16	0.79	1.64	2.9	2.3	3.6	3.4	2.8
63	Saanich	37	47.86	0.77	0.54	1.07	2.5	1.1	2.7	0.6	2.3
64	Gulf Islands	12	14.12	0.85	0.44	1.48	1.8	2.7	4.3	0.6	2.7
65	Cowichan	35	32.06	1.09	0.76	1.52	1.4	3.7	3.5	2.3	2.8
66	Lake Cowichan	4	3.64	1.10	0.30	2.81	-	3.6	7.2	2.7	-
67	Ladysmith	15	13.36	1.12	0.63	1.85	2.3	-	3.2	2.2	4.7
68	Nanaimo	73	57.59	1.27	0.99	1.59	4.3	2.7	2.5	4.0	2.9
69	Qualicum	39	30.62	1.27	0.91	1.74	0.7	3.8	3.7	4.5	5.4
70	Alberni	23	21.31	1.08	0.68	1.62	-	2.7	4.8	4.1	1.5
71	Courtenay	43	32.98	1.30	0.94	1.76	2.7	3.3	4.1	5.5	1.4
72	Campbell River	18	18.21	0.99	0.59	1.56	4.8	1.4	2.0	2.6	1.9
75	Mission	22	19.13	1.15	0.72	1.74	3.4	2.2	4.6	2.4	2.6
76	Agassiz-Harrison	1	4.16	0.24	0.00	1.34	-	♦	-	-	-
77	Summerland	14	12.01	1.17	0.64	1.96	1.9	1.7	7.4	0.8	2.6
78	Enderby	5	5.34	0.94	0.30	2.18	3.0	-	7.1	-	3.2
80	Kitimat	2	4.10	0.49	0.05	1.76	-	-	1.9	5.3	-
81	Fort Nelson	2	1.07	1.87	0.21	6.74	-	12.7	-	-	-
84	Vancouver Island West	2	0.77	2.60	0.29	9.37	19.5	♦	-	-	-
85	Vancouver Island North	6	4.25	1.41	0.52	3.08	5.1	4.5	-	1.6	4.4
87	Slikine	1	0.56	1.78	0.02	9.91	-	-	♦	-	♦
88	Terrace	6	8.95	0.67	0.24	1.46	3.2	-	1.1	2.0	0.9
92	Nishga	1	0.56	1.80	0.02	10.00	-	-	-	-	♦
94	Telegraph Creek	0	0.23	-	-	-	-	-	-	-	-
	Provincial Total	**2,568**	♦	1.00	♦	♦	2.2	2.5	2.5	2.6	2.7

180

Breast Cancer: Female

	Local Health Area	Observed Deaths	Expected Deaths	SMR (p)	95% C.I. Lower	Upper	1985	1986	ASMR 1987	1988	1989
1	Fernie	13	7.34	1.77	0.94	3.03	-	3.6	8.2	1.7	8.6
2	Cranbrook	14	13.19	1.06	0.58	1.78	2.1	4.2	1.8	2.0	2.8
3	Kimberley	11	7.38	1.49	0.74	2.67	1.4	3.4	3.2	5.0	4.3
4	Windermere	1	3.96	0.25	0.00	1.41	-	-	-	♦	-
5	Creston	11	11.50	0.96	0.48	1.71	4.5	0.7	2.8	2.4	0.7
6	Kootenay Lake	6	3.06	1.96	0.72	4.27	8.5	-	3.7	7.6	3.9
7	Nelson	20	17.41	1.15	0.70	1.77	3.0	6.9	1.7	0.5	2.6
9	Castlegar	10	8.86	1.13	0.54	2.07	1.3	5.2	4.5	-	2.6
10	Arrow Lakes	0	3.83	-	-	-	-	-	-	-	-
11	Trail	21	18.53	1.13	0.70	1.73	2.5	3.4	1.2	2.0	3.5
12	Grand Forks	5	7.29	0.69	0.22	1.60	2.2	-	1.3	1.7	5.7
13	Kettle Valley	3	2.28	1.32	0.26	3.85	4.9	-	-	8.0	-
14	Southern Okanagan	11	17.34	0.63	0.32	1.13	0.5	2.5	2.1	1.9	-
15	Penticton	30	35.84	0.84	0.56	1.20	1.9	1.9	3.2	1.7	2.0
16	Keremeos	2	3.76	0.53	0.06	1.92	-	-	-	-	5.2
17	Princeton	1	3.60	0.28	0.00	1.55	♦	-	-	-	-
18	Golden	5	3.21	1.56	0.50	3.64	10.2	-	3.2	-	3.3
19	Revelstoke	6	4.85	1.24	0.45	2.69	-	2.9	4.7	5.8	1.7
20	Salmon Arm	24	23.54	1.02	0.65	1.52	3.1	2.3	3.2	2.5	1.9
21	Armstrong-Spallumcheen	3	5.82	0.52	0.10	1.51	1.9	-	2.1	1.7	-
22	Vernon	49	39.26	1.25	0.92	1.65	2.5	2.3	3.6	3.4	3.9
23	Central Okanagan	83	94.74	0.88	0.70	1.09	1.8	1.8	2.2	2.0	2.9
24	Kamloops	54	49.17	1.10	0.82	1.43	2.2	3.5	2.0	2.2	3.8
26	North Thompson	2	2.26	0.88	0.10	3.19	-	-	5.0	-	5.7
27	Cariboo-Chilcotin	20	18.35	1.09	0.67	1.68	3.5	4.7	1.4	1.4	2.0
28	Quesnel	10	11.88	0.84	0.40	1.55	4.1	3.1	1.6	1.0	1.9
29	Lillooet	3	2.47	1.21	0.24	3.55	-	5.0	-	3.9	3.3
30	South Cariboo	6	4.30	1.40	0.51	3.04	2.8	2.8	5.4	2.8	2.5
31	Merritt	4	5.55	0.72	0.19	1.84	3.7	2.2	-	1.8	-
32	Hope	5	5.30	0.94	0.30	2.20	1.7	3.1	-	5.8	-
33	Chilliwack	48	43.03	1.12	0.82	1.48	1.4	3.0	1.6	3.7	3.9
34	Abbotsford	57	58.90	0.97	0.73	1.25	2.8	2.1	2.0	1.9	3.1
35	Langley	58	50.03	1.16	0.88	1.50	3.7	3.7	2.4	3.2	1.6
36	Surrey	146	161.30	0.91	0.76	1.06	2.5	2.7	1.8	1.7	2.3
37	Delta	44	51.32	0.86	0.62	1.15	2.5	3.0	1.5	1.7	2.5
38	Richmond	85	83.17	1.02	0.82	1.26	1.8	2.3	2.2	3.2	3.0
39	Vancouver	402	434.45	0.93	0.84	1.02	2.8	2.0	2.5	2.5	2.0
40	New Westminster	47	46.62	1.01	0.74	1.34	1.9	3.0	2.7	3.6	2.4
41	Burnaby	128	138.79	0.92	0.77	1.10	2.7	2.8	2.2	1.8	1.8
42	Maple Ridge	29	32.59	0.89	0.60	1.28	2.7	1.2	1.8	1.7	3.3
43	Coquitlam	71	73.17	0.97	0.76	1.22	2.4	2.3	2.0	2.6	2.7
44	North Vancouver	96	86.36	1.11	0.90	1.36	3.0	2.1	3.2	3.2	2.1
45	West Vancouver-Bowen Is	51	52.07	0.98	0.73	1.29	1.5	3.1	2.3	2.8	2.0
46	Sechelt	15	17.48	0.86	0.48	1.42	2.3	2.3	0.9	2.9	4.2
47	Powell River	24	14.83	1.62 *	1.04	2.41	3.2	1.8	8.1	4.7	2.5
48	Howe Sound	11	7.40	1.49	0.74	2.66	9.9	1.6	6.6	1.3	-
49	Central Coast	1	1.48	0.67	0.01	3.75	♦	-	-	-	-
50	Queen Charlotte	5	1.90	2.63	0.85	6.14	19.2	7.1	6.8	13.5	-
52	Prince Rupert	8	8.34	0.96	0.41	1.89	4.2	2.8	-	2.8	2.1
54	Smithers	5	6.05	0.83	0.27	1.93	2.0	5.1	-	-	3.6
55	Burns Lake	4	3.26	1.23	0.33	3.14	3.3	9.3	-	-	3.2
56	Nechako	3	6.72	0.45	0.09	1.30	1.8	-	1.7	-	3.0
57	Prince George	32	35.90	0.89	0.61	1.26	4.3	3.2	1.3	0.9	2.6
59	Peace River South	8	12.89	0.62	0.27	1.22	1.0	1.0	1.0	1.4	2.8
60	Peace River North	6	10.06	0.60	0.22	1.30	1.3	2.3	-	2.2	1.3
61	Greater Victoria	235	226.06	1.04	0.91	1.18	2.2	2.7	2.2	3.1	2.2
62	Sooke	34	26.88	1.26	0.88	1.77	2.5	5.3	4.2	2.7	1.7
63	Saanich	42	44.07	0.95	0.69	1.29	1.2	1.8	2.3	2.4	3.6
64	Gulf Islands	19	12.49	1.52	0.92	2.38	6.8	1.7	3.5	2.8	1.2
65	Cowichan	41	30.09	1.36	0.98	1.85	3.6	2.6	2.3	4.5	3.0
66	Lake Cowichan	5	3.45	1.45	0.47	3.38	4.2	-	7.8	5.5	-
67	Ladysmith	18	12.17	1.48	0.88	2.34	6.3	3.6	2.3	2.8	4.1
68	Nanaimo	64	53.63	1.19	0.92	1.52	2.7	2.2	2.9	3.5	4.3
69	Qualicum	37	27.23	1.36	0.96	1.87	2.3	3.2	4.2	1.6	2.8
70	Alberni	22	20.41	1.08	0.68	1.63	2.4	2.1	1.9	4.3	2.1
71	Courtenay	22	31.31	0.70	0.44	1.06	1.8	1.6	1.8	2.1	1.7
72	Campbell River	23	17.97	1.28	0.81	1.92	4.3	3.9	0.7	3.8	3.7
75	Mission	19	18.31	1.04	0.62	1.62	3.1	3.8	3.7	1.5	1.6
76	Agassiz-Harrison	4	3.83	1.04	0.28	2.68	3.3	2.6	5.3	-	2.3
77	Summerland	8	10.77	0.74	0.32	1.46	1.5	6.5	3.4	-	1.1
78	Enderby	2	4.87	0.41	0.05	1.48	-	3.1	-	3.9	-
80	Kitimat	6	4.57	1.31	0.48	2.85	3.9	2.1	-	2.0	1.9
81	Fort Nelson	0	1.29	-	-	-	-	-	-	-	-
84	Vancouver Island West	0	0.96	-	-	-	-	-	-	-	-
85	Vancouver Island North	5	4.80	1.04	0.34	2.43	-	4.3	-	8.7	5.0
87	Stikine	0	0.63	-	-	-	-	-	-	-	-
88	Terrace	16	9.54	1.68	0.96	2.72	3.1	4.2	3.0	3.5	6.9
92	Nishga	1	0.54	1.84	0.02	10.22	-	♦	-	-	-
94	Telegraph Creek	0	0.24	-	-	-	-	-	-	-	-
	Provincial Total	**2,440**	♦	1.00	♦	♦	2.5	2.6	2.3	2.5	2.4

Endocrine, Nutritional, and Metabolic Diseases and Immunity Disorders: Male

	Local Health Area	Observed Deaths	Expected Deaths	SMR	(p)	95% C.I. Lower	95% C.I. Upper	ASMR 1985	ASMR 1986	ASMR 1987	ASMR 1988	ASMR 1989
1	Fernie	1	4.30	0.23		0.00	1.29	-	◆	-	-	-
2	Cranbrook	4	6.39	0.63		0.17	1.60	0.9	-	-	2.3	0.9
3	Kimberley	5	3.73	1.34		0.43	3.13	1.9	1.8	1.1	-	6.0
4	Windermere	0	2.37	-		-	-	-	-	-	-	-
5	Creston	11	7.15	1.54		0.77	2.75	0.7	4.8	1.3	1.2	0.5
6	Kootenay Lake	0	1.92	-		-	-	-	-	-	-	-
7	Nelson	4	9.64	0.41		0.11	1.06	0.9	0.7	0.5	-	0.8
9	Castlegar	7	4.72	1.48		0.59	3.05	-	2.3	1.0	4.7	-
10	Arrow Lakes	1	2.29	0.44		0.01	2.43	-	-	-	◆	-
11	Trail	10	9.91	1.01		0.48	1.86	0.7	1.1	2.1	-	1.3
12	Grand Forks	6	4.24	1.41		0.52	3.08	3.1	-	1.0	2.0	1.7
13	Kettle Valley	2	1.61	1.24		0.14	4.48	-	-	-	2.9	2.8
14	Southern Okanagan	18	10.17	1.77	*	1.05	2.80	2.7	1.9	1.8	2.3	1.2
15	Penticton	21	19.57	1.07		0.66	1.64	1.3	0.6	1.5	2.0	0.7
16	Keremeos	2	2.70	0.74		0.08	2.68	4.5	-	-	1.7	-
17	Princeton	1	1.86	0.54		0.01	3.00	◆	-	-	-	-
18	Golden	1	1.93	0.52		0.01	2.89	-	◆	-	-	-
19	Revelstoke	1	2.49	0.40		0.01	2.23	-	-	-	-	◆
20	Salmon Arm	8	13.28	0.60		0.26	1.19	-	0.9	0.9	1.5	0.3
21	Armstrong-Spallumcheen	2	3.36	0.59		0.07	2.15	-	-	1.5	1.7	-
22	Vernon	27	21.26	1.27		0.84	1.85	1.0	1.3	1.7	1.3	3.1
23	Central Okanagan	46	51.62	0.89		0.65	1.19	0.9	1.4	1.4	0.7	1.2
24	Kamloops	22	24.63	0.89		0.56	1.35	0.7	1.0	1.7	1.0	1.2
26	North Thompson	3	1.28	2.34		0.47	6.85	-	4.6	4.3	5.2	-
27	Cariboo-Chilcotin	12	9.73	1.23		0.64	2.15	5.2	1.2	1.1	1.0	0.6
28	Quesnel	8	6.73	1.19		0.51	2.34	0.9	2.0	-	1.6	2.5
29	Lillooet	0	1.67	-		-	-	-	-	-	-	-
30	South Cariboo	2	2.71	0.74		0.08	2.67	2.5	1.9	-	-	-
31	Merritt	3	3.02	0.99		0.20	2.90	1.7	-	2.0	-	3.8
32	Hope	4	2.93	1.37		0.37	3.50	-	1.7	-	2.9	3.4
33	Chilliwack	24	22.45	1.07		0.68	1.59	2.1	0.7	1.4	1.2	0.6
34	Abbotsford	30	31.44	0.95		0.64	1.36	2.1	0.7	1.2	0.7	1.1
35	Langley	32	25.81	1.24		0.85	1.75	0.9	1.5	1.2	1.4	2.1
36	Surrey	79	80.61	0.98		0.78	1.22	1.4	1.4	0.8	1.1	1.2
37	Delta	14	23.02	0.61		0.33	1.02	0.3	0.9	1.0	0.7	0.6
38	Richmond	36	36.07	1.00		0.70	1.38	1.5	1.4	1.9	0.7	0.8
39	Vancouver	262	206.40	1.27	***	1.12	1.43	1.6	2.2	0.7	2.1	1.5
40	New Westminster	21	20.27	1.04		0.64	1.58	0.6	1.5	1.4	0.8	2.2
41	Burnaby	64	62.73	1.02		0.79	1.30	0.8	1.2	0.8	1.3	2.0
42	Maple Ridge	17	16.31	1.04		0.61	1.67	2.3	1.0	0.8	1.8	0.7
43	Coquitlam	25	33.31	0.75		0.49	1.11	1.0	0.6	1.0	1.1	0.9
44	North Vancouver	37	35.41	1.04		0.74	1.44	1.1	1.0	2.9	0.3	1.1
45	West Vancouver-Bowen Is	13	22.60	0.58	*	0.31	0.98	0.6	1.0	0.9	0.4	0.4
46	Sechelt	11	9.54	1.15		0.57	2.06	1.6	1.5	3.4	0.6	-
47	Powell River	3	7.97	0.38		0.08	1.10	-	-	-	0.7	1.7
48	Howe Sound	7	3.88	1.80		0.72	3.71	4.4	3.2	0.9	3.3	-
49	Central Coast	2	0.97	2.06		0.23	7.44	-	-	6.2	-	4.9
50	Queen Charlotte	1	1.33	0.75		0.01	4.20	-	-	-	-	◆
52	Prince Rupert	9	4.54	1.98		0.90	3.76	-	2.6	2.9	1.4	5.3
54	Smithers	3	3.24	0.93		0.19	2.70	2.6	2.2	-	1.9	-
55	Burns Lake	3	2.11	1.42		0.29	4.16	-	6.4	-	-	2.8
56	Nechako	5	4.00	1.25		0.40	2.91	-	4.1	3.0	-	-
57	Prince George	24	18.48	1.30		0.83	1.93	1.4	2.3	2.0	2.8	1.0
59	Peace River South	8	7.45	1.07		0.46	2.12	3.1	2.9	0.8	-	1.0
60	Peace River North	2	5.87	0.34		0.04	1.23	0.9	-	-	-	1.1
61	Greater Victoria	98	104.42	0.94		0.76	1.14	1.0	1.4	1.0	1.1	1.0
62	Sooke	10	13.54	0.74		0.35	1.36	0.7	1.3	0.9	0.7	0.7
63	Saanich	16	22.06	0.73		0.41	1.18	1.4	0.4	0.3	1.5	0.8
64	Gulf Islands	4	6.84	0.58		0.16	1.50	-	0.7	-	2.4	1.4
65	Cowichan	13	15.73	0.83		0.44	1.41	2.6	-	0.9	0.4	1.2
66	Lake Cowichan	0	1.89	-		-	-	-	-	-	-	-
67	Ladysmith	5	6.87	0.73		0.23	1.70	-	1.0	0.7	0.7	1.4
68	Nanaimo	27	26.85	1.01		0.66	1.46	0.2	1.0	1.6	0.8	2.0
69	Qualicum	7	14.75	0.47	*	0.19	0.98	0.3	0.3	-	0.5	1.5
70	Alberni	14	9.97	1.40		0.77	2.36	2.3	0.5	2.3	1.7	1.7
71	Courtenay	21	15.86	1.32		0.82	2.02	1.2	1.7	1.7	2.4	1.3
72	Campbell River	3	8.83	0.34	+	0.07	0.99	0.6	1.4	0.6	-	-
75	Mission	6	10.37	0.58		0.21	1.26	1.4	1.7	0.6	0.6	-
76	Agassiz-Harrison	0	2.36	-		-	-	-	-	-	-	-
77	Summerland	6	6.38	0.94		0.34	2.05	-	4.0	-	2.2	-
78	Enderby	2	2.89	0.69		0.08	2.50	4.7	-	-	-	-
80	Kitimat	0	2.25					-	-	-	-	-
81	Fort Nelson	1	0.82	1.22		0.02	6.80	-	-	-	◆	-
84	Vancouver Island West	1	0.59	1.69		0.02	9.42	-	◆	-	-	-
85	Vancouver Island North	3	2.65	1.13		0.23	3.31	4.7	-	5.4	-	-
87	Stikine	0	0.38	-		-	-	-	-	-	-	*
88	Terrace	5	5.92	0.84		0.27	1.97	-	1.2	0.8	3.0	-
92	Nishga	0	0.37	-		-	-	-	-	-	-	-
94	Telegraph Creek	0	0.14	-		-	-	-	-	-	-	-
	Provincial Total	**1,208**	◆	1.00		◆	◆	1.2	1.3	1.1	1.2	1.2

182

Endocrine, Nutritional, and Metabolic Diseases and Immunity Disorders: Female

	Local Health Area	Observed Deaths	Expected Deaths	SMR (p)	95% C.I. Lower	Upper	ASMR 1985	1986	1987	1988	1989
1	Fernie	8	3.14	2.55 *	1.10	5.03	6.6	4.3	2.1	1.6	1.5
2	Cranbrook	14	6.29	2.23 *	1.22	3.74	3.1	3.1	1.8	2.8	3.2
3	Kimberley	7	3.74	1.87	0.75	3.86	1.2	2.8	3.0	1.6	1.2
4	Windermere	4	1.59	2.52	0.68	6.45	-	2.7	6.4	5.9	-
5	Creston	11	6.22	1.77	0.88	3.16	1.9	0.7	0.9	2.5	2.9
6	Kootenay Lake	0	1.59	-	-	-	-	-	-	-	-
7	Nelson	9	9.39	0.96	0.44	1.82	1.2	1.2	0.6	2.0	-
9	Castlegar	4	4.37	0.91	0.25	2.34	1.4	-	1.2	-	2.5
10	Arrow Lakes	0	2.19	-	-	-	-	-	-	-	-
11	Trail	15	9.41	1.59	0.89	2.63	1.8	1.2	3.5	0.9	1.4
12	Grand Forks	2	3.72	0.54	0.06	1.94	-	1.9	-	1.7	-
13	Kettle Valley	1	0.92	1.08	0.01	6.03	-	-	◆	-	-
14	Southern Okanagan	10	9.37	1.07	0.51	1.96	0.6	0.5	1.7	2.0	0.4
15	Penticton	16	20.11	0.80	0.45	1.29	1.1	1.1	1.1	0.7	0.4
16	Keremeos	2	1.88	1.06	0.12	3.84	-	-	3.0	-	6.8
17	Princeton	2	1.75	1.14	0.13	4.12	-	-	2.7	2.5	-
18	Golden	0	1.26	-	-	-	-	-	-	-	-
19	Revelstoke	5	2.33	2.15	0.69	5.01	6.2	-	-	2.1	5.1
20	Salmon Arm	12	11.20	1.07	0.55	1.87	2.9	2.0	-	0.4	0.9
21	Armstrong-Spallumcheen	0	2.84	-	-	-	-	-	-	-	-
22	Vernon	20	20.32	0.98	0.60	1.52	1.8	0.8	1.7	1.5	0.3
23	Central Okanagan	41	48.64	0.84	0.60	1.14	1.1	0.5	1.1	1.6	0.6
24	Kamloops	39	21.95	1.78 **	1.26	2.43	1.7	1.9	2.3	2.4	1.9
26	North Thompson	1	0.92	1.09	0.01	6.04	-	-	◆	-	-
27	Cariboo-Chilcotin	13	7.08	1.84	0.98	3.14	3.4	2.5	0.6	1.5	3.0
28	Quesnel	7	4.72	1.48	0.59	3.05	-	1.8	3.2	2.5	2.1
29	Lillooet	2	1.07	1.87	0.21	6.74	-	5.1	-	5.9	-
30	South Cariboo	1	1.87	0.53	0.01	2.97	-	-	-	-	◆
31	Merritt	2	2.46	0.81	0.09	2.93	2.1	-	-	2.8	-
32	Hope	5	2.27	2.21	0.71	5.15	-	2.9	3.2	3.2	3.0
33	Chilliwack	22	21.75	1.01	0.63	1.53	0.8	1.6	1.5	1.4	0.4
34	Abbotsford	26	31.72	0.82	0.54	1.20	0.6	1.1	0.7	0.8	1.2
35	Langley	28	24.11	1.16	0.77	1.68	1.7	1.1	1.3	0.8	1.8
36	Surrey	78	80.29	0.97	0.77	1.21	0.6	1.2	1.0	1.3	1.5
37	Delta	21	23.19	0.91	0.56	1.38	0.6	1.6	0.2	0.7	1.9
38	Richmond	35	37.72	0.93	0.65	1.29	1.0	1.6	0.6	1.0	1.0
39	Vancouver	248	254.90	0.97	0.86	1.10	0.9	1.3	1.1	1.2	1.2
40	New Westminster	27	28.72	0.94	0.62	1.37	0.7	0.4	1.1	1.3	1.7
41	Burnaby	83	75.82	1.09	0.87	1.36	1.3	0.7	1.6	1.4	1.4
42	Maple Ridge	20	16.71	1.20	0.73	1.85	1.2	1.9	1.7	0.9	1.1
43	Coquitlam	33	32.05	1.03	0.71	1.45	0.6	1.0	1.6	0.9	1.8
44	North Vancouver	37	41.66	0.89	0.63	1.22	1.4	0.5	1.3	0.7	1.2
45	West Vancouver-Bowen Is	20	29.71	0.67	0.41	1.04	-	0.9	1.0	1.2	0.2
46	Sechelt	2	8.59	0.23 +	0.03	0.84	0.5	-	-	-	0.7
47	Powell River	8	7.68	1.04	0.45	2.05	1.6	1.3	0.6	1.7	0.6
48	Howe Sound	3	2.87	1.05	0.21	3.06	-	-	4.4	-	2.2
49	Central Coast	1	0.56	1.80	0.02	10.01	-	-	-	-	◆
50	Queen Charlotte	0	0.83	-	-	-	-	-	-	-	-
52	Prince Rupert	9	3.57	2.52 *	1.15	4.79	3.4	4.5	-	4.5	1.3
54	Smithers	7	2.53	2.77 *	1.11	5.70	6.3	6.5	3.1	-	2.6
55	Burns Lake	2	1.26	1.58	0.18	5.71	-	◆	5.5	-	4.5
56	Nechako	1	2.81	0.36	0.00	1.98	-	◆	-	-	-
57	Prince George	27	13.22	2.04 **	1.35	2.97	1.4	3.2	2.4	2.2	2.5
59	Peace River South	13	5.66	2.30 *	1.22	3.93	3.3	2.1	3.1	2.8	2.0
60	Peace River North	4	4.11	0.97	0.26	2.49	0.6	-	-	-	3.7
61	Greater Victoria	117	147.74	0.79 *	0.65	0.95	0.6	0.7	1.1	1.1	1.1
62	Sooke	16	11.71	1.37	0.78	2.22	2.6	0.9	1.8	0.5	2.4
63	Saanich	20	21.55	0.93	0.57	1.43	-	1.3	1.7	1.5	0.8
64	Gulf Islands	4	6.15	0.65	0.17	1.66	-	1.0	1.2	-	1.6
65	Cowichan	21	15.35	1.37	0.85	2.09	1.1	1.2	1.4	1.5	2.5
66	Lake Cowichan	2	1.45	1.38	0.16	4.99	-	-	-	2.7	3.0
67	Ladysmith	7	6.12	1.14	0.46	2.35	2.1	2.6	1.0	-	0.7
68	Nanaimo	21	26.38	0.80	0.49	1.22	0.5	1.2	1.4	0.8	1.1
69	Qualicum	5	13.46	0.37 *	0.12	0.87	-	1.4	0.3	0.5	0.4
70	Alberni	6	9.24	0.65	0.24	1.41	0.7	2.2	0.7	-	0.5
71	Courtenay	15	14.84	1.01	0.57	1.67	1.6	1.7	0.4	2.3	0.3
72	Campbell River	9	7.71	1.17	0.53	2.22	0.8	2.2	1.2	1.5	0.6
75	Mission	8	9.16	0.87	0.38	1.72	1.7	-	0.5	1.2	1.0
76	Agassiz-Harrison	0	1.82	-	-	-	-	-	-	-	-
77	Summerland	5	6.08	0.82	0.27	1.92	0.9	-	1.6	0.8	0.8
78	Enderby	5	2.47	2.02	0.65	4.71	-	4.3	-	4.4	1.8
80	Kitimat	3	1.55	1.93	0.39	5.64	7.2	-	-	-	15.2
81	Fort Nelson	1	0.40	2.49	0.03	13.84	-	-	-	◆	-
84	Vancouver Island West	0	0.34	-	-	-	-	-	-	-	-
85	Vancouver Island North	0	1.72	-	-	-	-	-	-	-	-
87	Stikine	0	0.20	-	-	-	-	-	-	-	-
88	Terrace	2	3.58	0.56	0.06	2.01	2.5	-	-	1.2	-
92	Nishga	1	0.23	4.32	0.06	24.04	-	-	-	-	◆
94	Telegraph Creek	0	0.10	-	-	-	-	-	-	-	-
	Provincial Total	**1,276**	◆	1.00	◆	◆	1.0	1.1	1.1	1.2	1.2

Diabetes: Male

#	Local Health Area	Observed Deaths	Expected Deaths	SMR (p)	95% C.I. Lower	Upper	ASMR 1985	1986	1987	1988	1989
1	Fernie	0	2.88	-	-	-	-	-	-	-	-
2	Cranbrook	3	4.47	0.67	0.13	1.96	-	-	-	2.3	0.9
3	Kimberley	3	2.76	1.09	0.22	3.18	-	1.8	1.1	-	4.2
4	Windermere	0	1.70	-	-	-	-	-	-	-	-
5	Creston	8	5.48	1.46	0.63	2.88	0.7	3.0	1.3	-	0.5
6	Kootenay Lake	0	1.45	-	-	-	-	-	-	-	-
7	Nelson	3	7.15	0.42	0.08	1.23	-	0.7	0.5	-	0.8
9	Castlegar	6	3.46	1.73	0.63	3.77	-	2.3	1.0	3.6	-
10	Arrow Lakes	1	1.71	0.59	0.01	3.26	-	-	-	♦	-
11	Trail	9	7.40	1.22	0.56	2.31	0.7	0.5	2.1	-	1.3
12	Grand Forks	5	3.23	1.55	0.50	3.61	2.0	-	1.0	2.0	1.7
13	Kettle Valley	2	1.21	1.66	0.19	5.98	-	-	-	2.9	2.8
14	Southern Okanagan	15	7.82	1.92 *	1.07	3.16	1.0	1.4	1.8	1.9	1.2
15	Penticton	13	14.97	0.87	0.46	1.49	0.7	0.3	0.7	0.9	0.7
16	Keremeos	1	2.09	0.48	0.01	2.66	-	-	-	♦	-
17	Princeton	1	1.35	0.74	0.01	4.12	♦	-	-	-	-
18	Golden	0	1.31	-	-	-	-	-	-	-	-
19	Revelstoke	1	1.70	0.59	0.01	3.27	-	-	-	-	♦
20	Salmon Arm	4	10.03	0.40	0.11	1.02	-	0.3	0.6	0.4	0.3
21	Armstrong-Spallumcheen	1	2.49	0.40	0.01	2.23	-	-	♦	-	-
22	Vernon	20	15.84	1.26	0.77	1.95	0.5	1.0	0.8	1.3	1.7
23	Central Okanagan	30	39.05	0.77	0.52	1.10	0.5	0.7	0.6	0.7	0.7
24	Kamloops	16	17.39	0.92	0.53	1.49	0.6	0.7	1.1	0.8	0.9
26	North Thompson	3	0.88	3.42	0.69	10.00	-	4.6	4.3	5.2	-
27	Cariboo-Chilcotin	8	6.62	1.21	0.52	2.38	3.9	-	0.5	0.4	0.6
28	Quesnel	4	4.64	0.86	0.23	2.21	-	0.8	-	0.8	1.6
29	Lillooet	0	1.20	-	-	-	-	-	-	-	-
30	South Cariboo	2	1.94	1.03	0.12	3.72	2.5	1.9	-	-	-
31	Merritt	2	2.12	0.94	0.11	3.41	-	-	2.0	-	3.8
32	Hope	4	2.15	1.86	0.50	4.76	-	1.7	-	2.9	3.4
33	Chilliwack	18	16.75	1.07	0.64	1.70	1.9	0.7	0.7	0.5	0.6
34	Abbotsford	28	23.29	1.20	0.80	1.74	2.1	0.7	1.0	0.7	0.9
35	Langley	28	18.52	1.51 *	1.00	2.19	0.9	1.1	1.2	1.2	1.9
36	Surrey	68	58.59	1.16	0.90	1.47	1.3	1.0	0.7	0.9	1.0
37	Delta	13	15.97	0.81	0.43	1.39	0.3	0.9	1.0	0.7	0.4
38	Richmond	29	25.56	1.13	0.76	1.63	1.5	0.9	1.7	0.5	0.4
39	Vancouver	161	151.65	1.06	0.90	1.24	0.8	0.8	0.6	1.5	1.1
40	New Westminster	20	15.06	1.33	0.81	2.05	0.6	1.5	1.4	0.8	1.9
41	Burnaby	57	45.94	1.24	0.94	1.61	0.7	0.8	0.8	1.2	1.7
42	Maple Ridge	14	11.64	1.20	0.66	2.02	1.8	0.6	0.8	1.8	0.4
43	Coquitlam	14	22.82	0.61	0.34	1.03	0.4	0.1	0.8	0.7	0.5
44	North Vancouver	29	25.10	1.16	0.77	1.66	0.7	0.5	2.4	0.3	1.0
45	West Vancouver-Bowen Is	8	17.09	0.47 *	0.20	0.92	0.6	0.3	0.5	0.4	0.2
46	Sechelt	6	7.21	0.83	0.30	1.81	0.4	-	2.5	0.6	-
47	Powell River	3	5.86	0.51	0.10	1.50	-	-	-	0.7	1.7
48	Howe Sound	5	2.58	1.94	0.63	4.53	3.0	3.2	-	3.3	-
49	Central Coast	1	0.68	1.46	0.02	8.15	-	-	♦	-	-
50	Queen Charlotte	1	0.85	1.18	0.02	6.55	-	-	-	-	♦
52	Prince Rupert	7	3.03	2.31	0.92	4.75	-	1.4	2.9	1.4	3.8
54	Smithers	3	2.12	1.42	0.28	4.14	2.6	2.2	-	1.9	-
55	Burns Lake	2	1.43	1.40	0.16	5.04	-	3.2	-	-	2.8
56	Nechako	3	2.72	1.10	0.22	3.22	-	3.1	1.7	-	-
57	Prince George	20	11.83	1.69 *	1.03	2.61	1.2	1.9	2.0	2.4	0.8
59	Peace River South	7	5.11	1.37	0.55	2.82	3.1	2.9	0.8	-	-
60	Peace River North	2	3.87	0.52	0.06	1.87	0.9	-	-	-	1.1
61	Greater Victoria	68	78.84	0.86	0.67	1.09	0.6	0.8	0.6	0.9	0.7
62	Sooke	8	9.63	0.83	0.36	1.64	0.7	1.3	0.9	0.7	-
63	Saanich	13	16.66	0.78	0.41	1.33	1.0	-	-	1.5	0.8
64	Gulf Islands	2	5.31	0.38	0.04	1.36	-	-	-	-	1.4
65	Cowichan	9	11.62	0.77	0.35	1.47	1.3	-	0.6	0.4	1.2
66	Lake Cowichan	0	1.35	-	-	-	-	-	-	-	-
67	Ladysmith	5	5.19	0.96	0.31	2.25	-	1.0	0.7	0.7	1.4
68	Nanaimo	20	19.84	1.01	0.62	1.56	-	1.0	1.2	0.6	1.4
69	Qualicum	6	11.34	0.53	0.19	1.15	0.3	0.3	-	0.3	1.5
70	Alberni	8	7.07	1.13	0.49	2.23	1.0	0.5	1.2	1.1	0.5
71	Courtenay	13	11.60	1.12	0.60	1.92	0.4	1.7	0.7	2.0	0.3
72	Campbell River	1	6.12	0.16 +	0.00	0.91	♦	-	-	-	-
75	Mission	2	7.54	0.27 +	0.03	0.96	-	-	0.6	0.6	-
76	Agassiz-Harrison	0	1.71	-	-	-	-	-	-	-	-
77	Summerland	4	4.92	0.81	0.22	2.08	-	2.6	-	2.2	-
78	Enderby	2	2.17	0.92	0.10	3.33	4.7	-	-	-	-
80	Kitimat	0	1.37	-	-	-	-	-	-	-	-
81	Fort Nelson	1	0.47	2.12	0.03	11.82	-	-	-	♦	-
84	Vancouver Island West	1	0.31	3.18	0.04	17.71	-	♦	-	-	-
85	Vancouver Island North	3	1.57	1.91	0.38	5.57	4.7	-	5.4	-	-
87	Stikine	0	0.23	-	-	-	-	-	-	-	-
88	Terrace	3	3.90	0.77	0.15	2.25	-	-	0.8	2.1	-
92	Nishga	0	0.25	-	-	-	-	-	-	-	-
94	Telegraph Creek	0	0.09	-	-	-	-	-	-	-	-
	Provincial Total	**881**	♦	1.00	♦	♦	0.8	0.8	0.8	1.0	0.9

Diabetes: Female

	Local Health Area	Observed Deaths	Expected Deaths	SMR	(p)	95% C.I. Lower	Upper	ASMR 1985	1986	1987	1988	1989
1	Fernie	8	2.25	3.55	**	1.53	7.00	6.6	4.3	2.1	1.6	1.5
2	Cranbrook	9	4.58	1.96		0.90	3.73	3.1	2.0	0.8	2.0	0.8
3	Kimberley	6	2.78	2.16		0.79	4.70	1.2	2.8	3.0	1.6	-
4	Windermere	1	1.18	0.85		0.01	4.70	-	-	-	♦	-
5	Creston	9	4.69	1.92		0.88	3.64	1.9	0.7	0.9	2.5	1.5
6	Kootenay Lake	0	1.20	-		-	-	-	-	-	-	-
7	Nelson	7	6.99	1.00		0.40	2.06	1.2	0.6	0.6	1.6	-
9	Castlegar	4	3.26	1.23		0.33	3.14	1.4	-	1.2	-	2.5
10	Arrow Lakes	0	1.62	-		-	-	-	-	-	-	-
11	Trail	11	7.03	1.56		0.78	2.80	0.7	-	3.5	0.9	1.4
12	Grand Forks	1	2.82	0.36		0.00	1.98	-	-	-	♦	-
13	Kettle Valley	1	0.69	1.45		0.02	8.08	-	-	♦	-	-
14	Southern Okanagan	9	7.02	1.28		0.59	2.43	0.6	0.5	1.7	2.0	-
15	Penticton	9	15.12	0.60		0.27	1.13	0.6	0.5	0.2	0.5	0.4
16	Keremeos	2	1.41	1.41		0.16	5.11	-	-	3.0	-	6.8
17	Princeton	2	1.28	1.56		0.18	5.65	-	-	2.7	2.5	-
18	Golden	0	0.88	-		-	-	-	-	-	-	-
19	Revelstoke	4	1.69	2.36		0.64	6.05	6.2	-	-	2.1	3.0
20	Salmon Arm	7	8.32	0.84		0.34	1.73	1.5	1.0	-	0.4	0.4
21	Armstrong-Spallumcheen	0	2.11	-		-	-	-	-	-	-	-
22	Vernon	12	15.15	0.79		0.41	1.38	1.0	0.5	0.8	1.1	-
23	Central Okanagan	31	36.39	0.85		0.58	1.21	1.0	0.1	1.1	1.0	0.5
24	Kamloops	32	16.01	2.00	***	1.37	2.82	1.7	1.1	2.1	1.7	1.7
26	North Thompson	1	0.68	1.47		0.02	8.18	-	-	♦	-	-
27	Cariboo-Chilcotin	9	5.03	1.79		0.82	3.40	1.9	1.1	0.6	1.5	3.0
28	Quesnel	5	3.39	1.47		0.47	3.44	-	1.8	-	2.5	2.1
29	Lillooet	1	0.77	1.30		0.02	7.23	-	-	-	♦	-
30	South Cariboo	1	1.37	0.73		0.01	4.05	-	-	-	-	♦
31	Merritt	2	1.77	1.13		0.13	4.08	2.1	-	-	2.8	-
32	Hope	5	1.69	2.97		0.96	6.92	-	2.9	3.2	3.2	3.0
33	Chilliwack	19	16.29	1.17		0.70	1.82	0.8	1.4	1.0	1.4	0.4
34	Abbotsford	19	23.48	0.81		0.49	1.26	0.6	0.8	0.7	0.5	0.7
35	Langley	18	17.72	1.02		0.60	1.61	1.0	1.1	0.7	0.4	1.0
36	Surrey	65	59.50	1.09		0.84	1.39	0.5	0.8	1.0	1.1	1.2
37	Delta	14	16.80	0.83		0.46	1.40	0.6	1.3	-	0.7	0.8
38	Richmond	30	27.77	1.08		0.73	1.54	1.0	1.3	0.5	0.8	0.9
39	Vancouver	172	188.62	0.91		0.78	1.06	0.5	1.0	0.8	0.9	0.8
40	New Westminster	23	21.51	1.07		0.68	1.60	0.7	0.4	0.8	1.0	1.7
41	Burnaby	68	55.85	1.22		0.95	1.54	1.3	0.6	1.1	0.8	1.2
42	Maple Ridge	15	12.18	1.23		0.69	2.03	0.8	1.5	1.0	0.9	0.9
43	Coquitlam	25	23.24	1.08		0.70	1.59	0.6	0.8	1.0	0.4	1.7
44	North Vancouver	28	30.59	0.92		0.61	1.32	1.0	0.4	0.8	0.4	1.2
45	West Vancouver-Bowen Is	18	22.02	0.82		0.48	1.29	-	0.9	0.9	1.1	0.2
46	Sechelt	1	6.45	0.16	+	0.00	0.86	-	-	-	-	♦
47	Powell River	6	5.68	1.06		0.39	2.30	1.6	-	0.6	1.7	0.6
48	Howe Sound	3	2.05	1.46		0.29	4.28	-	-	4.4	-	2.2
49	Central Coast	1	0.40	2.51		0.03	13.99	-	-	-	-	♦
50	Queen Charlotte	0	0.58	-		-	-	-	-	-	-	-
52	Prince Rupert	5	2.54	1.97		0.63	4.60	3.4	2.0	-	1.8	1.3
54	Smithers	4	1.79	2.23		0.60	5.71	6.3	3.1	-	-	2.6
55	Burns Lake	1	0.87	1.15		0.02	6.40	-	-	-	-	♦
56	Nechako	0	1.97	-		-	-	-	-	-	-	-
57	Prince George	20	9.25	2.16	**	1.32	3.34	1.4	3.2	1.7	1.3	1.6
59	Peace River South	11	4.06	2.71	**	1.35	4.85	3.3	1.2	3.1	2.8	1.1
60	Peace River North	2	2.90	0.69		0.08	2.49	-	-	-	-	2.3
61	Greater Victoria	81	109.30	0.74	**	0.59	0.92	0.3	0.5	0.9	0.7	0.9
02	Sooke	13	8.53	1.52		0.81	2.61	1.5	0.9	1.8	0.5	1.7
63	Saanich	16	16.01	1.00		0.57	1.62	-	1.0	1.4	1.3	0.6
64	Gulf Islands	2	4.65	0.43		0.05	1.55	-	-	1.2	-	0.7
65	Cowichan	14	11.39	1.23		0.67	2.06	0.8	0.8	0.4	1.5	1.6
66	Lake Cowichan	2	1.08	1.85		0.21	6.68	-	-	-	2.7	3.0
67	Ladysmith	4	4.61	0.87		0.23	2.22	0.9	1.7	-	-	0.7
68	Nanaimo	14	19.60	0.71		0.39	1.20	-	1.1	0.6	0.8	0.7
69	Qualicum	3	10.10	0.30	+	0.06	0.87	-	-	0.3	0.5	0.4
70	Alberni	3	6.81	0.44		0.09	1.29	0.7	0.7	0.7	-	-
71	Courtenay	10	10.95	0.91		0.44	1.68	1.2	0.5	-	1.9	0.3
72	Campbell River	7	5.59	1.25		0.50	2.58	0.8	0.9	1.2	1.5	0.6
75	Mission	4	6.70	0.60		0.16	1.53	0.6	-	-	1.2	0.5
76	Agassiz-Harrison	0	1.36	-		-	-	-	-	-	-	-
77	Summerland	3	4.57	0.66		0.13	1.92	0.9	-	-	0.8	0.8
78	Enderby	5	1.88	2.66		0.86	6.22	-	4.3	-	4.4	1.8
80	Kitimat	2	1.05	1.91		0.21	6.88	-	-	-	-	15.2
81	Fort Nelson	1	0.25	3.97		0.05	22.07	-	-	-	♦	-
84	Vancouver Island West	0	0.22	-		-	-	-	-	-	-	-
85	Vancouver Island North	0	1.16	-		-	-	-	-	-	-	-
87	Stikine	0	0.14	-		-	-	-	-	-	-	-
88	Terrace	1	2.48	0.40		0.01	2.24	♦	-	-	-	-
92	Nishga	0	0.16	-		-	-	-	-	-	-	-
94	Telegraph Creek	0	0.07	-		-	-	-	-	-	-	-
	Provincial Total	942	♦	1.00		♦	♦	0.7	0.8	0.8	0.9	0.9

Circulatory System: Male

	Local Health Area	Observed Deaths	Expected Deaths	SMR (p)	95% C.I. Lower	Upper	1985	1986	ASMR 1987	1988	1989
1	Fernie	81	73.98	1.09	0.87	1.36	19.9	23.4	19.1	26.8	36.2
2	Cranbrook	125	117.05	1.07	0.89	1.27	33.1	29.2	15.9	21.5	26.4
3	Kimberley	80	71.76	1.11	0.88	1.39	29.5	41.8	29.0	14.1	28.9
4	Windermere	31	44.44	0.70 *	0.47	0.99	18.0	22.3	11.9	8.7	21.1
5	Creston	146	150.69	0.97	0.82	1.14	22.4	21.2	19.4	23.0	26.9
6	Kootenay Lake	19	38.24	0.50 ***	0.30	0.78	4.7	9.6	21.6	15.4	8.3
7	Nelson	218	192.45	1.13	0.99	1.29	24.6	31.9	25.1	23.6	27.8
9	Castlegar	89	91.50	0.97	0.78	1.20	23.1	15.5	25.5	17.5	25.3
10	Arrow Lakes	44	46.22	0.95	0.69	1.28	24.8	18.8	26.1	13.4	23.1
11	Trail	216	198.17	1.09	0.95	1.25	31.0	24.4	23.7	25.6	22.2
12	Grand Forks	108	85.90	1.26 *	1.03	1.52	27.8	31.0	28.0	19.7	34.4
13	Kettle Valley	24	32.61	0.74	0.47	1.10	11.7	14.9	18.7	20.6	21.6
14	Southern Okanagan	223	212.66	1.05	0.92	1.20	27.3	26.4	18.8	24.0	24.4
15	Penticton	346	407.41	0.85 **	0.76	0.94	18.4	17.9	27.2	21.0	17.3
16	Keremeos	43	55.21	0.78	0.56	1.05	16.8	15.4	13.6	18.3	18.9
17	Princeton	59	35.89	1.64 ***	1.25	2.12	62.7	36.9	18.4	33.3	41.6
18	Golden	26	34.24	0.76	0.50	1.11	20.1	13.8	27.1	14.7	20.7
19	Revelstoke	48	44.35	1.08	0.80	1.43	27.2	23.7	37.2	20.7	24.9
20	Salmon Arm	221	266.75	0.83 **	0.72	0.95	20.4	14.3	23.0	21.3	18.1
21	Armstrong-Spallumcheen	62	67.17	0.92	0.71	1.18	33.8	21.4	15.6	20.3	20.3
22	Vernon	410	426.84	0.96	0.87	1.06	24.1	23.1	26.2	22.8	17.3
23	Central Okanagan	845	1051.72	0.80 ***	0.75	0.86	18.9	18.8	17.4	17.9	18.0
24	Kamloops	522	457.07	1.14 **	1.05	1.24	35.0	24.2	25.0	22.3	26.0
26	North Thompson	23	22.62	1.02	0.64	1.53	34.6	8.8	22.7	21.1	16.0
27	Cariboo-Chilcotin	177	169.95	1.04	0.89	1.21	23.3	26.3	17.5	26.4	21.5
28	Quesnel	143	121.38	1.18	0.99	1.39	33.7	27.8	19.1	25.8	28.7
29	Lillooet	32	32.09	1.00	0.68	1.41	43.5	33.7	12.9	20.6	13.2
30	South Cariboo	55	52.09	1.06	0.80	1.37	23.9	29.7	20.0	23.2	24.2
31	Merritt	77	55.53	1.39 **	1.09	1.73	35.6	50.4	26.7	17.4	32.0
32	Hope	60	55.70	1.08	0.82	1.39	20.7	25.4	23.2	39.3	19.3
33	Chilliwack	491	449.38	1.09	1.00	1.19	31.3	27.2	23.2	21.6	22.7
34	Abbotsford	580	621.92	0.93	0.86	1.01	24.6	22.4	22.0	18.9	18.3
35	Langley	430	486.79	0.88 **	0.80	0.97	19.1	19.9	21.0	21.9	18.8
36	Surrey	1582	1545.60	1.02	0.97	1.08	25.7	25.0	25.6	21.0	21.0
37	Delta	418	411.40	1.02	0.92	1.12	26.7	22.1	27.3	17.4	25.2
38	Richmond	609	660.68	0.92 *	0.85	1.00	23.1	25.8	21.8	20.0	17.8
39	Vancouver	4317	4119.31	1.05 **	1.02	1.08	26.1	23.6	25.5	23.7	22.6
40	New Westminster	462	404.11	1.14 **	1.04	1.25	33.2	22.9	23.5	26.0	27.3
41	Burnaby	1321	1229.17	1.07 **	1.02	1.13	24.7	26.8	24.8	25.0	22.1
42	Maple Ridge	341	306.10	1.11	1.00	1.24	28.7	30.8	26.4	22.6	21.2
43	Coquitlam	624	593.55	1.05	0.97	1.14	28.5	26.8	24.4	22.6	21.0
44	North Vancouver	691	655.27	1.05	0.98	1.14	28.3	25.2	24.8	24.6	21.5
45	West Vancouver-Bowen Is	354	458.57	0.77 ***	0.69	0.86	18.5	13.3	18.5	18.6	18.7
46	Sechelt	187	190.27	0.98	0.85	1.13	23.3	19.8	21.7	23.1	24.6
47	Powell River	190	157.47	1.21 *	1.04	1.39	28.8	31.7	30.2	26.5	22.4
48	Howe Sound	69	64.43	1.07	0.83	1.36	36.4	17.8	40.4	25.9	16.6
49	Central Coast	22	16.93	1.30	0.81	1.97	44.2	17.8	28.6	12.3	23.2
50	Queen Charlotte	20	22.39	0.89	0.55	1.38	25.9	17.4	14.6	29.1	12.7
52	Prince Rupert	101	79.92	1.26 *	1.03	1.54	28.3	29.9	26.2	32.4	27.7
54	Smithers	74	54.01	1.37 *	1.08	1.72	40.8	27.7	32.2	40.8	18.1
55	Burns Lake	41	37.39	1.10	0.79	1.49	15.4	30.2	20.0	28.5	29.5
56	Nechako	63	71.48	0.88	0.68	1.13	18.7	13.6	26.7	22.1	19.4
57	Prince George	371	298.93	1.24 ***	1.12	1.37	27.9	31.1	25.3	24.9	32.2
59	Peace River South	159	134.46	1.18 *	1.01	1.38	30.4	29.8	31.8	18.4	25.3
60	Peace River North	123	101.48	1.21 *	1.01	1.45	29.4	28.6	27.0	29.9	24.4
61	Greater Victoria	1994	2169.23	0.92 ***	0.88	0.96	22.6	22.3	21.7	20.9	19.3
62	Sooke	193	248.18	0.78 ***	0.67	0.90	20.3	17.9	14.4	19.3	16.8
63	Saanich	318	436.37	0.73 ***	0.65	0.81	18.7	18.7	16.8	15.0	17.9
64	Gulf Islands	108	139.76	0.77 **	0.63	0.93	17.5	17.4	20.6	15.6	15.8
65	Cowichan	294	309.40	0.95	0.84	1.07	27.5	21.8	21.1	18.9	20.9
66	Lake Cowichan	35	35.48	0.99	0.69	1.37	38.9	11.7	11.9	22.9	20.4
67	Ladysmith	151	139.04	1.09	0.92	1.27	26.5	29.8	21.9	19.4	27.7
68	Nanaimo	576	521.66	1.10 *	1.02	1.20	29.2	26.6	23.9	28.3	20.6
69	Qualicum	302	297.64	1.01	0.90	1.14	23.5	21.6	22.4	26.7	21.9
70	Alberni	195	184.09	1.06	0.92	1.22	26.2	25.7	26.6	27.9	16.6
71	Courtenay	311	308.34	1.01	0.90	1.13	26.5	25.2	18.2	27.1	18.9
72	Campbell River	180	156.16	1.15	0.99	1.33	36.5	33.3	26.0	28.2	18.2
75	Mission	176	199.03	0.88	0.76	1.03	23.7	19.8	15.6	25.0	19.4
76	Agassiz-Harrison	45	44.68	1.01	0.73	1.35	11.4	29.5	27.4	30.2	17.4
77	Summerland	114	135.48	0.84	0.69	1.01	12.7	31.0	26.2	15.3	14.2
78	Enderby	62	59.57	1.04	0.80	1.33	36.2	30.6	15.8	17.9	22.6
80	Kitimat	37	33.78	1.10	0.77	1.51	16.7	22.4	22.6	20.1	20.4
81	Fort Nelson	9	11.72	0.77	0.35	1.46	-	-	44.9	6.7	44.9
84	Vancouver Island West	8	7.17	1.12	0.48	2.20	46.7	-	15.0	10.1	21.1
85	Vancouver Island North	59	38.44	1.54 **	1.17	1.98	18.4	53.7	33.3	13.2	33.4
87	Stikine	4	5.67	0.71	0.19	1.01	38.8	-	37.8	-	-
88	Terrace	97	102.85	0.94	0.76	1.15	15.8	21.7	26.9	18.0	22.4
92	Nishga	12	6.71	1.79	0.92	3.12	23.3	45.7	98.1	37.0	34.0
94	Telegraph Creek	1	2.18	0.46	0.01	2.55	-	-	♦	-	-
	Provincial Total	23,481	♦	1.00	♦	♦	25.2	23.6	23.1	22.1	21.3

186

Circulatory System: Female

	Local Health Area	Observed Deaths	Expected Deaths	SMR	(p)	95% C.I. Lower	95% C.I. Upper	ASMR 1985	ASMR 1986	ASMR 1987	ASMR 1988	ASMR 1989
1	Fernie	60	46.49	1.29		0.98	1.66	23.5	32.4	24.9	18.5	15.2
2	Cranbrook	101	97.73	1.03		0.84	1.26	33.1	18.1	13.4	17.5	12.5
3	Kimberley	59	59.75	0.99		0.75	1.27	16.6	24.1	15.4	14.6	15.9
4	Windermere	20	21.64	0.92		0.56	1.43	25.2	6.4	22.4	16.2	2.3
5	Creston	91	100.68	0.90		0.73	1.11	17.6	10.9	21.4	15.8	11.3
6	Kootenay Lake	13	25.17	0.52	*	0.27	0.88	13.4	7.5	2.6	6.6	15.5
7	Nelson	180	154.57	1.16	*	1.00	1.35	23.6	25.3	15.2	19.9	17.6
9	Castlegar	75	67.81	1.11		0.87	1.39	17.7	20.4	20.6	24.0	16.3
10	Arrow Lakes	34	36.96	0.92		0.64	1.29	18.5	20.4	9.6	14.5	16.1
11	Trail	204	149.62	1.36	***	1.18	1.56	19.7	22.4	24.1	27.9	24.5
12	Grand Forks	82	58.55	1.40	**	1.11	1.74	33.2	24.5	27.9	21.7	13.4
13	Kettle Valley	6	12.79	0.47		0.17	1.02	4.2	9.3	4.7	-	9.4
14	Southern Okanagan	144	152.83	0.94		0.79	1.11	15.5	15.5	15.9	16.0	19.8
15	Penticton	247	331.79	0.74	***	0.65	0.84	19.0	12.5	11.6	14.0	10.5
16	Keremeos	23	29.57	0.78		0.49	1.17	22.1	12.7	9.9	11.7	17.1
17	Princeton	28	28.29	0.99		0.66	1.43	25.9	15.5	18.2	13.2	18.6
18	Golden	21	17.71	1.19		0.73	1.81	42.1	-	33.0	14.2	24.7
19	Revelstoke	40	37.18	1.08		0.77	1.47	19.3	18.4	16.9	25.4	14.7
20	Salmon Arm	152	173.67	0.88		0.74	1.03	18.9	16.4	12.6	16.4	14.6
21	Armstrong-Spallumcheen	41	44.59	0.92		0.66	1.25	18.7	10.0	16.0	18.4	17.8
22	Vernon	298	325.91	0.91		0.81	1.02	17.8	20.3	15.2	14.1	12.9
23	Central Okanagan	634	776.36	0.82	***	0.75	0.88	15.7	13.6	15.5	13.9	13.3
24	Kamloops	337	333.59	1.01		0.91	1.12	19.2	19.5	18.1	17.3	14.7
26	North Thompson	9	12.45	0.72		0.33	1.37	27.3	9.6	-	10.7	14.2
27	Cariboo-Chilcotin	85	97.53	0.87		0.70	1.08	14.3	18.3	6.2	19.8	15.9
28	Quesnel	97	66.07	1.47	***	1.19	1.79	26.6	21.2	36.6	20.8	27.0
29	Lillooet	20	16.24	1.23		0.75	1.90	12.8	28.4	24.1	31.1	18.1
30	South Cariboo	23	27.86	0.83		0.52	1.24	6.3	16.9	20.9	8.8	15.4
31	Merritt	47	37.46	1.25		0.92	1.67	25.7	25.4	23.0	27.7	13.7
32	Hope	31	32.47	0.95		0.65	1.36	22.9	11.1	25.8	18.6	8.3
33	Chilliwack	381	343.24	1.11	*	1.00	1.23	20.8	20.0	21.9	17.3	17.3
34	Abbotsford	475	515.45	0.92		0.84	1.01	19.7	18.2	16.0	16.3	11.3
35	Langley	401	375.42	1.07		0.97	1.18	20.0	19.5	17.3	21.3	16.5
36	Surrey	1239	1262.28	0.98		0.93	1.04	18.8	19.5	16.8	16.6	14.6
37	Delta	378	357.78	1.06		0.95	1.17	18.3	16.9	22.1	16.6	19.2
38	Richmond	545	578.51	0.94		0.86	1.02	18.1	16.9	17.4	16.2	14.3
39	Vancouver	4341	4417.38	0.98		0.95	1.01	17.3	17.6	17.5	17.4	16.8
40	New Westminster	510	497.25	1.03		0.94	1.12	19.4	17.7	17.5	18.3	15.7
41	Burnaby	1376	1279.43	1.08	**	1.02	1.13	21.5	20.1	19.0	17.1	16.7
42	Maple Ridge	298	272.19	1.09		0.97	1.23	18.5	23.8	20.0	17.5	18.2
43	Coquitlam	579	485.29	1.19	***	1.10	1.29	23.8	24.0	21.3	18.6	18.3
44	North Vancouver	751	668.94	1.12	**	1.04	1.21	22.8	20.5	17.7	19.2	17.6
45	West Vancouver-Bowen Is	508	512.01	0.99		0.91	1.08	15.7	17.1	17.8	16.8	16.0
46	Sechelt	147	133.48	1.10		0.93	1.29	17.3	23.8	23.2	11.6	19.1
47	Powell River	117	124.11	0.94		0.78	1.13	16.1	21.7	20.2	11.0	15.4
48	Howe Sound	43	38.86	1.11		0.80	1.49	22.6	31.7	14.8	17.8	12.0
49	Central Coast	10	7.20	1.39		0.66	2.55	16.1	58.9	-	6.7	13.9
50	Queen Charlotte	17	11.79	1.44		0.84	2.31	33.8	23.0	29.1	25.9	21.5
52	Prince Rupert	69	51.77	1.33	*	1.04	1.69	26.5	21.4	31.9	21.3	14.9
54	Smithers	30	36.40	0.82		0.56	1.18	19.7	14.9	10.3	17.0	10.8
55	Burns Lake	19	17.75	1.07		0.64	1.67	16.7	46.9	5.5	10.0	26.3
56	Nechako	40	40.45	0.99		0.71	1.35	17.0	11.5	20.4	24.5	17.7
57	Prince George	205	176.29	1.16	*	1.01	1.33	26.7	21.0	22.1	14.4	16.0
59	Peace River South	107	85.10	1.26	*	1.03	1.52	25.1	24.5	26.5	17.8	16.5
60	Peace River North	65	56.80	1.14		0.88	1.46	15.3	23.2	13.1	23.8	21.5
61	Greater Victoria	2377	2650.67	0.90	***	0.86	0.93	17.5	15.6	16.0	16.4	13.6
62	Sooke	183	174.35	1.05		0.90	1.21	22.9	19.0	19.4	15.2	16.6
63	Saanich	299	340.13	0.88	*	0.78	0.98	18.0	14.5	15.1	13.0	16.1
64	Gulf Islands	90	95.71	0.94		0.76	1.16	17.4	16.9	13.2	19.5	19.2
65	Cowichan	248	245.76	1.01		0.89	1.14	19.7	16.3	19.8	16.7	16.6
66	Lake Cowichan	26	20.81	1.25		0.82	1.83	16.7	14.8	9.7	9.9	43.9
67	Ladysmith	127	95.68	1.33	**	1.11	1.58	23.8	20.6	27.3	22.9	22.0
68	Nanaimo	463	414.40	1.12	*	1.02	1.22	25.5	14.9	19.3	19.6	18.8
69	Qualicum	205	210.25	0.98		0.85	1.12	15.5	15.2	22.9	13.2	17.1
70	Alberni	175	137.73	1.27	**	1.09	1.47	28.6	14.6	18.8	23.4	24.0
71	Courtenay	259	231.25	1.12		0.99	1.27	21.4	20.9	16.7	16.4	23.2
72	Campbell River	121	113.61	1.07		0.88	1.27	18.3	16.9	23.0	17.7	19.0
75	Mission	127	145.38	0.87		0.73	1.04	20.8	17.3	12.4	11.5	15.3
76	Agassiz-Harrison	28	27.39	1.02		0.68	1.48	26.1	6.4	7.3	32.2	15.7
77	Summerland	125	101.05	1.24	*	1.03	1.47	22.1	25.8	16.5	25.7	18.8
78	Enderby	40	38.52	1.04		0.74	1.41	25.2	13.4	13.1	28.9	14.6
80	Kitimat	24	20.52	1.17		0.75	1.74	43.0	5.0	30.1	23.5	11.9
81	Fort Nelson	3	4.49	0.67		0.13	1.95	-	-	-	41.8	6.4
84	Vancouver Island West	3	4.43	0.68		0.14	1.98	-	14.4	3.8	-	-
85	Vancouver Island North	26	22.48	1.16		0.76	1.69	4.3	13.8	21.5	24.6	26.7
87	Stikine	1	2.21	0.45		0.01	2.51	-	♦	-	-	-
88	Terrace	59	47.63	1.24		0.94	1.60	22.7	24.0	19.6	23.1	18.2
92	Nishga	0	2.92	-		-	-	-	-	-	-	-
94	Telegraph Creek	2	1.44	1.39		0.16	5.03	22.9	-	38.4	-	-
	Provincial Total	**20,865**	♦	1.00		♦	♦	19.0	18.1	17.7	17.1	16.0

187

Ischaemic Heart Disease: Male

	Local Health Area	Observed Deaths	Expected Deaths	SMR	(p)	95% C.I. Lower	Upper	1985	1986	ASMR 1987	1988	1989
1	Fernie	62	47.82	1.30		0.99	1.66	17.2	19.6	10.4	18.0	31.6
2	Cranbrook	68	75.89	0.90		0.70	1.14	20.6	16.4	7.7	8.0	15.8
3	Kimberley	46	46.62	0.99		0.72	1.32	21.0	14.5	19.3	8.7	10.9
4	Windermere	19	28.81	0.66		0.40	1.03	7.3	4.7	9.5	8.7	18.5
5	Creston	87	95.22	0.91		0.73	1.13	14.5	14.3	10.8	9.8	17.2
6	Kootenay Lake	12	24.68	0.49	**	0.25	0.85	4.7	6.1	3.8	13.4	5.7
7	Nelson	124	122.58	1.01		0.84	1.21	12.6	17.1	12.6	14.2	19.6
9	Castlegar	53	59.04	0.90		0.67	1.17	14.7	12.2	11.9	11.2	14.7
10	Arrow Lakes	27	29.40	0.92		0.61	1.34	13.2	12.1	21.5	2.4	16.1
11	Trail	141	126.63	1.11		0.94	1.31	21.4	17.2	16.6	17.1	12.4
12	Grand Forks	72	54.96	1.31	*	1.03	1.65	15.2	26.9	21.6	13.8	13.9
13	Kettle Valley	15	20.83	0.72		0.40	1.19	-	11.6	18.7	18.2	5.6
14	Southern Okanagan	146	135.34	1.08		0.91	1.27	19.2	18.2	12.6	11.0	18.5
15	Penticton	211	257.82	0.82	**	0.71	0.94	12.9	11.8	16.7	12.2	9.2
16	Keremeos	29	35.36	0.82		0.55	1.18	12.6	7.8	13.6	11.1	9.3
17	Princeton	40	23.38	1.71	**	1.22	2.33	38.5	20.2	15.2	11.7	41.6
18	Golden	14	21.97	0.64		0.35	1.07	20.1	11.1	9.9	2.5	10.7
19	Revelstoke	27	28.65	0.94		0.62	1.37	24.8	15.0	19.3	8.0	12.6
20	Salmon Arm	138	172.39	0.80	**	0.67	0.95	13.1	9.7	15.6	11.3	10.3
21	Armstrong-Spallumcheen	42	42.90	0.98		0.71	1.32	16.2	16.3	14.3	15.0	13.6
22	Vernon	244	271.69	0.90		0.79	1.02	16.0	15.0	13.4	15.1	9.5
23	Central Okanagan	504	669.38	0.75	***	0.69	0.82	12.0	10.6	10.6	10.8	10.4
24	Kamloops	336	295.77	1.14	*	1.02	1.26	25.3	15.7	16.8	12.6	14.1
26	North Thompson	18	14.80	1.22		0.72	1.92	25.6	3.9	14.7	21.1	16.0
27	Cariboo-Chilcotin	116	111.69	1.04		0.86	1.25	13.7	17.1	11.9	15.9	12.9
28	Quesnel	100	78.53	1.27	*	1.04	1.55	20.7	19.9	18.2	15.3	20.9
29	Lillooet	21	20.54	1.02		0.63	1.56	22.2	25.5	9.1	13.2	9.8
30	South Cariboo	33	33.49	0.99		0.68	1.38	16.4	21.2	8.9	8.5	18.2
31	Merritt	49	36.18	1.35	*	1.00	1.79	30.2	30.5	9.0	9.4	20.8
32	Hope	36	36.43	0.99		0.69	1.37	13.1	17.7	16.4	29.2	3.6
33	Chilliwack	317	287.46	1.10		0.98	1.23	20.0	18.8	13.4	13.8	15.3
34	Abbotsford	399	394.59	1.01		0.91	1.12	17.4	13.7	15.9	14.2	12.5
35	Langley	288	312.32	0.92		0.82	1.04	12.5	12.6	16.8	15.5	10.4
36	Surrey	1081	988.56	1.09	**	1.03	1.16	18.9	17.5	18.4	13.9	13.0
37	Delta	296	268.44	1.10		0.98	1.24	16.3	13.9	22.0	12.7	17.5
38	Richmond	410	430.00	0.95		0.86	1.05	14.8	18.9	14.9	12.5	11.8
39	Vancouver	2717	2616.03	1.04		1.00	1.08	17.2	14.7	15.8	15.1	13.9
40	New Westminster	321	256.58	1.25	***	1.12	1.40	24.9	16.2	16.2	18.4	16.7
41	Burnaby	894	787.81	1.13	***	1.06	1.21	17.2	18.8	17.8	15.8	13.8
42	Maple Ridge	213	196.01	1.09		0.95	1.24	17.8	20.1	15.9	14.6	13.1
43	Coquitlam	410	384.14	1.07		0.97	1.18	19.5	18.3	14.9	14.8	13.2
44	North Vancouver	459	426.65	1.08		0.98	1.18	18.8	17.0	16.9	17.0	12.9
45	West Vancouver-Bowen Is	213	294.70	0.72	***	0.63	0.83	11.9	8.5	12.0	11.1	9.4
46	Sechelt	124	122.68	1.01		0.84	1.21	14.7	13.4	15.7	13.4	18.1
47	Powell River	125	100.82	1.24	*	1.03	1.48	19.5	22.5	20.8	14.5	15.1
48	Howe Sound	43	42.60	1.01		0.73	1.36	18.6	10.2	18.1	22.4	6.8
49	Central Coast	16	11.04	1.45		0.83	2.35	36.5	11.6	28.6	-	9.6
50	Queen Charlotte	11	14.21	0.77		0.39	1.39	14.2	7.6	14.6	18.1	6.1
52	Prince Rupert	75	51.48	1.46	**	1.15	1.83	19.4	25.5	22.4	21.7	18.7
54	Smithers	42	35.17	1.19		0.86	1.61	24.0	15.5	21.0	20.1	7.0
55	Burns Lake	28	24.18	1.16		0.77	1.67	6.1	18.5	20.0	14.7	23.4
56	Nechako	38	46.20	0.82		0.58	1.13	9.7	6.2	16.4	12.0	14.8
57	Prince George	230	196.92	1.17	*	1.02	1.33	13.9	19.2	16.1	13.0	20.1
59	Peace River South	107	86.26	1.24	*	1.02	1.50	19.8	18.4	24.7	14.2	14.2
60	Peace River North	77	65.59	1.17		0.93	1.47	18.0	19.0	14.2	20.8	16.0
61	Greater Victoria	1182	1362.33	0.87	***	0.82	0.92	14.2	15.5	13.3	11.7	10.8
62	Sooke	121	161.73	0.75	***	0.62	0.89	14.1	12.1	7.2	12.2	8.8
63	Saanich	187	282.49	0.66	***	0.57	0.76	10.6	11.7	10.5	6.9	9.6
64	Gulf Islands	66	90.28	0.73	**	0.57	0.93	12.9	8.3	12.3	12.5	9.6
65	Cowichan	179	198.52	0.90		0.77	1.04	17.9	12.1	13.8	11.4	12.0
66	Lake Cowichan	24	23.21	1.03		0.66	1.54	31.7	9.2	9.5	14.4	7.0
67	Ladysmith	95	89.03	1.07		0.86	1.30	15.2	18.0	16.1	13.5	16.6
68	Nanaimo	352	336.37	1.05		0.94	1.16	18.3	17.1	15.3	15.1	12.0
69	Qualicum	196	192.70	1.02		0.88	1.17	15.5	13.7	13.7	18.4	13.8
70	Alberni	136	120.17	1.13		0.95	1.34	17.7	18.6	18.2	19.2	12.4
71	Courtenay	199	198.86	1.00		0.87	1.15	18.2	17.3	12.9	14.9	10.9
72	Campbell River	113	102.31	1.10		0.91	1.33	25.8	16.8	19.4	16.0	9.7
75	Mission	123	127.64	0.96		0.80	1.15	16.8	14.8	11.1	17.6	12.4
76	Agassiz-Harrison	28	28.83	0.97		0.65	1.40	11.4	26.8	12.4	9.3	13.5
77	Summerland	77	85.26	0.90		0.71	1.13	6.8	23.4	16.4	9.9	9.8
78	Enderby	37	37.80	0.98		0.69	1.35	14.5	24.7	6.4	14.8	13.9
80	Kitimat	22	22.76	0.97		0.61	1.46	3.1	22.4	5.5	8.1	13.7
81	Fort Nelson	4	7.67	0.52		0.14	1.34	-	-	12.5	6.7	9.1
84	Vancouver Island West	6	4.86	1.24		0.45	2.69	7.5	-	15.0	10.1	4.9
85	Vancouver Island North	46	25.38	1.81	***	1.33	2.42	17.1	34.2	21.6	9.2	32.3
87	Stikine	4	3.72	1.07		0.29	2.75	38.8	-	37.8	-	-
88	Terrace	63	66.18	0.95		0.73	1.22	13.1	15.3	10.9	12.7	15.2
92	Nishga	8	4.29	1.87		0.80	3.68	14.6	38.1	82.9	37.0	17.1
94	Telegraph Creek	1	1.47	0.68		0.01	3.78	-	-	◆	-	-
	Provincial Total	**15,036**	◆	1.00		◆	◆	16.7	15.5	15.1	13.9	13.0

188

Ischaemic Heart Disease: Female

	Local Health Area	Observed Deaths	Expected Deaths	SMR	(p)	95% C.I. Lower	95% C.I. Upper	ASMR 1985	1986	1987	1988	1989
1	Fernie	39	24.30	1.61	**	1.14	2.19	16.6	17.4	16.1	15.7	9.1
2	Cranbrook	50	51.13	0.98		0.73	1.29	10.9	11.0	5.4	10.8	7.3
3	Kimberley	35	31.61	1.11		0.77	1.54	9.8	15.8	9.7	7.3	8.9
4	Windermere	10	11.55	0.87		0.41	1.59	10.7	2.7	13.7	6.4	2.3
5	Creston	46	53.45	0.86		0.63	1.15	12.6	6.5	10.5	6.2	3.6
6	Kootenay Lake	8	13.31	0.60		0.26	1.18	9.6	3.8	-	6.6	9.2
7	Nelson	100	81.24	1.23	*	1.00	1.50	14.2	15.2	8.1	11.5	8.3
9	Castlegar	37	35.80	1.03		0.73	1.42	3.9	11.0	7.7	14.7	10.4
10	Arrow Lakes	14	19.40	0.72		0.39	1.21	10.9	7.2	2.8	8.2	4.9
11	Trail	108	79.27	1.36	**	1.12	1.64	10.3	13.7	10.1	12.5	14.1
12	Grand Forks	47	31.17	1.51	**	1.11	2.00	20.8	16.9	15.3	12.7	4.2
13	Kettle Valley	4	6.83	0.59		0.16	1.50	-	9.3	4.7	-	4.6
14	Southern Okanagan	70	80.89	0.87		0.67	1.09	6.5	7.7	6.1	8.9	9.4
15	Penticton	128	175.26	0.73	***	0.61	0.87	10.8	7.3	6.1	5.8	5.0
16	Keremeos	13	15.70	0.83		0.44	1.42	15.7	9.6	6.7	5.8	5.6
17	Princeton	15	14.81	1.01		0.57	1.67	7.9	10.0	14.7	2.5	10.8
18	Golden	7	9.23	0.76		0.30	1.56	16.3	-	4.8	5.5	8.6
19	Revelstoke	23	19.41	1.18		0.75	1.78	7.2	11.6	7.5	12.6	14.7
20	Salmon Arm	74	91.99	0.80		0.63	1.01	9.9	8.1	6.8	5.7	7.4
21	Armstrong-Spallumcheen	22	23.52	0.94		0.59	1.42	6.6	7.8	6.2	7.9	14.5
22	Vernon	148	171.79	0.86		0.73	1.01	8.8	11.3	6.2	7.2	6.4
23	Central Okanagan	322	410.51	0.78	***	0.70	0.87	8.0	7.0	6.7	6.8	7.6
24	Kamloops	171	174.87	0.98		0.84	1.14	9.0	9.6	9.1	10.4	6.9
26	North Thompson	3	6.60	0.45		0.09	1.33	27.3	5.5	-	-	-
27	Cariboo-Chilcotin	35	50.90	0.69	*	0.48	0.96	7.0	6.2	1.4	10.2	4.0
28	Quesnel	48	34.64	1.39	*	1.02	1.84	13.6	9.1	21.2	6.3	13.2
29	Lillooet	9	8.52	1.06		0.48	2.00	5.9	10.2	5.9	16.7	12.2
30	South Cariboo	11	14.72	0.75		0.37	1.34	-	10.5	11.4	5.5	3.5
31	Merritt	27	19.58	1.38		0.91	2.01	18.5	7.3	14.8	17.9	7.6
32	Hope	13	17.30	0.75		0.40	1.29	1.7	5.1	10.6	9.5	5.3
33	Chilliwack	229	181.90	1.26	***	1.10	1.43	12.7	13.0	13.1	7.2	11.8
34	Abbotsford	271	270.67	1.00		0.89	1.13	11.9	11.1	10.2	7.7	5.9
35	Langley	194	196.90	0.99		0.85	1.13	10.0	8.8	8.5	10.2	8.0
36	Surrey	720	663.78	1.08	*	1.01	1.17	11.4	11.2	10.1	9.4	7.9
37	Delta	202	186.32	1.08		0.94	1.24	9.5	10.7	11.3	7.6	9.9
38	Richmond	283	303.32	0.93		0.83	1.05	8.2	8.4	9.8	8.7	7.7
39	Vancouver	2307	2311.03	1.00		0.96	1.04	9.7	9.6	9.3	8.6	8.8
40	New Westminster	298	261.39	1.14	*	1.01	1.28	11.8	9.9	9.6	11.9	9.2
41	Burnaby	753	669.01	1.13	**	1.05	1.21	13.4	12.0	10.1	8.4	8.2
42	Maple Ridge	159	141.83	1.12		0.95	1.31	13.7	12.4	9.8	8.5	9.5
43	Coquitlam	360	253.04	1.42	***	1.28	1.58	15.3	15.9	13.5	11.8	10.0
44	North Vancouver	398	349.89	1.14	*	1.03	1.25	11.3	11.1	9.8	10.2	9.3
45	West Vancouver-Bowen Is	263	267.94	0.98		0.87	1.11	8.6	8.7	9.0	8.8	8.2
46	Sechelt	74	70.96	1.04		0.82	1.31	8.0	16.6	8.5	7.0	7.6
47	Powell River	61	65.22	0.94		0.72	1.20	8.0	10.0	10.8	5.6	9.8
48	Howe Sound	20	20.31	0.98		0.60	1.52	15.4	6.3	7.6	10.2	5.8
49	Central Coast	5	3.82	1.31		0.42	3.05	7.6	26.9	-	-	7.3
50	Queen Charlotte	9	6.08	1.48		0.68	2.81	19.0	7.7	20.2	9.6	14.3
52	Prince Rupert	39	27.00	1.44	*	1.03	1.97	17.3	12.4	15.3	11.9	9.9
54	Smithers	8	18.84	0.42	**	0.18	0.84	11.0	3.1	2.8	2.9	1.7
55	Burns Lake	7	9.21	0.76		0.30	1.57	3.3	21.9	-	4.3	7.7
56	Nechako	14	21.09	0.66		0.36	1.11	3.8	5.1	8.9	5.3	8.8
57	Prince George	92	91.36	1.01		0.81	1.23	12.3	7.8	9.4	5.1	8.3
59	Peace River South	55	44.31	1.24		0.94	1.62	17.6	12.3	12.3	9.4	7.1
60	Peace River North	37	29.50	1.25		0.88	1.73	12.4	12.6	7.6	13.7	9.8
61	Greater Victoria	1157	1383.96	0.84	***	0.79	0.89	8.9	8.4	8.9	6.8	5.9
62	Sooke	96	91.63	1.05		0.85	1.28	10.9	10.9	11.2	9.0	7.0
63	Saanich	141	179.48	0.79	**	0.66	0.93	8.2	8.3	7.0	5.1	7.8
64	Gulf Islands	43	51.12	0.84		0.61	1.13	7.1	9.5	3.9	10.5	9.2
65	Cowichan	121	129.32	0.94		0.78	1.12	11.1	7.5	8.9	6.1	9.2
66	Lake Cowichan	14	11.08	1.26		0.69	2.12	10.4	10.7	6.6	2.7	21.0
67	Ladysmith	66	50.90	1.30	*	1.00	1.65	8.1	12.5	17.7	11.4	9.6
68	Nanaimo	253	218.90	1.16	*	1.02	1.31	13.5	7.9	10.1	11.6	10.2
69	Qualicum	83	111.78	0.74	**	0.59	0.92	7.0	6.8	7.2	4.7	7.3
70	Alberni	76	72.69	1.05		0.82	1.31	13.3	5.3	9.1	9.0	9.8
71	Courtenay	130	121.62	1.07		0.89	1.27	11.8	11.2	7.0	8.8	11.2
72	Campbell River	63	59.56	1.06		0.81	1.35	9.6	6.4	11.2	10.7	10.5
75	Mission	61	76.21	0.80		0.61	1.03	9.1	9.8	5.8	6.3	6.3
76	Agassiz-Harrison	10	14.58	0.69		0.33	1.26	10.3	-	4.5	8.0	6.2
77	Summerland	69	53.50	1.29	*	1.00	1.63	11.3	13.1	13.1	11.5	10.6
78	Enderby	22	20.51	1.07		0.67	1.62	12.0	13.4	4.4	17.7	10.5
80	Kitimat	10	10.43	0.96		0.46	1.76	8.4	-	12.3	19.6	3.7
81	Fort Nelson	0	2.22	-		-	-	-	-	-	-	-
84	Vancouver Island West	1	2.22	0.45		0.01	2.51	-	-	◆	-	-
85	Vancouver Island North	12	11.48	1.05		0.54	1.83	-	11.2	3.5	20.5	7.0
87	Stikine	1	1.15	0.87		0.01	4.82	-	◆	-	-	-
88	Terrace	20	24.73	0.81		0.49	1.25	5.5	6.8	8.7	9.4	7.0
92	Nishga	0	1.53	-		-	-	-	-	-	-	-
94	Telegraph Creek	0	0.74	-		-	-	-	-	-	-	-
	Provincial Total	10,944	◆	1.00		◆	◆	10.3	9.9	9.3	8.5	8.1

Cerebrovascular Disease/Stroke: Male

	Local Health Area	Observed Deaths	Expected Deaths	SMR	(p)	95% C.I. Lower	95% C.I. Upper	ASMR 1985	1986	1987	1988	1989
1	Fernie	8	11.60	0.69		0.30	1.36	1.3	0.7	2.9	4.0	3.1
2	Cranbrook	32	18.27	1.75	**	1.20	2.47	10.3	6.2	5.6	6.0	4.9
3	Kimberley	17	11.22	1.52		0.88	2.43	5.7	13.6	2.8	3.6	5.1
4	Windermere	6	6.89	0.87		0.32	1.90	5.6	9.2	-	-	2.6
5	Creston	30	25.31	1.19		0.00	1.69	5.6	4.8	4.6	3.9	3.4
6	Kootenay Lake	1	6.07	0.16	+	0.00	0.92	-	-	♦	-	-
7	Nelson	50	31.62	1.58	**	1.17	2.08	5.1	8.8	4.7	6.3	4.8
9	Castlegar	14	14.53	0.96		0.53	1.62	2.0	2.0	4.4	3.7	4.7
10	Arrow Lakes	7	7.62	0.92		0.37	1.89	5.1	2.0	-	4.5	5.0
11	Trail	47	32.28	1.46	*	1.07	1.94	5.6	6.0	5.0	5.6	4.2
12	Grand Forks	14	14.02	1.00		0.55	1.68	10.8	1.0	4.0	2.3	1.3
13	Kettle Valley	2	5.28	0.38		0.04	1.37	-	3.4	-	-	4.4
14	Southern Okanagan	29	35.02	0.83		0.55	1.19	3.7	2.5	3.5	3.3	1.4
15	Penticton	56	68.10	0.82		0.62	1.07	2.8	2.0	3.1	4.2	3.9
16	Keremeos	6	8.99	0.67		0.24	1.45	-	-	-	5.6	4.6
17	Princeton	12	5.51	2.18	*	1.12	3.80	24.2	14.0	-	4.8	-
18	Golden	7	5.45	1.28		0.51	2.65	-	2.6	4.5	12.2	5.2
19	Revelstoke	9	6.96	1.29		0.59	2.45	2.4	3.4	7.5	2.8	7.6
20	Salmon Arm	39	42.13	0.93		0.66	1.27	3.8	1.5	2.3	5.7	4.8
21	Armstrong-Spallumcheen	5	10.92	0.46		0.15	1.07	7.9	1.5	-	-	-
22	Vernon	61	70.06	0.87		0.67	1.12	1.9	2.4	6.0	2.4	3.5
23	Central Okanagan	144	172.85	0.83	*	0.70	0.98	2.6	3.1	3.4	2.9	3.0
24	Kamloops	65	71.53	0.91		0.70	1.16	4.3	3.1	2.6	3.4	3.7
26	North Thompson	0	3.44	-		-	-	-	-	-	-	-
27	Cariboo-Chilcotin	22	25.26	0.87		0.55	1.32	0.9	3.3	3.0	4.1	4.2
28	Quesnel	20	18.90	1.06		0.65	1.63	3.5	4.9	0.9	7.3	1.6
29	Lillooet	3	5.15	0.58		0.12	1.70	4.8	5.1	3.8	-	-
30	South Cariboo	6	8.31	0.72		0.26	1.57	5.2	-	2.3	6.1	-
31	Merritt	12	8.50	1.41		0.73	2.47	3.0	10.7	11.7	-	5.4
32	Hope	7	8.52	0.82		0.33	1.69	1.6	-	1.6	2.4	9.0
33	Chilliwack	89	72.89	1.22		0.98	1.50	5.9	4.6	4.0	4.2	4.0
34	Abbotsford	105	102.74	1.02		0.84	1.24	3.5	5.5	3.2	2.8	3.5
35	Langley	55	77.86	0.71	**	0.53	0.92	2.9	2.3	1.8	3.3	2.4
36	Surrey	219	249.20	0.88		0.77	1.00	3.2	2.7	3.1	3.3	3.6
37	Delta	64	62.89	1.02		0.78	1.30	5.1	4.6	2.6	2.1	5.0
38	Richmond	92	101.60	0.91		0.73	1.11	4.2	2.4	3.7	3.2	3.3
39	Vancouver	750	680.54	1.10	**	1.02	1.18	4.1	4.2	4.6	4.1	3.6
40	New Westminster	71	67.02	1.06		0.83	1.34	3.3	3.2	4.0	3.8	5.4
41	Burnaby	223	197.76	1.13		0.98	1.29	4.0	4.5	3.9	4.2	4.3
42	Maple Ridge	61	49.34	1.24		0.95	1.59	4.5	4.9	4.6	3.6	4.9
43	Coquitlam	94	92.35	1.02		0.82	1.25	3.7	4.7	3.9	3.4	3.0
44	North Vancouver	115	100.69	1.14		0.94	1.37	4.6	3.6	4.2	3.3	5.1
45	West Vancouver-Bowen Is	66	73.44	0.90		0.69	1.14	3.2	2.2	2.6	2.7	5.2
46	Sechelt	24	30.24	0.79		0.51	1.18	3.4	3.8	1.2	4.3	1.4
47	Powell River	31	25.47	1.22		0.83	1.73	4.1	3.4	6.5	5.1	2.6
48	Howe Sound	9	9.35	0.96		0.44	1.83	5.3	1.3	2.5	1.4	3.9
49	Central Coast	4	2.61	1.54		0.41	3.93	-	6.3	-	12.3	6.0
50	Queen Charlotte	2	3.66	0.55		0.06	1.97	4.2	7.6	-	-	-
52	Prince Rupert	7	12.58	0.56		0.22	1.15	4.1	-	0.8	1.4	2.2
54	Smithers	11	8.24	1.33		0.67	2.39	-	7.8	4.0	8.0	6.1
55	Burns Lake	2	5.85	0.34		0.04	1.23	-	3.2	-	1.8	-
56	Nechako	11	11.17	0.98		0.49	1.76	2.9	3.8	7.0	2.8	1.7
57	Prince George	50	44.09	1.13		0.84	1.50	5.4	3.9	4.5	3.7	4.1
59	Peace River South	18	21.54	0.84		0.50	1.32	4.2	5.5	0.8	0.8	3.6
60	Peace River North	26	15.82	1.64	*	1.07	2.41	9.4	4.9	3.9	5.5	5.1
61	Greater Victoria	337	368.67	0.91		0.82	1.02	4.0	2.3	3.5	3.8	3.2
62	Sooke	30	37.98	0.79		0.53	1.13	2.5	3.5	2.6	2.3	4.0
63	Saanich	59	68.23	0.86		0.66	1.12	3.9	4.3	3.0	3.5	2.8
64	Gulf Islands	19	22.13	0.86		0.52	1.34	1.3	7.8	2.3	1.1	1.6
65	Cowichan	45	49.58	0.91		0.66	1.21	4.5	4.0	3.6	3.0	2.0
66	Lake Cowichan	5	5.39	0.93		0.30	2.17	3.6	2.5	-	3.0	6.7
67	Ladysmith	21	22.50	0.93		0.58	1.43	4.7	4.8	1.6	3.6	3.4
68	Nanaimo	102	82.97	1.23	*	1.01	1.50	5.5	3.6	3.6	5.7	4.5
69	Qualicum	55	46.74	1.18		0.89	1.53	5.8	4.3	4.7	3.9	3.3
70	Alberni	27	28.19	0.96		0.63	1.39	2.5	3.5	4.0	4.4	2.5
71	Courtenay	44	48.78	0.90		0.66	1.21	3.3	3.4	2.1	3.9	3.6
72	Campbell River	26	23.55	1.10		0.72	1.62	2.3	7.7	2.9	5.8	2.8
75	Mission	30	31.97	0.94		0.63	1.34	3.9	2.7	2.7	4.0	3.7
76	Agassiz-Harrison	3	7.07	0.42		0.09	1.24	-	-	2.4	5.0	-
77	Summerland	18	22.91	0.79		0.47	1.24	3.3	4.7	3.9	2.1	1.3
78	Enderby	5	9.83	0.51		0.16	1.19	4.4	-	-	1.7	1.6
80	Kitimat	7	4.62	1.51		0.61	3.12	4.5	♦	1.3	7.0	3.6
81	Fort Nelson	2	1.73	1.16		0.13	4.17	-	-	32.4	-	7.1
84	Vancouver Island West	1	0.95	1.05		0.01	5.87	♦	-	-	-	-
85	Vancouver Island North	5	5.57	0.90		0.29	2.09	1.3	4.3	0.9	1.3	1.1
87	Stikine	0	0.85	-		-	-	-	-	-	-	-
88	Terrace	12	16.15	0.74		0.38	1.30	2.1	1.4	5.7	0.6	2.8
92	Nishga	3	1.08	2.78		0.56	8.11	8.6	7.7	-	-	16.8
94	Telegraph Creek	0	0.30	-		-	-	-	-	-	-	-
	Provincial Total	**3,788**	♦	**1.00**		♦	♦	**3.9**	**3.6**	**3.6**	**3.6**	**3.6**

190

Cerebrovascular Disease/Stroke: Female

	Local Health Area	Observed Deaths	Expected Deaths	SMR (p)	95% C.I. Lower	95% C.I. Upper	ASMR 1985	1986	1987	1988	1989
1	Fernie	12	11.23	1.07	0.55	1.87	1.6	11.9	6.5	-	4.0
2	Cranbrook	29	23.51	1.23	0.83	1.77	8.2	6.2	6.1	4.1	2.4
3	Kimberley	10	14.21	0.70	0.34	1.29	2.7	3.4	2.6	4.5	1.6
4	Windermere	6	5.09	1.18	0.43	2.56	10.7	-	3.0	9.8	-
5	Creston	24	23.89	1.00	0.64	1.49	3.0	1.7	4.8	4.0	6.1
6	Kootenay Lake	3	5.97	0.50	0.10	1.47	3.8	3.7	-	-	3.5
7	Nelson	36	37.12	0.97	0.68	1.34	5.2	5.2	2.0	3.9	3.7
9	Castlegar	18	16.18	1.11	0.66	1.76	8.1	3.9	5.6	3.9	3.7
10	Arrow Lakes	7	8.89	0.79	0.32	1.62	2.3	7.1	-	2.2	4.7
11	Trail	37	35.56	1.04	0.73	1.43	3.4	2.7	4.8	5.2	6.0
12	Grand Forks	17	13.87	1.23	0.71	1.96	5.8	4.4	10.1	4.0	1.3
13	Kettle Valley	0	3.00	-	-	-	-	-	-	-	-
14	Southern Okanagan	31	36.28	0.85	0.58	1.21	4.5	3.1	3.8	3.1	5.0
15	Penticton	61	79.15	0.77 *	0.59	0.99	3.9	3.9	3.2	3.1	2.8
16	Keremeos	3	7.00	0.43	0.09	1.25	3.7	-	3.2	-	3.0
17	Princeton	6	6.81	0.88	0.32	1.92	8.2	3.0	-	4.1	5.3
18	Golden	7	4.27	1.64	0.66	3.38	10.1	-	13.8	5.1	3.3
19	Revelstoke	10	9.01	1.11	0.53	2.04	8.8	4.7	6.7	5.2	-
20	Salmon Arm	36	41.13	0.88	0.61	1.21	3.3	5.1	1.4	3.6	5.2
21	Armstrong-Spallumcheen	7	10.64	0.66	0.26	1.36	-	2.2	3.8	5.3	1.7
22	Vernon	74	77.88	0.95	0.75	1.19	4.7	5.1	4.0	2.7	3.5
23	Central Okanagan	174	184.81	0.94	0.81	1.09	4.7	3.7	4.4	3.7	3.6
24	Kamloops	71	80.20	0.89	0.69	1.12	5.6	3.4	4.0	2.8	3.3
26	North Thompson	3	2.97	1.01	0.20	2.96	-	4.1	-	5.4	4.2
27	Cariboo-Chilcotin	24	23.44	1.02	0.66	1.52	3.8	7.3	2.6	5.3	4.2
28	Quesnel	33	15.85	2.08 ***	1.43	2.92	11.4	8.4	9.0	8.9	7.6
29	Lillooet	4	3.90	1.03	0.28	2.62	6.9	5.1	11.3	-	-
30	South Cariboo	6	6.65	0.90	0.33	1.97	2.9	-	6.7	-	9.0
31	Merritt	13	9.02	1.44	0.77	2.46	7.2	13.8	2.1	5.1	6.1
32	Hope	10	7.64	1.31	0.63	2.41	7.5	2.8	9.8	9.1	-
33	Chilliwack	93	81.60	1.14	0.92	1.40	4.3	4.2	5.4	6.8	3.6
34	Abbotsford	116	123.58	0.94	0.78	1.13	4.6	3.8	3.9	4.6	2.7
35	Langley	96	90.22	1.06	0.86	1.30	5.5	4.7	4.8	4.3	3.4
36	Surrey	292	302.43	0.97	0.86	1.08	4.2	4.4	3.6	4.1	4.1
37	Delta	87	86.58	1.00	0.80	1.24	3.6	1.8	5.4	4.1	5.9
38	Richmond	124	138.98	0.89	0.74	1.06	4.3	3.5	3.3	3.6	4.1
39	Vancouver	1057	1067.13	0.99	0.93	1.05	4.1	4.1	4.2	4.6	3.9
40	New Westminster	107	119.59	0.89	0.73	1.08	4.2	4.2	3.8	3.1	2.8
41	Burnaby	341	308.53	1.11	0.99	1.23	4.5	5.3	4.2	5.0	4.3
42	Maple Ridge	77	65.88	1.17	0.92	1.46	3.6	6.5	4.6	4.8	5.1
43	Coquitlam	109	117.40	0.93	0.76	1.12	4.7	4.8	2.0	3.8	4.5
44	North Vancouver	199	161.28	1.23 **	1.07	1.42	7.1	5.2	4.7	4.8	4.4
45	West Vancouver-Bowen Is	137	123.42	1.11	0.93	1.31	3.7	5.2	5.9	4.1	3.5
46	Sechelt	38	31.55	1.20	0.85	1.65	5.7	3.9	7.1	2.7	5.1
47	Powell River	31	29.75	1.04	0.71	1.48	5.7	2.9	5.8	4.1	3.0
48	Howe Sound	9	9.32	0.97	0.44	1.83	1.6	9.2	2.8	4.5	3.3
49	Central Coast	1	1.71	0.58	0.01	3.25	-	◆	-	-	-
50	Queen Charlotte	3	2.88	1.04	0.21	3.04	2.5	6.7	-	-	7.2
52	Prince Rupert	17	12.50	1.36	0.79	2.18	7.9	3.5	8.8	4.8	4.1
54	Smithers	11	8.87	1.24	0.62	2.22	2.8	8.6	-	6.2	9.2
55	Burns Lake	6	4.29	1.40	0.51	3.04	6.5	19.3	5.5	-	-
56	Nechako	11	9.75	1.13	0.56	2.02	2.0	4.6	7.4	4.1	4.8
57	Prince George	46	42.85	1.07	0.79	1.43	8.2	3.8	4.4	2.6	4.0
59	Peace River South	25	20.63	1.21	0.78	1.79	5.2	7.4	5.0	5.2	1.8
60	Peace River North	11	13.75	0.80	0.40	1.43	1.6	2.8	1.3	7.1	2.7
61	Greater Victoria	554	641.24	0.86 ***	0.79	0.94	4.1	3.2	3.5	4.4	3.4
62	Sooke	40	41.69	0.96	0.69	1.31	3.0	4.1	4.8	4.7	3.7
63	Saanich	81	80.93	1.00	0.79	1.24	5.5	3.5	3.5	4.3	4.2
64	Gulf Islands	29	22.48	1.29	0.86	1.85	7.9	2.4	8.1	2.9	5.3
65	Cowichan	53	58.84	0.90	0.67	1.18	4.9	4.8	3.5	3.9	2.8
66	Lake Cowichan	6	4.92	1.22	0.45	2.65	3.9	4.1	-	4.1	11.1
67	Ladysmith	25	22.64	1.10	0.71	1.63	4.2	3.3	4.2	2.4	7.3
68	Nanaimo	111	98.68	1.12	0.93	1.35	6.3	3.6	4.9	4.8	4.4
69	Qualicum	56	49.54	1.13	0.85	1.47	5.7	4.0	6.2	3.3	4.2
70	Alberni	47	32.81	1.43 *	1.05	1.91	5.5	5.0	3.8	7.8	6.9
71	Courtenay	63	55.29	1.14	0.88	1.46	3.3	6.9	5.1	4.1	4.7
72	Campbell River	29	27.24	1.06	0.71	1.53	4.0	7.7	5.1	3.0	3.7
75	Mission	30	34.88	0.86	0.58	1.23	3.9	4.2	3.0	3.5	3.1
76	Agassiz-Harrison	8	6.47	1.24	0.53	2.44	4.3	-	2.9	13.2	4.7
77	Summerland	29	24.07	1.20	0.81	1.73	7.2	7.6	2.5	7.0	2.4
78	Enderby	6	9.13	0.66	0.24	1.43	4.4	-	4.9	3.5	-
80	Kitimat	6	5.09	1.18	0.43	2.57	8.6	-	13.2	2.0	3.7
81	Fort Nelson	1	1.14	0.88	0.01	4.89	-	-	-	◆	-
84	Vancouver Island West	0	1.12	-	-	-	-	-	-	-	-
85	Vancouver Island North	9	5.56	1.62	0.74	3.07	-	-	18.0	1.1	14.4
87	Stikine	0	0.54	-	-	-	-	-	-	-	-
88	Terrace	15	11.55	1.30	0.73	2.14	8.5	5.2	5.7	4.1	3.1
92	Nishga	0	0.69	-	-	-	-	-	-	-	-
94	Telegraph Creek	1	0.36	2.81	0.04	15.61	-	-	◆	-	-
	Provincial Total	5,016	◆	1.00	◆	◆	4.5	4.2	4.2	4.3	3.9

Diseases of Arteries, Arterioles, and Capillaries: Male

	Local Health Area	Observed Deaths	Expected Deaths	SMR (p)	95% C.I. Lower	Upper	ASMR 1985	1986	1987	1988	1989
1	Fernie	6	4.79	1.25	0.46	2.72	1.5	1.5	-	4.8	1.5
2	Cranbrook	9	7.67	1.17	0.54	2.23	0.9	1.4	1.0	3.1	2.6
3	Kimberley	4	4.88	0.82	0.22	2.10	1.5	-	2.8	-	5.4
4	Windermere	1	2.91	0.34	0.00	1.91	-	◆	-	-	-
5	Creston	9	10.76	0.84	0.38	1.59	0.7	-	1.9	3.0	0.7
6	Kootenay Lake	2	2.68	0.75	0.08	2.70	-	-	5.7	1.9	-
7	Nelson	16	13.34	1.20	0.68	1.95	1.8	1.2	5.1	1.0	0.4
9	Castlegar	8	6.20	1.29	0.56	2.54	1.0	-	4.0	2.6	2.0
10	Arrow Lakes	1	3.24	0.31	0.00	1.72	-	◆	-	-	-
11	Trail	13	13.77	0.94	0.50	1.61	1.7	0.6	1.1	1.5	2.2
12	Grand Forks	6	6.00	1.00	0.37	2.18	-	-	1.0	1.1	5.6
13	Kettle Valley	1	2.25	0.44	0.01	2.47	◆	-	-	-	-
14	Southern Okanagan	21	15.11	1.39	0.86	2.13	2.4	1.8	1.8	4.5	1.3
15	Penticton	28	28.99	0.97	0.64	1.40	1.2	1.7	2.7	1.2	0.7
16	Keremeos	5	3.89	1.28	0.41	3.00	2.0	4.2	-	-	4.9
17	Princeton	1	2.40	0.42	0.01	2.32	-	◆	-	-	-
18	Golden	2	2.20	0.91	0.10	3.28	-	-	7.3	-	-
19	Revelstoke	3	2.87	1.05	0.21	3.06	-	2.6	2.8	-	2.3
20	Salmon Arm	23	18.38	1.25	0.79	1.88	1.7	1.5	2.1	2.3	0.9
21	Armstrong-Spallumcheen	6	4.62	1.30	0.47	2.83	3.0	2.0	-	1.7	2.7
22	Vernon	28	29.65	0.94	0.63	1.36	0.8	2.5	2.1	1.2	0.6
23	Central Okanagan	54	73.62	0.73 *	0.55	0.96	1.2	1.6	1.1	1.1	0.4
24	Kamloops	38	29.94	1.27	0.90	1.74	1.0	1.5	1.9	1.6	3.5
26	North Thompson	1	1.44	0.70	0.01	3.88	◆	-	-	-	-
27	Cariboo-Chilcotin	7	10.66	0.66	0.26	1.35	2.0	-	1.0	1.8	-
28	Quesnel	5	7.89	0.63	0.20	1.48	3.3	-	-	0.8	1.1
29	Lillooet	4	2.18	1.83	0.49	4.69	6.8	-	-	4.3	3.4
30	South Cariboo	4	3.51	1.14	0.31	2.92	-	-	6.5	1.7	-
31	Merritt	4	3.62	1.11	0.30	2.83	2.5	5.7	-	-	-
32	Hope	7	3.70	1.89	0.76	3.90	4.2	2.0	3.7	1.5	3.6
33	Chilliwack	35	31.07	1.13	0.78	1.57	2.6	1.6	2.7	0.8	1.4
34	Abbotsford	27	43.39	0.62 *	0.41	0.91	1.1	1.4	1.4	0.4	0.6
35	Langley	19	32.81	0.58 *	0.35	0.90	1.6	0.9	0.2	0.8	1.2
36	Surrey	107	105.01	1.02	0.84	1.23	1.3	2.2	1.6	1.6	1.2
37	Delta	21	26.17	0.80	0.50	1.23	1.8	1.4	1.1	1.0	0.7
38	Richmond	25	42.83	0.58 **	0.38	0.86	0.8	1.3	0.8	0.9	0.7
39	Vancouver	273	286.07	0.95	0.84	1.07	1.5	1.6	1.4	1.4	1.4
40	New Westminster	26	28.27	0.92	0.60	1.35	2.2	1.5	0.8	1.6	1.6
41	Burnaby	70	83.55	0.84	0.65	1.06	1.8	1.2	1.2	1.2	1.1
42	Maple Ridge	31	20.50	1.51 *	1.03	2.15	3.9	2.9	2.7	1.0	1.5
43	Coquitlam	43	37.96	1.13	0.82	1.53	2.3	1.9	2.7	1.0	0.9
44	North Vancouver	47	42.47	1.11	0.81	1.47	2.3	2.6	1.4	1.0	1.2
45	West Vancouver-Bowen Is	32	31.46	1.02	0.70	1.44	2.0	1.6	1.0	2.2	1.1
46	Sechelt	16	13.14	1.22	0.70	1.98	1.3	1.7	2.5	3.2	0.4
47	Powell River	15	10.78	1.39	0.78	2.30	3.2	1.6	0.8	3.8	2.1
48	Howe Sound	5	3.92	1.28	0.41	2.98	8.4	1.1	8.4	-	-
49	Central Coast	0	1.10	-	-	-	-	-	-	-	-
50	Queen Charlotte	1	1.45	0.69	0.01	3.83	◆	-	-	-	-
52	Prince Rupert	9	5.14	1.75	0.80	3.33	3.1	2.9	1.6	3.1	3.2
54	Smithers	5	3.38	1.48	0.48	3.45	5.1	-	5.2	2.7	-
55	Burns Lake	4	2.41	1.66	0.45	4.24	3.2	2.7	-	2.8	2.8
56	Nechako	3	4.62	0.65	0.13	1.90	3.0	-	1.4	-	-
57	Prince George	22	17.92	1.23	0.77	1.86	2.8	2.5	0.9	2.5	1.9
59	Peace River South	10	8.78	1.14	0.55	2.09	1.5	3.9	-	1.8	1.6
60	Peace River North	10	6.50	1.54	0.74	2.83	1.4	2.3	3.0	3.7	1.0
61	Greater Victoria	174	155.23	1.12	0.96	1.30	2.0	1.6	1.5	1.7	1.6
62	Sooke	17	16.23	1.05	0.61	1.68	1.2	-	2.5	2.4	1.7
63	Saanich	25	29.61	0.84	0.55	1.25	1.1	0.7	0.4	1.4	3.1
64	Gulf Islands	5	9.75	0.51	0.17	1.20	1.0	-	2.6	-	0.6
65	Cowichan	22	21.14	1.04	0.65	1.58	1.6	2.3	0.6	2.0	1.2
66	Lake Cowichan	1	2.32	0.43	0.01	2.40	-	-	-	-	◆
67	Ladysmith	11	9.65	1.14	0.57	2.04	0.7	0.6	0.7	1.6	4.0
68	Nanaimo	49	35.43	1.38 *	1.02	1.83	1.5	2.3	1.8	2.6	2.0
69	Qualicum	20	20.66	0.97	0.59	1.50	1.3	1.7	1.3	1.5	1.5
70	Alberni	17	11.95	1.42	0.83	2.28	4.1	1.8	1.0	2.6	1.1
71	Courtenay	31	20.73	1.50 *	1.02	2.12	2.1	2.2	1.7	3.1	2.4
72	Campbell River	18	9.95	1.81 *	1.07	2.86	3.8	3.1	3.1	2.8	2.0
75	Mission	8	13.50	0.59	0.26	1.17	1.6	0.5	1.8	0.5	0.5
76	Agassiz-Harrison	4	3.01	1.33	0.36	3.40	-	-	4.1	2.5	1.8
77	Summerland	7	9.76	0.72	0.29	1.48	1.7	0.8	-	1.3	1.8
78	Enderby	8	4.21	1.90	0.82	3.75	7.5	-	5.4	1.4	1.6
80	Kitimat	4	1.82	2.19	0.59	5.61	4.5	-	10.2	-	1.7
81	Fort Nelson	0	0.67	-	-	-	-	-	-	-	-
84	Vancouver Island West	1	0.34	2.95	0.04	16.42	-	-	-	-	◆
85	Vancouver Island North	2	2.16	0.93	0.10	3.34	-	-	6.2	-	-
87	Stikine	0	0.33	-	-	-	-	-	-	-	-
88	Terrace	2	6.58	0.30	0.03	1.10	-	1.4	-	0.9	-
92	Nishga	0	0.46	-	-	-	-	-	-	-	-
94	Telegraph Creek	0	0.13	-	-	-	-	-	-	-	-
	Provincial Total	**1,600**	◆	**1.00**	◆	◆	1.7	1.6	1.6	1.5	1.3

Diseases of Arteries, Arterioles, and Capillaries: Female

	Local Health Area	Observed Deaths	Expected Deaths	SMR (p)	95% C.I. Lower	Upper	ASMR 1985	1986	1987	1988	1989
1	Fernie	0	3.07	-	-	-	-	-	-	-	-
2	Cranbrook	5	6.56	0.76	0.25	1.78	4.2	-	-	0.8	-
3	Kimberley	4	4.00	1.00	0.27	2.56	-	1.4	1.5	1.4	1.3
4	Windermere	1	1.34	0.75	0.01	4.16	-	-	◆	-	-
5	Creston	8	6.69	1.20	0.52	2.36	-	1.8	3.5	1.6	-
6	Kootenay Lake	0	1.67	-	-	-	-	-	-	-	-
7	Nelson	15	10.41	1.44	0.81	2.38	1.6	1.1	1.1	2.5	1.7
9	Castlegar	3	4.45	0.67	0.14	1.97	2.0	-	-	1.8	1.1
10	Arrow Lakes	1	2.51	0.40	0.01	2.21	-	-	◆	-	-
11	Trail	27	9.95	2.71 ***	1.79	3.95	3.9	2.3	5.2	3.8	1.6
12	Grand Forks	5	3.82	1.31	0.42	3.06	2.5	-	2.6	1.7	-
13	Kettle Valley	1	0.81	1.23	0.02	6.86	◆	-	-	-	-
14	Southern Okanagan	8	10.30	0.78	0.33	1.53	0.6	1.1	1.2	0.5	0.9
15	Penticton	12	22.33	0.54 *	0.28	0.94	1.7	-	-	2.2	-
16	Keremeos	3	1.96	1.53	0.31	4.48	2.7	3.1	-	2.9	-
17	Princeton	2	1.92	1.04	0.12	3.77	-	2.6	3.4	-	-
18	Golden	1	1.17	0.85	0.01	4.74	-	-	◆	-	-
19	Revelstoke	2	2.50	0.80	0.09	2.89	1.6	-	-	2.7	-
20	Salmon Arm	14	11.54	1.21	0.66	2.04	2.3	-	1.1	3.3	0.4
21	Armstrong-Spallumcheen	3	2.97	1.01	0.20	2.95	4.0	-	-	2.0	-
22	Vernon	24	21.82	1.10	0.70	1.64	1.9	1.4	1.3	1.2	0.8
23	Central Okanagan	25	51.78	0.48 ***	0.31	0.71	0.7	0.5	0.8	0.7	0.2
24	Kamloops	19	22.11	0.86	0.52	1.34	-	1.6	1.1	1.2	1.0
26	North Thompson	0	0.77	-	-	-	-	-	-	-	-
27	Cariboo-Chilcotin	7	6.33	1.11	0.44	2.28	1.4	1.8	-	1.5	0.8
28	Quesnel	5	4.27	1.17	0.38	2.73	-	1.8	3.0	1.3	1.1
29	Lillooet	1	1.09	0.92	0.01	5.12	-	-	-	-	◆
30	South Cariboo	0	1.81	-	-	-	-	-	-	-	-
31	Merritt	2	2.50	0.80	0.09	2.89	-	2.1	-	2.8	-
32	Hope	0	2.08	-	-	-	-	-	-	-	-
33	Chilliwack	28	22.71	1.23	0.82	1.78	1.1	1.6	1.5	2.2	0.7
34	Abbotsford	28	34.86	0.80	0.53	1.16	1.3	1.1	0.7	0.9	0.7
35	Langley	20	25.05	0.80	0.49	1.23	1.7	0.8	0.8	0.9	0.7
36	Surrey	63	84.34	0.75 *	0.57	0.96	1.0	0.9	0.7	1.2	0.5
37	Delta	23	23.95	0.96	0.61	1.44	1.1	1.3	1.0	1.6	0.6
38	Richmond	43	38.44	1.12	0.81	1.51	1.9	1.8	1.4	1.1	0.5
39	Vancouver	330	304.80	1.08	0.97	1.21	1.2	1.3	1.2	1.3	1.1
40	New Westminster	39	33.99	1.15	0.82	1.57	1.6	1.5	1.2	0.6	1.8
41	Burnaby	98	87.82	1.12	0.91	1.36	1.2	1.1	1.4	1.2	1.4
42	Maple Ridge	16	18.52	0.86	0.49	1.40	-	2.1	1.6	0.9	0.5
43	Coquitlam	22	32.28	0.68	0.43	1.03	1.0	0.7	0.9	0.9	0.5
44	North Vancouver	55	45.23	1.22	0.92	1.58	2.2	1.2	0.9	1.6	1.4
45	West Vancouver-Bowen Is	38	35.27	1.08	0.76	1.48	1.4	1.7	1.1	1.3	0.8
46	Sechelt	9	8.82	1.02	0.47	1.94	1.6	0.5	2.3	-	1.0
47	Powell River	7	8.34	0.84	0.34	1.73	-	2.2	1.0	0.6	1.3
48	Howe Sound	2	2.51	0.80	0.09	2.88	-	-	1.5	-	1.4
49	Central Coast	0	0.45	-	-	-	-	-	-	-	-
50	Queen Charlotte	1	0.77	1.29	0.02	7.20	-	-	-	◆	-
52	Prince Rupert	1	3.43	0.29	0.00	1.62	-	-	-	◆	-
54	Smithers	2	2.41	0.83	0.09	2.99	2.3	-	-	1.9	-
55	Burns Lake	0	1.18	-	-	-	-	-	-	-	-
56	Nechako	2	2.68	0.75	0.08	2.69	1.9	-	-	2.2	-
57	Prince George	15	11.36	1.32	0.74	2.18	1.8	2.9	0.6	2.3	-
59	Peace River South	1	5.67	0.18 +	0.00	0.98	◆	-	-	-	-
60	Peace River North	7	3.69	1.90	0.76	3.91	-	1.9	-	1.6	7.1
61	Greater Victoria	169	185.13	0.91	0.78	1.06	1.8	0.9	0.6	1.2	1.1
62	Sooke	13	11.54	1.13	0.60	1.93	2.6	0.5	1.0	-	2.3
63	Saanich	18	22.84	0.79	0.47	1.25	0.5	0.2	1.2	1.2	1.2
64	Gulf Islands	1	6.31	0.16 +	0.00	0.88	-	-	-	-	◆
65	Cowichan	20	16.44	1.22	0.74	1.88	0.9	0.7	2.5	1.6	1.5
66	Lake Cowichan	2	1.33	1.50	0.17	5.43	-	-	-	3.1	2.8
67	Ladysmith	16	6.29	2.54 **	1.45	4.13	3.4	3.1	5.3	2.7	0.9
68	Nanaimo	36	27.60	1.30	0.91	1.81	1.0	1.6	1.8	1.3	1.8
69	Qualicum	24	13.99	1.72 *	1.10	2.55	1.5	1.3	2.9	2.1	1.9
70	Alberni	13	9.00	1.44	0.77	2.47	2.7	1.5	-	2.9	1.6
71	Courtenay	25	15.44	1.62 *	1.05	2.39	4.6	0.8	1.0	1.5	1.6
72	Campbell River	4	7.49	0.53	0.14	1.37	1.0	-	0.7	0.7	0.7
75	Mission	9	9.81	0.92	0.42	1.74	1.2	0.5	1.2	0.5	1.5
76	Agassiz-Harrison	4	1.78	2.25	0.60	5.75	8.9	-	-	-	4.8
77	Summerland	7	6.83	1.03	0.41	2.11	0.7	2.6	-	2.3	-
78	Enderby	3	2.51	1.19	0.24	3.49	4.5	-	-	1.6	-
80	Kitimat	1	1.33	0.75	0.01	4.18	-	◆	-	-	-
81	Fort Nelson	0	0.29	-	-	-	-	-	-	-	-
84	Vancouver Island West	0	0.28	-	-	-	-	-	-	-	-
85	Vancouver Island North	0	1.46	-	-	-	-	-	-	-	-
87	Stikine	0	0.13	-	-	-	-	-	-	-	-
88	Terrace	1	3.08	0.32	0.00	1.81	-	-	-	-	◆
92	Nishga	0	0.18	-	-	-	-	-	-	-	-
94	Telegraph Creek	0	0.09	-	-	-	-	-	-	-	-
	Provincial Total	1,414	◆	1.00	◆	◆	1.3	1.1	1.1	1.3	1.0

Respiratory System: Male

#	Local Health Area	Observed Deaths	Expected Deaths	SMR	(p)	95% C.I. Lower	Upper	1985	1986	ASMR 1987	1988	1989
1	Fernie	20	16.62	1.20		0.73	1.86	1.5	6.5	4.3	14.9	4.6
2	Cranbrook	52	26.30	1.98	***	1.48	2.59	11.5	12.0	9.2	13.9	6.0
3	Kimberley	14	16.32	0.86		0.47	1.44	2.6	1.3	8.5	7.2	6.1
4	Windermere	7	10.02	0.70		0.28	1.44	-	-	9.6	4.9	2.4
5	Creston	24	37.81	0.63	*	0.41	0.94	3.8	6.7	2.6	2.0	3.2
6	Kootenay Lake	8	9.03	0.89		0.38	1.74	9.7	4.0	6.7	3.9	10.5
7	Nelson	40	46.57	0.86		0.61	1.17	5.8	4.3	3.0	7.0	4.1
9	Castlegar	16	21.22	0.75		0.43	1.22	7.7	7.0	3.2	-	2.2
10	Arrow Lakes	19	11.30	1.68	*	1.01	2.63	9.9	12.1	10.5	4.7	11.0
11	Trail	46	47.71	0.96		0.71	1.29	6.8	2.7	4.7	5.2	4.7
12	Grand Forks	11	20.65	0.53	*	0.27	0.95	2.6	3.1	2.1	1.4	4.3
13	Kettle Valley	3	7.81	0.38		0.08	1.12	12.9	3.4	-	-	-
14	Southern Okanagan	49	52.28	0.94		0.69	1.24	2.3	7.6	10.4	3.7	4.1
15	Penticton	80	101.57	0.79	*	0.62	0.98	6.7	3.4	2.5	3.2	5.1
16	Keremeos	15	13.36	1.12		0.63	1.85	10.5	11.6	1.7	8.7	-
17	Princeton	15	8.06	1.86	*	1.04	3.07	16.3	3.4	14.9	9.3	6.5
18	Golden	6	7.77	0.77		0.28	1.68	-	15.1	-	7.3	-
19	Revelstoke	6	9.95	0.60		0.22	1.31	7.7	-	-	2.4	5.3
20	Salmon Arm	60	62.23	0.96		0.74	1.24	7.6	2.9	4.6	5.0	4.7
21	Armstrong-Spallumcheen	23	16.10	1.43		0.91	2.14	6.6	1.5	9.9	12.2	9.8
22	Vernon	119	103.68	1.15		0.95	1.37	8.4	5.5	5.7	5.0	6.1
23	Central Okanagan	217	256.28	0.85	*	0.74	0.97	4.3	4.6	4.8	4.0	4.8
24	Kamloops	121	103.26	1.17		0.97	1.40	6.6	6.0	6.8	5.8	5.9
26	North Thompson	4	4.89	0.82		0.22	2.09	7.6	3.8	10.1	-	-
27	Cariboo-Chilcotin	36	35.95	1.00		0.70	1.39	5.5	3.8	4.8	5.3	6.7
28	Quesnel	39	27.30	1.43	*	1.02	1.95	9.0	2.4	9.6	5.2	9.8
29	Lillooet	8	7.57	1.06		0.45	2.08	11.3	-	11.4	3.3	6.7
30	South Cariboo	8	12.12	0.66		0.28	1.30	6.9	4.4	1.9	3.7	-
31	Merritt	11	12.24	0.90		0.45	1.61	2.4	7.0	8.0	5.6	2.5
32	Hope	13	12.36	1.05		0.56	1.80	-	10.4	14.1	6.5	1.4
33	Chilliwack	105	107.70	0.97		0.80	1.18	5.5	5.6	5.1	5.1	5.4
34	Abbotsford	119	152.13	0.78	**	0.65	0.94	5.2	3.3	4.6	4.8	3.2
35	Langley	116	113.70	1.02		0.84	1.22	4.5	7.5	4.8	6.0	4.9
36	Surrey	333	364.91	0.91		0.82	1.02	4.7	5.3	3.9	5.7	4.8
37	Delta	81	89.46	0.91		0.72	1.13	6.1	5.4	4.1	5.9	3.3
38	Richmond	149	145.66	1.02		0.87	1.20	4.9	6.2	5.5	5.2	5.2
39	Vancouver	1112	1001.92	1.11	***	1.05	1.18	6.7	5.6	5.4	5.8	6.7
40	New Westminster	103	98.76	1.04		0.85	1.26	6.7	4.5	8.3	5.8	4.8
41	Burnaby	287	289.26	0.99		0.88	1.11	4.7	3.9	5.7	6.1	5.7
42	Maple Ridge	100	71.51	1.40	**	1.14	1.70	9.5	4.8	7.1	8.8	7.1
43	Coquitlam	190	131.60	1.44	***	1.25	1.66	7.6	6.8	9.8	7.6	6.9
44	North Vancouver	159	144.08	1.10		0.94	1.29	5.9	6.1	7.8	5.3	5.6
45	West Vancouver-Bowen Is	70	108.16	0.65	***	0.50	0.82	3.8	3.6	3.4	2.7	3.6
46	Sechelt	36	44.60	0.81		0.57	1.12	5.7	5.7	3.4	3.9	4.7
47	Powell River	28	37.34	0.75		0.50	1.08	3.0	8.3	3.7	3.4	2.0
48	Howe Sound	23	13.09	1.76	*	1.11	2.64	3.6	11.5	12.8	15.4	2.0
49	Central Coast	2	3.72	0.54		0.06	1.94	5.3	-	12.6	-	-
50	Queen Charlotte	2	5.24	0.38		0.04	1.38	-	-	-	3.5	3.2
52	Prince Rupert	26	18.03	1.44		0.94	2.11	4.6	6.6	10.3	4.9	10.0
54	Smithers	11	11.64	0.94		0.47	1.69	5.4	3.4	5.0	11.4	2.8
55	Burns Lake	8	8.42	0.95		0.41	1.87	3.0	5.6	2.6	2.6	9.0
56	Nechako	9	16.12	0.56		0.25	1.06	5.6	5.5	0.9	1.6	1.5
57	Prince George	77	61.17	1.26		0.99	1.57	4.9	7.0	9.2	3.4	8.8
59	Peace River South	33	30.86	1.07		0.74	1.50	3.4	6.4	3.6	6.7	8.5
60	Peace River North	21	22.77	0.92		0.57	1.41	5.2	3.8	4.4	2.6	8.3
61	Greater Victoria	551	550.81	1.00		0.92	1.09	5.6	4.4	5.4	6.0	5.2
62	Sooke	37	54.82	0.67	*	0.48	0.93	6.3	1.2	1.5	4.8	4.4
63	Saanich	78	100.10	0.78	*	0.62	0.97	5.4	3.4	5.4	4.2	3.4
64	Gulf Islands	25	32.78	0.76		0.49	1.13	9.8	7.2	2.0	1.5	3.2
65	Cowichan	73	72.90	1.00		0.78	1.26	5.6	7.2	4.0	6.1	4.1
66	Lake Cowichan	3	7.82	0.38		0.08	1.12	-	-	-	8.3	-
67	Ladysmith	25	33.27	0.75		0.49	1.11	2.4	4.4	4.3	4.4	5.8
68	Nanaimo	117	121.04	0.97		0.80	1.16	4.4	5.9	6.7	3.0	5.7
69	Qualicum	54	69.33	0.78		0.59	1.02	4.7	3.4	2.8	4.4	4.7
70	Alberni	42	40.47	1.04		0.75	1.40	4.1	3.4	5.0	7.0	7.5
71	Courtenay	53	71.15	0.74	*	0.56	0.97	3.2	6.2	3.2	3.1	4.3
72	Campbell River	45	33.51	1.34		0.98	1.80	12.9	9.4	5.5	7.8	4.3
75	Mission	44	46.76	0.94		0.68	1.26	5.8	1.9	6.5	9.9	1.7
76	Agassiz-Harrison	10	10.28	0.97		0.47	1.79	2.8	12.8	5.8	2.5	5.5
77	Summerland	29	34.34	0.84		0.57	1.21	5.1	4.4	6.2	4.1	1.2
78	Enderby	18	14.70	1.22		0.73	1.94	7.7	5.2	5.4	7.7	4.9
80	Kitimat	8	6.07	1.32		0.57	2.60	-	3.7	1.1	12.6	21.6
81	Fort Nelson	3	2.38	1.26		0.25	3.68	-	-	46.0	-	12.6
84	Vancouver Island West	0	1.19	-		-	-	-	-	-	-	-
85	Vancouver Island North	2	7.43	0.27	+	0.03	0.97	-	0.9	-	3.6	-
87	Stikine	3	1.15	2.61		0.52	7.63	29.6	-	-	16.1	-
88	Terrace	37	23.17	1.60	**	1.12	2.20	7.9	11.6	8.8	4.6	9.9
92	Nishga	1	1.63	0.61		0.01	3.41	-	-	-	♦	-
94	Telegraph Creek	0	0.43	-		-	-	-	-	-	-	-
	Provincial Total	5,550	♦	1.00		♦	♦	5.7	5.1	5.3	5.4	5.2

194

Respiratory System: Female

	Local Health Area	Observed Deaths	Expected Deaths	SMR (p)	95% C.I. Lower	Upper	ASMR 1985	1986	1987	1988	1989
1	Fernie	10	9.92	1.01	0.48	1.85	4.3	5.0	4.4	1.5	3.9
2	Cranbrook	26	20.62	1.26	0.82	1.85	5.4	5.3	3.3	3.4	6.0
3	Kimberley	13	12.51	1.04	0.55	1.78	4.6	3.3	2.8	7.0	1.3
4	Windermere	5	4.60	1.09	0.35	2.54	6.6	-	6.2	-	2.5
5	Creston	17	20.91	0.81	0.47	1.30	3.7	1.8	1.8	4.8	4.2
6	Kootenay Lake	5	5.27	0.95	0.31	2.21	2.6	-	-	6.0	6.2
7	Nelson	22	32.18	0.68	0.43	1.04	2.2	2.8	2.0	3.6	3.3
9	Castlegar	13	14.22	0.91	0.49	1.56	6.4	2.2	2.4	4.1	2.0
10	Arrow Lakes	14	7.71	1.82	0.99	3.05	8.1	9.2	9.1	6.9	-
11	Trail	30	31.32	0.96	0.65	1.37	5.1	2.1	2.8	2.6	6.1
12	Grand Forks	7	12.17	0.58	0.23	1.19	-	4.5	3.5	-	2.7
13	Kettle Valley	3	2.74	1.09	0.22	3.19	-	-	-	7.0	8.8
14	Southern Okanagan	28	32.01	0.87	0.58	1.26	2.3	2.7	2.0	3.0	7.3
15	Penticton	60	69.17	0.87	0.66	1.12	4.9	3.0	3.3	1.7	3.0
16	Keremeos	9	6.16	1.46	0.67	2.77	2.8	3.1	6.7	13.0	2.7
17	Princeton	10	5.95	1.68	0.80	3.09	3.1	4.4	12.7	7.4	3.1
18	Golden	6	3.85	1.56	0.57	3.39	-	9.3	8.5	5.5	13.7
19	Revelstoke	8	7.87	1.02	0.44	2.00	-	8.7	-	4.9	4.5
20	Salmon Arm	28	36.51	0.77	0.51	1.11	3.7	3.2	3.8	1.2	2.3
21	Armstrong-Spallumcheen	6	9.37	0.64	0.23	1.39	2.3	-	2.1	3.9	3.3
22	Vernon	79	68.03	1.16	0.92	1.45	4.8	3.4	4.9	4.4	3.5
23	Central Okanagan	132	162.55	0.81 *	0.68	0.96	3.1	3.4	3.3	2.8	2.5
24	Kamloops	73	70.52	1.04	0.81	1.30	2.4	4.5	4.4	3.5	4.3
26	North Thompson	4	2.65	1.51	0.41	3.87	-	-	9.6	11.2	-
27	Cariboo-Chilcotin	24	21.12	1.14	0.73	1.69	3.5	2.5	5.5	4.2	7.1
28	Quesnel	12	14.21	0.84	0.44	1.48	6.9	-	1.4	5.6	1.3
29	Lillooet	7	3.45	2.03	0.81	4.18	-	12.3	16.2	5.9	7.9
30	South Cariboo	12	5.87	2.04 *	1.05	3.57	7.0	7.5	12.6	9.6	2.9
31	Merritt	11	7.99	1.38	0.69	2.46	2.1	4.8	5.2	4.8	8.8
32	Hope	10	6.86	1.46	0.70	2.68	5.5	-	6.3	4.2	8.6
33	Chilliwack	56	71.82	0.78	0.59	1.01	3.3	3.6	3.5	1.4	2.6
34	Abbotsford	93	108.36	0.86	0.69	1.05	2.6	3.8	2.9	2.9	3.6
35	Langley	76	79.21	0.96	0.76	1.20	4.3	4.4	3.2	3.3	3.1
36	Surrey	270	265.62	1.02	0.90	1.15	3.6	3.6	3.9	3.9	3.6
37	Delta	59	75.78	0.78	0.59	1.00	2.8	2.8	1.9	4.0	2.6
38	Richmond	112	122.03	0.92	0.76	1.10	3.7	4.0	3.0	3.1	3.3
39	Vancouver	931	917.26	1.01	0.95	1.08	3.9	3.9	3.1	3.8	4.1
40	New Westminster	85	103.00	0.83	0.66	1.02	3.6	3.6	2.8	3.1	3.9
41	Burnaby	253	267.32	0.95	0.83	1.07	3.2	3.0	3.8	3.5	4.1
42	Maple Ridge	66	57.47	1.15	0.89	1.46	5.2	4.8	3.2	4.8	4.0
43	Coquitlam	131	102.79	1.27 **	1.07	1.51	5.7	2.9	5.1	4.4	5.8
44	North Vancouver	167	140.54	1.19 *	1.01	1.38	3.8	3.1	4.6	5.1	4.9
45	West Vancouver-Bowen Is	112	106.58	1.05	0.87	1.26	3.2	3.1	3.5	4.8	3.4
46	Sechelt	27	27.99	0.96	0.64	1.40	1.3	4.0	3.3	3.5	4.8
47	Powell River	21	26.00	0.81	0.50	1.23	4.4	2.5	5.3	1.2	1.9
48	Howe Sound	6	8.44	0.71	0.26	1.55	-	4.2	4.4	2.3	2.2
49	Central Coast	4	1.54	2.59	0.70	6.64	7.9	22.0	-	-	25.8
50	Queen Charlotte	0	2.53	-	-	-	-	-	-	-	-
52	Prince Rupert	14	11.06	1.27	0.69	2.12	1.9	3.4	6.7	4.8	5.9
54	Smithers	8	7.84	1.02	0.44	2.01	9.8	2.9	2.7	-	5.4
55	Burns Lake	4	3.93	1.02	0.27	2.61	♦	3.2	-	9.0	-
56	Nechako	11	8.73	1.26	0.63	2.26	4.0	10.6	3.7	4.4	-
57	Prince George	53	38.27	1.38 *	1.04	1.81	6.5	7.3	3.4	4.1	4.9
59	Peace River South	21	18.11	1.16	0.72	1.77	3.8	4.3	6.5	3.9	3.0
60	Peace River North	9	12.31	0.73	0.33	1.39	2.6	1.9	1.6	1.5	4.8
61	Greater Victoria	575	549.81	1.05	0.96	1.13	4.2	3.4	3.3	4.3	4.1
62	Sooke	45	37.08	1.21	0.89	1.62	4.5	7.0	4.8	3.9	2.4
63	Saanich	76	71.57	1.06	0.84	1.33	2.9	2.4	5.9	4.4	4.2
64	Gulf Islands	21	20.09	1.05	0.65	1.60	4.8	3.6	1.4	4.9	4.1
65	Cowichan	37	51.34	0.72 *	0.51	0.99	2.3	1.9	2.6	1.6	5.0
66	Lake Cowichan	4	4.42	0.90	0.24	2.32	6.9	-	3.5	-	4.6
67	Ladysmith	15	20.02	0.75	0.42	1.24	2.0	3.8	1.8	5.1	2.3
68	Nanaimo	92	87.13	1.06	0.85	1.29	4.5	3.7	3.0	3.7	3.9
69	Qualicum	40	44.23	0.90	0.65	1.23	5.6	3.7	2.0	2.1	3.1
70	Alberni	31	29.08	1.07	0.72	1.51	3.8	2.2	3.6	7.1	3.1
71	Courtenay	43	48.64	0.88	0.64	1.19	6.0	2.4	3.1	3.6	2.0
72	Campbell River	23	24.15	0.95	0.60	1.43	1.7	2.3	2.7	4.9	5.1
75	Mission	32	30.67	1.04	0.71	1.47	4.2	0.7	6.3	2.7	5.2
76	Agassiz-Harrison	8	5.76	1.39	0.60	2.74	4.3	2.6	5.5	8.8	2.4
77	Summerland	25	21.06	1.19	0.77	1.75	7.0	5.8	1.6	4.0	3.8
78	Enderby	6	8.08	0.74	0.27	1.62	-	-	-	10.7	4.1
80	Kitimat	5	4.53	1.10	0.36	2.58	-	13.4	1.1	3.7	4.6
81	Fort Nelson	1	1.06	0.95	0.01	5.26	-	-	-	-	♦
84	Vancouver Island West	2	1.00	2.00	0.22	7.22	-	6.4	-	38.4	-
85	Vancouver Island North	2	4.99	0.40	0.05	1.45	-	-	5.7	-	-
87	Stikine	0	0.49	-	-	-	-	-	-	-	-
88	Terrace	10	10.40	0.96	0.46	1.77	3.5	1.9	6.1	2.3	2.7
92	Nishga	1	0.66	1.53	0.02	8.49	-	♦	-	-	-
94	Telegraph Creek	1	0.32	3.16	0.04	17.56	♦	-	-	-	-
	Provincial Total	**4,369**	♦	**1.00**	♦	♦	3.8	3.5	3.5	3.8	3.8

Pneumonia and Influenza: Male

	Local Health Area	Observed Deaths	Expected Deaths	SMR (p)	95% C.I. Lower	Upper	ASMR 1985	1986	1987	1988	1989
1	Fernie	3	6.37	0.47	0.09	1.38	-	-	-	2.0	3.1
2	Cranbrook	16	9.99	1.60	0.91	2.60	6.9	3.0	3.2	2.7	-
3	Kimberley	2	5.95	0.34	0.04	1.21	-	-	-	1.9	3.6
4	Windermere	1	3.81	0.26	0.00	1.46	-	-	-	-	♦
5	Creston	9	15.24	0.59	0.27	1.12	1.5	2.1	-	1.3	1.4
6	Kootenay Lake	1	3.35	0.30	0.00	1.66	-	-	-	♦	-
7	Nelson	10	18.42	0.54 *	0.26	1.00	1.2	0.5	1.0	1.5	1.1
9	Castlegar	4	8.00	0.50	0.13	1.28	1.3	2.0	1.0	-	1.1
10	Arrow Lakes	3	4.50	0.67	0.13	1.95	4.7	-	2.2	-	-
11	Trail	10	18.61	0.54 *	0.26	0.99	2.4	0.5	0.5	0.9	0.8
12	Grand Forks	7	7.86	0.89	0.36	1.83	1.1	3.1	1.0	-	3.5
13	Kettle Valley	1	3.11	0.32	0.00	1.79	-	♦	-	-	-
14	Southern Okanagan	22	20.60	1.07	0.67	1.62	0.9	3.9	4.6	1.4	2.3
15	Penticton	24	40.55	0.59 **	0.38	0.88	2.4	0.5	0.7	1.9	0.7
16	Keremeos	6	5.04	1.19	0.43	2.59	2.7	3.1	-	5.6	-
17	Princeton	6	3.06	1.96	0.72	4.27	12.3	-	6.3	-	3.8
18	Golden	3	3.10	0.97	0.19	2.83	-	12.5	-	-	-
19	Revelstoke	3	3.86	0.78	0.16	2.27	2.5	-	-	2.4	2.6
20	Salmon Arm	14	23.34	0.60	0.33	1.01	0.9	-	2.0	2.1	1.1
21	Armstrong-Spallumcheen	7	6.31	1.11	0.44	2.29	1.9	-	3.3	6.0	4.4
22	Vernon	46	41.20	1.12	0.82	1.49	3.4	3.3	1.7	2.3	1.7
23	Central Okanagan	99	100.99	0.98	0.80	1.19	2.3	2.5	2.3	1.1	2.1
24	Kamloops	36	39.86	0.90	0.63	1.25	2.2	1.9	1.5	2.3	1.7
26	North Thompson	3	1.80	1.66	0.33	4.86	3.8	3.8	10.1	-	-
27	Cariboo-Chilcotin	9	13.36	0.67	0.31	1.28	2.5	1.8	1.6	-	2.1
28	Quesnel	12	10.69	1.12	0.58	1.96	2.6	-	7.0	1.3	1.1
29	Lillooet	3	3.04	0.99	0.20	2.88	11.3	-	-	3.3	-
30	South Cariboo	1	4.81	0.21	0.00	1.16	-	-	-	♦	-
31	Merritt	4	4.69	0.85	0.23	2.18	-	5.3	2.1	2.0	-
32	Hope	4	4.39	0.91	0.25	2.33	-	8.8	4.6	-	-
33	Chilliwack	41	42.14	0.97	0.70	1.32	1.7	1.8	1.7	3.2	2.2
34	Abbotsford	57	60.52	0.94	0.71	1.22	2.4	1.3	1.8	3.0	1.4
35	Langley	44	44.34	0.99	0.72	1.33	1.3	2.5	1.7	2.3	2.5
36	Surrey	110	143.37	0.77 **	0.63	0.92	1.3	1.7	1.7	2.0	1.6
37	Delta	26	33.19	0.78	0.51	1.15	2.7	2.3	1.3	1.1	1.2
38	Richmond	52	54.73	0.95	0.71	1.25	2.8	2.6	1.3	1.6	1.8
39	Vancouver	489	407.69	1.20 ***	1.10	1.31	2.8	2.2	2.6	2.6	2.8
40	New Westminster	37	39.26	0.94	0.66	1.30	2.8	2.1	1.9	2.7	2.1
41	Burnaby	105	114.46	0.92	0.75	1.11	1.6	1.9	2.4	2.6	1.3
42	Maple Ridge	46	28.19	1.63 **	1.19	2.18	3.9	2.5	3.5	3.4	4.0
43	Coquitlam	92	51.72	1.78 ***	1.43	2.18	4.3	4.6	4.7	2.8	2.9
44	North Vancouver	63	54.67	1.15	0.89	1.47	2.6	2.8	3.3	1.9	2.1
45	West Vancouver-Bowen Is	34	41.88	0.81	0.56	1.13	2.3	2.2	1.0	0.8	2.1
46	Sechelt	13	16.75	0.78	0.41	1.33	2.3	2.2	2.0	2.0	0.7
47	Powell River	13	14.69	0.88	0.47	1.51	1.5	5.1	0.8	1.3	0.7
48	Howe Sound	8	4.77	1.68	0.72	3.31	0.8	7.8	4.2	2.6	1.3
49	Central Coast	0	1.31	-	-	-	-	-	-	-	-
50	Queen Charlotte	0	2.21	-	-	-	-	-	-	-	-
52	Prince Rupert	10	7.30	1.37	0.66	2.52	1.2	2.4	4.2	2.6	3.2
54	Smithers	5	4.46	1.12	0.36	2.61	3.2	-	1.8	7.8	-
55	Burns Lake	4	3.29	1.22	0.33	3.12	3.0	2.6	2.6	-	2.8
56	Nechako	2	6.33	0.32	0.04	1.14	1.8	-	0.9	-	-
57	Prince George	30	22.92	1.31	0.88	1.87	0.7	3.3	2.6	2.0	4.8
59	Peace River South	13	12.35	1.05	0.56	1.80	1.5	2.6	1.9	3.4	1.8
60	Peace River North	7	9.11	0.77	0.31	1.58	1.4	1.3	1.2	-	4.0
61	Greater Victoria	240	227.40	1.06	0.93	1.20	2.4	1.6	2.3	2.4	2.4
62	Sooke	11	20.28	0.54 *	0.27	0.97	2.5	1.2	-	1.2	0.7
63	Saanich	37	37.16	1.00	0.70	1.37	2.9	1.3	2.4	2.1	1.9
64	Gulf Islands	10	12.06	0.83	0.40	1.52	4.7	5.0	-	-	0.9
65	Cowichan	26	28.42	0.91	0.60	1.34	1.2	1.9	1.5	2.5	2.8
66	Lake Cowichan	0	2.91	-	-	-	-	-	-	-	-
67	Ladysmith	10	12.86	0.78	0.37	1.43	1.7	2.7	-	1.3	2.7
68	Nanaimo	46	45.75	1.01	0.74	1.34	2.4	2.6	3.1	0.8	1.5
69	Qualicum	18	25.39	0.71	0.42	1.12	1.1	2.1	1.3	1.7	1.2
70	Alberni	19	14.96	1.27	0.76	1.98	0.6	1.1	2.8	3.9	3.6
71	Courtenay	12	27.47	0.44 **	0.23	0.76	1.2	0.7	1.3	0.4	1.1
72	Campbell River	13	12.28	1.06	0.56	1.81	6.6	1.3	1.8	2.9	1.1
75	Mission	14	18.16	0.77	0.42	1.29	4.6	0.7	1.9	1.6	-
76	Agassiz-Harrison	5	3.89	1.28	0.41	3.00	2.8	5.1	5.8	-	1.8
77	Summerland	15	13.96	1.07	0.60	1.77	4.3	1.5	3.5	1.2	0.6
78	Enderby	7	6.00	1.17	0.47	2.41	2.7	1.7	1.5	4.7	1.7
80	Kitimat	7	2.13	3.28 *	1.32	6.76	-	3.7	1.1	12.6	16.8
81	Fort Nelson	2	0.97	2.06	0.23	7.43	-	-	32.4	-	12.6
84	Vancouver Island West	0	0.43	-	-	-	-	-	-	-	-
85	Vancouver Island North	0	2.82	-	-	-	-	-	-	-	-
87	Stikine	0	0.41	-	-	-	-	-	-	-	-
88	Terrace	22	9.45	2.33 ***	1.46	3.52	2.6	6.1	3.7	4.6	8.9
92	Nishga	0	0.67	-	-	-	-	-	-	-	-
94	Telegraph Creek	0	0.13	-	-	-	-	-	-	-	-
	Provincial Total	2,185	♦	1.00	♦	♦	2.3	2.1	2.1	2.1	2.0

196

Pneumonia and Influenza: Female

#	Local Health Area	Observed Deaths	Expected Deaths	SMR	(p)	95% C.I. Lower	95% C.I. Upper	ASMR 1985	1986	1987	1988	1989
1	Fernie	6	5.19	1.16		0.42	2.52	1.6	1.2	2.1	1.5	3.9
2	Cranbrook	15	11.13	1.35		0.75	2.22	3.1	3.5	2.3	0.8	3.2
3	Kimberley	1	6.64	0.15	+	0.00	0.84	-	-	-	♦	-
4	Windermere	1	2.11	0.47		0.01	2.64	♦	-	-	-	-
5	Creston	5	11.06	0.45		0.15	1.06	1.1	-	0.9	0.8	3.1
6	Kootenay Lake	2	2.76	0.72		0.08	2.62	-	-	-	-	6.2
7	Nelson	12	17.69	0.68		0.35	1.19	1.1	0.8	2.0	2.5	1.5
9	Castlegar	5	7.42	0.67		0.22	1.57	3.0	-	-	2.3	1.1
10	Arrow Lakes	6	4.32	1.39		0.51	3.02	2.3	4.4	6.8	-	-
11	Trail	12	16.46	0.73		0.38	1.27	2.3	1.1	1.1	0.6	3.1
12	Grand Forks	4	6.25	0.64		0.17	1.64	-	1.3	1.9	-	2.7
13	Kettle Valley	2	1.26	1.59		0.18	5.73	-	-	-	-	8.8
14	Southern Okanagan	14	17.16	0.82		0.45	1.37	1.2	1.6	-	1.5	4.8
15	Penticton	27	37.45	0.72		0.47	1.05	2.3	1.6	1.0	0.2	1.7
16	Keremeos	0	3.21	-		-	-	-	-	-	-	-
17	Princeton	8	3.30	2.42	*	1.04	4.77	3.1	4.4	8.9	5.0	3.1
18	Golden	3	1.98	1.52		0.30	4.43	-	4.7	8.5	5.5	-
19	Revelstoke	4	4.35	0.92		0.25	2.35	-	8.7	-	-	-
20	Salmon Arm	15	18.98	0.79		0.44	1.30	1.5	2.8	1.4	1.2	0.9
21	Armstrong-Spallumcheen	2	4.95	0.40		0.05	1.46	-	-	2.1	-	1.7
22	Vernon	50	36.57	1.37	*	1.01	1.80	2.4	2.5	3.1	3.4	1.6
23	Central Okanagan	80	86.12	0.93		0.74	1.16	1.8	2.1	2.4	1.4	1.4
24	Kamloops	39	37.29	1.05		0.74	1.43	1.3	1.7	3.3	2.1	1.9
26	North Thompson	1	1.25	0.80		0.01	4.44	-	-	♦	-	-
27	Cariboo-Chilcotin	13	10.65	1.22		0.65	2.09	1.2	2.5	4.5	1.7	3.1
28	Quesnel	4	7.08	0.56		0.15	1.45	4.7	-	-	1.3	-
29	Lillooet	5	1.83	2.73		0.88	6.38	-	12.3	5.4	5.9	7.9
30	South Cariboo	8	2.98	2.69	*	1.16	5.29	7.0	7.5	7.2	3.1	2.9
31	Merritt	5	4.31	1.16		0.37	2.71	-	2.2	2.6	-	7.2
32	Hope	4	3.33	1.20		0.32	3.08	2.5	-	3.5	4.2	-
33	Chilliwack	34	37.59	0.90		0.63	1.26	2.8	2.6	1.8	0.3	1.7
34	Abbotsford	51	59.39	0.86		0.64	1.13	1.5	2.3	1.4	1.5	1.7
35	Langley	35	42.46	0.82		0.57	1.15	1.7	1.5	1.7	1.7	1.7
36	Surrey	126	141.91	0.89		0.74	1.06	1.4	1.8	2.2	1.7	1.5
37	Delta	26	41.11	0.63	*	0.41	0.93	1.2	1.6	0.6	2.4	0.4
38	Richmond	52	64.64	0.80		0.60	1.05	1.8	1.8	1.1	1.1	2.1
39	Vancouver	556	526.37	1.06		0.97	1.15	2.3	2.0	1.9	1.9	2.5
40	New Westminster	38	58.25	0.65	**	0.46	0.90	1.6	2.0	1.2	1.5	1.5
41	Burnaby	147	151.58	0.97		0.82	1.14	1.7	1.4	2.0	2.3	2.3
42	Maple Ridge	37	32.22	1.15		0.81	1.58	2.5	2.0	1.5	3.5	2.2
43	Coquitlam	83	55.11	1.51	***	1.20	1.87	4.1	2.0	3.4	2.8	3.2
44	North Vancouver	100	77.23	1.29	*	1.05	1.57	1.8	1.5	3.0	3.0	3.3
45	West Vancouver-Bowen Is	70	60.91	1.15		0.90	1.45	1.3	2.1	2.4	2.7	2.6
46	Sechelt	16	14.34	1.12		0.64	1.81	1.3	1.2	2.7	2.3	2.5
47	Powell River	6	14.10	0.43	*	0.16	0.93	2.1	-	0.6	-	1.1
48	Howe Sound	3	4.18	0.72		0.14	2.10	-	-	4.4	-	2.2
49	Central Coast	2	0.70	2.86		0.32	10.32	7.9	-	-	-	6.6
50	Queen Charlotte	0	1.35	-		-	-	-	-	-	-	-
52	Prince Rupert	5	5.82	0.86		0.28	2.00	1.9	-	3.7	1.1	0.9
54	Smithers	4	4.19	0.95		0.26	2.44	-	2.9	2.7	-	3.4
55	Burns Lake	2	2.07	0.97		0.11	3.49	♦	-	-	4.5	-
56	Nechako	4	4.57	0.87		0.24	2.24	2.0	2.2	-	4.4	-
57	Prince George	28	19.21	1.46		0.97	2.11	2.0	4.6	0.6	3.2	4.0
59	Peace River South	4	9.74	0.41		0.11	1.05	1.9	-	1.9	-	-
60	Peace River North	3	6.31	0.48		0.10	1.39	-	-	-	1.5	2.4
61	Greater Victoria	361	323.36	1.12	*	1.00	1.24	2.3	1.6	1.7	2.7	2.2
62	Sooke	27	19.17	1.41		0.93	2.05	3.6	4.3	3.1	1.8	1.2
63	Saanich	45	37.99	1.18		0.86	1.59	1.9	1.3	3.4	3.4	2.3
64	Gulf Islands	11	10.12	1.09		0.54	1.95	4.0	3.6	0.8	1.7	0.9
65	Cowichan	15	27.81	0.54	*	0.30	0.89	1.1	1.1	1.1	-	2.2
66	Lake Cowichan	2	2.14	0.93		0.10	3.37	3.5	-	3.5	-	-
67	Ladysmith	9	10.24	0.88		0.40	1.67	1.2	3.0	1.8	1.7	1.3
68	Nanaimo	46	45.89	1.00		0.73	1.34	2.6	1.5	1.4	2.0	2.3
69	Qualicum	20	22.78	0.88		0.54	1.36	2.4	3.1	0.4	0.8	2.2
70	Alberni	16	14.89	1.07		0.61	1.75	2.2	1.5	1.2	4.3	1.3
71	Courtenay	21	25.91	0.81		0.50	1.24	2.2	2.1	0.8	1.8	1.4
72	Campbell River	7	12.49	0.56		0.22	1.15	1.7	0.8	1.4	0.8	0.7
75	Mission	13	16.70	0.78		0.41	1.33	2.8	-	1.2	1.7	2.1
76	Agassiz-Harrison	5	2.88	1.74		0.56	4.05	4.3	-	3.0	6.5	2.4
77	Summerland	11	11.42	0.96		0.48	1.72	3.3	2.4	0.8	0.8	1.6
78	Enderby	3	4.12	0.73		0.15	2.13	-	-	-	2.7	4.1
80	Kitimat	3	2.40	1.25		0.25	3.66	-	7.7	-	3.7	4.6
81	Fort Nelson	1	0.55	1.82		0.02	10.15	-	-	-	-	♦
84	Vancouver Island West	1	0.55	1.83		0.02	10.16	-	♦	-	-	-
85	Vancouver Island North	2	2.57	0.78		0.09	2.81	-	-	5.7	-	-
87	Stikine	0	0.20	-		-	-	-	-	-	-	-
88	Terrace	5	5.22	0.96		0.31	2.23	-	-	3.4	2.3	2.0
92	Nishga	0	0.32	-		-	-	-	-	-	-	-
94	Telegraph Creek	0	0.17	-		-	-	-	-	-	-	-
	Provincial Total	2,410	♦	1.00		♦	♦	2.0	1.8	1.9	2.0	2.1

Chronic Lung Disease: Male

	Local Health Area	Observed Deaths	Expected Deaths	SMR	(p)	95% C.I. Lower	95% C.I. Upper	ASMR 1985	1986	1987	1988	1989
1	Fernie	13	7.84	1.66		0.88	2.84	1.5	5.1	4.3	9.8	-
2	Cranbrook	32	12.58	2.54	***	1.74	3.59	4.6	9.0	6.0	7.9	4.7
3	Kimberley	11	8.15	1.35		0.67	2.42	2.6	1.3	7.1	5.4	2.5
4	Windermere	5	4.80	1.04		0.34	2.43	-	-	7.1	4.9	-
5	Creston	13	17.83	0.73		0.39	1.25	2.4	2.0	2.6	0.6	1.2
6	Kootenay Lake	3	4.50	0.67		0.13	1.95	3.0	4.0	1.7	-	-
7	Nelson	19	22.08	0.86		0.52	1.34	3.3	2.4	2.0	2.3	1.2
9	Castlegar	6	10.34	0.58		0.21	1.26	4.4	3.6	-	-	-
10	Arrow Lakes	12	5.35	2.24	*	1.16	3.92	5.2	9.8	2.0	4.7	6.5
11	Trail	29	22.87	1.27		0.85	1.82	2.1	1.7	3.8	4.3	3.4
12	Grand Forks	3	10.10	0.30	+	0.06	0.87	1.5	-	1.0	1.4	-
13	Kettle Valley	0	3.69	-		-	-	-	-	-	-	-
14	Southern Okanagan	21	25.06	0.84		0.52	1.28	0.9	1.0	5.4	1.9	0.9
15	Penticton	41	48.19	0.85		0.61	1.15	2.4	2.4	1.8	0.8	3.2
16	Keremeos	8	6.60	1.21		0.52	2.39	5.6	8.5	1.7	3.1	-
17	Princeton	9	3.89	2.31	*	1.06	4.39	4.0	3.4	8.6	9.3	2.8
18	Golden	3	3.57	0.84		0.17	2.46	-	2.6	-	7.3	-
19	Revelstoke	3	4.66	0.64		0.13	1.88	5.2	-	-	-	2.6
20	Salmon Arm	35	30.63	1.14		0.80	1.59	5.6	2.5	1.5	1.6	3.1
21	Armstrong-Spallumcheen	13	7.67	1.70		0.90	2.90	4.8	1.5	4.8	6.2	2.6
22	Vernon	52	48.99	1.06		0.79	1.39	3.0	1.9	3.5	1.5	3.0
23	Central Okanagan	94	122.25	0.77	**	0.62	0.94	1.4	1.6	2.1	2.3	2.2
24	Kamloops	67	48.89	1.37	*	1.06	1.74	3.1	3.8	3.8	2.4	3.8
26	North Thompson	1	2.37	0.42		0.01	2.35	♦	-	-	-	-
27	Cariboo-Chilcotin	22	17.18	1.28		0.80	1.94	1.0	2.0	3.3	5.3	3.3
28	Quesnel	24	12.70	1.89	**	1.21	2.81	5.5	1.7	2.5	4.0	7.9
29	Lillooet	5	3.51	1.42		0.46	3.32	-	-	11.4	-	6.7
30	South Cariboo	5	5.68	0.88		0.28	2.05	4.6	4.4	1.9	-	-
31	Merritt	5	5.81	0.86		0.28	2.01	2.4	1.7	2.0	1.8	2.5
32	Hope	8	6.23	1.28		0.55	2.53	-	1.6	7.7	6.5	1.4
33	Chilliwack	57	51.37	1.11		0.84	1.44	2.8	3.5	3.1	1.9	2.7
34	Abbotsford	48	71.77	0.67	**	0.49	0.89	2.1	1.3	2.4	1.6	1.0
35	Langley	58	53.84	1.08		0.82	1.39	3.0	3.8	2.9	2.2	2.0
36	Surrey	174	172.50	1.01		0.86	1.17	2.7	3.1	1.7	2.7	2.4
37	Delta	44	43.10	1.02		0.74	1.37	3.2	2.9	1.9	3.6	1.6
38	Richmond	80	70.16	1.14		0.90	1.42	1.7	3.0	2.9	3.2	2.9
39	Vancouver	472	465.33	1.01		0.92	1.11	3.1	2.5	2.2	2.4	2.7
40	New Westminster	54	46.82	1.15		0.87	1.50	3.9	2.1	4.7	2.4	2.0
41	Burnaby	139	136.41	1.02		0.86	1.20	2.5	1.6	2.0	2.6	3.7
42	Maple Ridge	42	33.56	1.25		0.90	1.69	4.9	1.5	2.9	3.6	2.8
43	Coquitlam	84	60.97	1.38	**	1.10	1.71	2.6	1.8	4.9	4.4	3.1
44	North Vancouver	76	69.02	1.10		0.87	1.38	2.1	2.8	3.7	2.9	2.8
45	West Vancouver-Bowen Is	25	52.04	0.48	***	0.31	0.71	1.3	0.8	1.7	1.3	0.9
46	Sechelt	15	21.96	0.68		0.38	1.13	2.1	1.4	1.4	1.0	2.6
47	Powell River	9	17.69	0.51	*	0.23	0.97	0.8	2.5	1.6	1.4	0.5
48	Howe Sound	10	6.29	1.59		0.76	2.93	-	3.6	6.4	9.8	-
49	Central Coast	2	1.86	1.07		0.12	3.88	5.3	-	12.6	-	-
50	Queen Charlotte	1	2.28	0.44		0.01	2.44	-	-	-	-	♦
52	Prince Rupert	11	8.15	1.35		0.67	2.42	3.4	4.2	4.7	-	4.2
54	Smithers	4	5.41	0.74		0.20	1.89	2.2	3.4	3.2	2.1	-
55	Burns Lake	3	3.92	0.77		0.15	2.24	-	-	-	2.6	6.2
56	Nechako	6	7.46	0.80		0.29	1.75	3.8	3.8	-	1.6	1.5
57	Prince George	39	28.50	1.37		0.97	1.87	4.1	3.6	4.6	1.0	3.4
59	Peace River South	17	14.18	1.20		0.70	1.92	2.0	2.9	1.7	3.3	5.1
60	Peace River North	12	10.33	1.16		0.60	2.03	3.8	2.5	1.2	2.6	4.3
61	Greater Victoria	240	254.66	0.94		0.83	1.07	2.3	2.2	2.4	2.6	2.4
62	Sooke	21	26.72	0.79		0.49	1.20	2.8	-	0.7	3.2	3.1
63	Saanich	31	49.42	0.63	**	0.43	0.89	2.1	1.6	1.9	1.1	1.2
64	Gulf Islands	9	16.45	0.55		0.25	1.04	3.2	0.7	2.0	-	0.9
65	Cowichan	40	34.77	1.15		0.82	1.57	3.9	4.5	1.8	3.3	1.0
66	Lake Cowichan	2	3.80	0.53		0.06	1.90	-	-	-	6.0	-
67	Ladysmith	13	16.07	0.81		0.43	1.38	0.7	1.7	2.4	3.1	2.4
68	Nanaimo	56	58.93	0.95		0.72	1.23	1.9	2.6	2.3	1.8	3.1
69	Qualicum	30	34.80	0.86		0.58	1.23	3.3	1.4	1.6	2.7	1.8
70	Alberni	18	19.71	0.91		0.54	1.44	2.5	2.3	2.2	2.1	2.5
71	Courtenay	33	34.03	0.97		0.67	1.36	1.6	4.8	1.6	2.3	2.1
72	Campbell River	22	16.30	1.35		0.85	2.04	5.3	4.5	2.5	3.6	2.0
75	Mission	28	22.31	1.26		0.83	1.81	1.2	1.2	4.1	7.8	1.7
76	Agassiz-Harrison	2	5.00	0.40		0.04	1.45	-	-	-	2.5	1.8
77	Summerland	11	16.12	0.68		0.34	1.22	-	2.9	2.1	2.0	0.6
78	Enderby	10	6.84	1.46		0.70	2.69	5.0	3.5	3.9	1.4	3.2
80	Kitimat	1	2.83	0.35		0.00	1.97	-	-	-	-	♦
81	Fort Nelson	0	1.00	-		-	-	-	-	-	-	-
84	Vancouver Island West	0	0.50	-		-	-	-	-	-	-	-
85	Vancouver Island North	2	3.33	0.60		0.07	2.17	-	0.9	-	3.6	-
87	Stikine	2	0.54	3.70		0.42	13.35	21.2	-	-	16.1	-
88	Terrace	10	10.34	0.97		0.46	1.78	3.4	4.3	3.6	-	1.0
92	Nishga	0	0.73	-		-	-	-	-	-	-	-
94	Telegraph Creek	0	0.22	-		-	-	-	-	-	-	-
	Provincial Total	**2,625**	♦	1.00		♦	♦	2.6	2.4	2.5	2.5	2.4

Chronic Lung Disease: Female

	Local Health Area	Observed Deaths	Expected Deaths	SMR (p)	95% C.I. Lower	95% C.I. Upper	ASMR 1985	1986	1987	1988	1989
1	Fernie	4	3.10	1.29	0.35	3.31	2.7	3.8	2.3	-	-
2	Cranbrook	7	6.33	1.11	0.44	2.28	1.1	1.0	1.0	0.8	2.8
3	Kimberley	10	4.01	2.49 *	1.19	4.58	3.0	3.3	2.8	4.2	1.3
4	Windermere	3	1.70	1.76	0.35	5.15	3.8	-	3.2	-	2.5
5	Creston	7	6.82	1.03	0.41	2.11	1.6	0.8	0.9	2.4	-
6	Kootenay Lake	3	1.73	1.73	0.35	5.07	2.6	-	-	6.0	-
7	Nelson	6	9.82	0.61	0.22	1.33	0.5	0.6	-	0.6	1.8
9	Castlegar	4	4.63	0.86	0.23	2.21	2.0	2.2	-	-	0.9
10	Arrow Lakes	4	2.29	1.75	0.47	4.47	5.8	2.6	2.3	-	-
11	Trail	16	10.21	1.57	0.90	2.55	1.7	1.0	1.0	2.0	3.0
12	Grand Forks	2	4.11	0.49	0.05	1.76	-	1.3	1.6	-	-
13	Kettle Valley	0	1.03	-	-	-	-	-	-	-	-
14	Southern Okanagan	9	10.27	0.88	0.40	1.66	0.5	0.6	1.5	1.6	0.6
15	Penticton	18	21.87	0.82	0.49	1.30	0.9	0.6	1.5	1.0	0.6
16	Keremeos	6	2.04	2.94 *	1.07	6.39	2.8	-	3.2	8.9	2.7
17	Princeton	1	1.77	0.57	0.01	3.15	-	-	-	♦	-
18	Golden	1	1.21	0.82	0.01	4.58	-	♦	-	-	-
19	Revelstoke	3	2.31	1.30	0.26	3.80	-	-	-	2.8	4.5
20	Salmon Arm	10	12.05	0.83	0.40	1.53	1.6	0.4	1.3	-	1.4
21	Armstrong-Spallumcheen	4	3.00	1.33	0.36	3.41	2.3	-	-	3.9	1.7
22	Vernon	21	21.46	0.98	0.61	1.50	1.7	0.6	0.5	1.0	1.6
23	Central Okanagan	39	52.58	0.74	0.53	1.01	1.0	0.7	0.7	1.1	0.8
24	Kamloops	20	22.16	0.90	0.55	1.39	1.0	1.4	0.3	0.7	1.6
26	North Thompson	3	0.93	3.23	0.65	9.43	-	-	4.8	11.2	-
27	Cariboo-Chilcotin	7	6.84	1.02	0.41	2.11	1.2	-	1.0	0.9	3.3
28	Quesnel	5	4.69	1.07	0.34	2.49	1.0	-	1.4	2.5	1.3
29	Lillooet	2	1.06	1.89	0.21	6.81	-	-	10.8	-	-
30	South Cariboo	3	1.94	1.54	0.31	4.51	-	-	2.7	6.6	-
31	Merritt	3	2.42	1.24	0.25	3.62	-	2.6	-	4.8	-
32	Hope	2	2.42	0.83	0.09	2.98	-	-	-	-	4.4
33	Chilliwack	16	23.51	0.68	0.39	1.11	0.5	1.0	0.8	0.7	0.9
34	Abbotsford	27	33.27	0.81	0.53	1.18	0.4	1.2	1.1	1.3	1.0
35	Langley	27	24.71	1.09	0.72	1.59	1.1	1.6	0.9	1.6	1.2
36	Surrey	95	83.95	1.13	0.92	1.38	1.3	1.3	1.2	1.3	1.4
37	Delta	22	22.98	0.96	0.60	1.45	0.5	1.0	0.7	1.2	1.8
38	Richmond	39	38.64	1.01	0.72	1.38	1.1	1.6	1.4	1.5	0.4
39	Vancouver	256	262.97	0.97	0.86	1.10	1.1	1.6	0.8	1.1	1.1
40	New Westminster	35	30.51	1.15	0.80	1.60	1.7	1.3	1.2	1.5	1.4
41	Burnaby	72	77.83	0.93	0.72	1.17	0.9	1.0	1.3	0.8	1.3
42	Maple Ridge	25	16.79	1.49	0.96	2.20	2.3	2.0	1.4	1.3	1.8
43	Coquitlam	30	31.47	0.95	0.64	1.36	0.6	0.6	1.5	1.2	1.5
44	North Vancouver	43	42.43	1.01	0.73	1.36	1.0	1.3	0.8	1.4	1.1
45	West Vancouver-Bowen Is	31	30.90	1.00	0.68	1.42	0.8	0.9	1.2	1.6	0.7
46	Sechelt	10	9.45	1.06	0.51	1.95	-	2.8	0.5	0.7	2.2
47	Powell River	10	8.08	1.24	0.59	2.28	1.6	1.6	2.3	1.2	0.7
48	Howe Sound	2	2.80	0.72	0.08	2.58	-	2.6	-	2.3	-
49	Central Coast	0	0.56	-	-	-	-	-	-	-	-
50	Queen Charlotte	0	0.75	-	-	-	-	-	-	-	-
52	Prince Rupert	6	3.41	1.76	0.64	3.83	-	3.4	1.6	-	5.0
54	Smithers	2	2.33	0.86	0.10	3.10	3.5	-	-	-	1.9
55	Burns Lake	2	1.18	1.70	0.19	6.13	-	3.2	-	4.5	-
56	Nechako	5	2.68	1.87	0.60	4.35	2.0	6.2	1.6	-	-
57	Prince George	17	12.11	1.40	0.82	2.25	3.0	1.4	1.8	1.0	0.9
59	Peace River South	10	5.45	1.83	0.88	3.37	-	2.2	3.4	2.1	3.0
60	Peace River North	5	3.86	1.30	0.42	3.02	2.0	1.9	1.6	-	2.4
61	Greater Victoria	144	152.59	0.94	0.80	1.11	1.1	1.2	0.9	1.0	1.3
62	Sooke	15	12.05	1.25	0.70	2.05	0.9	2.7	0.4	2.1	1.1
63	Saanich	21	23.04	0.91	0.56	1.39	0.8	1.1	1.0	0.5	1.7
64	Gulf Islands	9	7.00	1.29	0.59	2.44	0.8	-	0.6	2.4	3.1
65	Cowichan	16	15.95	1.00	0.57	1.63	1.2	0.8	1.5	0.7	1.7
66	Lake Cowichan	0	1.55	-	-	-	-	-	-	-	-
67	Ladysmith	2	6.77	0.30	0.03	1.07	-	-	-	0.7	1.0
68	Nanaimo	33	28.20	1.17	0.81	1.64	1.5	2.2	1.0	0.8	1.3
69	Qualicum	10	14.92	0.67	0.32	1.23	2.1	0.3	0.3	0.5	0.6
70	Alberni	12	9.61	1.25	0.64	2.18	0.9	0.7	1.7	2.3	1.8
71	Courtenay	15	15.38	0.98	0.55	1.61	2.1	0.4	1.1	1.8	0.3
72	Campbell River	12	7.78	1.54	0.80	2.70	-	0.7	0.6	2.7	4.5
75	Mission	9	9.39	0.96	0.44	1.82	0.8	0.7	2.6	-	1.6
76	Agassiz-Harrison	2	1.99	1.00	0.11	3.62	-	2.6	2.5	-	-
77	Summerland	5	6.65	0.75	0.24	1.75	-	0.8	0.8	0.8	1.5
78	Enderby	2	2.75	0.73	0.08	2.63	-	-	-	5.2	-
80	Kitimat	1	1.28	0.78	0.01	4.36	-	♦	-	-	-
81	Fort Nelson	0	0.27	-	-	-	-	-	-	-	-
84	Vancouver Island West	0	0.25	-	-	-	-	-	-	-	-
85	Vancouver Island North	0	1.47	-	-	-	-	-	-	-	-
87	Stikine	0	0.18	-	-	-	-	-	-	-	-
88	Terrace	3	3.28	0.91	0.18	2.67	1.9	1.9	2.7	-	-
92	Nishga	0	0.22	-	-	-	-	-	-	-	-
94	Telegraph Creek	1	0.10	10.33	0.14	57.48	♦	-	-	-	-
	Provincial Total	**1,322**	♦	**1.00**	♦	♦	**1.1**	**1.2**	**1.0**	**1.2**	**1.2**

199

Digestive System: Male

	Local Health Area	Observed Deaths	Expected Deaths	SMR	(p)	95% C.I. Lower	95% C.I. Upper	ASMR 1985	1986	1987	1988	1989
1	Fernie	5	7.45	0.67		0.22	1.57	1.3	3.3	1.7	1.4	-
2	Cranbrook	17	11.41	1.49		0.87	2.38	1.9	6.4	2.0	3.4	3.3
3	Kimberley	3	6.49	0.46		0.09	1.35	2.9	-	-	-	3.6
4	Windermere	2	4.30	0.47		0.05	1.68	3.0	-	2.3	-	-
5	Creston	8	12.49	0.64		0.28	1.26	2.6	0.7	0.6	0.8	1.1
6	Kootenay Lake	4	3.28	1.22		0.33	3.12	7.1	-	3.8	9.6	-
7	Nelson	10	16.90	0.59		0.28	1.09	1.9	1.8	0.5	1.0	0.6
9	Castlegar	7	8.37	0.84		0.34	1.72	1.3	2.0	1.2	1.7	2.5
10	Arrow Lakes	7	3.97	1.76		0.71	3.63	-	4.5	4.5	4.1	1.8
11	Trail	17	17.31	0.98		0.57	1.57	0.7	3.1	2.1	3.1	2.2
12	Grand Forks	8	7.38	1.08		0.47	2.14	1.1	1.0	2.7	2.3	4.1
13	Kettle Valley	4	2.91	1.37		0.37	3.52	3.3	-	3.8	2.4	2.8
14	Southern Okanagan	13	17.73	0.73		0.39	1.25	2.5	2.2	1.0	0.8	1.6
15	Penticton	29	33.86	0.86		0.57	1.23	2.4	0.4	2.7	1.9	2.3
16	Keremeos	3	4.62	0.65		0.13	1.90	-	-	1.4	3.0	-
17	Princeton	5	3.41	1.47		0.47	3.42	2.6	5.5	3.2	-	2.5
18	Golden	1	3.47	0.29		0.00	1.60	-	♦	-	-	-
19	Revelstoke	8	4.45	1.80		0.77	3.54	2.4	4.1	-	4.9	7.6
20	Salmon Arm	16	23.59	0.68		0.39	1.10	1.3	2.8	1.5	1.9	1.1
21	Armstrong-Spallumcheen	3	5.95	0.50		0.10	1.47	-	4.3	-	1.7	-
22	Vernon	29	37.33	0.78		0.52	1.12	1.4	1.4	1.1	2.0	2.7
23	Central Okanagan	65	90.42	0.72	**	0.55	0.92	1.5	1.6	1.2	1.0	2.3
24	Kamloops	42	44.51	0.94		0.68	1.28	2.4	1.0	2.2	2.4	2.3
26	North Thompson	2	2.31	0.86		0.10	3.12	-	14.7	-	-	-
27	Cariboo-Chilcotin	25	17.86	1.40		0.91	2.07	3.4	1.9	1.1	4.9	5.3
28	Quesnel	12	12.09	0.99		0.51	1.73	2.3	0.6	4.7	1.6	2.0
29	Lillooet	7	2.98	2.35		0.94	4.84	8.5	3.2	9.1	3.3	-
30	South Cariboo	8	4.90	1.63		0.70	3.22	2.4	-	8.3	6.0	2.1
31	Merritt	8	5.51	1.45		0.62	2.86	1.7	9.2	3.9	-	1.7
32	Hope	8	5.25	1.52		0.66	3.00	4.1	3.8	3.9	2.4	2.4
33	Chilliwack	35	39.57	0.88		0.62	1.23	1.7	1.7	1.7	2.6	2.3
34	Abbotsford	38	54.12	0.70	*	0.50	0.96	1.9	1.6	1.3	1.9	1.2
35	Langley	32	45.36	0.71	*	0.48	1.00	1.1	2.0	1.1	1.8	1.4
36	Surrey	144	141.46	1.02		0.86	1.20	2.5	2.2	2.4	1.8	2.2
37	Delta	22	41.86	0.53	**	0.33	0.80	1.8	0.7	1.9	0.7	1.0
38	Richmond	59	65.27	0.90		0.69	1.17	1.9	2.4	1.9	1.7	1.9
39	Vancouver	465	363.72	1.28	***	1.16	1.40	4.0	2.7	2.6	2.6	2.6
40	New Westminster	58	34.96	1.66	***	1.26	2.15	6.9	2.2	3.3	2.9	3.4
41	Burnaby	128	112.31	1.14		0.95	1.36	2.0	3.8	2.9	2.2	1.4
42	Maple Ridge	38	28.77	1.32		0.93	1.81	2.4	3.2	2.8	1.1	4.7
43	Coquitlam	53	60.45	0.88		0.66	1.15	2.9	2.6	2.0	1.1	1.7
44	North Vancouver	53	65.05	0.81		0.61	1.07	1.7	1.9	2.2	2.0	1.3
45	West Vancouver-Bowen Is	26	40.85	0.64	*	0.42	0.93	1.0	2.2	0.7	1.5	1.5
46	Sechelt	14	16.75	0.84		0.46	1.40	2.2	2.3	1.0	1.2	2.6
47	Powell River	12	14.22	0.84		0.44	1.47	1.6	1.8	3.8	1.1	2.0
48	Howe Sound	5	7.07	0.71		0.23	1.65	2.4	-	1.4	2.1	-
49	Central Coast	5	1.66	3.02		0.97	7.05	5.6	7.3	7.7	7.0	10.1
50	Queen Charlotte	2	2.30	0.87		0.10	3.14	-	-	4.1	-	6.4
52	Prince Rupert	16	8.14	1.97	*	1.12	3.19	5.6	5.3	4.8	3.2	2.8
54	Smithers	3	5.77	0.52		0.10	1.52	1.8	-	3.3	2.0	-
55	Burns Lake	3	3.72	0.81		0.16	2.36	-	5.3	3.2	-	-
56	Nechako	8	7.16	1.12		0.48	2.20	3.0	3.8	-	4.9	1.5
57	Prince George	46	33.63	1.37	*	1.00	1.82	4.0	3.5	4.2	2.4	1.8
59	Peace River South	13	13.27	0.98		0.52	1.67	1.8	1.5	1.7	1.8	3.6
60	Peace River North	9	10.43	0.86		0.39	1.64	0.9	1.8	0.9	4.3	1.1
61	Greater Victoria	185	179.66	1.03		0.89	1.19	2.6	1.9	2.7	2.2	2.2
62	Sooke	22	24.25	0.91		0.57	1.37	1.1	3.0	1.5	1.8	2.4
63	Saanich	25	39.43	0.63	*	0.41	0.94	1.7	1.6	1.8	1.5	0.7
64	Gulf Islands	13	12.02	1.08		0.58	1.85	1.9	1.8	1.8	2.1	1.8
65	Cowichan	30	27.94	1.07		0.72	1.53	2.6	3.5	0.3	3.5	2.3
66	Lake Cowichan	4	3.42	1.17		0.31	2.99	-	2.6	8.8	-	-
67	Ladysmith	17	12.12	1.40		0.82	2.25	5.5	2.8	3.3	0.7	3.7
68	Nanaimo	47	47.50	0.99		0.73	1.32	2.7	1.9	2.2	2.0	2.4
69	Qualicum	17	25.89	0.66		0.38	1.05	0.9	2.0	1.3	1.6	1.0
70	Alberni	19	18.09	1.05		0.63	1.64	2.2	3.0	2.8	1.1	2.3
71	Courtenay	18	28.65	0.63	*	0.37	0.99	1.1	1.6	1.5	1.7	0.7
72	Campbell River	11	15.97	0.69		0.34	1.23	3.4	0.6	1.2	1.0	1.1
75	Mission	19	18.22	1.04		0.63	1.63	1.5	1.0	3.7	3.1	1.7
76	Agassiz-Harrison	2	4.12	0.49		0.05	1.75	-	-	-	-	5.3
77	Summerland	8	11.07	0.72		0.31	1.42	1.5	0.8	3.4	1.7	-
78	Enderby	5	5.08	0.98		0.32	2.30	-	6.4	4.0	1.6	-
80	Kitimat	4	4.29	0.93		0.25	2.39	1.4	1.2	1.5	5.0	-
81	Fort Nelson	2	1.44	1.39		0.16	5.03	-	-	6.9	8.0	-
84	Vancouver Island West	0	1.05	-		-	-	-	-	-	-	-
85	Vancouver Island North	8	4.79	1.67		0.72	3.29	2.4	1.4	-	4.9	1.2
87	Stikine	1	0.07	1.48		0.02	8.26	-	♦	-	-	-
88	Terrace	17	10.65	1.60		0.93	2.55	3.6	5.8	3.1	3.1	2.5
92	Nishga	0	0.62	-		-	-	-	-	-	-	-
94	Telegraph Creek	0	0.24	-		-	-	-	-	-	-	-
	Provincial Total	**2,138**	♦	**1.00**		♦	♦	2.5	2.3	2.2	2.0	2.0

200

Digestive System: Female

	Local Health Area	Observed Deaths	Expected Deaths	SMR (p)	95% C.I. Lower	95% C.I. Upper	1985	1986	1987	1988	1989
1	Fernie	6	5.11	1.17	0.43	2.55	-	2.0	6.4	-	3.6
2	Cranbrook	8	10.09	0.79	0.34	1.56	0.9	0.9	0.8	2.8	1.5
3	Kimberley	8	5.95	1.35	0.58	2.65	3.9	4.7	2.5	3.6	-
4	Windermere	0	2.51	-	-	-	-	-	-	-	-
5	Creston	18	9.75	1.85 *	1.09	2.92	4.7	5.3	0.8	6.5	0.8
6	Kootenay Lake	2	2.49	0.80	0.09	2.90	3.1	7.7	-	-	-
7	Nelson	8	14.93	0.54	0.23	1.06	0.5	2.3	0.6	-	0.9
9	Castlegar	7	6.91	1.01	0.41	2.09	1.1	1.4	2.9	1.0	2.0
10	Arrow Lakes	2	3.49	0.57	0.06	2.07	-	-	-	2.2	2.1
11	Trail	19	14.89	1.28	0.77	1.99	2.5	1.1	3.4	1.3	2.6
12	Grand Forks	5	5.81	0.86	0.28	2.01	1.2	1.3	1.3	1.7	1.3
13	Kettle Valley	2	1.46	1.37	0.15	4.94	-	4.7	-	-	6.5
14	Southern Okanagan	18	14.74	1.22	0.72	1.93	2.8	2.6	1.6	3.0	2.7
15	Penticton	28	31.52	0.89	0.59	1.28	3.5	1.4	1.9	1.2	0.7
16	Keremeos	3	2.96	1.01	0.20	2.96	3.7	3.1	-	3.0	-
17	Princeton	2	2.85	0.70	0.08	2.54	-	-	-	2.5	2.5
18	Golden	2	2.05	0.97	0.11	3.52	5.6	11.0	-	-	-
19	Revelstoke	5	3.79	1.32	0.43	3.08	5.7	-	5.4	-	2.9
20	Salmon Arm	16	17.81	0.90	0.51	1.46	1.3	2.6	0.9	1.5	1.3
21	Armstrong-Spallumcheen	3	4.52	0.66	0.13	1.94	-	-	-	5.8	-
22	Vernon	32	32.16	1.00	0.68	1.40	1.8	1.1	2.4	1.0	2.4
23	Central Okanagan	55	76.67	0.72 *	0.54	0.93	1.3	1.1	2.0	0.8	1.4
24	Kamloops	36	35.45	1.02	0.71	1.41	1.5	1.2	1.0	2.8	2.7
26	North Thompson	2	1.45	1.38	0.15	4.97	-	-	12.8	-	-
27	Cariboo-Chilcotin	11	11.52	0.95	0.48	1.71	2.2	1.2	-	2.0	2.8
28	Quesnel	13	7.66	1.70	0.90	2.90	1.0	1.8	2.1	3.6	5.2
29	Lillooet	7	1.77	3.96 **	1.59	8.17	-	-	21.7	-	13.1
30	South Cariboo	8	3.02	2.64 *	1.14	5.21	-	2.6	9.2	5.5	6.4
31	Merritt	4	4.01	1.00	0.27	2.55	-	5.4	-	1.9	2.1
32	Hope	2	3.58	0.56	0.06	2.02	-	1.7	3.5	-	-
33	Chilliwack	45	34.25	1.31	0.96	1.76	2.4	2.8	3.1	1.6	2.3
34	Abbotsford	47	49.99	0.94	0.69	1.25	1.5	1.7	1.6	1.9	1.4
35	Langley	31	38.34	0.81	0.55	1.15	2.0	2.1	0.9	0.8	1.7
36	Surrey	112	126.94	0.88	0.73	1.06	3.0	1.2	1.9	1.5	0.7
37	Delta	47	37.57	1.25	0.92	1.66	2.6	2.5	2.3	1.6	2.1
38	Richmond	65	60.68	1.07	0.83	1.37	2.0	2.9	1.2	2.4	1.4
39	Vancouver	420	409.70	1.03	0.93	1.13	2.1	2.1	2.0	1.6	1.8
40	New Westminster	48	45.43	1.06	0.78	1.40	1.7	5.0	1.8	1.8	2.2
41	Burnaby	124	122.18	1.01	0.84	1.21	2.2	2.3	1.4	1.5	1.6
42	Maple Ridge	35	26.86	1.30	0.91	1.81	3.7	2.5	1.8	2.5	1.8
43	Coquitlam	52	52.06	1.00	0.75	1.31	2.4	1.9	1.7	1.6	1.9
44	North Vancouver	81	67.61	1.20	0.95	1.49	2.0	2.2	2.7	2.2	1.6
45	West Vancouver-Bowen Is	31	47.76	0.65 *	0.44	0.92	1.8	0.8	0.9	1.0	1.4
46	Sechelt	19	13.50	1.41	0.85	2.20	4.3	5.2	2.1	3.0	1.1
47	Powell River	15	12.24	1.23	0.69	2.02	1.6	1.5	2.0	3.2	2.7
48	Howe Sound	5	4.62	1.08	0.35	2.53	1.8	1.5	-	5.0	1.5
49	Central Coast	4	0.89	4.49 +	1.21	11.51	8.1	4.2	26.9	-	-
50	Queen Charlotte	4	1.33	3.01	0.81	7.70	-	10.5	7.0	-	8.6
52	Prince Rupert	7	5.76	1.21	0.49	2.50	2.9	-	4.1	1.1	1.7
54	Smithers	4	4.11	0.97	0.26	2.49	5.1	-	5.3	-	-
55	Burns Lake	1	2.08	0.48	0.01	2.68	♦	-	-	-	-
56	Nechako	2	4.57	0.44	0.05	1.58	-	1.8	-	1.9	-
57	Prince George	31	21.76	1.42	0.97	2.02	1.5	3.9	4.9	1.7	1.5
59	Peace River South	9	9.21	0.98	0.45	1.86	1.0	2.2	1.9	2.1	1.9
60	Peace River North	7	6.62	1.06	0.42	2.18	6.1	1.3	-	1.5	2.8
61	Greater Victoria	220	236.23	0.93	0.81	1.06	1.7	1.9	1.3	1.8	1.6
62	Sooke	13	18.84	0.69	0.37	1.18	0.7	3.1	1.1	1.0	0.7
63	Saanich	27	34.20	0.79	0.52	1.15	1.1	0.7	2.0	2.0	1.3
64	Gulf Islands	9	9.62	0.94	0.43	1.78	1.4	1.7	1.6	2.8	0.9
65	Cowichan	30	24.38	1.23	0.83	1.76	3.4	2.1	2.7	2.1	1.2
66	Lake Cowichan	2	2.31	0.86	0.10	3.12	6.5	-	-	-	2.8
67	Ladysmith	6	9.58	0.63	0.23	1.36	0.8	-	-	1.6	2.8
68	Nanaimo	38	41.84	0.91	0.64	1.25	1.8	1.6	1.4	1.7	2.1
69	Qualicum	21	21.10	1.00	0.62	1.52	1.6	0.4	2.9	2.0	2.4
70	Alberni	15	14.68	1.02	0.57	1.69	2.9	1.3	3.0	1.9	0.5
71	Courtenay	19	23.71	0.80	0.48	1.25	0.7	1.4	1.5	1.7	1.5
72	Campbell River	13	12.42	1.05	0.56	1.79	3.8	2.1	2.7	0.6	0.6
75	Mission	19	14.59	1.30	0.78	2.03	0.7	1.1	3.3	4.4	2.5
76	Agassiz-Harrison	3	2.85	1.05	0.21	3.08	4.6	-	2.5	-	2.4
77	Summerland	7	9.54	0.73	0.29	1.51	-	2.8	2.0	1.9	-
78	Enderby	3	3.86	0.78	0.16	2.27	2.3	-	-	1.6	1.4
80	Kitimat	3	2.66	1.13	0.23	3.30	-	1.3	-	12.2	-
81	Fort Nelson	1	0.68	1.46	0.02	8.15	-	-	♦	-	-
84	Vancouver Island West	2	0.57	3.48	0.39	12.57	25.5	-	-	-	-
85	Vancouver Island North	4	2.87	1.39	0.37	3.57	2.5	5.3	4.3	-	-
87	Stikine	0	0.32	-	-	-	-	-	-	-	-
88	Terrace	7	5.83	1.20	0.48	2.47	0.8	-	3.3	0.7	2.9
92	Nishga	0	0.36	-	-	-	-	-	-	-	-
94	Telegraph Creek	0	0.16	-	-	-	-	-	-	-	-
	Provincial Total	**2,040**	♦	1.00	♦	♦	2.0	1.9	1.8	1.7	1.7

Motor Vehicle Traffic Accidents: Male

	Local Health Area	Observed Deaths	Expected Deaths	SMR	(p)	95% C.I. Lower	Upper	ASMR 1985	1986	1987	1988	1989
1	Fernie	8	9.67	0.83		0.36	1.63	0.6	2.3	1.0	1.5	5.7
2	Cranbrook	13	12.12	1.07		0.57	1.83	6.7	-	3.0	1.2	1.9
3	Kimberley	8	4.68	1.71		0.74	3.37	1.5	5.1	10.3	2.9	9.3
4	Windermere	6	3.97	1.51		0.55	3.29	6.1	-	2.5	8.5	-
5	Creston	7	5.76	1.22		0.49	2.50	2.8	1.3	3.4	-	6.5
6	Kootenay Lake	2	1.74	1.15		0.13	4.14	-	4.4	-	-	6.0
7	Nelson	12	11.35	1.06		0.55	1.85	1.7	3.8	-	2.6	4.7
9	Castlegar	7	6.66	1.05		0.42	2.17	4.4	-	3.6	2.4	2.2
10	Arrow Lakes	4	2.68	1.49		0.40	3.82	4.7	4.6	9.3	-	-
11	Trail	10	11.58	0.86		0.41	1.59	-	2.6	1.6	0.8	5.1
12	Grand Forks	8	4.09	1.96		0.84	3.86	-	4.1	10.2	7.7	1.4
13	Kettle Valley	6	1.87	3.22	*	1.17	7.00	17.3	-	9.4	-	10.7
14	Southern Okanagan	8	7.90	1.01		0.44	2.00	2.7	2.3	2.7	3.0	-
15	Penticton	23	17.38	1.32		0.84	1.99	5.1	1.8	4.0	4.1	1.7
16	Keremeos	9	2.20	4.09	**	1.87	7.76	-	19.1	18.4	-	10.8
17	Princeton	10	2.86	3.49	**	1.67	6.43	4.1	14.6	4.2	3.4	17.5
18	Golden	6	4.34	1.38		0.50	3.01	3.6	8.6	3.0	3.8	-
19	Revelstoke	9	5.33	1.69		0.77	3.21	2.1	2.9	4.9	6.8	-
20	Salmon Arm	27	14.10	1.91	**	1.26	2.79	3.5	5.5	4.7	5.1	3.4
21	Armstrong-Spallumcheen	8	4.09	1.96		0.84	3.86	-	7.8	3.3	10.0	3.7
22	Vernon	38	25.33	1.50	*	1.06	2.06	3.2	2.4	9.0	3.1	0.6
23	Central Okanagan	75	54.14	1.39	**	1.09	1.74	3.3	2.9	3.5	4.0	3.3
24	Kamloops	65	45.85	1.42	**	1.09	1.81	3.9	2.8	5.6	1.2	3.4
26	North Thompson	6	2.76	2.18		0.79	4.74	-	-	8.1	10.3	11.4
27	Cariboo-Chilcotin	55	21.84	2.52	***	1.90	3.28	5.1	7.0	2.5	7.2	7.2
28	Quesnel	23	14.06	1.64	*	1.04	2.45	3.4	4.2	2.7	2.9	6.7
29	Lillooet	5	2.85	1.76		0.57	4.10	5.6	3.7	8.5	-	3.7
30	South Cariboo	20	4.45	4.49	***	2.74	6.94	8.8	5.5	16.9	16.8	5.8
31	Merritt	7	5.84	1.20		0.48	2.47	8.1	1.5	-	2.3	2.6
32	Hope	5	4.42	1.13		0.36	2.64	6.9	-	6.7	-	2.7
33	Chilliwack	29	27.94	1.04		0.70	1.49	1.8	2.3	1.8	4.0	3.0
34	Abbotsford	55	42.85	1.28		0.97	1.67	3.2	2.5	6.6	2.0	2.0
35	Langley	60	43.14	1.39	*	1.06	1.79	2.0	6.3	2.9	3.4	2.7
36	Surrey	122	124.54	0.98		0.81	1.17	2.0	2.1	2.2	2.8	2.4
37	Delta	34	47.08	0.72		0.50	1.01	1.5	0.9	2.0	2.1	2.6
38	Richmond	30	66.63	0.45	***	0.30	0.64	0.5	1.4	2.1	1.1	0.6
39	Vancouver	177	284.05	0.62	***	0.53	0.72	0.9	1.7	1.5	1.3	1.4
40	New Westminster	23	26.68	0.86		0.55	1.29	1.8	3.2	1.8	3.3	0.9
41	Burnaby	59	92.72	0.64	***	0.48	0.82	1.2	1.3	2.3	1.3	1.8
42	Maple Ridge	21	28.41	0.74		0.46	1.13	1.6	2.2	2.0	1.0	2.0
43	Coquitlam	40	74.05	0.54	***	0.39	0.74	0.8	1.0	2.0	1.2	2.0
44	North Vancouver	36	64.79	0.56	***	0.39	0.77	1.3	2.0	1.5	1.0	1.1
45	West Vancouver-Bowen Is	10	23.85	0.42	**	0.20	0.77	0.8	-	0.4	2.1	0.6
46	Sechelt	9	9.63	0.93		0.43	1.77	1.4	0.8	3.2	3.4	1.6
47	Powell River	13	10.82	1.20		0.64	2.05	5.7	3.4	3.7	1.2	1.0
48	Howe Sound	17	9.90	1.72		1.00	2.75	3.8	6.8	3.6	6.7	0.7
49	Central Coast	2	1.95	1.03		0.12	3.71	-	-	-	18.4	-
50	Queen Charlotte	8	3.51	2.28		0.98	4.49	8.8	3.3	3.9	9.1	-
52	Prince Rupert	14	10.94	1.28		0.70	2.15	2.7	3.2	1.2	7.2	1.0
54	Smithers	22	8.87	2.48	***	1.55	3.76	8.1	6.3	5.8	6.3	3.4
55	Burns Lake	11	4.75	2.32	*	1.15	4.14	8.8	2.8	4.0	12.1	-
56	Nechako	24	9.33	2.57	***	1.65	3.83	4.4	5.4	6.4	6.8	8.3
57	Prince George	92	53.37	1.72	***	1.39	2.11	3.3	4.7	4.8	5.0	3.5
59	Peace River South	30	16.74	1.79	**	1.21	2.56	4.1	3.1	0.5	6.0	6.9
60	Peace River North	26	14.73	1.77	*	1.15	2.59	5.2	3.4	2.8	7.5	3.1
61	Greater Victoria	39	111.22	0.35	***	0.25	0.48	1.0	0.9	0.8	0.8	0.5
62	Sooke	19	23.79	0.80		0.48	1.25	2.0	4.0	3.5	0.7	-
63	Saanich	11	23.81	0.46	**	0.23	0.83	3.0	0.7	0.8	0.3	1.0
64	Gulf Islands	3	5.01	0.60		0.12	1.75	-	-	0.5	4.3	1.5
65	Cowichan	25	20.74	1.21		0.78	1.78	1.2	2.3	3.3	4.7	3.6
66	Lake Cowichan	1	2.86	0.35		0.00	1.95	-	-	-	-	◆
67	Ladysmith	8	7.28	1.10		0.47	2.16	2.2	5.8	4.4	-	2.0
68	Nanaimo	35	36.16	0.97		0.67	1.35	0.3	3.5	4.3	1.6	2.1
69	Qualicum	14	12.56	1.11		0.61	1.87	3.6	3.6	3.8	1.4	2.9
70	Alberni	23	17.98	1.28		0.81	1.92	1.8	4.4	5.5	1.9	1.9
71	Courtenay	22	22.61	0.97		0.61	1.47	2.5	2.7	2.8	0.8	2.0
72	Campbell River	23	18.29	1.26		0.80	1.89	1.8	3.0	3.5	2.8	2.6
75	Mission	26	15.66	1.66	*	1.08	2.43	5.5	2.4	4.2	6.5	2.8
76	Agassiz-Harrison	4	3.72	1.08		0.29	2.75	-	8.0	-	-	2.4
77	Summerland	9	4.88	1.84		0.84	3.50	3.1	3.8	9.1	4.3	3.0
78	Enderby	16	3.08	5.20	***	2.97	8.45	18.2	2.0	2.3	26.9	14.8
80	Kitimat	9	7.49	1.20		0.55	2.28	3.8	5.2	-	-	3.0
81	Fort Nelson	2	3.31	0.60		0.07	2.18	-	-	4.8	-	5.6
84	Vancouver Island West	1	2.33	0.43		0.01	2.39	-	-	◆	-	-
85	Vancouver Island North	10	9.22	1.08		0.52	1.99	2.7	-	-	5.6	6.5
87	Stikine	2	1.17	1.72		0.19	6.19	-	-	14.0	10.1	-
88	Terrace	28	15.29	1.83	**	1.22	2.65	5.6	2.3	6.4	3.7	4.4
92	Nishga	0	1.02	-		-	-	-	-	-	-	-
94	Telegraph Creek	2	0.45	4.40		0.49	15.88	59.2	-	-	-	-
	Provincial Total	**1,787**	◆	1.00		◆	◆	2.1	2.4	2.7	2.5	2.2

Motor Vehicle Traffic Accidents: Female

	Local Health Area	Observed Deaths	Expected Deaths	SMR	(p)	95% C.I. Lower	95% C.I. Upper	1985	1986	1987	1988	1989
1	Fernie	3	3.47	0.86		0.17	2.53	-	-	-	3.2	1.8
2	Cranbrook	5	4.94	1.01		0.33	2.36	2.1	-	-	-	2.6
3	Kimberley	0	2.04	-		-	-	-	-	-	-	-
4	Windermere	2	1.50	1.34		0.15	4.82	5.3	-	-	-	-
5	Creston	7	2.71	2.59	*	1.04	5.33	-	8.4	1.6	0.8	-
6	Kootenay Lake	3	0.76	3.96		0.80	11.57	2.6	-	-	3.4	2.7
7	Nelson	6	4.98	1.20		0.44	2.62	0.5	0.6	3.1	0.8	-
9	Castlegar	0	2.76	-		-	-	-	-	-	-	-
10	Arrow Lakes	5	1.07	4.69	*	1.51	10.94	-	12.1	16.9	-	-
11	Trail	2	5.10	0.39		0.04	1.42	-	-	-	2.9	-
12	Grand Forks	1	1.83	0.55		0.01	3.05	-	-	-	♦	-
13	Kettle Valley	0	0.72	-		-	-	-	-	-	-	-
14	Southern Okanagan	6	3.76	1.60		0.58	3.47	0.6	8.4	2.3	-	-
15	Penticton	7	8.48	0.83		0.33	1.70	-	0.2	0.5	2.2	1.0
16	Keremeos	1	0.87	1.15		0.02	6.40	-	♦	-	-	-
17	Princeton	3	1.12	2.68		0.54	7.83	-	9.9	-	2.5	-
18	Golden	1	1.54	0.65		0.01	3.60	-	♦	-	-	-
19	Revelstoke	3	1.94	1.54		0.31	4.51	2.9	-	2.2	-	3.4
20	Salmon Arm	10	6.20	1.61		0.77	2.97	-	2.9	1.8	1.0	0.8
21	Armstrong-Spallumcheen	6	1.75	3.42	*	1.25	7.45	1.7	3.3	-	2.7	8.3
22	Vernon	12	11.19	1.07		0.55	1.87	0.3	-	2.2	1.7	1.0
23	Central Okanagan	34	24.63	1.38		0.96	1.93	2.0	1.6	0.9	1.3	0.6
24	Kamloops	23	18.41	1.25		0.79	1.88	1.4	1.2	0.5	0.6	2.2
26	North Thompson	7	1.02	6.88	***	2.76	14.18	11.0	5.2	12.8	-	3.5
27	Cariboo-Chilcotin	26	8.26	3.15	***	2.05	4.61	0.6	2.3	2.8	5.6	4.0
28	Quesnel	9	5.39	1.67		0.76	3.17	-	5.0	0.6	1.3	0.6
29	Lillooet	7	0.99	7.11	***	2.85	14.64	5.3	5.0	19.1	-	6.6
30	South Cariboo	8	1.62	4.95	***	2.13	9.76	3.5	2.1	8.9	2.8	5.2
31	Merritt	7	2.19	3.20	*	1.28	6.59	2.3	4.3	-	6.4	1.6
32	Hope	1	1.70	0.59		0.01	3.28	-	-	-	-	♦
33	Chilliwack	21	12.29	1.71	*	1.06	2.61	2.2	0.3	1.7	1.3	2.2
34	Abbotsford	12	18.12	0.66		0.34	1.16	0.4	1.1	1.4	-	0.4
35	Langley	19	17.89	1.06		0.64	1.66	1.4	1.1	0.7	0.5	1.8
36	Surrey	47	52.40	0.90		0.66	1.19	0.5	0.5	1.9	0.5	0.9
37	Delta	15	19.26	0.78		0.44	1.28	0.5	1.1	0.8	0.7	0.8
38	Richmond	10	28.05	0.36	***	0.17	0.66	0.2	0.4	0.3	0.8	0.1
39	Vancouver	86	123.01	0.70	***	0.56	0.86	0.7	0.7	0.9	0.6	0.5
40	New Westminster	7	11.86	0.59		0.24	1.22	-	1.5	-	0.5	0.2
41	Burnaby	29	40.05	0.72		0.48	1.04	0.7	0.8	0.6	0.4	0.4
42	Maple Ridge	10	11.60	0.86		0.41	1.59	-	0.8	1.1	1.5	0.5
43	Coquitlam	19	29.04	0.65		0.39	1.02	0.6	0.8	0.2	0.5	1.1
44	North Vancouver	15	27.61	0.54	*	0.30	0.90	0.5	0.3	0.6	0.4	0.5
45	West Vancouver-Bowen Is	6	11.84	0.51		0.18	1.10	0.2	-	-	1.2	0.2
46	Sechelt	5	4.37	1.14		0.37	2.67	0.8	-	0.8	4.7	-
47	Powell River	1	4.46	0.22		0.00	1.25	-	-	-	-	♦
48	Howe Sound	4	3.41	1.17		0.32	3.00	1.0	-	3.3	1.5	-
49	Central Coast	1	0.70	1.42		0.02	7.90	-	-	-	♦	-
50	Queen Charlotte	0	1.08	-		-	-	-	-	-	-	-
52	Prince Rupert	6	4.01	1.50		0.55	3.26	1.0	2.1	-	2.3	-
54	Smithers	6	3.12	1.92		0.70	4.18	2.0	3.5	1.6	3.5	-
55	Burns Lake	8	1.67	4.79	***	2.06	9.45	4.0	10.8	2.6	1.9	3.2
56	Nechako	16	3.33	4.81	***	2.75	7.81	2.6	1.7	-	8.0	9.2
57	Prince George	28	19.66	1.42		0.95	2.06	0.8	1.1	0.8	2.7	1.4
59	Peace River South	6	6.09	0.98		0.36	2.14	-	-	3.1	-	2.3
60	Peace River North	9	5.37	1.68		0.76	3.18	2.0	2.4	2.0	1.0	0.8
61	Greater Victoria	35	53.87	0.65	**	0.45	0.90	0.1	1.2	0.7	0.3	0.3
62	Sooke	5	9.64	0.52		0.17	1.21	0.6	1.7	-	0.7	-
63	Saanich	5	10.93	0.46		0.15	1.07	-	-	1.8	0.7	0.3
64	Gulf Islands	2	2.53	0.79		0.09	2.85	-	-	1.4	0.8	-
65	Cowichan	12	9.03	1.33		0.69	2.32	0.5	3.5	0.7	0.8	0.7
66	Lake Cowichan	0	1.14	-		-	-	-	-	-	-	-
67	Ladysmith	5	3.24	1.54		0.50	3.60	-	2.9	2.6	1.9	-
68	Nanaimo	16	15.78	1.01		0.58	1.65	-	1.7	0.8	0.6	2.6
69	Qualicum	2	6.03	0.33		0.04	1.20	-	-	-	3.2	-
70	Alberni	8	7.07	1.13		0.49	2.23	-	1.6	2.0	2.4	-
71	Courtenay	16	9.52	1.68		0.96	2.73	3.5	0.3	2.3	1.8	0.7
72	Campbell River	10	7.10	1.41		0.67	2.59	1.7	2.4	0.4	1.4	1.5
75	Mission	12	6.19	1.94	*	1.00	3.39	3.6	0.6	1.2	0.9	1.0
76	Agassiz-Harrison	2	1.16	1.72		0.19	6.22	-	-	4.1	5.3	-
77	Summerland	1	2.34	0.43		0.01	2.38	-	-	-	♦	-
78	Enderby	2	1.30	1.54		0.17	5.55	-	7.6	-	-	-
80	Kitimat	4	2.72	1.47		0.40	3.76	-	3.0	2.4	-	-
81	Fort Nelson	6	1.08	5.58	**	2.04	12.14	8.8	-	-	6.6	8.5
84	Vancouver Island West	2	0.75	2.66		0.30	9.61	-	2.9	16.7	-	-
85	Vancouver Island North	3	3.08	0.97		0.20	2.85	-	-	-	4.1	1.2
87	Stikine	0	0.38	-		-	-	-	-	-	-	-
88	Terrace	14	5.42	2.58	**	1.41	4.33	0.6	3.7	3.8	1.5	1.5
92	Nishga	0	0.32	-		-	-	-	-	-	-	-
94	Telegraph Creek	1	0.14	7.04		0.09	39.18	-	♦	-	-	-
	Provincial Total	**754**	♦	1.00		♦	♦	0.7	1.2	1.0	1.0	0.9

Accidental Falls: Male

	Local Health Area	Observed Deaths	Expected Deaths	SMR (p)	95% C.I. Lower	Upper	ASMR 1985	1986	1987	1988	1989
1	Fernie	1	2.45	0.41	0.01	2.27	-	♦	-	-	-
2	Cranbrook	2	3.57	0.56	0.06	2.02	0.9	1.4	-	-	-
3	Kimberley	4	1.89	2.12	0.57	5.42	3.7	-	1.3	1.4	-
4	Windermere	1	1.32	1.52	0.17	5.49	2.6	3.1	-	-	-
5	Creston	7	4.19	1.67	0.67	3.44	1.5	1.6	1.3	0.8	-
6	Kootenay Lake	1	0.96	1.04	0.01	5.77	-	-	♦	-	-
7	Nelson	3	5.54	0.54	0.11	1.58	-	0.5	0.5	-	0.6
9	Castlegar	2	2.58	0.77	0.09	2.80	-	-	1.6	-	1.4
10	Arrow Lakes	1	1.32	0.76	0.01	4.20	-	-	-	♦	-
11	Trail	4	5.58	0.72	0.19	1.83	-	-	0.9	0.6	0.8
12	Grand Forks	1	2.31	0.43	0.01	2.41	♦	-	-	-	-
13	Kettle Valley	1	0.95	1.06	0.01	5.87	-	♦	-	-	-
14	Southern Okanagan	5	5.66	0.88	0.28	2.06	1.4	0.5	0.5	-	-
15	Penticton	10	11.28	0.89	0.42	1.63	0.5	1.1	-	0.4	0.7
16	Keremeos	0	1.41	-	-	-	-	-	-	-	-
17	Princeton	0	1.02	-	-	-	-	-	-	-	-
18	Golden	1	1.16	0.86	0.01	4.80	-	♦	-	-	-
19	Revelstoke	1	1.46	0.69	0.01	3.82	-	-	-	-	♦
20	Salmon Arm	4	7.01	0.57	0.15	1.46	0.5	0.9	0.3	-	-
21	Armstrong-Spallumcheen	1	1.90	0.53	0.01	2.92	-	-	-	♦	-
22	Vernon	11	12.26	0.90	0.45	1.61	0.6	0.9	0.3	1.0	0.4
23	Central Okanagan	32	29.31	1.09	0.75	1.54	1.0	0.4	0.9	1.1	0.7
24	Kamloops	16	14.01	1.14	0.65	1.85	1.5	1.0	1.3	0.3	0.2
26	North Thompson	1	0.71	1.41	0.02	7.86	-	-	-	♦	-
27	Cariboo-Chilcotin	5	5.37	0.93	0.30	2.17	1.1	0.8	1.0	-	0.8
28	Quesnel	3	3.89	0.77	0.15	2.25	1.3	-	1.8	-	-
29	Lillooet	4	0.99	4.03 +	1.08	10.31	5.0	-	2.7	4.3	3.0
30	South Cariboo	3	1.60	1.87	0.38	5.46	-	2.5	-	-	4.2
31	Merritt	2	1.70	1.18	0.13	4.25	-	2.2	-	2.5	-
32	Hope	2	1.50	1.34	0.15	4.82	1.6	2.0	-	-	-
33	Chilliwack	15	12.60	1.19	0.67	1.96	1.4	0.5	1.2	0.2	0.9
34	Abbotsford	10	18.20	0.55	0.26	1.01	0.7	0.5	0.3	0.2	0.3
35	Langley	17	14.60	1.16	0.68	1.86	0.8	1.3	0.7	0.8	0.6
36	Surrey	36	45.65	0.79	0.55	1.09	0.4	0.5	0.6	0.8	0.5
37	Delta	10	12.66	0.79	0.38	1.45	-	0.9	1.1	0.9	0.5
38	Richmond	17	19.63	0.87	0.50	1.39	0.7	0.6	0.8	0.9	0.3
39	Vancouver	177	122.84	1.44 ***	1.24	1.67	1.1	1.2	1.3	1.2	0.7
40	New Westminster	12	11.71	1.03	0.53	1.79	1.0	0.8	0.3	1.6	0.7
41	Burnaby	34	36.05	0.94	0.65	1.32	0.8	0.5	0.9	0.2	0.9
42	Maple Ridge	8	9.31	0.86	0.37	1.69	0.7	0.4	-	1.3	0.7
43	Coquitlam	21	19.33	1.09	0.67	1.66	0.9	1.6	0.8	0.2	0.9
44	North Vancouver	17	19.53	0.87	0.51	1.39	0.3	0.5	0.5	1.9	0.4
45	West Vancouver-Bowen Is	11	12.55	0.88	0.44	1.57	0.3	0.6	1.1	0.2	0.6
46	Sechelt	1	5.00	0.20	0.00	1.11	-	-	-	♦	-
47	Powell River	3	4.58	0.66	0.13	1.92	1.0	0.8	-	0.7	-
48	Howe Sound	0	2.07	-	-	-	-	-	-	-	-
49	Central Coast	1	0.51	1.98	0.03	11.01	-	-	-	♦	-
50	Queen Charlotte	0	0.85	-	-	-	-	-	-	-	-
52	Prince Rupert	3	2.76	1.09	0.22	3.18	0.8	2.0	1.3	-	-
54	Smithers	2	1.87	1.07	0.12	3.85	-	3.4	-	3.2	-
55	Burns Lake	2	1.21	1.66	0.19	5.99	2.7	-	-	4.6	-
56	Nechako	3	2.36	1.27	0.26	3.71	1.5	2.0	-	-	1.7
57	Prince George	11	10.55	1.04	0.52	1.87	0.3	0.9	1.3	1.7	0.7
59	Peace River South	3	4.48	0.67	0.13	1.96	-	0.8	1.9	-	-
60	Peace River North	3	3.52	0.85	0.17	2.49	-	-	2.0	0.5	-
61	Greater Victoria	56	63.55	0.88	0.67	1.14	0.6	0.7	0.5	0.8	0.4
62	Sooke	4	7.17	0.56	0.15	1.43	-	0.8	2.2	-	-
63	Saanich	10	11.40	0.88	0.42	1.61	-	1.4	1.8	-	0.6
64	Gulf Islands	4	3.45	1.16	0.31	2.97	1.3	-	-	5.8	0.6
65	Cowichan	2	8.81	0.23 +	0.03	0.82	-	-	-	0.4	0.3
66	Lake Cowichan	0	0.99	-	-	-	-	-	-	-	-
67	Ladysmith	6	3.78	1.59	0.58	3.46	4.3	-	-	0.9	0.7
68	Nanaimo	17	14.50	1.17	0.68	1.88	1.0	0.8	0.9	0.4	1.1
69	Qualicum	6	7.38	0.81	0.30	1.77	1.9	-	0.3	0.5	1.0
70	Alberni	7	5.39	1.30	0.52	2.68	1.8	-	1.1	1.5	1.1
71	Courtenay	6	8.81	0.68	0.25	1.48	-	-	0.8	1.4	0.3
72	Campbell River	4	4.73	0.85	0.23	2.16	1.3	0.6	0.6	-	-
75	Mission	3	5.80	0.52	0.10	1.51	0.6	-	0.5	0.6	-
76	Agassiz-Harrison	0	1.28	-	-	-	-	-	-	-	-
77	Summerland	3	3.80	0.79	0.16	2.31	-	-	-	2.2	-
78	Enderby	3	1.70	1.76	0.35	5.15	4.4	3.3	1.5	-	-
80	Kitimat	0	1.27	-	-	-	-	-	-	-	-
81	Fort Nelson	2	0.52	3.88	0.44	14.00	3.2	-	3.5	-	-
84	Vancouver Island West	1	0.33	3.02	0.04	16.78	-	-	-	-	♦
85	Vancouver Island North	3	1.57	1.91	0.38	5.58	1.3	0.7	-	-	4.3
87	Stikine	1	0.21	4.75	0.06	26.41	-	-	♦	-	-
88	Terrace	3	3.65	0.82	0.17	2.40	0.6	1.2	1.0	-	-
92	Nishga	1	0.23	4.36	0.06	24.28	-	♦	-	-	-
94	Telegraph Creek	0	0.07	-	-	-	-	-	-	-	-
	Provincial Total	**690**	♦	1.00	♦	♦	0.8	0.7	0.8	0.7	0.6

Accidental Falls: Female

	Local Health Area	Observed Deaths	Expected Deaths	SMR (p)	95% C.I. Lower	Upper	ASMR 1985	1986	1987	1988	1989
1	Fernie	2	1.48	1.35	0.15	4.87	-	3.7	-	-	-
2	Cranbrook	6	3.08	1.95	0.71	4.24	2.0	-	0.8	0.8	1.6
3	Kimberley	1	1.82	0.55	0.01	3.06	-	♦	-	-	-
4	Windermere	0	0.60	-	-	-	-	-	-	-	-
5	Creston	7	2.99	2.34	0.94	4.82	4.4	-	-	0.8	2.3
6	Kootenay Lake	1	0.76	1.32	0.02	7.37	-	♦	-	-	-
7	Nelson	5	4.80	1.04	0.34	2.43	0.6	0.6	1.2	-	1.1
9	Castlegar	1	2.03	0.49	0.01	2.74	-	-	-	♦	-
10	Arrow Lakes	0	1.17	-	-	-	-	-	-	-	-
11	Trail	5	4.47	1.12	0.36	2.61	-	0.6	-	0.6	1.6
12	Grand Forks	0	1.70	-	-	-	-	-	-	-	-
13	Kettle Valley	0	0.35	-	-	-	-	-	-	-	-
14	Southern Okanagan	5	4.62	1.08	0.35	2.53	0.6	0.8	1.0	0.5	-
15	Penticton	8	10.06	0.79	0.34	1.57	0.3	0.8	0.2	0.2	0.6
16	Keremeos	0	0.87	-	-	-	-	-	-	-	-
17	Princeton	0	0.90	-	-	-	-	-	-	-	-
18	Golden	1	0.57	1.75	0.02	9.76	-	-	♦	-	-
19	Revelstoke	2	1.20	1.66	0.19	6.00	4.6	-	2.7	-	-
20	Salmon Arm	3	5.19	0.58	0.12	1.69	-	-	0.5	-	0.9
21	Armstrong-Spallumcheen	2	1.36	1.47	0.17	5.32	-	-	-	1.6	1.7
22	Vernon	11	9.96	1.10	0.55	1.98	0.9	0.6	-	0.5	0.9
23	Central Okanagan	27	23.32	1.16	0.76	1.68	0.6	0.7	0.9	0.3	0.5
24	Kamloops	14	10.39	1.35	0.74	2.26	1.7	0.5	0.5	0.2	1.1
26	North Thompson	2	0.36	5.60	0.63	20.22	-	15.4	2.8	-	-
27	Cariboo-Chilcotin	4	3.04	1.32	0.35	3.37	-	1.9	1.4	0.8	-
28	Quesnel	2	2.04	0.98	0.11	3.54	1.6	-	-	1.3	-
29	Lillooet	0	0.51	-	-	-	-	-	-	-	-
30	South Cariboo	4	0.84	4.76 +	1.28	12.19	3.0	2.8	-	2.9	2.9
31	Merritt	1	1.20	0.83	0.01	4.62	-	-	♦	-	-
32	Hope	0	0.93	-	-	-	-	-	-	-	-
33	Chilliwack	11	10.23	1.08	0.54	1.92	0.8	1.4	-	0.2	0.5
34	Abbotsford	4	16.06	0.25 +	0.07	0.64	-	-	0.3	0.1	0.1
35	Langley	12	11.67	1.03	0.53	1.80	-	0.7	0.4	1.3	0.2
36	Surrey	23	38.72	0.59 **	0.38	0.89	0.4	0.5	0.3	-	0.5
37	Delta	6	11.41	0.53	0.19	1.14	0.6	-	-	0.2	0.4
38	Richmond	17	17.87	0.95	0.55	1.52	0.6	0.5	0.4	0.6	0.5
39	Vancouver	172	143.15	1.20 *	1.03	1.40	0.9	0.6	0.7	0.7	0.5
40	New Westminster	12	15.72	0.76	0.39	1.33	0.7	0.2	0.7	0.1	0.4
41	Burnaby	36	41.30	0.87	0.61	1.21	0.3	0.4	0.7	0.3	0.5
42	Maple Ridge	3	8.84	0.34 +	0.07	0.99	0.6	-	-	-	0.2
43	Coquitlam	19	15.48	1.23	0.74	1.92	1.2	0.2	0.9	0.5	0.7
44	North Vancouver	21	21.27	0.99	0.61	1.51	0.7	0.4	0.5	0.4	0.7
45	West Vancouver-Bowen Is	19	16.42	1.16	0.70	1.81	1.0	1.3	0.5	0.1	0.3
46	Sechelt	6	3.89	1.54	0.56	3.36	-	1.9	1.5	-	0.7
47	Powell River	3	3.85	0.78	0.16	2.28	-	0.7	0.6	-	0.6
48	Howe Sound	0	1.21	-	-	-	-	-	-	-	-
49	Central Coast	0	0.21	-	-	-	-	-	-	-	-
50	Queen Charlotte	0	0.39	-	-	-	-	-	-	-	-
52	Prince Rupert	4	1.66	2.42	0.65	6.18	4.0	-	-	2.1	-
54	Smithers	0	1.19	-	-	-	-	-	-	-	-
55	Burns Lake	0	0.60	-	-	-	-	-	-	-	-
56	Nechako	0	1.31	-	-	-	-	-	-	-	-
57	Prince George	6	5.72	1.05	0.38	2.28	0.6	0.6	0.6	0.4	0.8
59	Peace River South	3	2.76	1.09	0.22	3.17	-	-	-	1.0	1.7
60	Peace River North	1	1.82	0.55	0.01	3.06	-	♦	-	-	-
61	Greater Victoria	86	86.85	0.99	0.79	1.22	0.6	0.5	0.4	0.6	0.5
62	Sooke	4	5.35	0.75	0.20	1.91	0.6	1.8	-	-	-
63	Saanich	9	10.29	0.88	0.40	1.66	0.9	-	0.8	-	0.6
64	Gulf Islands	5	2.73	1.83	0.59	4.28	-	1.0	1.0	1.0	1.9
65	Cowichan	7	7.57	0.92	0.37	1.91	0.4	0.4	0.4	0.9	0.3
66	Lake Cowichan	0	0.60	-	-	-	-	-	-	-	-
67	Ladysmith	1	2.79	0.36	0.00	1.99	-	-	♦	-	0.3
68	Nanaimo	12	12.54	0.96	0.49	1.67	0.5	0.9	0.9	-	0.3
69	Qualicum	8	6.14	1.30	0.56	2.57	3.2	-	1.3	0.4	-
70	Alberni	7	4.13	1.70	0.68	3.49	0.7	0.8	2.0	1.2	-
71	Courtenay	3	7.12	0.42	0.08	1.23	-	0.8	-	0.5	-
72	Campbell River	3	3.52	0.85	0.17	2.49	-	1.5	0.7	-	0.5
75	Mission	4	4.58	0.87	0.23	2.24	0.7	0.7	0.5	-	0.5
76	Agassiz-Harrison	0	0.78	-	-	-	-	-	-	-	-
77	Summerland	7	3.05	2.30	0.92	4.73	2.7	-	0.8	4.8	-
78	Enderby	2	1.10	1.81	0.20	6.54	-	3.1	1.7	-	-
80	Kitimat	1	0.72	1.38	0.02	7.69	-	-	♦	-	-
81	Fort Nelson	0	0.18	-	-	-	-	-	-	-	-
84	Vancouver Island West	0	0.17	-	-	-	-	-	-	-	-
85	Vancouver Island North	0	0.78	-	-	-	-	-	-	-	-
87	Stikine	0	0.07	-	-	-	-	-	-	-	-
88	Terrace	7	1.55	4.52 **	1.81	9.32	2.4	3.1	2.7	4.5	0.6
92	Nishga	0	0.09	-	-	-	-	-	-	-	-
94	Telegraph Creek	0	0.04	-	-	-	-	-	-	-	-
	Provincial Total	**659**	♦	**1.00**	♦	♦	0.7	0.6	0.5	0.5	0.5

Suicide: Male

#	Local Health Area	Observed Deaths	Expected Deaths	SMR (p)	95% C.I. Lower	95% C.I. Upper	ASMR 1985	1986	1987	1988	1989
1	Fernie	8	8.66	0.92	0.40	1.82	2.7	3.8	1.7	1.7	-
2	Cranbrook	15	10.84	1.38	0.77	2.28	3.9	1.0	4.8	1.0	3.2
3	Kimberley	3	4.44	0.68	0.14	1.97	-	2.1	4.6	-	-
4	Windermere	2	3.63	0.55	0.06	1.99	-	-	-	-	6.6
5	Creston	4	5.66	0.71	0.19	1.81	3.0	-	5.5	-	2.1
6	Kootenay Lake	3	1.76	1.70	0.34	4.97	-	6.7	-	5.7	13.5
7	Nelson	8	10.81	0.74	0.32	1.46	1.4	0.7	2.0	0.8	0.9
9	Castlegar	4	6.12	0.65	0.18	1.67	1.3	2.3	1.6	1.5	-
10	Arrow Lakes	2	2.47	0.81	0.09	2.92	-	-	4.2	4.0	-
11	Trail	10	10.89	0.92	0.44	1.69	2.3	1.3	1.8	2.1	2.2
12	Grand Forks	7	4.00	1.75	0.70	3.60	3.4	5.2	6.9	-	2.5
13	Kettle Valley	2	1.78	1.12	0.13	4.05	-	5.4	-	3.9	-
14	Southern Okanagan	7	7.90	0.89	0.36	1.83	1.0	3.0	0.9	-	4.6
15	Penticton	21	16.73	1.25	0.78	1.92	1.5	1.8	1.5	4.3	3.0
16	Keremeos	2	2.16	0.93	0.10	3.35	7.8	4.6	-	-	-
17	Princeton	7	2.67	2.62 *	1.05	5.40	6.8	-	2.9	2.5	14.1
18	Golden	3	3.88	0.77	0.16	2.26	-	2.9	2.3	2.5	-
19	Revelstoke	8	4.80	1.67	0.72	3.28	6.1	1.7	5.5	-	6.3
20	Salmon Arm	7	13.58	0.52	0.21	1.06	1.7	1.2	2.3	-	-
21	Armstrong-Spallumcheen	2	3.80	0.53	0.06	1.90	-	-	2.6	-	4.1
22	Vernon	24	23.58	1.02	0.65	1.51	0.6	3.7	3.2	2.7	0.7
23	Central Okanagan	54	51.29	1.05	0.79	1.37	2.4	2.8	1.8	1.5	1.8
24	Kamloops	52	41.19	1.26	0.94	1.66	3.6	2.3	2.8	2.7	1.5
26	North Thompson	1	2.44	0.41	0.01	2.28	-	-	♦	-	-
27	Cariboo-Chilcotin	36	19.43	1.85 **	1.30	2.57	2.6	4.4	1.4	4.0	6.7
28	Quesnel	15	12.43	1.21	0.67	1.99	1.8	4.8	2.5	-	3.5
29	Lillooet	6	2.49	2.41	0.88	5.24	8.2	4.5	-	7.3	2.6
30	South Cariboo	9	4.01	2.25 *	1.03	4.27	2.0	-	6.6	8.7	8.6
31	Merritt	13	5.21	2.50 **	1.33	4.27	3.6	3.5	6.1	6.9	5.0
32	Hope	7	4.01	1.75	0.70	3.60	2.1	3.2	-	8.1	6.3
33	Chilliwack	30	25.69	1.17	0.79	1.67	4.4	2.6	2.4	1.8	2.2
34	Abbotsford	32	38.54	0.83	0.57	1.17	2.1	1.9	1.8	1.8	0.8
35	Langley	27	39.24	0.69	0.45	1.00	2.5	1.5	0.5	1.2	1.3
36	Surrey	106	114.77	0.92	0.76	1.12	2.6	1.2	1.5	2.5	1.3
37	Delta	24	42.23	0.57 **	0.36	0.85	0.7	2.0	2.2	0.7	0.2
38	Richmond	40	62.12	0.64 **	0.46	0.88	1.5	1.7	1.1	1.0	1.0
39	Vancouver	293	269.15	1.09	0.97	1.22	2.5	2.2	2.0	1.7	2.2
40	New Westminster	19	25.17	0.76	0.45	1.18	2.4	1.3	1.1	1.5	1.5
41	Burnaby	60	87.27	0.69 **	0.52	0.88	1.0	1.6	1.3	0.9	1.7
42	Maple Ridge	27	26.05	1.04	0.68	1.51	3.3	0.9	2.4	2.8	1.4
43	Coquitlam	56	66.65	0.84	0.63	1.09	1.6	2.3	1.7	2.0	1.2
44	North Vancouver	50	60.99	0.82	0.61	1.08	2.1	1.8	1.2	1.0	1.5
45	West Vancouver-Bowen Is	14	23.65	0.59 *	0.32	0.99	2.4	2.2	0.9	0.7	0.2
46	Sechelt	11	9.68	1.14	0.57	2.03	4.3	-	0.9	2.6	5.0
47	Powell River	12	10.02	1.20	0.62	2.09	2.5	2.9	1.2	5.5	-
48	Howe Sound	11	8.90	1.24	0.62	2.21	1.5	2.0	2.2	1.4	5.4
49	Central Coast	10	1.74	5.74 ***	2.75	10.55	6.6	25.3	19.2	-	3.9
50	Queen Charlotte	6	3.13	1.92	0.70	4.18	-	7.3	-	9.7	5.9
52	Prince Rupert	12	9.54	1.26	0.65	2.20	2.9	2.1	2.3	3.5	2.0
54	Smithers	5	7.67	0.65	0.21	1.52	1.0	2.2	3.0	1.9	-
55	Burns Lake	6	4.07	1.48	0.54	3.21	4.7	-	9.2	-	2.3
56	Nechako	11	7.89	1.40	0.70	2.50	5.0	3.0	3.6	-	2.3
57	Prince George	63	46.56	1.35 *	1.04	1.73	4.1	1.9	2.1	2.1	4.1
59	Peace River South	12	14.79	0.81	0.42	1.42	3.0	1.6	0.6	2.3	1.2
60	Peace River North	16	12.54	1.28	0.73	2.07	2.3	1.8	3.1	1.9	3.7
61	Greater Victoria	71	102.93	0.69 **	0.54	0.87	1.4	1.5	1.4	1.3	1.0
62	Sooke	21	22.07	0.95	0.59	1.45	1.1	2.7	2.7	1.3	2.2
63	Saanich	21	23.57	0.89	0.55	1.36	-	2.6	3.3	1.7	1.6
64	Gulf Islands	6	5.43	1.11	0.40	2.41	2.2	-	6.4	0.5	2.4
65	Cowichan	31	19.39	1.60 *	1.09	2.27	4.4	3.4	4.1	3.5	1.9
66	Lake Cowichan	2	2.68	0.75	0.08	2.70	-	2.6	-	7.2	-
67	Ladysmith	9	6.98	1.29	0.59	2.45	0.9	1.7	2.3	1.0	6.0
68	Nanaimo	37	33.95	1.09	0.77	1.50	1.2	2.0	2.3	2.3	2.2
69	Qualicum	14	12.84	1.09	0.60	1.83	0.3	3.5	0.4	2.8	5.5
70	Alberni	20	16.26	1.23	0.75	1.90	3.3	4.8	0.5	2.1	1.6
71	Courtenay	35	21.43	1.63 **	1.14	2.27	4.6	4.6	3.9	2.2	1.3
72	Campbell River	13	16.71	0.78	0.41	1.33	1.1	2.1	2.7	1.0	1.0
75	Mission	11	14.37	0.77	0.38	1.37	2.4	1.8	0.7	1.6	1.4
76	Agassiz-Harrison	1	3.47	0.29	0.00	1.60	-	-	-	-	♦
77	Summerland	3	4.76	0.63	0.13	1.84	-	4.7	-	0.6	-
78	Enderby	3	2.85	1.05	0.21	3.07	-	-	1.9	4.9	3.7
80	Kitimat	13	6.56	1.98 *	1.05	3.39	-	6.5	2.2	4.8	7.2
81	Fort Nelson	0	2.76	-	-	-	-	-	-	-	-
84	Vancouver Island West	0	2.10	-	-	-	-	-	-	-	-
85	Vancouver Island North	21	8.15	2.58 ***	1.59	3.94	3.8	5.8	11.1	2.9	4.3
87	Stikine	2	1.04	1.92	0.22	6.92	-	4.6	-	-	4.9
88	Terrace	18	13.00	1.38	0.82	2.19	4.7	3.5	-	4.8	1.7
92	Nishga	0	0.76	-	-	-	-	-	-	-	-
94	Telegraph Creek	1	0.36	2.82	0.04	15.67	-	-	-	-	♦
	Provincial Total	1,655	♦	1.00	♦	♦	2.2	2.2	1.9	1.9	1.9

Suicide: Female

	Local Health Area	Observed Deaths	Expected Deaths	SMR (p)	95% C.I. Lower	Upper	ASMR 1985	1986	1987	1988	1989
1	Fernie	2	2.19	0.91	0.10	3.29	0.7	0.8	-	-	-
2	Cranbrook	3	3.17	0.95	0.19	2.76	-	0.6	-	2.4	-
3	Kimberley	1	1.36	0.73	0.01	4.08	-	-	-	◆	-
4	Windermere	1	0.98	1.02	0.01	5.70	-	-	-	-	◆
5	Creston	1	1.82	0.55	0.01	3.06	◆	-	-	-	-
6	Kootenay Lake	0	0.52	-	-	-	-	-	-	-	-
7	Nelson	3	3.31	0.91	0.18	2.65	0.7	-	-	0.8	0.8
9	Castlegar	0	1.82	-	-	-	-	-	-	-	-
10	Arrow Lakes	0	0.70	-	-	-	-	-	-	-	-
11	Trail	2	3.39	0.59	0.07	2.13	-	0.6	0.7	-	-
12	Grand Forks	0	1.24	-	-	-	-	-	-	-	-
13	Kettle Valley	2	0.47	4.23	0.47	15.26	-	-	5.6	5.4	-
14	Southern Okanagan	0	2.58	-	-	-	-	-	-	-	-
15	Penticton	7	5.68	1.23	0.49	2.54	1.3	-	1.3	1.2	1.0
16	Keremeos	2	0.61	3.30	0.37	11.93	5.6	-	-	4.5	-
17	Princeton	4	0.75	5.33 +	1.43	13.64	-	4.8	-	-	12.4
18	Golden	0	0.96	-	-	-	-	-	-	-	-
19	Revelstoke	0	1.25	-	-	-	-	-	-	-	-
20	Salmon Arm	4	4.20	0.95	0.26	2.44	0.9	-	1.1	-	0.7
21	Armstrong-Spallumcheen	0	1.15	-	-	-	-	-	-	-	-
22	Vernon	3	7.43	0.40	0.08	1.18	-	0.4	0.9	-	-
23	Central Okanagan	12	16.71	0.72	0.37	1.25	-	0.5	0.4	0.7	0.7
24	Kamloops	15	12.02	1.25	0.70	2.06	0.9	0.2	-	1.0	1.4
26	North Thompson	1	0.64	1.57	0.02	8.72	-	-	-	◆	2.1
27	Cariboo-Chilcotin	7	5.18	1.35	0.54	2.79	1.2	1.0	-	-	2.1
28	Quesnel	10	3.37	2.97 **	1.42	5.46	1.9	1.9	3.6	2.9	-
29	Lillooet	0	0.61	-	-	-	-	-	-	-	-
30	South Cariboo	0	1.05	-	-	-	-	-	-	-	-
31	Merritt	1	1.39	0.72	0.01	3.99	-	-	-	-	◆
32	Hope	0	1.13	-	-	-	-	-	-	-	-
33	Chilliwack	6	8.05	0.74	0.27	1.62	0.2	0.2	0.2	0.6	0.3
34	Abbotsford	12	11.62	1.03	0.53	1.80	1.5	1.0	0.2	-	0.3
35	Langley	10	11.67	0.86	0.41	1.58	0.4	1.4	0.4	0.3	-
36	Surrey	34	34.60	0.98	0.68	1.37	1.0	0.7	0.4	0.6	0.2
37	Delta	10	12.75	0.78	0.38	1.44	1.2	0.3	0.3	0.5	0.4
38	Richmond	19	19.27	0.99	0.59	1.54	0.7	0.8	0.9	0.1	0.3
39	Vancouver	105	82.81	1.27 *	1.04	1.53	0.7	0.6	1.0	0.6	0.7
40	New Westminster	20	7.95	2.51 ***	1.54	3.88	1.5	2.0	1.1	0.7	1.4
41	Burnaby	20	27.21	0.73	0.45	1.14	0.8	0.2	0.3	0.4	0.2
42	Maple Ridge	8	7.57	1.06	0.46	2.08	0.3	0.8	-	0.6	1.1
43	Coquitlam	13	19.33	0.67	0.36	1.15	0.6	0.7	0.2	-	0.6
44	North Vancouver	20	19.10	1.05	0.64	1.62	0.4	0.6	0.6	0.6	0.8
45	West Vancouver-Bowen Is	8	8.37	0.96	0.41	1.88	0.2	0.6	0.4	0.8	0.4
46	Sechelt	2	3.01	0.66	0.07	2.40	-	-	0.6	0.8	-
47	Powell River	0	2.93	-	-	-	-	-	-	-	-
48	Howe Sound	2	2.20	0.91	0.10	3.28	1.8	-	0.9	-	-
49	Central Coast	1	0.44	2.29	0.03	12.72	-	◆	-	-	-
50	Queen Charlotte	1	0.66	1.51	0.02	8.42	◆	-	-	-	-
52	Prince Rupert	2	2.47	0.81	0.09	2.93	1.5	1.6	-	-	-
54	Smithers	2	1.92	1.04	0.12	3.75	-	1.0	-	1.2	-
55	Burns Lake	1	1.00	1.00	0.01	5.56	-	-	◆	-	-
56	Nechako	6	1.97	3.04 *	1.11	6.62	0.9	7.0	1.7	-	-
57	Prince George	16	12.21	1.31	0.75	2.13	0.3	0.8	0.4	0.3	1.6
59	Peace River South	4	3.81	1.05	0.28	2.69	1.2	-	0.8	0.5	-
60	Peace River North	3	3.22	0.93	0.19	2.73	0.9	-	0.6	-	0.8
61	Greater Victoria	36	35.47	1.01	0.71	1.40	0.8	0.4	0.6	0.8	0.4
62	Sooke	7	6.41	1.09	0.44	2.25	1.8	0.7	-	0.6	0.7
63	Saanich	1	7.66	0.13 +	0.00	0.73	-	◆	-	-	-
64	Gulf Islands	0	1.85	-	-	-	-	0.5	-	0.4	1.2
65	Cowichan	5	5.95	0.84	0.27	1.96	-	-	-	◆	-
66	Lake Cowichan	1	0.75	1.33	0.02	7.43	-	-	-	◆	-
67	Ladysmith	1	2.15	0.47	0.01	2.59	-	-	-	◆	-
68	Nanaimo	10	10.57	0.95	0.45	1.74	0.6	-	0.8	0.3	0.7
69	Qualicum	4	4.22	0.95	0.25	2.42	0.3	0.3	-	0.5	0.4
70	Alberni	6	4.58	1.31	0.48	2.85	1.1	-	1.2	-	1.7
71	Courtenay	9	6.41	1.40	0.64	2.66	0.7	1.2	1.6	-	0.3
72	Campbell River	1	4.62	0.22	0.00	1.20	-	-	-	-	◆
75	Mission	2	3.99	0.50	0.06	1.81	0.9	-	0.8	-	-
76	Agassiz-Harrison	0	0.75	-	-	-	-	-	-	-	-
77	Summerland	1	1.58	0.63	0.01	3.53	-	-	◆	-	-
78	Enderby	1	0.86	1.16	0.02	6.47	-	-	-	◆	-
80	Kitimat	0	1.65	-	-	-	-	-	-	-	-
81	Fort Nelson	1	0.62	1.61	0.02	8.93	-	-	-	◆	-
84	Vancouver Island West	1	0.44	2.28	0.03	12.66	-	-	-	◆	-
85	Vancouver Island North	0	1.87	-	-	-	-	-	-	-	-
87	Stikine	2	0.25	8.16	0.92	29.47	-	12.6	-	9.7	-
88	Terrace	4	3.25	1.23	0.33	3.15	1.1	0.9	-	0.6	0.9
92	Nishga	0	0.17	-	-	-	-	-	-	◆	-
94	Telegraph Creek	1	0.08	12.20	0.16	67.90	-	-	-	-	-
	Provincial Total	**500**	◆	**1.00**	◆	◆	0.7	0.6	0.5	0.5	0.6

207

Alcohol-Related Deaths: Male

	Local Health Area	Observed Deaths	Expected Deaths	SMR (p)	95% C.I. Lower	95% C.I. Upper	ASMR 1985	1986	1987	1988	1989
1	Fernie	15	11.40	1.32	0.74	2.17	2.9	6.1	6.6	5.0	-
2	Cranbrook	20	16.56	1.21	0.74	1.87	1.9	4.5	5.3	1.1	5.1
3	Kimberley	5	8.63	0.58	0.19	1.35	1.3	1.3	2.8	3.3	-
4	Windermere	9	6.07	1.48	0.68	2.81	7.2	8.7	3.0	1.8	2.1
5	Creston	8	13.44	0.60	0.26	1.17	2.0	3.0	0.8	0.8	2.0
6	Kootenay Lake	3	4.06	0.74	0.15	2.16	7.1	3.5	-	-	6.0
7	Nelson	10	20.58	0.49 *	0.23	0.89	0.7	-	3.4	1.1	1.0
9	Castlegar	7	11.04	0.63	0.25	1.31	2.0	-	4.7	1.7	1.1
10	Arrow Lakes	4	4.76	0.84	0.23	2.15	-	4.6	4.2	-	3.8
11	Trail	20	21.13	0.95	0.58	1.46	1.7	2.8	2.1	4.8	1.6
12	Grand Forks	6	8.71	0.69	0.25	1.50	2.4	1.0	6.8	-	-
13	Kettle Valley	2	3.60	0.56	0.06	2.01	3.3	-	-	2.9	-
14	Southern Okanagan	25	19.74	1.27	0.82	1.87	3.6	4.0	-	5.4	6.2
15	Penticton	31	37.37	0.83	0.56	1.18	2.8	2.7	2.8	1.9	2.5
16	Keremeos	6	5.28	1.14	0.41	2.47	-	11.3	-	4.4	4.3
17	Princeton	4	4.79	0.84	0.22	2.14	-	2.9	3.5	-	6.1
18	Golden	1	5.19	0.19	0.00	1.07	-	♦	-	-	-
19	Revelstoke	7	6.67	1.05	0.42	2.16	2.4	4.1	-	2.2	7.5
20	Salmon Arm	18	29.75	0.60 *	0.36	0.96	1.2	4.4	1.1	2.8	1.1
21	Armstrong-Spallumcheen	5	7.35	0.68	0.22	1.59	-	2.8	4.0	1.7	1.4
22	Vernon	32	45.26	0.71 *	0.48	1.00	0.6	2.1	1.8	2.9	2.9
23	Central Okanagan	73	106.68	0.68 ***	0.54	0.86	2.8	2.7	1.4	1.4	2.1
24	Kamloops	74	63.99	1.16	0.91	1.45	4.2	3.7	3.7	3.2	2.8
26	North Thompson	6	3.56	1.69	0.62	3.67	2.8	16.9	3.4	-	-
27	Cariboo-Chilcotin	52	28.48	1.83 ***	1.36	2.39	9.2	8.5	5.3	2.1	5.4
28	Quesnel	16	18.00	0.89	0.51	1.44	1.2	5.0	2.1	0.7	4.6
29	Lillooet	7	4.00	1.75	0.70	3.60	13.3	-	-	12.4	3.6
30	South Cariboo	13	6.63	1.96 *	1.04	3.35	6.7	4.6	11.3	5.2	3.8
31	Merritt	22	8.18	2.69 ***	1.68	4.07	5.3	12.5	8.9	2.2	11.1
32	Hope	11	7.36	1.50	0.75	2.68	1.8	5.4	1.7	11.3	2.4
33	Chilliwack	44	49.01	0.90	0.65	1.21	3.7	4.8	0.9	3.2	1.5
34	Abbotsford	37	66.64	0.56 ***	0.39	0.77	2.8	1.6	1.2	2.2	0.8
35	Langley	36	62.54	0.58 ***	0.40	0.80	1.6	1.2	1.5	1.8	2.7
36	Surrey	173	189.03	0.92	0.78	1.06	3.2	2.7	3.2	2.5	2.1
37	Delta	28	63.87	0.44 ***	0.29	0.63	1.8	1.6	1.4	1.2	1.1
38	Richmond	68	97.27	0.70 **	0.54	0.89	2.0	2.3	2.1	2.0	2.1
39	Vancouver	713	452.74	1.57 ***	1.46	1.69	5.4	5.1	4.4	4.7	4.8
40	New Westminster	54	42.62	1.27	0.95	1.65	5.8	2.8	3.1	2.9	4.2
41	Burnaby	129	147.80	0.87	0.73	1.04	2.2	3.7	2.5	2.9	1.7
42	Maple Ridge	33	39.82	0.83	0.57	1.16	1.6	5.5	2.3	2.1	1.6
43	Coquitlam	78	92.84	0.84	0.66	1.05	2.3	3.3	3.4	1.7	2.3
44	North Vancouver	63	96.38	0.65 ***	0.50	0.84	1.1	2.0	2.8	2.2	1.7
45	West Vancouver-Bowen Is	40	50.78	0.79	0.56	1.07	1.6	3.4	2.2	2.1	1.7
46	Sechelt	22	21.10	1.04	0.65	1.58	6.3	0.9	1.9	2.0	5.9
47	Powell River	27	18.18	1.49	0.98	2.16	3.9	7.8	5.3	3.0	4.2
48	Howe Sound	13	12.06	1.08	0.57	1.84	3.2	1.6	6.7	3.0	-
49	Central Coast	9	2.51	3.59 **	1.64	6.81	7.7	28.5	10.6	7.0	-
50	Queen Charlotte	7	3.56	1.97	0.79	4.06	6.0	11.1	2.5	-	3.8
52	Prince Rupert	25	12.47	2.01 **	1.30	2.96	8.8	6.8	5.7	4.8	3.2
54	Smithers	8	9.51	0.84	0.36	1.66	2.8	1.2	1.9	2.7	5.5
55	Burns Lake	7	5.58	1.25	0.50	2.58	8.6	5.3	3.2	2.6	-
56	Nechako	9	10.77	0.84	0.38	1.59	4.6	1.8	1.4	3.0	2.7
57	Prince George	71	58.07	1.22	0.95	1.54	6.3	3.5	4.1	3.2	3.4
59	Peace River South	20	19.56	1.02	0.62	1.58	1.5	4.8	3.3	0.8	4.9
60	Peace River North	12	16.16	0.74	0.38	1.30	2.7	1.9	1.7	4.0	1.6
61	Greater Victoria	191	197.51	0.97	0.83	1.11	2.7	2.8	4.0	2.4	3.0
62	Sooke	30	35.90	0.84	0.56	1.19	0.8	2.8	2.7	3.3	2.4
63	Saanich	29	51.46	0.56 ***	0.38	0.81	2.4	1.1	2.7	1.9	0.8
64	Gulf Islands	12	14.55	0.82	0.43	1.44	1.1	2.2	2.4	5.3	3.0
65	Cowichan	30	36.14	0.83	0.56	1.19	2.3	2.4	1.2	2.2	4.3
66	Lake Cowichan	3	4.87	0.62	0.12	1.80	-	2.6	3.0	3.3	-
67	Ladysmith	15	14.71	1.02	0.57	1.68	1.3	5.6	2.4	1.4	8.4
68	Nanaimo	71	62.83	1.13	0.88	1.43	1.6	2.9	6.0	2.9	4.6
69	Qualicum	18	32.18	0.56 **	0.33	0.88	1.3	2.2	2.2	2.4	2.0
70	Alberni	23	26.42	0.87	0.55	1.31	3.3	1.6	3.6	2.1	2.6
71	Courtenay	28	38.58	0.73	0.48	1.05	1.9	3.3	2.9	2.0	0.6
72	Campbell River	24	24.91	0.96	0.62	1.43	4.9	1.3	3.6	2.0	3.1
75	Mission	19	24.21	0.78	0.47	1.23	2.7	0.5	4.5	2.6	1.4
76	Aggassiz-Harrison	5	5.67	0.88	0.28	2.06	-	2.6	-	8.6	2.9
77	Summerland	10	11.70	0.85	0.41	1.57	2.4	5.3	2.8	3.9	2.0
78	Enderby	6	5.94	1.01	0.37	2.20	-	12.6	2.5	-	3.9
80	Kitimat	8	8.05	0.99	0.43	1.96	1.4	4.4	4.2	1.7	3.0
81	Fort Nelson	5	2.75	1.82	0.59	4.25	-	4.6	42.8	-	5.2
84	Vancouver Island West	1	2.21	0.45	0.01	2.52	-	-	♦	-	-
85	Vancouver Island North	19	9.06	2.10 **	1.26	3.28	3.9	6.5	2.1	7.1	7.2
87	Stikine	3	1.19	2.52	0.51	7.36	-	19.1	-	-	-
88	Terrace	15	16.60	0.90	0.51	1.49	-	3.5	3.5	3.6	3.2
92	Nishga	1	0.90	1.12	0.01	6.21	-	♦	-	-	-
94	Telegraph Creek	0	0.44	-	-	-	-	-	-	-	-
	Provincial Total	**2,808**	♦	1.00	♦	♦	3.0	3.4	3.1	2.8	2.8

208

Alcohol-Related Deaths: Female

	Local Health Area	Observed Deaths	Expected Deaths	SMR	(p)	95% C.I. Lower	Upper	ASMR 1985	1986	1987	1988	1989
1	Fernie	7	3.42	2.05		0.82	4.22	-	2.0	6.2	-	5.3
2	Cranbrook	6	5.80	1.03		0.38	2.25	2.1	1.0	0.8	1.2	1.0
3	Kimberley	3	3.10	0.97		0.19	2.82	4.5	1.6	-	-	-
4	Windermere	0	1.80	-		-	-	-	-	-	-	-
5	Creston	7	4.67	1.50		0.60	3.09	2.3	2.3	0.8	4.1	0.8
6	Kootenay Lake	1	1.27	0.79		0.01	4.37	◆	-	-	-	-
7	Nelson	7	7.19	0.97		0.39	2.01	1.5	1.2	-	0.8	1.2
9	Castlegar	3	3.79	0.79		0.16	2.31	-	-	2.9	1.0	-
10	Arrow Lakes	0	1.56	-		-	-	-	-	-	-	-
11	Trail	4	7.76	0.52		0.14	1.32	1.5	-	0.5	-	0.9
12	Grand Forks	3	3.00	1.00		0.20	2.92	1.9	-	2.1	1.7	-
13	Kettle Valley	2	1.01	1.98		0.22	7.16	-	-	-	-	9.0
14	Southern Okanagan	7	7.00	1.00		0.40	2.06	-	1.0	0.5	2.0	2.6
15	Penticton	11	14.44	0.76		0.38	1.36	1.6	0.8	0.6	0.6	-
16	Keremeos	3	1.56	1.93		0.39	5.63	-	3.1	3.4	-	2.2
17	Princeton	1	1.54	0.65		0.01	3.61	-	◆	-	-	-
18	Golden	0	1.51	-		-	-	-	-	-	2.7	3.3
19	Revelstoke	2	2.14	0.93		0.10	3.37	-	-	-	-	-
20	Salmon Arm	4	9.96	0.40		0.11	1.03	0.4	1.5	0.4	-	-
21	Armstrong-Spallumcheen	2	2.48	0.81		0.09	2.91	-	3.3	-	2.1	-
22	Vernon	11	16.43	0.67		0.33	1.20	0.3	0.5	0.3	1.2	0.9
23	Central Okanagan	21	39.33	0.53	**	0.33	0.82	0.6	0.5	0.7	0.6	0.5
24	Kamloops	26	21.89	1.19		0.78	1.74	1.1	1.0	0.5	2.0	1.9
26	North Thompson	2	1.05	1.91		0.21	6.89	-	-	12.8	-	-
27	Cariboo-Chilcotin	10	8.57	1.17		0.56	2.15	4.0	0.5	-	-	2.0
28	Quesnel	7	5.53	1.27		0.51	2.61	-	0.8	2.0	3.7	-
29	Lillooet	11	1.11	9.94	***	4.96	17.79	5.3	-	16.0	8.5	27.6
30	South Cariboo	7	1.92	3.64	**	1.46	7.50	-	7.4	2.9	8.3	-
31	Merritt	7	2.49	2.81	*	1.13	5.79	-	8.2	2.1	4.1	-
32	Hope	2	2.34	0.85		0.10	3.09	-	3.5	-	-	-
33	Chilliwack	14	18.08	0.77		0.42	1.30	1.0	1.0	1.1	0.4	0.2
34	Abbotsford	17	24.64	0.69		0.40	1.10	0.4	1.0	1.0	0.6	0.4
35	Langley	19	21.87	0.87		0.52	1.36	1.2	1.1	0.7	0.7	1.1
36	Surrey	53	69.27	0.77		0.57	1.00	1.3	0.6	1.0	0.8	0.4
37	Delta	23	22.79	1.01		0.64	1.51	0.7	1.7	1.0	0.6	1.4
38	Richmond	19	36.56	0.52	**	0.31	0.81	-	0.8	0.1	1.0	0.8
39	Vancouver	244	176.25	1.38	***	1.22	1.57	1.2	1.9	1.8	1.4	1.3
40	New Westminster	28	18.46	1.52	*	1.01	2.19	2.4	4.3	1.8	0.6	0.6
41	Burnaby	38	57.48	0.66	**	0.47	0.91	0.5	1.0	0.3	0.7	0.7
42	Maple Ridge	11	14.01	0.78		0.39	1.40	1.3	1.0	0.5	0.3	1.2
43	Coquitlam	18	33.02	0.55	**	0.32	0.86	0.6	0.8	0.7	0.9	0.3
44	North Vancouver	39	37.19	1.05		0.75	1.43	1.1	1.3	1.0	1.2	0.9
45	West Vancouver-Bowen Is	18	20.71	0.87		0.51	1.37	1.5	1.2	0.6	-	1.2
46	Sechelt	12	7.31	1.64		0.85	2.87	3.4	4.9	1.0	0.5	0.6
47	Powell River	6	6.24	0.96		0.35	2.09	2.6	0.7	-	0.9	0.7
48	Howe Sound	6	3.48	1.72		0.63	3.75	-	3.0	3.4	1.4	1.5
49	Central Coast	2	0.70	2.85		0.32	10.31	-	-	26.9	-	-
50	Queen Charlotte	3	0.91	3.29		0.66	9.60	6.9	-	-	7.3	3.1
52	Prince Rupert	7	3.88	1.81		0.72	3.72	1.0	0.8	3.5	3.0	-
54	Smithers	2	2.86	0.70		0.08	2.53	-	-	2.0	1.8	-
55	Burns Lake	1	1.54	0.65		0.01	3.60	◆	-	-	-	-
56	Nechako	6	3.13	1.92		0.70	4.17	-	1.1	-	1.9	6.0
57	Prince George	22	17.48	1.26		0.79	1.91	0.3	1.5	1.4	1.1	2.4
59	Peace River South	7	5.96	1.17		0.47	2.42	1.5	1.1	1.0	1.0	1.8
60	Peace River North	12	4.81	2.50	**	1.29	4.36	4.1	1.4	3.9	1.0	1.2
61	Greater Victoria	69	87.04	0.79		0.62	1.00	0.8	1.0	1.0	1.0	0.6
62	Sooke	5	12.01	0.42	*	0.13	0.97	0.4	1.9	-	-	-
63	Saanich	15	18.45	0.81		0.45	1.34	0.6	0.7	0.8	0.9	0.9
64	Gulf Islands	5	5.14	0.97		0.31	2.27	-	1.7	0.8	0.8	2.1
65	Cowichan	16	12.70	1.26		0.72	2.05	0.4	2.5	1.2	0.6	-
66	Lake Cowichan	0	1.53	-		-	-	-	-	-	-	-
67	Ladysmith	3	5.08	0.59		0.12	1.73	2.2	-	-	0.7	0.7
68	Nanaimo	29	22.82	1.27		0.85	1.83	0.8	1.1	2.3	1.5	1.1
69	Qualicum	7	11.28	0.62		0.25	1.28	0.5	-	-	2.6	0.4
70	Alberni	13	8.97	1.45		0.77	2.48	1.4	1.3	3.8	1.3	0.6
71	Courtenay	12	13.45	0.89		0.46	1.56	0.3	1.0	0.4	2.0	0.9
72	Campbell River	12	8.14	1.47		0.76	2.58	-	3.1	2.5	2.1	-
75	Mission	9	7.85	1.15		0.52	2.18	-	-	2.8	1.2	2.0
76	Aggassiz-Harrison	1	1.64	0.61		0.01	3.38	-	-	◆	-	-
77	Summerland	5	4.29	1.17		0.38	2.72	1.0	2.0	1.1	1.1	-
78	Enderby	1	2.04	0.49		0.01	2.73	-	-	◆	-	-
80	Kitimat	2	2.27	0.88		0.10	3.18	1.3	1.3	-	-	-
81	Fort Nelson	6	0.70	8.57	***	3.13	18.64	-	-	3.1	16.0	13.1
84	Vancouver Island West	0	0.50	-		-	-	-	-	-	-	-
85	Vancouver Island North	4	2.42	1.65		0.44	4.23	2.5	2.7	-	-	2.8
87	Stikine	0	0.32	-		-	-	-	-	-	-	-
88	Terrace	10	4.63	2.16	*	1.03	3.97	0.8	1.9	2.1	1.3	5.0
92	Nishga	0	0.26	-		-	-	-	-	-	-	-
94	Telegraph Creek	0	0.12	-		-	-	-	-	-	-	-
	Provincial Total	**1,028**	◆	1.00		◆	◆	1.0	1.2	1.1	1.1	1.0

Age Under 1 Year: Male

	Local Health Area	Observed Deaths	Expected Deaths	SMR (p)	95% C.I. Lower	Upper	1985	1986	ASMR 1987	1988	1989
1	Fernie	3	7.38	0.41	0.08	1.19	2.0	1.0	-	-	-
2	Cranbrook	3	8.17	0.37	0.07	1.07	-	-	0.8	0.9	1.3
3	Kimberley	2	2.77	0.72	0.08	2.60	-	3.1	-	2.8	-
4	Windermere	0	3.27	-	-	-	-	-	-	-	-
5	Creston	2	3.32	0.60	0.07	2.18	-	2.1	2.5	-	
6	Kootenay Lake	3	1.08	2.78	0.56	8.13	20.3	-	-	-	-
7	Nelson	3	6.41	0.47	0.09	1.37	1.1	-	-	1.3	1.5
9	Castlegar	5	3.62	1.38	0.44	3.22	2.1	-	3.9	-	5.3
10	Arrow Lakes	0	1.36	-	-	-	-	-	-	-	-
11	Trail	1	6.34	0.16 +	0.00	0.88	-	-	-	-	♦
12	Grand Forks	3	2.13	1.41	0.28	4.11	3.6	4.8	-	-	5.0
13	Kettle Valley	2	0.82	2.43	0.27	8.76	-	-	14.1	-	9.9
14	Southern Okanagan	5	3.66	1.37	0.44	3.19	2.2	4.2	2.1	-	2.3
15	Penticton	2	8.49	0.24 +	0.03	0.85	-	1.8	-	-	-
16	Keremeos	0	1.05	-	-	-	-	-	-	-	-
17	Princeton	1	1.28	0.78	0.01	4.36	-	♦	-	-	-
18	Golden	1	3.04	0.33	0.00	1.83	-	-	-	-	♦
19	Revelstoke	1	3.86	0.26	0.00	1.44	-	-	-	-	♦
20	Salmon Arm	2	8.01	0.25 +	0.03	0.90	-	-	0.8	1.0	-
21	Armstrong-Spallumcheen	4	2.46	1.62	0.44	4.16	-	-	-	2.6	13.3
22	Vernon	17	15.23	1.12	0.65	1.79	1.1	2.6	1.5	1.8	1.7
23	Central Okanagan	32	26.67	1.20	0.82	1.69	1.7	1.5	3.3	1.5	1.5
24	Kamloops	28	26.95	1.04	0.69	1.50	2.0	1.2	1.4	1.9	1.6
26	North Thompson	3	1.81	1.66	0.33	4.84	8.4	3.8	-	-	-
27	Cariboo-Chilcotin	23	16.37	1.40	0.89	2.11	1.0	2.1	2.2	2.9	2.9
28	Quesnel	15	10.98	1.37	0.76	2.25	1.3	0.8	4.5	2.6	0.9
29	Lillooet	4	1.64	2.44	0.66	6.26	15.3	8.4	-	-	4.1
30	South Cariboo	6	2.89	2.07	0.76	4.51	2.4	2.4	2.7	5.8	3.3
31	Merritt	6	3.95	1.52	0.55	3.31	2.1	1.8	-	8.1	-
32	Hope	7	3.20	2.19	0.88	4.51	-	3.8	3.6	3.9	6.8
33	Chilliwack	12	18.28	0.66	0.34	1.15	1.2	1.8	-	0.9	1.3
34	Abbotsford	26	27.59	0.94	0.62	1.38	1.7	1.9	1.3	1.9	0.6
35	Langley	23	27.03	0.85	0.54	1.28	0.3	0.6	3.0	0.9	2.1
36	Surrey	66	81.76	0.81	0.62	1.03	1.1	1.4	1.5	1.4	1.0
37	Delta	19	26.27	0.72	0.44	1.13	2.4	0.6	1.2	0.8	0.6
38	Richmond	28	36.12	0.78	0.52	1.12	1.3	1.0	2.1	1.6	0.2
39	Vancouver	158	116.56	1.36 ***	1.15	1.58	1.2	2.0	2.5	2.6	2.3
40	New Westminster	14	10.88	1.29	0.70	2.16	0.8	1.5	2.3	3.0	2.4
41	Burnaby	29	42.59	0.68 *	0.46	0.98	0.9	1.1	1.7	1.3	0.3
42	Maple Ridge	17	18.84	0.90	0.53	1.44	2.6	0.9	0.4	1.3	1.8
43	Coquitlam	40	46.45	0.86	0.62	1.17	1.7	1.5	1.8	1.4	0.3
44	North Vancouver	25	31.41	0.80	0.51	1.18	1.1	1.0	1.1	2.6	0.6
45	West Vancouver-Bowen Is	6	8.47	0.71	0.26	1.54	-	1.8	0.9	0.9	1.9
46	Sechelt	6	5.17	1.16	0.42	2.53	3.0	-	3.4	1.6	1.4
47	Powell River	5	5.35	0.93	0.30	2.18	1.5	-	2.9	1.6	1.4
48	Howe Sound	8	7.38	1.08	0.47	2.14	1.3	-	3.8	1.8	1.0
49	Central Coast	3	1.62	1.85	0.37	5.40	-	-	6.8	4.7	4.4
50	Queen Charlotte	1	2.57	0.39	0.01	2.16	-	-	-	♦	-
52	Prince Rupert	12	8.35	1.44	0.74	2.51	3.9	2.9	1.9	0.9	1.9
54	Smithers	16	6.73	2.38 **	1.36	3.86	6.4	1.0	-	6.3	4.6
55	Burns Lake	7	4.22	1.66	0.66	3.42	1.8	2.6	1.4	4.9	2.3
56	Nechako	15	7.52	1.99 *	1.12	3.29	4.6	2.0	3.0	3.2	2.4
57	Prince George	34	39.81	0.85	0.59	1.19	2.3	0.6	1.5	0.5	1.8
59	Peace River South	7	10.47	0.67	0.27	1.38	2.0	1.3	-	0.9	0.8
60	Peace River North	9	14.04	0.64	0.29	1.22	0.5	0.6	0.9	0.5	3.1
61	Greater Victoria	47	46.00	1.02	0.75	1.36	1.9	1.2	1.6	1.5	1.8
62	Sooke	20	15.44	1.30	0.79	2.00	1.9	2.5	1.5	2.1	2.1
63	Saanich	12	10.97	1.09	0.56	1.91	3.5	-	3.5	0.7	0.7
64	Gulf Islands	1	2.29	0.44	0.01	2.43	-	-	-	-	♦
65	Cowichan	19	12.44	1.53	0.92	2.39	3.2	2.4	0.6	3.7	2.0
66	Lake Cowichan	0	2.69	-	-	-	-	-	-	-	-
67	Ladysmith	7	3.53	1.98	0.79	4.09	4.8	2.3	4.3	2.3	2.0
68	Nanaimo	19	19.37	0.98	0.59	1.53	1.6	2.1	1.3	-	2.8
69	Qualicum	1	7.27	0.14 +	0.00	0.77	-	♦	-	-	-
70	Alberni	22	11.51	1.91 **	1.20	2.89	1.3	5.4	5.2	1.2	2.4
71	Courtenay	14	12.85	1.09	0.60	1.83	2.3	3.8	-	0.6	1.9
72	Campbell River	9	12.18	0.74	0.34	1.40	-	3.4	1.2	0.6	0.7
75	Mission	10	10.72	0.93	0.45	1.72	1.6	0.7	1.5	-	3.5
76	Agassiz-Harrison	0	1.47	-	-	-	-	-	-	-	-
77	Summerland	0	2.30	-	-	-	-	-	-	-	-
78	Enderby	0	1.67	-	-	-	-	-	-	-	-
80	Kitimat	6	5.13	1.17	0.43	2.55	-	4.4	-	1.7	3.8
81	Fort Nelson	2	2.76	0.72	0.08	2.61	2.5	-	-	-	3.4
84	Vancouver Island West	2	2.41	0.83	0.09	3.00	-	4.8	-	2.6	-
85	Vancouver Island North	6	7.12	0.84	0.31	1.83	1.1	-	1.9	-	4.0
87	Stikine	2	0.87	2.29	0.26	8.28	8.4	-	-	7.3	-
88	Terrace	11	12.29	0.89	0.45	1.60	0.7	0.6	2.3	1.2	2.1
92	Nishga	1	0.94	1.06	0.01	5.89	♦	-	-	-	-
94	Telegraph Creek	0	0.53	-	-	-	-	-	-	-	-
	Provincial Total	**999**	♦	**1.00**	♦	♦	**1.5**	**1.5**	**1.7**	**1.6**	**1.6**

210

Age Under 1 Year: Female

	Local Health Area	Observed Deaths	Expected Deaths	SMR (p)	95% C.I. Lower	Upper	1985	1986	ASMR 1987	1988	1989
1	Fernie	3	4.82	0.62	0.13	1.82	-	2.4	-	1.2	-
2	Cranbrook	4	5.56	0.72	0.19	1.84	-	2.4	-	2.0	-
3	Kimberley	3	1.46	2.06	0.41	6.01	-	4.6	-	4.4	4.4
4	Windermere	1	1.72	0.58	0.01	3.24	-	♦	-	-	-
5	Creston	1	2.54	0.39	0.01	2.19	-	-	-	-	♦
6	Kootenay Lake	0	0.89	-	-	-	-	-	-	-	-
7	Nelson	6	4.43	1.35	0.49	2.95	3.6	-	1.2	-	3.1
9	Castlegar	1	3.04	0.33	0.00	1.83	♦	-	-	-	-
10	Arrow Lakes	0	1.13	-	-	-	-	-	-	-	-
11	Trail	6	5.37	1.12	0.41	2.43	4.0	-	1.0	-	1.5
12	Grand Forks	0	1.50	-	-	-	-	-	-	-	-
13	Kettle Valley	1	0.63	1.59	0.02	8.82	-	-	-	-	♦
14	Southern Okanagan	3	2.82	1.06	0.21	3.11	-	4.3	-	-	2.3
15	Penticton	6	5.94	1.01	0.37	2.20	0.9	-	1.1	2.1	1.9
16	Keremeos	1	0.93	1.08	0.01	6.00	♦	-	-	-	-
17	Princeton	2	1.06	1.89	0.21	6.83	-	5.4	-	4.9	-
18	Golden	2	2.60	0.77	0.09	2.78	-	5.9	-	-	-
19	Revelstoke	3	2.87	1.05	0.21	3.06	-	4.3	-	-	3.1
20	Salmon Arm	2	5.22	0.38	0.04	1.38	1.0	1.1	-	-	-
21	Armstrong-Spallumcheen	0	1.56	-	-	-	-	-	-	-	-
22	Vernon	13	10.23	1.27	0.68	2.17	2.3	-	2.8	1.1	1.2
23	Central Okanagan	21	19.55	1.07	0.66	1.64	0.3	1.2	0.9	2.1	1.8
24	Kamloops	13	20.07	0.65	0.34	1.11	0.6	0.6	0.5	0.8	1.3
26	North Thompson	2	1.38	1.45	0.16	5.22	3.8	-	-	4.4	-
27	Cariboo-Chilcotin	14	11.60	1.21	0.66	2.03	-	0.6	0.5	2.2	4.1
28	Quesnel	9	7.37	1.22	0.56	2.32	1.5	2.7	1.4	0.7	0.9
29	Lillooet	3	1.91	1.57	0.32	4.59	-	-	1.8	2.4	4.1
30	South Cariboo	2	1.80	1.11	0.12	4.00	-	-	-	7.0	-
31	Merritt	1	2.90	0.35	0.00	1.92	-	-	♦	-	-
32	Hope	0	2.18	-	-	-	-	-	-	-	-
33	Chilliwack	7	12.02	0.58	0.23	1.20	0.4	1.5	0.5	0.5	0.5
34	Abbotsford	13	19.57	0.66	0.35	1.14	0.9	0.3	1.0	1.5	0.3
35	Langley	19	20.57	0.92	0.56	1.44	1.3	0.6	1.3	1.2	1.0
36	Surrey	46	58.63	0.78	0.57	1.05	0.9	1.2	0.8	0.8	0.9
37	Delta	13	20.16	0.64	0.34	1.10	0.9	0.9	1.1	0.5	0.3
38	Richmond	30	26.59	1.13	0.76	1.61	0.9	2.3	1.0	1.0	1.4
39	Vancouver	100	86.89	1.15	0.94	1.40	1.4	1.6	1.5	1.1	1.2
40	New Westminster	15	8.83	1.70	0.95	2.80	2.1	2.0	2.8	1.3	1.8
41	Burnaby	21	31.33	0.67	0.41	1.02	0.7	1.0	1.0	0.4	0.9
42	Maple Ridge	17	14.59	1.17	0.68	1.87	0.8	2.5	1.2	1.6	0.7
43	Coquitlam	37	33.33	1.11	0.78	1.53	1.0	1.4	1.5	1.1	1.5
44	North Vancouver	28	24.60	1.14	0.76	1.64	3.0	0.9	1.8	0.5	0.6
45	West Vancouver-Bowen Is	5	5.54	0.90	0.29	2.11	-	1.0	1.1	1.1	1.9
46	Sechelt	5	4.13	1.21	0.39	2.83	1.4	3.7	1.5	-	-
47	Powell River	8	4.27	1.87	0.81	3.69	1.4	4.2	2.5	1.4	1.3
48	Howe Sound	4	5.35	0.75	0.20	1.91	-	-	-	1.9	2.0
49	Central Coast	2	1.26	1.58	0.18	5.71	-	4.5	6.2	-	-
50	Queen Charlotte	4	1.96	2.05	0.55	5.24	2.6	5.0	3.3	-	-
52	Prince Rupert	12	6.26	1.92	0.99	3.35	2.0	3.8	1.9	3.4	-
54	Smithers	6	4.62	1.30	0.47	2.83	1.2	1.1	4.7	-	1.2
55	Burns Lake	4	3.39	1.18	0.32	3.02	-	2.3	2.6	1.4	-
56	Nechako	6	5.32	1.13	0.41	2.46	-	1.1	-	1.1	4.9
57	Prince George	29	29.50	0.98	0.66	1.41	1.0	0.6	1.5	1.3	1.4
59	Peace River South	12	8.32	1.44	0.74	2.52	1.9	0.6	-	4.3	2.3
60	Peace River North	6	9.33	0.64	0.23	1.40	0.6	0.7	1.1	0.5	0.8
61	Greater Victoria	28	34.26	0.82	0.54	1.18	0.3	1.2	1.1	1.2	1.0
62	Sooke	11	10.66	1.03	0.51	1.85	1.6	-	2.2	1.1	1.0
63	Saanich	3	7.99	0.38	0.08	1.10	0.7	0.8	-	0.7	-
64	Gulf Islands	2	1.51	1.32	0.15	4.77	-	3.6	4.2	-	-
65	Cowichan	13	8.69	1.50	0.80	2.56	-	0.7	1.4	5.4	1.3
66	Lake Cowichan	1	1.58	0.63	0.01	3.52	-	♦	-	-	-
67	Ladysmith	5	2.87	1.74	0.56	4.06	4.4	4.2	-	1.9	-
68	Nanaimo	18	15.38	1.17	0.69	1.85	0.7	0.8	1.5	1.8	2.0
69	Qualicum	5	4.85	1.03	0.33	2.41	1.2	3.1	1.1	-	1.3
70	Alberni	11	8.40	1.31	0.65	2.34	2.7	1.5	2.7	-	0.8
71	Courtenay	4	9.63	0.42	0.11	1.06	-	-	-	1.2	1.3
72	Campbell River	11	8.80	1.25	0.62	2.24	0.7	1.4	1.2	2.5	1.4
75	Mission	7	7.47	0.94	0.38	1.93	0.9	2.4	1.6	0.8	-
76	Agassiz-Harrison	3	1.25	2.40	0.48	7.02	-	4.0	-	4.4	5.2
77	Summerland	0	1.58	-	-	-	-	-	-	-	-
78	Enderby	2	1.27	1.58	0.18	5.69	-	5.2	-	-	4.9
80	Kitimat	4	4.08	0.98	0.26	2.51	2.9	-	1.1	1.5	-
81	Fort Nelson	2	2.20	0.91	0.10	3.29	-	-	-	5.9	-
84	Vancouver Island West	2	1.52	1.32	0.15	4.75	-	6.4	-	3.0	-
85	Vancouver Island North	9	5.81	1.55	0.71	2.94	3.0	1.0	-	0.9	5.1
87	Stikine	1	0.59	1.69	0.02	9.40	♦	-	-	-	-
88	Terrace	7	9.00	0.78	0.31	1.60	-	0.7	1.2	1.3	1.4
92	Nishga	0	0.66	-	-	-	-	-	-	-	-
94	Telegraph Creek	0	0.24	-	-	-	-	-	-	-	-
	Provincial Total	721	♦	1.00	♦	♦	1.1	1.3	1.1	1.2	1.2

Age 1 - 14 Years: Male

	Local Health Area	Observed Deaths	Expected Deaths	SMR (p)	95% C.I. Lower	Upper	ASMR 1985	1986	1987	1988	1989
1	Fernie	3	3.32	0.90	0.18	2.64	2.4	-	-	-	1.1
2	Cranbrook	4	3.93	1.02	0.27	2.60	-	-	2.1	1.0	1.2
3	Kimberley	1	1.34	0.75	0.01	4.16	-	-	-	-	◆
4	Windermere	0	1.11	-	-	-	-	-	-	-	-
5	Creston	0	1.54	-	-	-	-	-	-	-	-
6	Kootenay Lake	2	0.46	4.34	0.49	15.66	-	-	-	-	18.6
7	Nelson	4	3.43	1.17	0.31	2.99	2.4	1.2	-	-	1.2
9	Castlegar	2	2.00	1.00	0.11	3.60	-	-	1.7	-	2.1
10	Arrow Lakes	3	0.81	3.70	0.74	10.82	-	9.2	-	-	5.9
11	Trail	2	3.35	0.60	0.07	2.16	1.4	-	-	-	1.3
12	Grand Forks	1	1.07	0.94	0.01	5.21	-	-	-	◆	-
13	Kettle Valley	0	0.55	-	-	-	-	-	-	-	-
14	Southern Okanagan	3	1.95	1.54	0.31	4.49	-	2.7	2.5	2.5	-
15	Penticton	2	3.89	0.51	0.06	1.86	-	-	1.2	0.9	-
16	Keremeos	1	0.52	1.91	0.02	10.62	-	-	◆	-	-
17	Princeton	4	0.76	5.25 +	1.41	13.45	-	11.4	-	-	11.5
18	Golden	0	1.26	-	-	-	-	-	-	-	-
19	Revelstoke	3	1.61	1.86	0.37	5.43	2.9	-	-	3.0	3.1
20	Salmon Arm	4	3.88	1.03	0.28	2.64	-	1.3	0.9	0.9	0.9
21	Armstrong-Spallumcheen	3	1.23	2.44	0.49	7.14	3.3	3.6	3.6	-	-
22	Vernon	7	7.11	0.98	0.39	2.03	0.6	2.6	1.1	-	-
23	Central Okanagan	13	13.08	0.99	0.53	1.70	-	1.3	0.6	1.2	0.9
24	Kamloops	19	13.93	1.36	0.82	2.13	1.6	0.7	1.6	0.3	1.5
26	North Thompson	1	1.02	0.98	0.01	5.45	-	-	-	-	◆
27	Cariboo-Chilcotin	9	7.34	1.23	0.56	2.33	0.6	0.5	0.5	0.7	2.9
28	Quesnel	13	4.72	2.76 **	1.47	4.71	2.2	3.0	1.7	3.2	2.6
29	Lillooet	4	0.92	4.32 +	1.16	11.07	3.2	-	9.4	-	6.4
30	South Cariboo	0	1.44	-	-	-	-	-	-	-	-
31	Merritt	0	1.97	-	-	-	-	-	-	-	-
32	Hope	1	1.30	0.77	0.01	4.29	◆	-	-	-	-
33	Chilliwack	7	7.80	0.90	0.36	1.85	1.7	-	-	1.5	0.4
34	Abbotsford	9	11.14	0.81	0.37	1.53	1.1	0.8	0.3	0.9	-
35	Langley	21	13.01	1.61	1.00	2.47	0.3	1.7	-	3.3	1.2
36	Surrey	21	32.59	0.64 *	0.40	0.99	0.4	0.9	0.4	0.3	0.7
37	Delta	7	14.60	0.48 *	0.19	0.99	-	0.3	0.9	0.3	0.6
38	Richmond	8	16.46	0.49 *	0.21	0.96	0.2	-	0.5	0.8	0.5
39	Vancouver	40	45.73	0.87	0.62	1.19	0.9	0.4	0.9	0.8	0.8
40	New Westminster	3	3.59	0.84	0.17	2.44	2.4	0.9	-	-	-
41	Burnaby	15	16.58	0.90	0.51	1.49	1.2	0.7	-	0.8	1.0
42	Maple Ridge	6	8.25	0.73	0.27	1.58	-	0.4	-	1.7	0.8
43	Coquitlam	14	19.37	0.72	0.39	1.21	0.6	1.0	0.5	0.4	0.6
44	North Vancouver	16	13.73	1.17	0.67	1.89	2.1	0.6	1.0	0.6	0.6
45	West Vancouver-Bowen Is	3	4.55	0.66	0.13	1.93	2.8	-	-	-	-
46	Sechelt	0	2.48	-	-	-	-	-	-	-	-
47	Powell River	2	2.99	0.67	0.08	2.41	-	-	1.5	-	1.4
48	Howe Sound	4	3.04	1.32	0.35	3.37	2.8	1.2	-	-	1.1
49	Central Coast	4	0.63	6.30 +	1.69	16.13	-	5.2	6.0	6.4	6.1
50	Queen Charlotte	3	1.22	2.46	0.49	7.18	4.6	-	4.9	-	2.7
52	Prince Rupert	6	3.66	1.64	0.60	3.57	-	2.4	-	4.8	-
54	Smithers	5	3.16	1.58	0.51	3.69	-	1.1	2.7	1.5	1.1
55	Burns Lake	0	1.73	-	-	-	-	-	-	-	-
56	Nechako	11	3.63	3.03 **	1.51	5.42	2.9	2.0	3.1	0.9	2.3
57	Prince George	20	18.23	1.10	0.67	1.69	0.7	0.9	1.1	1.3	0.7
59	Peace River South	6	4.90	1.23	0.45	2.67	-	1.5	1.1	1.1	1.8
60	Peace River North	10	5.59	1.79	0.86	3.29	1.9	-	1.9	2.9	1.6
61	Greater Victoria	15	19.59	0.77	0.43	1.26	0.9	0.9	0.6	0.6	0.2
62	Sooke	5	7.21	0.69	0.22	1.62	-	0.7	1.2	1.1	-
63	Saanich	3	5.45	0.55	0.11	1.61	0.8	0.8	-	-	0.8
64	Gulf Islands	2	1.07	1.88	0.21	6.77	3.0	-	4.9	-	-
65	Cowichan	8	5.86	1.36	0.59	2.69	0.6	1.4	3.0	-	0.8
66	Lake Cowichan	0	0.97	-	-	-	-	-	-	-	-
67	Ladysmith	1	1.98	0.51	0.01	2.81	-	-	-	◆	-
68	Nanaimo	8	9.52	0.84	0.36	1.66	-	0.8	2.2	-	0.5
69	Qualicum	3	2.94	1.02	0.21	2.98	-	-	-	2.8	1.2
70	Alberni	7	5.77	1.21	0.49	2.50	0.8	0.7	0.7	2.0	0.7
71	Courtenay	6	6.11	0.98	0.36	2.14	0.8	1.6	0.6	-	1.4
72	Campbell River	4	5.45	0.73	0.20	1.88	0.9	-	-	1.4	0.8
75	Mission	5	4.99	1.00	0.32	2.34	-	1.7	-	3.0	-
76	Agassiz-Harrison	0	0.83	-	-	-	-	-	-	-	-
77	Summerland	1	1.13	0.88	0.01	4.92	-	◆	-	-	-
78	Enderby	2	0.91	2.20	0.25	7.95	-	-	4.2	-	4.5
80	Kitimat	6	2.87	2.09	0.76	4.55	3.1	3.3	2.2	-	-
81	Fort Nelson	0	1.18	-	-	-	-	-	-	-	-
84	Vancouver Island West	3	0.94	3.20	0.64	9.34	6.0	-	-	6.0	4.2
85	Vancouver Island North	2	3.07	0.65	0.07	2.36	1.4	-	-	-	1.9
87	Stikine	1	0.44	2.30	0.03	12.78	-	-	-	◆	-
88	Terrace	8	5.62	1.42	0.61	2.80	-	2.4	0.6	3.3	-
92	Nishga	1	0.44	2.27	0.03	12.65	-	-	-	◆	-
94	Telegraph Creek	2	0.19	10.58 +	1.19	38.21	59.2	-	-	-	-
	Provincial Total	**444**	◆	1.00	◆	◆	0.8	0.8	0.8	0.9	0.8

212

Age 1 - 14 Years: Female

	Local Health Area	Observed Deaths	Expected Deaths	SMR (p)	95% C.I. Lower	Upper	ASMR 1985	1986	1987	1988	1989
1	Fernie	0	2.17	-	-	-	-	-	-	-	-
2	Cranbrook	2	2.53	0.79	0.09	2.86	1.1	-	-	-	1.1
3	Kimberley	0	0.91	-	-	-	-	-	-	-	-
4	Windermere	0	0.75	-	-	-	-	-	-	-	-
5	Creston	3	0.93	3.24	0.65	9.46	5.4	2.5	-	-	♦
6	Kootenay Lake	1	0.34	2.97	0.04	16.51	-	-	-	-	♦
7	Nelson	2	2.18	0.92	0.10	3.32	1.1	1.4	-	-	-
9	Castlegar	0	1.27	-	-	-	-	-	-	-	-
10	Arrow Lakes	0	0.47	-	-	-	-	-	-	-	-
11	Trail	2	2.13	0.94	0.11	3.39	1.1	-	1.2	-	-
12	Grand Forks	1	0.63	1.59	0.02	8.82	-	♦	-	-	-
13	Kettle Valley	0	0.32	-	-	-	-	-	-	-	-
14	Southern Okanagan	0	1.18	-	-	-	-	-	-	♦	-
15	Penticton	1	2.60	0.39	0.01	2.14	-	-	-	-	-
16	Keremeos	0	0.31	-	-	-	-	-	-	-	-
17	Princeton	1	0.49	2.06	0.03	11.46	-	♦	-	-	-
18	Golden	0	0.82	-	-	-	-	-	-	-	-
19	Revelstoke	0	1.05	-	-	-	-	-	-	-	-
20	Salmon Arm	2	2.36	0.85	0.10	3.06	1.2	-	1.3	-	-
21	Armstrong-Spallumcheen	0	0.82	-	-	-	-	-	-	-	-
22	Vernon	7	4.55	1.54	0.62	3.17	0.7	0.7	-	1.8	1.2
23	Central Okanagan	6	8.30	0.72	0.26	1.57	0.4	0.4	-	0.9	0.3
24	Kamloops	11	8.84	1.25	0.62	2.23	1.0	0.3	1.2	0.7	0.3
26	North Thompson	0	0.64	-	-	-	-	-	-	-	-
27	Cariboo-Chilcotin	6	4.96	1.21	0.44	2.63	0.5	0.5	-	1.1	1.3
28	Quesnel	3	3.09	0.97	0.19	2.83	0.8	1.7	-	-	-
29	Lillooet	2	0.59	3.39	0.38	12.26	-	-	9.1	-	-
30	South Cariboo	2	0.84	2.38	0.27	8.60	3.5	-	-	-	3.6
31	Merritt	0	1.17	-	-	-	-	-	-	-	-
32	Hope	1	0.81	1.23	0.02	6.86	♦	-	-	-	♦
33	Chilliwack	1	4.82	0.21	0.00	1.15	-	-	-	-	-
34	Abbotsford	12	7.17	1.67	0.86	2.92	-	0.8	3.6	-	0.6
35	Langley	8	8.38	0.95	0.41	1.88	0.4	0.7	1.1	-	0.5
36	Surrey	22	21.15	1.04	0.65	1.57	0.8	0.5	0.5	0.5	0.6
37	Delta	5	9.30	0.54	0.17	1.26	0.6	0.6	-	0.3	-
38	Richmond	14	10.63	1.32	0.72	2.21	0.8	1.3	0.3	0.3	1.0
39	Vancouver	25	29.32	0.85	0.55	1.26	0.9	0.5	0.2	0.4	0.2
40	New Westminster	2	2.42	0.83	0.09	2.98	1.5	-	-	-	1.4
41	Burnaby	8	10.96	0.73	0.31	1.44	1.0	-	0.2	0.5	0.3
42	Maple Ridge	5	5.16	0.97	0.31	2.26	2.2	-	0.5	-	-
43	Coquitlam	14	12.61	1.11	0.61	1.86	0.6	1.0	0.4	0.2	0.5
44	North Vancouver	8	8.82	0.91	0.39	1.79	0.6	0.8	0.3	0.6	-
45	West Vancouver-Bowen Is	3	2.72	1.10	0.22	3.22	1.0	-	-	-	1.9
46	Sechelt	3	1.60	1.87	0.38	5.47	1.4	1.5	1.5	-	-
47	Powell River	1	1.91	0.52	0.01	2.91	-	♦	-	-	-
48	Howe Sound	2	1.98	1.01	0.11	3.64	-	-	1.1	1.0	-
49	Central Coast	1	0.43	2.31	0.03	12.83	-	-	-	-	♦
50	Queen Charlotte	1	0.74	1.36	0.02	7.56	♦	-	-	-	-
52	Prince Rupert	1	2.39	0.42	0.01	2.33	-	-	-	♦	-
54	Smithers	3	2.03	1.48	0.30	4.32	-	-	-	1.5	2.4
55	Burns Lake	2	1.19	1.68	0.19	6.07	-	4.8	-	-	-
56	Nechako	6	2.33	2.58	0.94	5.61	1.2	1.4	-	2.0	2.4
57	Prince George	10	11.94	0.84	0.40	1.54	0.8	0.6	0.2	0.5	-
59	Peace River South	4	3.21	1.25	0.34	3.19	-	0.9	2.1	-	0.7
60	Peace River North	1	3.60	0.28	0.00	1.55	-	-	♦	-	-
61	Greater Victoria	13	12.64	1.03	0.55	1.76	0.7	0.2	0.8	0.6	0.4
62	Sooke	5	4.60	1.09	0.35	2.54	-	0.7	1.2	0.8	0.7
63	Saanich	3	3.51	0.85	0.17	2.49	-	0.7	0.7	0.7	-
64	Gulf Islands	0	0.70	-	-	-	-	-	-	-	-
65	Cowichan	4	3.87	1.03	0.28	2.65	-	0.8	1.6	-	0.6
66	Lake Cowichan	0	0.64	-	-	-	-	-	-	-	-
67	Ladysmith	3	1.38	2.17	0.44	6.35	1.9	2.4	1.6	-	-
68	Nanaimo	5	6.14	0.81	0.26	1.90	-	1.9	0.4	-	-
69	Qualicum	4	1.87	2.13	0.57	5.47	-	2.7	-	1.9	1.4
70	Alberni	3	3.66	0.82	0.16	2.40	-	-	1.4	0.6	-
71	Courtenay	6	3.94	1.52	0.56	3.31	1.5	0.8	0.6	1.4	-
72	Campbell River	2	3.52	0.57	0.06	2.05	-	1.4	-	-	-
75	Mission	2	3.18	0.63	0.07	2.27	-	-	-	1.9	-
76	Agassiz-Harrison	0	0.51	-	-	-	-	-	-	-	-
77	Summerland	0	0.69	-	-	-	-	-	-	-	-
78	Enderby	0	0.56	-	-	-	-	-	-	-	-
80	Kitimat	5	1.93	2.58	0.83	6.03	-	1.7	2.1	2.6	-
81	Fort Nelson	1	0.78	1.28	0.02	7.13	-	-	-	♦	-
84	Vancouver Island West	1	0.67	1.50	0.02	8.32	-	-	-	♦	-
85	Vancouver Island North	4	2.13	1.88	0.51	4.82	-	-	2.0	-	2.6
87	Stikine	0	0.25	-	-	-	-	-	-	-	-
88	Terrace	9	3.61	2.49 *	1.14	4.74	0.9	-	1.7	3.6	0.6
92	Nishga	1	0.26	3.82	0.05	21.25	-	♦	-	-	-
94	Telegraph Creek	0	0.09	-	-	-	-	-	-	-	-
	Provincial Total	**286**	♦	1.00	♦	♦	0.6	0.6	0.5	0.5	0.4

Age 15 - 24 Years: Male

	Local Health Area	Observed Deaths	Expected Deaths	SMR (p)	95% C.I. Lower	Upper	ASMR 1985	1986	1987	1988	1989
1	Fernie	6	8.08	0.74	0.27	1.62	-	3.0	1.5	-	5.7
2	Cranbrook	13	11.35	1.14	0.61	1.96	8.3	1.0	2.3	2.4	-
3	Kimberley	6	3.61	1.66	0.61	3.61	-	2.7	10.3	5.9	5.0
4	Windermere	4	3.52	1.14	0.31	2.91	6.9	3.7	-	-	3.7
5	Creston	4	4.11	0.97	0.26	2.49	5.8	-	3.5	-	3.5
6	Kootenay Lake	1	1.14	0.88	0.01	4.89	◆	-	-	-	-
7	Nelson	10	8.74	1.14	0.55	2.10	1.3	4.5	1.7	2.7	4.3
9	Castlegar	8	5.98	1.34	0.58	2.64	1.8	4.5	4.3	4.8	2.2
10	Arrow Lakes	2	2.25	0.89	0.10	3.21	10.4	-	-	-	-
11	Trail	6	9.18	0.65	0.24	1.42	1.3	1.5	1.6	1.7	2.7
12	Grand Forks	3	3.03	0.99	0.20	2.89	-	4.1	4.1	3.9	-
13	Kettle Valley	4	1.49	2.68	0.72	6.87	25.9	8.0	-	-	-
14	Southern Okanagan	6	5.47	1.10	0.40	2.39	4.4	2.3	-	-	7.2
15	Penticton	14	13.22	1.06	0.58	1.78	2.0	3.0	1.9	5.7	1.0
16	Keremeos	3	1.56	1.93	0.39	5.63	8.1	9.2	7.4	-	-
17	Princeton	2	2.58	0.77	0.09	2.80	-	-	-	-	11.0
18	Golden	9	3.96	2.28 *	1.04	4.32	7.3	9.5	6.0	7.5	-
19	Revelstoke	3	4.81	0.62	0.13	1.82	2.6	-	3.0	-	3.2
20	Salmon Arm	13	11.29	1.15	0.61	1.97	3.1	4.4	2.4	4.8	-
21	Armstrong-Spallumcheen	6	3.47	1.73	0.63	3.76	-	4.3	3.3	10.4	4.1
22	Vernon	33	21.34	1.55 *	1.06	2.17	4.5	1.8	7.5	3.2	3.2
23	Central Okanagan	36	44.64	0.81	0.56	1.12	1.9	2.0	2.6	2.1	1.8
24	Kamloops	48	42.91	1.12	0.82	1.48	2.1	2.7	3.4	2.8	3.4
26	North Thompson	6	2.50	2.40	0.88	5.23	8.9	-	4.3	7.1	12.0
27	Cariboo-Chilcotin	40	20.47	1.95 ***	1.40	2.66	3.4	4.8	1.9	7.1	8.2
28	Quesnel	22	13.14	1.67 *	1.05	2.53	3.8	5.8	1.0	3.0	8.1
29	Lillooet	4	2.68	1.49	0.40	3.82	5.6	-	11.6	4.9	-
30	South Cariboo	14	4.10	3.41 ***	1.87	5.73	2.4	5.5	23.0	7.6	6.6
31	Merritt	11	5.43	2.02 *	1.01	3.62	4.4	2.3	4.9	9.5	5.1
32	Hope	6	4.09	1.47	0.54	3.20	2.8	-	7.2	-	9.7
33	Chilliwack	33	24.19	1.36	0.94	1.92	2.5	3.5	2.1	5.5	3.8
34	Abbotsford	49	38.29	1.28	0.95	1.69	4.3	1.5	6.0	3.0	1.9
35	Langley	37	36.94	1.00	0.71	1.38	1.8	3.5	1.7	3.4	2.4
36	Surrey	96	103.66	0.93	0.75	1.13	2.3	2.3	2.5	2.8	2.1
37	Delta	25	45.32	0.55 **	0.36	0.81	1.2	1.1	2.2	1.4	1.2
38	Richmond	39	58.06	0.67 *	0.48	0.92	1.6	1.3	2.1	1.7	1.8
39	Vancouver	149	237.87	0.63 ***	0.53	0.74	1.7	1.6	1.3	1.4	1.7
40	New Westminster	24	22.33	1.07	0.69	1.60	3.0	5.1	1.4	3.6	0.9
41	Burnaby	53	79.59	0.67 **	0.50	0.87	1.4	1.7	1.6	1.0	2.3
42	Maple Ridge	20	23.02	0.87	0.53	1.34	1.1	2.2	2.7	2.9	2.1
43	Coquitlam	48	68.91	0.70 *	0.51	0.92	1.5	1.3	1.3	2.2	2.5
44	North Vancouver	28	56.95	0.49 ***	0.33	0.71	1.4	2.2	0.9	1.0	1.1
45	West Vancouver-Bowen Is	9	19.86	0.45 *	0.21	0.86	0.6	2.6	0.7	0.6	1.2
46	Sechelt	6	6.48	0.93	0.34	2.01	3.9	2.0	2.3	2.1	1.7
47	Powell River	11	9.51	1.16	0.58	2.07	6.6	2.4	3.7	1.2	-
48	Howe Sound	14	8.74	1.60	0.87	2.69	1.6	6.1	4.5	4.1	4.2
49	Central Coast	11	1.64	6.72 ***	3.35	12.02	13.2	15.2	32.1	26.2	-
50	Queen Charlotte	5	2.97	1.68	0.54	3.92	3.1	3.3	3.9	4.4	4.7
52	Prince Rupert	17	10.35	1.64	0.96	2.63	4.6	6.4	2.6	6.5	1.3
54	Smithers	14	8.26	1.69	0.93	2.84	2.9	4.4	1.7	6.6	6.1
55	Burns Lake	11	4.55	2.42 *	1.21	4.33	10.1	2.8	8.7	2.7	5.9
56	Nechako	19	9.28	2.05 **	1.23	3.20	8.4	4.1	2.9	6.9	3.1
57	Prince George	77	50.69	1.52 ***	1.20	1.90	3.0	4.3	3.9	3.5	4.9
59	Peace River South	19	15.07	1.26	0.76	1.97	3.8	2.1	-	5.9	5.3
60	Peace River North	29	14.50	2.00 **	1.34	2.87	6.4	5.7	1.8	6.7	4.9
61	Greater Victoria	60	99.00	0.61 ***	0.46	0.78	1.4	1.4	1.8	1.8	1.4
62	Sooke	16	19.20	0.83	0.48	1.35	3.2	1.9	2.1	1.8	1.4
63	Saanich	11	17.85	0.62	0.31	1.10	1.4	1.4	2.9	2.1	-
64	Gulf Islands	4	2.65	1.51	0.41	3.87	-	-	4.8	13.8	-
65	Cowichan	31	17.26	1.80 **	1.22	2.55	4.2	3.0	3.0	8.6	4.7
66	Lake Cowichan	5	2.37	2.11	0.68	4.92	4.3	-	6.5	11.7	7.0
67	Ladysmith	11	5.68	1.94	0.97	3.47	4.4	6.8	7.0	-	6.7
68	Nanaimo	31	30.34	1.02	0.69	1.45	1.6	3.9	3.4	1.7	2.6
69	Qualicum	10	7.92	1.26	0.60	2.32	3.1	6.5	1.8	1.4	3.3
70	Alberni	29	16.45	1.76 **	1.18	2.53	3.5	6.2	3.9	6.8	2.5
71	Courtenay	18	18.72	0.96	0.57	1.52	3.1	2.8	4.2	2.1	-
72	Campbell River	13	15.84	0.82	0.44	1.40	1.5	0.8	4.5	2.5	1.6
75	Mission	24	12.67	1.89 **	1.21	2.82	7.2	3.0	3.1	5.8	4.9
76	Agassiz-Harrison	4	3.14	1.27	0.34	3.26	3.0	6.6	-	-	3.9
77	Summerland	6	3.57	1.68	0.61	3.66	3.1	3.0	6.1	4.3	3.0
78	Enderby	8	2.59	3.09 *	1.33	6.08	14.1	-	-	11.7	13.3
80	Kitimat	14	7.25	1.93 *	1.05	3.24	2.8	8.4	-	3.7	9.4
81	Fort Nelson	3	3.22	0.93	0.19	2.72	6.3	-	-	-	5.6
84	Vancouver Island West	1	1.94	0.52	0.01	2.87	-	-	-	◆	-
85	Vancouver Island North	18	8.41	2.14 **	1.27	3.38	4.1	8.8	-	6.6	8.1
87	Stikine	1	1.03	0.97	0.01	5.40	-	-	◆	-	-
88	Terrace	28	15.12	1.85 **	1.23	2.68	5.7	2.6	4.5	8.0	3.3
92	Nishga	2	1.23	1.62	0.18	5.87	-	8.7	-	12.8	-
94	Telegraph Creek	3	0.52	5.74 +	1.15	16.76	-	-	-	52.9	33.6
	Provincial Total	1,541	◆	1.00	◆	◆	2.5	2.5	2.5	2.8	2.5

Age 15 - 24 Years: Female

	Local Health Area	Observed Deaths	Expected Deaths	SMR (p)	95% C.I. Lower	Upper	ASMR 1985	1986	1987	1988	1989
1	Fernie	1	2.56	0.39	0.01	2.17	♦	-	-	-	-
2	Cranbrook	5	3.80	1.31	0.42	3.07	2.1	1.0	-	1.3	1.1
3	Kimberley	0	1.18	-	-	-	-	-	-	-	-
4	Windermere	1	1.13	0.89	0.01	4.93	♦	-	-	-	-
5	Creston	2	1.46	1.37	0.15	4.94	2.8	2.9	-	-	-
6	Kootenay Lake	0	0.35	-	-	-	-	-	-	-	-
7	Nelson	1	2.98	0.34	0.00	1.87	-	-	♦	-	-
9	Castlegar	0	1.82	-	-	-	-	-	-	-	-
10	Arrow Lakes	3	0.61	4.89	0.98	14.29	-	12.1	6.0	-	-
11	Trail	3	3.04	0.99	0.20	2.88	-	-	1.6	3.1	-
12	Grand Forks	1	0.99	1.01	0.01	5.64	♦	-	-	-	-
13	Kettle Valley	1	0.49	2.05	0.03	11.42	-	-	-	-	♦
14	Southern Okanagan	7	1.74	4.02 **	1.61	8.29	2.3	7.4	2.3	2.2	2.9
15	Penticton	6	4.41	1.36	0.50	2.96	2.0	1.0	-	1.0	2.0
16	Keremeos	0	0.38	-	-	-	-	-	-	-	-
17	Princeton	0	0.72	-	-	-	-	-	-	-	-
18	Golden	0	1.26	-	-	-	-	-	-	-	-
19	Revelstoke	4	1.41	2.84	0.76	7.26	2.9	-	-	3.2	6.9
20	Salmon Arm	3	3.78	0.79	0.16	2.32	-	-	2.1	1.0	-
21	Armstrong-Spallumcheen	3	1.12	2.67	0.54	7.81	-	-	-	3.2	6.7
22	Vernon	4	7.10	0.56	0.15	1.44	-	0.6	0.6	-	1.2
23	Central Okanagan	14	14.24	0.98	0.54	1.65	0.9	0.6	0.3	1.3	1.3
24	Kamloops	12	13.96	0.86	0.44	1.50	0.3	0.9	0.6	0.3	1.6
26	North Thompson	2	0.79	2.52	0.28	9.09	-	-	5.0	7.4	-
27	Cariboo-Chilcotin	19	6.88	2.76 ***	1.66	4.31	2.4	1.3	4.0	2.5	2.1
28	Quesnel	5	4.45	1.12	0.36	2.62	-	3.8	-	1.1	-
29	Lillooet	4	0.73	5.46 +	1.47	13.98	-	-	11.6	-	14.3
30	South Cariboo	1	1.26	0.79	0.01	4.41	-	-	♦	-	-
31	Merritt	2	1.75	1.15	0.13	4.14	2.2	2.5	-	-	-
32	Hope	4	1.22	3.29	0.89	8.42	6.4	-	3.6	-	3.8
33	Chilliwack	12	8.02	1.50	0.77	2.61	1.1	1.1	1.6	1.1	1.7
34	Abbotsford	8	12.59	0.64	0.27	1.25	1.0	0.7	0.7	0.4	-
35	Langley	9	12.52	0.72	0.33	1.36	1.1	-	0.7	0.3	1.0
36	Surrey	30	34.12	0.88	0.59	1.26	0.1	0.8	0.6	1.0	1.2
37	Delta	6	14.76	0.41 *	0.15	0.88	0.5	0.3	0.7	-	0.3
38	Richmond	5	19.05	0.26 ***	0.08	0.61	0.5	-	0.2	0.2	0.2
39	Vancouver	75	78.84	0.95	0.75	1.19	0.7	0.8	0.8	0.9	0.8
40	New Westminster	10	7.14	1.40	0.67	2.58	1.6	0.4	1.5	0.4	1.5
41	Burnaby	16	26.57	0.60 *	0.34	0.98	0.5	0.5	0.9	0.4	0.4
42	Maple Ridge	5	7.89	0.63	0.20	1.48	-	0.6	0.6	0.5	0.9
43	Coquitlam	11	22.02	0.50 *	0.25	0.89	0.6	1.0	-	0.2	0.4
44	North Vancouver	14	18.81	0.74	0.41	1.25	0.8	0.5	0.9	0.7	0.3
45	West Vancouver-Bowen Is	3	6.20	0.48	0.10	1.41	-	-	1.5	-	0.6
46	Sechelt	2	2.17	0.92	0.10	3.33	-	-	-	3.5	-
47	Powell River	3	3.03	0.99	0.20	2.90	-	1.3	-	3.0	-
48	Howe Sound	2	2.48	0.81	0.09	2.91	1.4	1.4	-	-	-
49	Central Coast	3	0.59	5.08 +	1.02	14.86	-	11.5	-	7.3	-
50	Queen Charlotte	2	0.86	2.34	0.26	8.44	5.3	-	5.9	-	-
52	Prince Rupert	5	3.36	1.49	0.48	3.48	2.0	1.3	1.4	-	1.4
54	Smithers	5	2.53	1.97	0.64	4.61	-	3.5	1.6	3.5	-
55	Burns Lake	3	1.43	2.10	0.42	6.14	-	6.0	3.1	-	-
56	Nechako	6	2.90	2.07	0.76	4.50	2.7	-	1.7	5.0	-
57	Prince George	21	16.90	1.24	0.77	1.90	0.5	0.8	1.5	1.1	1.7
59	Peace River South	3	5.05	0.59	0.12	1.74	1.3	-	-	-	1.0
60	Peace River North	6	4.64	1.29	0.47	2.81	1.8	1.7	-	1.0	1.1
61	Greater Victoria	32	30.71	1.04	0.71	1.47	0.8	1.3	1.3	0.6	0.4
62	Sooke	9	6.37	1.41	0.64	2.68	-	2.1	1.2	1.2	1.4
63	Saanich	2	5.65	0.35	0.04	1.28	-	-	0.9	0.9	-
64	Gulf Islands	0	0.82	-	-	-	-	-	-	-	-
65	Cowichan	7	5.86	1.19	0.48	2.46	1.4	1.4	0.8	1.5	-
66	Lake Cowichan	1	0.72	1.40	0.02	7.78	-	-	-	-	♦
67	Ladysmith	3	1.85	1.62	0.33	4.73	-	2.0	2.0	1.9	-
68	Nanaimo	15	10.17	1.48	0.83	2.43	0.4	1.7	0.9	1.3	2.1
69	Qualicum	2	2.63	0.76	0.09	2.74	1.6	-	-	1.4	-
70	Alberni	8	5.00	1.60	0.69	3.15	1.5	1.6	0.8	1.9	1.1
71	Courtenay	8	5.89	1.36	0.58	2.68	2.8	0.7	0.8	0.9	0.9
72	Campbell River	4	5.25	0.76	0.20	1.95	-	0.8	-	0.9	1.6
75	Mission	8	4.07	1.97	0.85	3.88	2.4	1.1	2.1	1.0	2.1
76	Agassiz-Harrison	2	0.75	2.66	0.30	9.62	-	-	-	5.3	5.0
77	Summerland	1	1.04	0.96	0.01	5.35	-	-	-	♦	-
78	Enderby	1	0.78	1.29	0.02	7.17	-	♦	-	-	-
80	Kitimat	2	2.44	0.82	0.09	2.96	-	1.6	1.7	-	-
81	Fort Nelson	3	0.97	3.10	0.62	9.05	8.8	-	-	-	5.2
84	Vancouver Island West	2	0.62	3.24	0.36	11.70	5.5	6.8	-	-	-
85	Vancouver Island North	1	2.61	0.38	0.01	2.13	-	-	-	♦	-
87	Stikine	1	0.30	3.39	0.04	18.83	-	♦	-	-	-
88	Terrace	13	4.87	2.67 **	1.42	4.57	1.6	4.3	0.9	1.7	2.8
92	Nishga	0	0.35	-	-	-	-	-	-	-	-
94	Telegraph Creek	3	0.14	21.52 +	4.33	62.88	-	22.0	-	37.1	34.5
	Provincial Total	502	♦	1.00	♦	♦	0.8	0.9	0.8	0.9	0.9

215

Age 25 - 44 Years: Male

	Local Health Area	Observed Deaths	Expected Deaths	SMR	(p)	95% C.I. Lower	95% C.I. Upper	ASMR 1985	ASMR 1986	ASMR 1987	ASMR 1988	ASMR 1989
1	Fernie	16	27.03	0.59	*	0.34	0.96	2.0	4.0	1.7	3.6	1.6
2	Cranbrook	21	28.07	0.75		0.46	1.14	2.2	0.7	5.1	1.8	7.8
3	Kimberley	14	10.71	1.31		0.71	2.19	9.6	4.5	6.5	-	12.5
4	Windermere	6	8.94	0.67		0.25	1.46	4.3	2.0	2.5	5.8	-
5	Creston	7	10.39	0.67		0.27	1.39	2.4	-	2.0	4.0	7.0
6	Kootenay Lake	5	3.92	1.28		0.41	2.98	-	20.9	-	-	19.5
7	Nelson	23	26.22	0.88		0.56	1.32	3.5	3.2	4.1	3.1	6.3
9	Castlegar	15	13.87	1.08		0.60	1.78	5.3	2.9	6.8	3.1	5.7
10	Arrow Lakes	4	5.71	0.70		0.19	1.79	4.2	4.6	9.3	-	-
11	Trail	21	25.11	0.84		0.52	1.28	2.8	0.7	6.2	3.0	6.4
12	Grand Forks	10	8.09	1.24		0.59	2.27	12.0	3.4	6.1	2.5	5.0
13	Kettle Valley	4	3.91	1.02		0.28	2.62	-	5.4	5.7	-	10.7
14	Southern Okanagan	10	13.65	0.73		0.35	1.35	3.2	1.8	7.0	2.0	2.9
15	Penticton	30	33.46	0.90		0.60	1.28	7.8	0.8	3.4	5.1	3.4
16	Keremeos	8	3.99	2.01		0.86	3.95	12.3	14.5	4.5	-	9.8
17	Princeton	12	6.28	1.91		0.99	3.34	10.4	3.1	7.4	13.6	7.3
18	Golden	6	11.38	0.53		0.19	1.15	-	6.1	4.6	-	2.2
19	Revelstoke	16	13.51	1.18		0.68	1.92	9.9	7.4	6.3	1.6	-
20	Salmon Arm	30	27.14	1.11		0.75	1.58	5.8	3.2	4.6	3.9	8.1
21	Armstrong-Spallumcheen	7	8.54	0.82		0.33	1.69	6.3	-	8.8	-	5.0
22	Vernon	61	52.45	1.16		0.89	1.49	4.4	6.3	7.3	5.3	2.8
23	Central Okanagan	118	108.30	1.09		0.90	1.30	5.7	4.5	6.1	4.7	4.3
24	Kamloops	119	105.44	1.13		0.93	1.35	6.0	4.6	7.2	3.1	4.4
26	North Thompson	7	6.73	1.04		0.42	2.14	10.8	-	4.1	3.2	3.0
27	Cariboo-Chilcotin	73	52.69	1.39	**	1.09	1.74	5.8	8.0	6.0	6.9	5.1
28	Quesnel	52	33.78	1.54	**	1.15	2.02	7.2	9.7	4.5	6.3	6.8
29	Lillooet	16	6.26	2.56	**	1.46	4.15	24.3	8.1	6.3	5.9	16.1
30	South Cariboo	13	9.47	1.37		0.73	2.35	4.0	3.7	5.0	10.5	7.9
31	Merritt	16	13.06	1.23		0.70	1.99	3.3	2.9	5.1	4.3	11.8
32	Hope	15	8.99	1.67		0.93	2.75	4.4	6.8	2.7	16.7	7.3
33	Chilliwack	53	57.12	0.93		0.69	1.21	4.5	4.3	4.1	3.8	4.4
34	Abbotsford	81	96.09	0.84		0.67	1.05	3.6	3.5	4.9	3.5	3.6
35	Langley	77	109.48	0.70	**	0.56	0.88	4.0	5.0	2.1	3.0	2.5
36	Surrey	269	312.68	0.86	*	0.76	0.97	5.3	3.5	3.3	3.8	3.7
37	Delta	78	111.31	0.70	**	0.55	0.87	2.6	3.7	3.6	2.7	3.4
38	Richmond	104	167.82	0.62	***	0.51	0.75	2.8	2.8	3.5	2.9	2.3
39	Vancouver	942	692.10	1.36	***	1.28	1.45	6.0	5.2	6.4	6.2	7.1
40	New Westminster	76	64.77	1.17		0.92	1.47	5.2	3.7	5.6	6.0	6.8
41	Burnaby	147	215.86	0.68	***	0.58	0.80	2.3	3.2	2.8	3.7	3.7
42	Maple Ridge	59	75.88	0.78		0.59	1.00	4.1	2.8	3.9	3.5	3.3
43	Coquitlam	126	187.28	0.67	***	0.56	0.80	3.4	3.4	1.8	3.1	3.7
44	North Vancouver	100	160.67	0.62	***	0.51	0.76	2.8	3.5	2.8	2.4	2.5
45	West Vancouver-Bowen Is	24	45.95	0.52	***	0.33	0.78	4.1	2.5	2.0	2.2	1.3
46	Sechelt	22	22.61	0.97		0.61	1.47	5.8	5.9	5.1	4.3	6.8
47	Powell River	39	23.11	1.69	**	1.20	2.31	6.4	11.7	5.5	5.3	8.8
48	Howe Sound	37	27.06	1.37		0.96	1.89	5.3	5.0	4.2	9.3	6.9
49	Central Coast	17	4.98	3.41	***	1.99	5.47	-	45.8	12.1	4.8	12.8
50	Queen Charlotte	15	10.01	1.50		0.84	2.47	6.7	7.4	5.2	9.2	6.5
52	Prince Rupert	46	27.27	1.69	**	1.23	2.25	7.8	9.3	1.6	10.8	8.7
54	Smithers	31	23.00	1.35		0.92	1.91	5.5	6.4	6.2	9.5	4.2
55	Burns Lake	17	11.07	1.54		0.89	2.46	9.4	3.8	8.8	8.0	4.4
56	Nechako	31	21.04	1.47	*	1.00	2.09	6.7	5.2	9.2	7.8	5.7
57	Prince George	146	136.34	1.07		0.90	1.26	3.9	4.4	5.2	5.9	5.3
59	Peace River South	46	43.10	1.07		0.78	1.42	4.3	5.7	2.0	2.5	10.3
60	Peace River North	39	34.50	1.13		0.80	1.55	5.0	4.5	4.9	3.5	7.9
61	Greater Victoria	195	229.88	0.85	*	0.73	0.98	3.6	3.5	4.4	3.7	3.8
62	Sooke	35	62.10	0.56	***	0.39	0.78	2.5	3.1	3.4	3.2	0.8
63	Saanich	39	52.59	0.74		0.53	1.01	3.3	2.4	2.7	4.9	3.4
64	Gulf Islands	13	10.87	1.20		0.64	2.04	1.7	-	11.3	2.9	7.3
65	Cowichan	43	46.61	0.92		0.67	1.24	5.1	3.4	5.0	3.2	4.4
66	Lake Cowichan	4	6.28	0.64		0.17	1.63	3.9	3.0	-	-	8.9
67	Ladysmith	17	15.19	1.12		0.65	1.79	5.6	5.4	2.8	4.7	6.1
68	Nanaimo	73	82.27	0.89		0.70	1.12	2.7	3.6	3.7	5.9	4.2
69	Qualicum	23	26.09	0.88		0.56	1.32	5.2	4.4	1.7	4.0	6.2
70	Alberni	47	40.34	1.16		0.86	1.55	6.4	5.1	3.4	5.9	5.2
71	Courtenay	63	52.62	1.20		0.92	1.53	5.9	5.6	6.8	3.4	6.0
72	Campbell River	57	47.42	1.20		0.91	1.56	4.6	5.6	4.3	5.0	6.8
75	Mission	44	38.88	1.13		0.82	1.52	5.9	5.3	4.2	5.8	4.3
76	Agassiz-Harrison	9	9.32	0.97		0.44	1.83	2.5	6.9	2.4	2.1	6.8
77	Summerland	6	8.61	0.70		0.25	1.52	4.9	3.0	4.5	-	1.9
78	Enderby	10	5.86	1.71		0.82	3.14	8.8	4.1	3.8	18.3	8.0
80	Kitimat	22	18.73	1.17		0.74	1.78	2.4	6.5	6.9	2.8	7.8
81	Fort Nelson	4	8.79	0.46		0.12	1.17	-	-	7.0	4.7	-
84	Vancouver Island West	3	7.11	0.42		0.08	1.23	3.2	3.3	2.9	-	-
85	Vancouver Island North	44	26.52	1.66	**	1.21	2.23	6.8	6.7	9.4	5.3	10.2
87	Stikine	6	3.57	1.68		0.61	3.66	8.9	9.2	12.0	-	4.9
88	Terrace	51	36.80	1.39	*	1.03	1.82	5.9	3.5	9.0	6.7	5.5
92	Nishga	4	1.98	2.02		0.54	5.17	9.0	19.5	14.9	-	-
94	Telegraph Creek	1	0.91	1.10		0.01	6.11	-	-	-	-	◆
	Provincial Total	**4,207**	◆	**1.00**		◆	◆	4.5	4.3	4.5	4.4	4.7

216

Age 25 - 44 Years: Female

	Local Health Area	Observed Deaths	Expected Deaths	SMR (p)	95% C.I. Lower	95% C.I. Upper	ASMR 1985	1986	1987	1988	1989
1	Fernie	5	10.60	0.47	0.15	1.10	0.7	1.5	-	2.0	-
2	Cranbrook	13	13.28	0.98	0.52	1.67	3.3	2.0	1.4	-	3.0
3	Kimberley	5	4.74	1.05	0.34	2.46	1.6	4.1	-	1.9	1.9
4	Windermere	6	3.91	1.54	0.56	3.34	5.1	-	2.7	5.4	2.3
5	Creston	2	4.91	0.41	0.05	1.47	-	1.8	-	1.9	-
6	Kootenay Lake	3	1.75	1.72	0.35	5.02	-	4.8	-	9.9	-
7	Nelson	9	11.84	0.76	0.35	1.44	1.6	2.5	0.9	1.7	0.8
9	Castlegar	9	6.36	1.42	0.65	2.69	1.3	1.3	3.2	1.7	6.8
10	Arrow Lakes	4	2.49	1.61	0.43	4.11	-	3.1	4.5	4.0	4.4
11	Trail	12	10.84	1.11	0.57	1.93	3.5	0.8	1.6	2.1	3.0
12	Grand Forks	1	3.70	0.27	0.00	1.50	-	-	♦	-	-
13	Kettle Valley	3	1.67	1.79	0.36	5.24	-	-	5.6	5.4	5.7
14	Southern Okanagan	6	6.40	0.94	0.34	2.04	1.4	1.4	-	1.5	5.0
15	Penticton	23	16.12	1.43	0.90	2.14	2.7	1.7	3.6	3.6	2.5
16	Keremeos	3	1.70	1.77	0.36	5.16	5.6	-	5.8	4.5	-
17	Princeton	2	2.80	0.71	0.08	2.58	-	3.3	-	-	3.5
18	Golden	2	4.41	0.45	0.05	1.64	5.0	-	-	-	-
19	Revelstoke	5	5.45	0.92	0.30	2.14	-	2.2	4.4	1.7	1.7
20	Salmon Arm	10	12.91	0.77	0.37	1.42	0.9	4.0	-	1.1	1.4
21	Armstrong-Spallumcheen	4	4.26	0.94	0.25	2.40	-	4.3	2.0	2.1	-
22	Vernon	25	25.35	0.99	0.64	1.46	0.9	2.0	3.2	2.2	1.9
23	Central Okanagan	47	53.48	0.88	0.65	1.17	1.4	1.7	1.8	1.4	2.2
24	Kamloops	42	49.34	0.85	0.61	1.15	1.5	2.2	0.6	1.1	3.0
26	North Thompson	7	2.80	2.50 *	1.00	5.16	11.0	4.1	2.8	3.8	3.5
27	Cariboo-Chilcotin	36	22.61	1.59 *	1.12	2.20	3.4	3.3	2.5	2.5	4.9
28	Quesnel	14	14.74	0.95	0.52	1.59	1.4	0.8	1.3	3.5	2.9
29	Lillooet	6	2.40	2.50	0.91	5.45	10.6	6.5	4.9	-	3.3
30	South Cariboo	9	3.97	2.27 *	1.03	4.30	-	2.1	7.8	2.8	10.6
31	Merritt	14	5.66	2.47 **	1.35	4.15	3.4	3.4	3.7	9.8	5.2
32	Hope	3	3.95	0.76	0.15	2.22	-	-	2.6	5.0	-
33	Chilliwack	25	26.06	0.96	0.62	1.42	0.7	0.8	3.4	1.3	2.7
34	Abbotsford	28	41.83	0.67 *	0.44	0.97	1.9	1.3	1.8	1.4	0.4
35	Langley	36	51.04	0.71 *	0.49	0.98	1.0	2.1	1.3	1.4	1.1
36	Surrey	122	137.70	0.89	0.74	1.06	2.2	1.3	1.9	1.5	2.0
37	Delta	40	56.86	0.70 *	0.50	0.96	2.0	1.2	1.3	1.4	1.0
38	Richmond	57	80.52	0.71 **	0.54	0.92	1.6	1.6	1.4	1.5	0.9
39	Vancouver	329	294.40	1.12 *	1.00	1.25	2.2	2.3	2.3	2.1	2.1
40	New Westminster	46	25.29	1.82 ***	1.33	2.43	4.6	3.1	1.6	3.2	4.5
41	Burnaby	85	93.83	0.91	0.72	1.12	2.5	1.4	2.3	1.5	1.3
42	Maple Ridge	26	32.81	0.79	0.52	1.16	1.2	2.8	1.1	1.6	1.2
43	Coquitlam	63	85.95	0.73 *	0.56	0.94	1.2	1.3	1.8	1.6	1.3
44	North Vancouver	76	74.88	1.01	0.80	1.27	1.9	1.2	2.2	2.3	2.3
45	West Vancouver-Bowen Is	22	24.76	0.89	0.56	1.35	1.7	1.7	0.8	2.0	2.0
46	Sechelt	11	10.03	1.10	0.55	1.96	2.8	0.8	2.9	0.8	3.4
47	Powell River	9	10.04	0.90	0.41	1.70	1.9	1.8	2.0	2.2	0.9
48	Howe Sound	8	10.39	0.77	0.33	1.52	2.0	2.9	0.9	2.7	-
49	Central Coast	3	1.90	1.58	0.32	4.62	7.9	4.2	-	5.9	-
50	Queen Charlotte	2	3.48	0.58	0.06	2.08	2.5	-	-	-	3.1
52	Prince Rupert	22	10.95	2.01 **	1.26	3.04	0.8	4.3	2.0	7.0	5.4
54	Smithers	12	9.30	1.29	0.67	2.25	-	4.4	2.0	2.3	4.3
55	Burns Lake	9	4.49	2.00	0.91	3.80	8.3	1.9	2.6	1.9	4.1
56	Nechako	12	8.36	1.43	0.74	2.51	0.9	3.5	-	3.8	6.2
57	Prince George	70	59.34	1.18	0.92	1.49	2.6	3.4	2.1	1.3	2.3
59	Peace River South	11	16.92	0.65	0.32	1.16	1.2	1.6	0.6	1.4	1.1
60	Peace River North	17	14.61	1.16	0.68	1.86	1.2	2.5	2.9	2.3	3.0
61	Greater Victoria	88	105.70	0.83	0.67	1.03	1.7	1.7	0.8	1.9	2.0
62	Sooke	25	27.98	0.89	0.58	1.32	2.0	1.5	2.1	2.1	1.3
63	Saanich	20	26.05	0.77	0.47	1.19	1.9	0.7	1.9	1.3	1.5
64	Gulf Islands	7	5.27	1.33	0.53	2.73	3.3	4.6	1.4	1.2	1.5
65	Cowichan	33	21.27	1.55 *	1.07	2.18	3.4	3.4	1.7	3.8	3.3
66	Lake Cowichan	5	2.79	1.79	0.58	4.18	-	-	7.4	12.5	-
67	Ladysmith	11	6.89	1.60	0.80	2.86	4.0	1.5	1.9	7.6	1.3
68	Nanaimo	51	38.26	1.33	0.99	1.75	1.4	2.7	2.5	3.3	3.1
69	Qualicum	12	12.18	0.99	0.51	1.72	1.4	2.6	0.7	1.5	3.0
70	Alberni	19	17.26	1.10	0.66	1.72	1.7	2.8	3.2	2.3	1.1
71	Courtenay	25	23.92	1.05	0.68	1.54	0.9	2.1	2.9	2.0	2.1
72	Campbell River	13	20.25	0.64	0.34	1.10	1.2	2.3	1.4	0.8	0.4
75	Mission	19	16.04	1.18	0.71	1.85	4.2	1.4	2.9	2.0	1.6
76	Agassiz-Harrison	4	2.60	1.54	0.41	3.95	-	3.2	4.1	-	6.4
77	Summerland	5	4.26	1.17	0.38	2.74	-	2.5	2.3	6.6	-
78	Enderby	3	2.67	1.13	0.23	3.29	-	3.6	-	3.9	4.1
80	Kitimat	12	7.73	1.55	0.80	2.71	1.3	7.1	2.4	4.1	-
81	Fort Nelson	7	3.30	2.12	0.85	4.37	2.3	-	3.1	7.8	7.5
84	Vancouver Island West	3	2.46	1.22	0.24	3.56	2.9	2.9	3.8	-	-
85	Vancouver Island North	9	9.93	0.91	0.41	1.72	0.8	2.1	-	3.3	3.2
87	Stikine	4	1.39	2.88	0.78	7.38	-	12.5	-	17.0	-
88	Terrace	24	15.43	1.56	1.00	2.31	2.7	1.1	1.2	4.2	5.8
92	Nishga	1	0.61	1.65	0.02	9.17	-	♦	-	-	-
94	Telegraph Creek	2	0.41	4.93	0.55	17.80	-	36.4	-	20.6	-
	Provincial Total	1,875	♦	1.00	♦	♦	1.9	2.0	1.9	2.0	2.0

Age 45 - 64 Years: Male

	Local Health Area	Observed Deaths	Expected Deaths	SMR (p)	95% C.I. Lower	Upper	ASMR 1985	1986	1987	1988	1989
1	Fernie	43	46.54	0.92	0.67	1.24	10.1	13.4	12.6	18.6	10.7
2	Cranbrook	68	72.41	0.94	0.73	1.19	18.0	12.0	13.6	7.8	13.5
3	Kimberley	32	33.56	0.95	0.65	1.35	18.7	14.7	10.6	9.3	10.5
4	Windermere	25	27.47	0.91	0.59	1.34	12.4	7.8	9.9	10.5	23.6
5	Creston	51	48.68	1.05	0.78	1.38	7.9	15.4	15.1	13.8	20.7
6	Kootenay Lake	14	13.87	1.01	0.55	1.69	14.4	10.2	17.0	19.0	7.3
7	Nelson	82	81.03	1.01	0.80	1.26	12.4	14.6	16.5	11.5	15.1
9	Castlegar	34	45.75	0.74	0.51	1.04	7.3	10.1	10.9	12.4	10.8
10	Arrow Lakes	15	16.88	0.89	0.50	1.47	13.3	7.7	12.5	12.3	16.3
11	Trail	84	83.45	1.01	0.80	1.25	18.4	9.2	13.9	14.3	12.1
12	Grand Forks	36	33.23	1.08	0.76	1.50	5.9	8.8	22.5	13.8	21.8
13	Kettle Valley	20	15.37	1.30	0.79	2.01	15.6	8.4	18.9	15.7	26.4
14	Southern Okanagan	84	69.08	1.22	0.97	1.51	13.1	23.5	13.9	18.7	17.6
15	Penticton	130	128.50	1.01	0.85	1.20	12.0	11.4	17.8	13.1	16.0
16	Keremeos	12	18.87	0.64	0.33	1.11	9.1	11.8	14.7	-	11.5
17	Princeton	26	20.96	1.24	0.81	1.82	31.8	6.7	16.2	6.4	21.5
18	Golden	19	24.17	0.79	0.47	1.23	6.3	6.2	9.6	12.9	19.0
19	Revelstoke	42	30.08	1.40 *	1.01	1.89	22.5	10.6	31.9	14.6	20.0
20	Salmon Arm	106	117.68	0.90	0.74	1.09	12.2	10.2	18.7	7.7	11.3
21	Armstrong-Spallumcheen	23	27.82	0.83	0.52	1.24	19.1	16.1	-	15.4	7.5
22	Vernon	164	178.08	0.92	0.79	1.07	10.8	12.8	14.3	13.2	12.7
23	Central Okanagan	307	401.55	0.76 ***	0.68	0.86	8.5	10.9	10.8	11.6	11.0
24	Kamloops	315	292.29	1.08	0.96	1.20	19.1	13.8	12.1	14.7	14.9
26	North Thompson	17	16.06	1.06	0.62	1.69	9.0	8.8	21.6	22.8	12.5
27	Cariboo-Chilcotin	154	135.57	1.14	0.96	1.33	16.6	15.8	12.8	18.9	15.0
28	Quesnel	91	82.12	1.11	0.89	1.36	16.3	17.2	14.3	11.9	17.3
29	Lillooet	23	16.95	1.36	0.86	2.04	47.3	11.9	13.2	8.1	13.6
30	South Cariboo	42	30.00	1.40 *	1.01	1.89	17.1	12.8	19.0	26.3	24.5
31	Merritt	51	37.83	1.35 *	1.00	1.77	24.8	28.5	15.4	10.8	14.0
32	Hope	32	31.32	1.02	0.70	1.44	17.1	16.4	12.5	13.7	14.7
33	Chilliwack	199	196.40	1.01	0.88	1.16	15.5	18.5	12.3	10.2	13.9
34	Abbotsford	196	241.98	0.81 **	0.70	0.93	13.0	13.7	10.0	10.9	9.3
35	Langley	220	249.70	0.88	0.77	1.01	11.9	11.9	11.0	15.0	11.3
36	Surrey	713	756.39	0.94	0.87	1.01	13.8	14.8	13.0	12.1	11.8
37	Delta	230	292.54	0.79 ***	0.69	0.89	12.7	7.6	11.1	9.0	14.5
38	Richmond	350	441.39	0.79 ***	0.71	0.88	12.7	12.6	9.4	11.8	8.7
39	Vancouver	2250	1820.46	1.24 ***	1.19	1.29	19.9	16.6	16.9	16.8	16.2
40	New Westminster	184	159.83	1.15	0.99	1.33	19.5	10.8	14.7	17.1	19.0
41	Burnaby	593	642.58	0.92	0.85	1.00	13.4	14.8	11.9	12.2	11.2
42	Maple Ridge	205	168.85	1.21 **	1.05	1.39	23.5	19.6	14.8	15.4	12.9
43	Coquitlam	361	434.41	0.83 ***	0.75	0.92	13.1	9.9	12.9	11.2	10.6
44	North Vancouver	384	453.12	0.85 ***	0.76	0.94	11.5	13.9	11.8	11.7	10.0
45	West Vancouver-Bowen Is	135	220.73	0.61 ***	0.51	0.72	8.5	6.1	7.9	7.9	11.4
46	Sechelt	69	79.72	0.87	0.67	1.10	7.7	19.1	12.0	9.6	13.6
47	Powell River	84	77.88	1.08	0.86	1.34	15.9	19.8	9.9	19.5	10.2
48	Howe Sound	50	55.66	0.90	0.67	1.18	15.2	18.4	11.4	12.3	6.6
49	Central Coast	14	10.43	1.34	0.73	2.25	27.9	19.7	20.6	6.4	18.6
50	Queen Charlotte	22	14.61	1.51	0.94	2.28	27.8	17.6	15.0	28.0	13.4
52	Prince Rupert	78	57.32	1.36 *	1.08	1.70	22.9	13.3	22.2	9.9	25.9
54	Smithers	37	42.53	0.87	0.61	1.20	18.4	6.8	10.2	15.8	9.3
55	Burns Lake	40	24.91	1.61 **	1.15	2.19	16.5	34.5	30.0	16.3	13.8
56	Nechako	63	48.38	1.30 *	1.00	1.67	23.0	20.1	13.1	19.0	15.8
57	Prince George	326	279.55	1.17 **	1.04	1.30	16.8	17.5	14.2	17.4	14.8
59	Peace River South	103	88.09	1.17	0.95	1.42	13.6	26.0	13.0	16.6	12.5
60	Peace River North	88	75.26	1.17	0.94	1.44	8.4	17.1	21.1	17.4	16.4
61	Greater Victoria	695	679.75	1.02	0.95	1.10	11.3	13.8	13.7	14.5	17.4
62	Sooke	145	152.21	0.95	0.80	1.12	14.8	12.6	13.3	14.4	10.9
63	Saanich	146	207.60	0.70 ***	0.59	0.83	7.3	10.7	10.0	10.0	9.6
64	Gulf Islands	37	52.20	0.71 *	0.50	0.98	13.0	11.8	8.4	5.6	13.7
65	Cowichan	146	145.74	1.00	0.85	1.18	13.8	14.6	10.2	11.5	18.3
66	Lake Cowichan	22	22.04	1.00	0.63	1.51	15.6	5.1	17.7	19.2	10.7
67	Ladysmith	59	56.70	1.04	0.79	1.34	3.4	18.5	9.9	15.6	22.0
68	Nanaimo	265	252.36	1.05	0.93	1.18	15.0	13.3	15.8	14.8	14.4
69	Qualicum	74	115.59	0.64 ***	0.50	0.80	10.2	6.8	12.8	10.0	6.1
70	Alberni	129	120.28	1.07	0.90	1.27	15.6	12.8	18.6	15.2	12.1
71	Courtenay	151	167.32	0.90	0.76	1.06	11.5	10.8	13.3	14.5	12.1
72	Campbell River	125	112.75	1.11	0.92	1.32	22.6	16.3	12.2	13.0	13.5
75	Mission	102	96.65	1.06	0.86	1.28	17.2	14.3	17.2	10.3	15.1
76	Agassiz-Harrison	23	22.78	1.01	0.64	1.52	9.8	12.8	14.6	9.3	22.5
77	Summerland	38	38.60	0.98	0.70	1.35	7.3	23.0	24.3	7.4	9.8
78	Enderby	24	22.28	1.08	0.69	1.60	10.6	11.9	22.5	7.4	22.7
80	Kitimat	44	45.03	0.98	0.71	1.31	10.8	14.6	12.3	12.8	17.4
81	Fort Nelson	18	12.44	1.45	0.86	2.29	11.2	20.1	24.2	32.9	18.2
84	Vancouver Island West	12	11.94	1.00	0.52	1.76	19.8	7.1	36.0	10.1	4.9
85	Vancouver Island North	60	43.03	1.39 *	1.06	1.80	23.2	11.7	19.8	17.6	19.6
87	Stikine	9	5.34	1.68	0.77	3.20	17.7	28.7	11.4	48.2	
88	Terrace	95	75.49	1.26 *	1.02	1.54	17.0	18.5	19.5	13.9	17.1
92	Nishga	5	2.90	1.72	0.56	4.02	-	-	27.4	95.9	-
94	Telegraph Creek	2	1.96	1.02	0.11	3.68	-	-	35.5	-	26.7
	Provincial Total	**11,574**	♦	**1.00**	♦	♦	14.6	14.1	13.7	13.5	13.5

218

Age 45 - 64 Years: Female

	Local Health Area	Observed Deaths	Expected Deaths	SMR (p)	95% C.I. Lower	Upper	ASMR 1985	1986	1987	1988	1989
1	Fernie	29	22.81	1.27	0.85	1.83	4.6	15.3	9.6	7.8	15.0
2	Cranbrook	36	38.59	0.93	0.65	1.29	3.1	7.1	8.2	9.9	11.5
3	Kimberley	21	19.28	1.09	0.67	1.66	9.4	6.7	4.3	17.5	7.4
4	Windermere	14	13.85	1.01	0.55	1.70	2.9	3.2	10.6	19.6	8.5
5	Creston	29	28.96	1.00	0.67	1.44	10.0	5.7	11.2	7.0	7.8
6	Kootenay Lake	10	8.18	1.22	0.59	2.25	12.4	-	14.2	3.8	15.8
7	Nelson	49	45.75	1.07	0.79	1.42	6.6	12.0	5.7	5.1	13.6
9	Castlegar	25	25.54	0.98	0.63	1.45	10.9	10.6	6.8	8.3	2.9
10	Arrow Lakes	6	9.08	0.66	0.24	1.44	11.3	3.9	10.9	-	-
11	Trail	62	50.77	1.22	0.94	1.57	9.8	11.9	8.1	9.3	8.1
12	Grand Forks	16	20.15	0.79	0.45	1.29	8.6	1.7	3.7	5.0	12.8
13	Kettle Valley	8	7.76	1.03	0.44	2.03	13.9	-	10.0	4.0	8.8
14	Southern Okanagan	32	43.67	0.73	0.50	1.03	5.3	4.1	4.7	6.0	9.6
15	Penticton	81	87.56	0.93	0.73	1.15	11.9	9.7	7.2	5.0	4.2
16	Keremeos	11	10.67	1.03	0.51	1.84	8.3	9.5	4.5	7.1	14.8
17	Princeton	8	11.18	0.72	0.31	1.41	12.4	4.8	3.3	-	12.2
18	Golden	8	11.67	0.69	0.30	1.35	7.0	3.5	13.5	3.7	-
19	Revelstoke	19	15.12	1.26	0.76	1.96	5.2	7.6	8.6	15.1	17.4
20	Salmon Arm	60	71.51	0.84	0.64	1.08	8.4	8.8	8.1	6.3	7.3
21	Armstrong-Spallumcheen	14	16.26	0.86	0.47	1.44	4.7	8.5	6.4	7.2	8.5
22	Vernon	101	107.14	0.94	0.77	1.15	8.2	7.7	6.0	9.3	7.2
23	Central Okanagan	211	259.10	0.81 **	0.71	0.93	6.1	5.9	5.9	8.7	7.6
24	Kamloops	163	159.00	1.03	0.87	1.20	8.3	8.3	8.3	7.0	9.9
26	North Thompson	7	7.76	0.90	0.36	1.86	6.0	15.7	9.7	5.4	-
27	Cariboo-Chilcotin	78	67.63	1.15	0.91	1.44	6.0	7.5	12.4	10.4	9.5
28	Quesnel	48	42.17	1.14	0.84	1.51	5.9	11.3	8.3	17.3	15.3
29	Lillooet	12	8.99	1.33	0.69	2.33	8.2	13.3	14.4	8.8	9.2
30	South Cariboo	19	14.41	1.32	0.79	2.06	11.4	15.3	18.0	11.0	6.6
31	Merritt	28	18.48	1.52 *	1.01	2.19	9.6	13.4	17.3	7.4	13.9
32	Hope	25	16.99	1.47	0.95	2.17	5.6	7.3	6.3	10.1	8.5
33	Chilliwack	113	122.17	0.92	0.76	1.11	6.5	5.7	7.5	8.0	7.6
34	Abbotsford	132	153.86	0.86	0.72	1.02	9.7	11.5	7.7	10.3	9.3
35	Langley	168	139.97	1.20 *	1.03	1.40	9.0	8.7	8.1	6.8	6.9
36	Surrey	437	455.20	0.96	0.87	1.05	8.2	9.6	6.4	6.6	7.0
37	Delta	145	157.18	0.92	0.78	1.09	7.7	6.1	4.8	6.2	6.9
38	Richmond	206	263.82	0.78 ***	0.68	0.90	8.8	8.5	8.8	7.9	7.5
39	Vancouver	1076	1070.62	1.01	0.95	1.07	9.1	11.3	8.9	10.6	11.1
40	New Westminster	125	99.64	1.25 *	1.04	1.49	8.6	7.9	7.8	6.6	7.5
41	Burnaby	370	387.36	0.96	0.86	1.06	9.6	11.6	9.9	6.5	8.3
42	Maple Ridge	104	93.11	1.12	0.91	1.35	9.3	7.4	7.6	9.4	8.2
43	Coquitlam	246	241.16	1.02	0.90	1.16	8.5	8.2	7.7	8.8	4.0
44	North Vancouver	242	267.14	0.91	0.80	1.03	6.3	8.7	5.3	5.6	4.0
45	West Vancouver-Bowen Is	103	137.39	0.75 **	0.61	0.91	11.1	14.0	6.4	6.6	9.3
46	Sechelt	52	48.17	1.08	0.81	1.42	7.6	10.8	15.5	7.8	8.1
47	Powell River	51	42.15	1.21	0.90	1.59	16.9	6.3	14.0	12.0	2.8
48	Howe Sound	32	26.28	1.22	0.83	1.72	15.3	-	15.2	6.7	13.1
49	Central Coast	7	5.42	1.29	0.52	2.66	6.7	17.6	13.6	20.3	14.8
50	Queen Charlotte	10	5.99	1.67	0.80	3.07	4.3	11.5	11.6	12.8	4.1
52	Prince Rupert	31	28.40	1.09	0.74	1.55	13.3	4.1	6.0	4.0	7.8
54	Smithers	18	20.73	0.87	0.51	1.37	14.9	12.8	-	3.2	3.2
55	Burns Lake	10	11.71	0.85	0.41	1.57	7.1	9.0	3.2	6.8	3.6
56	Nechako	17	23.17	0.73	0.43	1.17	12.5	8.4	10.7	9.0	10.4
57	Prince George	160	130.07	1.23 *	1.05	1.44	9.8	11.7	9.2	9.2	15.6
59	Peace River South	59	43.21	1.37 *	1.04	1.76	4.6	9.7	13.6	10.6	4.6
60	Peace River North	36	34.27	1.05	0.74	1.45	9.1	7.4	7.3	9.0	8.9
61	Greater Victoria	473	466.87	1.01	0.92	1.11	11.3	11.8	11.3	7.8	6.6
62	Sooke	97	84.61	1.15	0.93	1.40	6.5	4.9	6.8	6.4	7.8
63	Saanich	105	128.45	0.82 *	0.67	0.99	6.8	8.9	4.6	4.9	6.0
64	Gulf Islands	28	33.59	0.83	0.55	1.20	9.1	8.9	11.7	7.9	6.6
65	Cowichan	91	85.07	1.07	0.86	1.31	14.8	12.0	20.6	6.2	24.4
66	Lake Cowichan	23	11.75	1.96 **	1.24	2.94	13.6	6.2	15.3	6.0	12.7
67	Ladysmith	42	32.96	1.27	0.92	1.72	9.3	9.4	8.3	9.4	8.7
68	Nanaimo	165	150.65	1.10	0.93	1.28	4.0	4.9	10.8	10.8	11.1
69	Qualicum	78	74.79	1.04	0.82	1.30	9.3	8.7	16.9	9.0	8.7
70	Alberni	80	63.91	1.25	0.99	1.56	10.7	8.2	9.1	6.5	6.2
71	Courtenay	94	98.20	0.96	0.77	1.17	11.0	12.4	7.0	6.3	9.9
72	Campbell River	66	58.63	1.13	0.87	1.43	11.4	5.7	11.5	9.9	9.7
75	Mission	63	52.20	1.21	0.93	1.54	-	5.4	5.3	20.2	11.0
76	Agassiz-Harrison	12	11.31	1.06	0.55	1.85	9.8	9.0	10.8	3.8	8.4
77	Summerland	25	25.48	0.98	0.63	1.45	9.0	5.3	15.8	18.6	8.6
78	Enderby	17	12.93	1.31	0.77	2.11	9.2	5.6	7.0	13.4	10.5
80	Kitimat	21	19.54	1.07	0.66	1.64	13.4	28.2	-	13.9	13.1
81	Fort Nelson	10	5.82	1.72	0.82	3.16	26.7	7.6	33.4	-	10.4
84	Vancouver Island West	6	3.66	1.64	0.60	3.57	10.3	17.7	7.8	11.8	6.9
85	Vancouver Island North	22	17.34	1.27	0.79	1.92	-	12.9	61.2	-	-
87	Stikine	2	1.97	1.02	0.11	3.67	8.6	10.5	6.0	9.8	11.7
88	Terrace	41	34.38	1.19	0.86	1.62	-	17.9	-	24.9	-
92	Nishga	2	1.96	1.02	0.11	3.68	♦	-	-	-	-
94	Telegraph Creek	1	0.87	1.15	0.02	6.40					
	Provincial Total	6,745	♦	1.00	♦	♦	8.6	8.4	8.0	8.0	7.9

219

Age 65 - 84 Years: Male

	Local Health Area	Observed Deaths	Expected Deaths	SMR	(p)	95% C.I. Lower	Upper	ASMR 1985	1986	1987	1988	1989
1	Fernie	104	97.62	1.07		0.87	1.29	29.2	28.4	25.1	35.7	36.1
2	Cranbrook	184	158.06	1.16	*	1.00	1.35	40.7	37.0	29.6	31.1	29.5
3	Kimberley	101	111.78	0.90		0.74	1.10	33.3	28.0	22.8	21.2	27.8
4	Windermere	40	59.73	0.67	**	0.48	0.91	24.4	21.4	27.8	14.0	12.2
5	Creston	187	214.03	0.87		0.75	1.01	24.7	24.8	29.3	21.7	28.1
6	Kootenay Lake	29	60.18	0.48	***	0.32	0.69	10.6	14.0	18.6	10.9	12.8
7	Nelson	272	269.20	1.01		0.89	1.14	30.2	27.9	28.5	28.1	31.4
9	Castlegar	144	132.82	1.08		0.91	1.28	44.6	22.9	33.0	21.4	35.8
10	Arrow Lakes	65	65.47	0.99		0.77	1.27	21.9	26.4	30.5	28.4	35.1
11	Trail	300	283.86	1.06		0.94	1.18	32.6	30.5	31.3	30.3	27.5
12	Grand Forks	149	130.66	1.14		0.96	1.34	38.0	29.1	35.7	24.5	36.3
13	Kettle Valley	34	43.33	0.78		0.54	1.10	9.1	23.0	29.7	19.5	28.9
14	Southern Okanagan	300	313.62	0.96		0.85	1.07	32.7	21.6	29.4	29.6	24.2
15	Penticton	516	591.99	0.87	**	0.80	0.95	23.1	22.7	27.9	28.3	22.6
16	Keremeos	80	86.85	0.92		0.73	1.15	22.0	30.7	27.4	32.7	28.9
17	Princeton	73	48.48	1.51	**	1.18	1.89	73.3	45.8	39.4	31.1	35.4
18	Golden	36	40.52	0.89		0.62	1.23	19.4	38.6	26.3	35.9	16.5
19	Revelstoke	50	55.47	0.90		0.67	1.19	29.3	29.2	24.1	22.8	26.3
20	Salmon Arm	310	400.61	0.77	***	0.69	0.86	23.2	25.0	22.1	21.7	19.3
21	Armstrong-Spallumcheen	78	96.47	0.81		0.64	1.01	24.6	19.5	26.6	21.0	25.9
22	Vernon	542	590.53	0.92	*	0.84	1.00	28.2	28.7	25.7	27.9	21.4
23	Central Okanagan	1305	1507.72	0.87	***	0.82	0.91	23.8	25.8	24.4	25.1	25.0
24	Kamloops	653	592.06	1.10	*	1.02	1.19	41.4	28.2	31.4	28.9	29.6
26	North Thompson	29	30.07	0.96		0.65	1.39	49.7	18.2	28.1	14.7	17.2
27	Cariboo-Chilcotin	246	211.52	1.16	*	1.02	1.32	37.8	32.9	27.8	35.3	30.1
28	Quesnel	187	148.92	1.26	**	1.08	1.45	50.5	29.8	31.2	36.6	33.9
29	Lillooet	39	40.83	0.96		0.68	1.31	30.8	41.4	21.5	31.5	17.2
30	South Cariboo	72	66.23	1.09		0.85	1.37	38.5	29.6	17.9	36.3	33.7
31	Merritt	92	70.38	1.31	*	1.05	1.60	41.0	54.6	41.4	17.4	44.5
32	Hope	90	85.66	1.05		0.84	1.29	33.4	38.8	29.3	35.6	16.4
33	Chilliwack	638	636.71	1.00		0.93	1.08	31.2	30.4	25.3	28.5	29.2
34	Abbotsford	749	871.47	0.86	***	0.80	0.92	27.3	23.9	24.7	24.8	22.5
35	Langley	659	659.61	1.00		0.92	1.08	24.4	31.6	30.8	27.7	29.4
36	Surrey	2090	2102.19	0.99		0.95	1.04	29.8	28.1	29.2	27.5	28.4
37	Delta	533	544.88	0.98		0.90	1.06	28.2	28.2	29.6	28.3	26.9
38	Richmond	849	873.17	0.97		0.91	1.04	30.7	30.2	25.9	26.3	27.7
39	Vancouver	5870	5392.72	1.09	***	1.06	1.12	31.8	31.3	31.0	31.4	31.9
40	New Westminster	672	569.35	1.18	***	1.09	1.27	35.8	34.7	31.8	35.0	34.5
41	Burnaby	1683	1624.40	1.04		0.99	1.09	27.9	30.7	31.5	31.3	27.6
42	Maple Ridge	447	402.91	1.11	*	1.01	1.22	32.7	31.7	31.9	32.4	31.8
43	Coquitlam	843	701.50	1.20	***	1.12	1.29	32.4	38.4	34.5	34.8	33.0
44	North Vancouver	906	843.45	1.07	*	1.01	1.15	32.7	29.2	32.5	31.2	30.7
45	West Vancouver-Bowen Is	489	642.32	0.76	***	0.70	0.83	22.4	23.3	22.8	22.8	18.4
46	Sechelt	280	287.16	0.98		0.86	1.10	29.2	21.5	27.6	30.4	30.8
47	Powell River	213	213.74	1.00		0.87	1.14	28.2	38.5	28.5	25.6	23.8
48	Howe Sound	89	79.41	1.12		0.90	1.38	51.0	31.5	39.3	42.2	14.6
49	Central Coast	29	25.68	1.13		0.76	1.62	46.5	18.6	38.6	40.9	23.2
50	Queen Charlotte	23	23.87	0.96		0.61	1.45	29.2	28.3	29.8	32.8	18.1
52	Prince Rupert	111	90.28	1.23	*	1.01	1.48	24.1	41.8	39.4	40.1	28.6
54	Smithers	86	64.23	1.34	*	1.07	1.65	41.1	35.9	37.2	46.7	31.7
55	Burns Lake	50	47.52	1.05		0.78	1.39	31.4	39.6	24.6	18.7	38.5
56	Nechako	76	88.01	0.86		0.68	1.08	22.6	20.6	30.0	17.6	32.3
57	Prince George	450	338.68	1.33	***	1.21	1.46	39.9	38.2	42.2	35.3	35.8
59	Peace River South	167	162.45	1.03		0.88	1.20	31.3	34.5	26.4	22.7	32.4
60	Peace River North	111	115.41	0.96		0.79	1.16	33.3	23.8	23.9	29.3	26.8
61	Greater Victoria	2698	2952.58	0.91	***	0.88	0.95	28.3	26.6	27.1	25.4	24.6
62	Sooke	285	346.31	0.82	***	0.73	0.92	23.2	23.6	18.3	25.7	24.7
63	Saanich	499	653.49	0.76	***	0.70	0.83	24.4	23.7	21.7	21.2	20.9
64	Gulf Islands	167	221.56	0.75	***	0.64	0.88	21.3	23.7	28.4	14.7	22.7
65	Cowichan	428	430.70	0.99		0.90	1.09	30.0	31.2	23.9	28.6	28.7
66	Lake Cowichan	44	49.22	0.89		0.65	1.20	31.3	16.9	27.5	25.7	31.2
67	Ladysmith	208	203.43	1.02		0.89	1.17	35.5	24.0	25.1	31.9	30.8
68	Nanaimo	830	760.03	1.09	*	1.02	1.17	28.2	36.6	31.7	30.6	29.6
69	Qualicum	453	472.07	0.96		0.87	1.05	31.2	30.5	26.4	26.7	28.1
70	Alberni	281	255.18	1.10		0.98	1.24	35.9	28.3	30.1	36.3	28.3
71	Courtenay	431	420.20	1.03		0.93	1.13	31.6	32.7	26.3	31.9	25.9
72	Campbell River	240	208.19	1.15	*	1.01	1.31	33.9	36.6	32.9	37.6	29.4
75	Mission	261	278.24	0.94		0.83	1.06	24.8	21.3	32.0	24.5	
76	Agassiz-Harrison	68	64.05	1.06		0.82	1.35	22.6	21.6	29.5	40.6	41.4
77	Summerland	159	191.84	0.83	*	0.70	0.97	22.0	36.1	24.6	22.5	14.6
78	Enderby	85	79.78	1.07		0.85	1.32	47.5	39.4	26.9	19.3	26.3
80	Kitimat	31	32.03	0.97		0.66	1.37	20.2	33.2	29.3	23.3	40.1
81	Fort Nelson	12	9.91	1.21		0.62	2.11	-	20.5	78.4	26.1	57.8
84	Vancouver Island West	7	4.45	1.57		0.63	3.24	39.2	54.8	26.5	62.2	39.1
85	Vancouver Island North	52	36.61	1.42	*	1.06	1.86	20.4	63.9	52.6	23.1	49.3
87	Stikine	6	6.77	0.89		0.32	1.93	12.3	19.0	26.5	-	
88	Terrace	119	112.48	1.06		0.88	1.27	21.8	37.4	44.9	28.7	23.2
92	Nishga	11	8.22	1.34		0.67	2.39	23.3	38.1	98.1	53.2	17.1
94	Telegraph Creek	0	3.11	-		-	-	-	-	-	-	-
	Provincial Total	**31,801**	♦	1.00		♦	♦	29.8	29.3	28.8	28.5	27.7

Age 65 - 84 Years: Female

	Local Health Area	Observed Deaths	Expected Deaths	SMR (p)	95% C.I. Lower	Upper	ASMR 1985	1986	1987	1988	1989
1	Fernie	71	55.85	1.27	0.99	1.60	29.0	29.2	29.6	28.0	18.2
2	Cranbrook	133	114.52	1.16	0.97	1.38	37.8	25.9	18.9	19.6	22.2
3	Kimberley	89	74.94	1.19	0.95	1.46	25.5	28.3	22.9	30.0	19.5
4	Windermere	32	32.99	0.97	0.66	1.37	44.7	9.2	32.4	11.7	5.3
5	Creston	131	132.63	0.99	0.83	1.17	22.8	14.3	24.2	24.9	16.9
6	Kootenay Lake	25	32.59	0.77	0.50	1.13	24.6	10.2	4.2	18.0	20.4
7	Nelson	167	185.45	0.90	0.77	1.05	23.0	20.4	18.2	21.1	12.5
9	Castlegar	90	88.98	1.01	0.81	1.24	17.5	22.6	19.1	25.9	22.7
10	Arrow Lakes	34	42.63	0.80	0.55	1.11	18.3	17.8	16.3	18.1	11.7
11	Trail	221	192.70	1.15 *	1.00	1.31	28.9	25.7	20.7	24.1	16.2
12	Grand Forks	91	81.13	1.12	0.90	1.38	28.5	22.9	20.4	9.4	19.6
13	Kettle Valley	17	18.90	0.90	0.52	1.44	16.7	20.6	17.0	19.7	17.6
14	Southern Okanagan	167	190.16	0.88	0.75	1.02	16.7	20.6	17.0	19.7	17.6
15	Penticton	348	415.38	0.84 ***	0.75	0.93	17.1	19.2	24.4	24.4	21.7
16	Keremeos	38	38.68	0.98	0.70	1.35	23.5	22.7	23.5	20.7	30.8
17	Princeton	34	30.27	1.12	0.78	1.57	23.5	22.7	23.5	20.7	30.8
18	Golden	28	19.81	1.41	0.94	2.04	74.2	25.0	29.6	12.4	33.2
19	Revelstoke	47	40.95	1.15	0.84	1.53	35.6	16.0	18.0	28.6	29.8
20	Salmon Arm	197	218.27	0.90	0.78	1.04	19.1	20.8	21.1	18.8	18.1
21	Armstrong-Spallumcheen	41	55.68	0.74 *	0.53	1.00	20.6	11.6	17.8	15.4	12.9
22	Vernon	380	403.47	0.94	0.85	1.04	21.6	21.1	20.1	17.7	18.8
23	Central Okanagan	803	986.96	0.81 ***	0.76	0.87	17.4	17.0	18.5	15.9	17.3
24	Kamloops	425	397.84	1.07	0.97	1.17	21.8	21.9	20.4	23.2	24.1
26	North Thompson	28	18.78	1.49	0.99	2.15	33.7	22.0	50.8	22.0	38.0
27	Cariboo-Chilcotin	140	115.46	1.21 *	1.02	1.43	25.4	25.3	18.8	28.1	27.5
28	Quesnel	100	82.94	1.21	0.98	1.47	27.1	29.0	22.4	27.9	22.3
29	Lillooet	26	18.25	1.43	0.93	2.09	14.0	48.5	35.3	26.8	28.9
30	South Cariboo	45	36.23	1.24	0.91	1.66	15.5	19.2	39.6	34.3	19.7
31	Merritt	65	41.43	1.57 ***	1.21	2.00	32.9	27.3	35.9	39.5	30.8
32	Hope	43	46.10	0.93	0.67	1.26	14.9	23.3	9.8	25.5	19.4
33	Chilliwack	446	448.32	0.99	0.90	1.09	20.6	23.1	18.1	22.1	20.4
34	Abbotsford	520	611.57	0.85 ***	0.78	0.93	19.3	20.8	16.7	16.8	16.4
35	Langley	453	456.72	0.99	0.90	1.09	19.2	25.3	17.8	21.8	20.1
36	Surrey	1502	1560.53	0.96	0.91	1.01	21.7	21.6	20.4	19.1	18.6
37	Delta	420	404.07	1.04	0.94	1.14	23.5	22.4	22.1	19.0	22.4
38	Richmond	726	694.49	1.05	0.97	1.12	23.1	25.3	19.3	22.4	20.3
39	Vancouver	4760	4730.10	1.01	0.98	1.04	20.9	20.9	21.1	22.2	20.6
40	New Westminster	556	576.06	0.97	0.89	1.05	19.3	20.3	20.1	20.5	22.6
41	Burnaby	1463	1364.17	1.07 **	1.02	1.13	24.7	22.4	21.4	22.8	21.6
42	Maple Ridge	343	294.20	1.17 **	1.05	1.30	29.3	27.5	20.4	23.6	22.2
43	Coquitlam	702	554.63	1.27 ***	1.17	1.36	27.0	26.7	26.0	26.9	26.6
44	North Vancouver	818	744.56	1.10 **	1.02	1.18	25.3	21.0	20.6	23.0	25.2
45	West Vancouver-Bowen Is	525	545.56	0.96	0.88	1.05	18.9	20.2	20.2	21.9	19.1
46	Sechelt	186	179.78	1.03	0.89	1.19	19.5	25.9	24.1	22.1	16.1
47	Powell River	137	147.96	0.93	0.78	1.09	19.0	16.9	20.1	18.7	22.3
48	Howe Sound	43	48.55	0.89	0.64	1.19	16.0	23.7	15.4	23.4	16.6
49	Central Coast	14	10.72	1.31	0.71	2.19	22.1	74.8	26.1	-	39.3
50	Queen Charlotte	18	13.74	1.31	0.78	2.07	31.5	15.3	45.3	44.8	14.3
52	Prince Rupert	80	60.14	1.33 *	1.05	1.66	41.8	23.0	31.3	15.8	30.1
54	Smithers	53	40.58	1.31	0.98	1.71	35.6	39.0	10.5	24.5	30.2
55	Burns Lake	24	18.07	1.33	0.85	1.98	15.9	42.8	-	43.1	28.1
56	Nechako	42	46.18	0.91	0.66	1.23	20.1	21.0	12.9	24.3	24.4
57	Prince George	295	209.19	1.41 ***	1.25	1.58	35.3	34.2	32.1	19.6	27.8
59	Peace River South	111	95.90	1.16	0.95	1.39	26.8	25.1	30.0	23.4	17.3
60	Peace River North	78	68.66	1.14	0.90	1.42	21.3	25.7	15.4	21.4	32.4
61	Greater Victoria	2452	2720.95	0.90 ***	0.87	0.94	19.5	18.7	19.2	19.2	18.0
62	Sooke	213	213.76	1.00	0.87	1.14	24.2	24.0	19.2	23.8	16.1
63	Saanich	349	413.29	0.84 **	0.76	0.94	14.8	15.6	21.4	15.4	20.8
64	Gulf Islands	118	132.29	0.89	0.74	1.07	12.9	23.5	17.0	25.3	22.2
65	Cowichan	327	298.26	1.10	0.98	1.22	24.4	19.8	23.4	21.2	26.2
66	Lake Cowichan	30	29.15	1.03	0.69	1.47	38.4	10.6	16.3	16.8	25.3
67	Ladysmith	153	130.62	1.17	0.99	1.37	22.3	22.1	25.0	27.6	25.0
68	Nanaimo	559	523.69	1.07	0.98	1.16	27.5	18.2	20.0	21.3	25.8
69	Qualicum	239	276.27	0.87 *	0.76	0.98	21.1	16.9	20.9	16.5	15.8
70	Alberni	222	179.53	1.24 **	1.08	1.41	23.3	15.3	21.3	34.5	31.5
71	Courtenay	290	275.67	1.05	0.93	1.18	22.5	20.6	19.1	21.8	26.4
72	Campbell River	151	138.21	1.09	0.93	1.28	25.0	21.0	23.9	23.9	21.2
75	Mission	156	167.87	0.93	0.79	1.09	24.3	17.7	15.8	19.4	20.2
76	Agassiz-Harrison	35	38.44	0.91	0.63	1.27	21.2	14.1	20.6	18.2	21.2
77	Summerland	117	126.07	0.93	0.77	1.11	22.5	20.8	21.7	19.2	14.2
78	Enderby	47	54.31	0.87	0.64	1.15	19.8	18.3	11.0	17.4	24.5
80	Kitimat	32	18.23	1.76 **	1.20	2.48	61.3	21.3	36.7	38.5	29.5
81	Fort Nelson	4	3.34	1.20	0.32	3.06	-	-	20.0	20.0	56.4
84	Vancouver Island West	3	3.88	0.77	0.16	2.26	20.0	♦	43.1	-	-
85	Vancouver Island North	24	23.79	1.01	0.65	1.50	8.3	21.4	22.1	15.2	35.9
87	Stikine	1	3.78	0.26	0.00	1.47	-	♦	-	-	-
88	Terrace	66	56.58	1.17	0.90	1.48	32.2	24.9	34.8	12.1	24.6
92	Nishga	7	3.92	1.79	0.72	3.68	♦	15.0	67.8	-	47.0
94	Telegraph Creek	2	1.70	1.17	0.13	4.24	100.2	-	-	-	18.3
	Provincial Total	23,969	♦	1.00	♦	♦	21.9	21.1	20.5	21.0	20.5

Age 85 Years and Over: Male

	Local Health Area	Observed Deaths	Expected Deaths	SMR (p)	95% C.I. Lower	Upper	ASMR 1985	1986	1987	1988	1989
1	Fernie	22	20.80	1.06	0.66	1.60	8.0	8.1	13.8	12.1	6.3
2	Cranbrook	47	33.79	1.39 *	1.02	1.85	12.3	14.4	8.8	21.7	7.8
3	Kimberley	28	16.33	1.71 *	1.14	2.48	11.7	27.0	22.5	6.3	14.4
4	Windermere	3	13.94	0.22 ı	0.04	0.63	-	3.4	-	5.3	-
5	Creston	66	69.78	0.95	0.73	1.20	11.9	11.6	5.1	9.9	5.9
6	Kootenay Lake	8	11.70	0.68	0.29	1.35	3.0	5.1	9.2	11.7	3.9
7	Nelson	69	77.02	0.90	0.70	1.13	8.9	13.0	6.7	10.2	3.6
9	Castlegar	16	27.53	0.58 *	0.33	0.94	3.9	4.0	8.7	1.4	8.2
10	Arrow Lakes	21	19.85	1.06	0.65	1.62	8.4	15.2	13.2	7.2	4.8
11	Trail	73	74.10	0.99	0.77	1.24	7.1	8.2	8.3	11.8	9.3
12	Grand Forks	31	28.03	1.11	0.75	1.57	8.4	14.2	5.1	10.9	11.7
13	Kettle Valley	9	14.37	0.63	0.29	1.19	14.4	10.1	3.0	7.2	-
14	Southern Okanagan	95	89.51	1.06	0.86	1.30	7.8	10.1	9.4	9.9	11.3
15	Penticton	155	179.41	0.86	0.73	1.01	7.6	7.2	7.3	10.0	7.3
16	Keremeos	15	17.61	0.85	0.48	1.41	10.6	10.1	6.3	7.2	5.8
17	Princeton	21	12.01	1.75 *	1.08	2.67	25.3	6.7	15.8	18.4	15.2
18	Golden	11	12.18	0.90	0.45	1.62	12.6	15.2	7.2	2.7	9.6
19	Revelstoke	19	14.37	1.32	0.80	2.07	21.7	6.7	14.0	8.4	13.8
20	Salmon Arm	72	82.95	0.87	0.68	1.09	6.7	5.6	10.6	11.1	6.4
21	Armstrong-Spallumcheen	22	25.50	0.86	0.54	1.31	11.0	6.1	10.1	10.5	3.9
22	Vernon	165	181.85	0.91	0.77	1.06	9.2	10.1	7.6	6.5	8.5
23	Central Okanagan	372	431.50	0.86 **	0.78	0.95	8.8	6.9	8.1	7.6	8.0
24	Kamloops	180	149.08	1.21 *	1.04	1.40	13.0	10.4	11.1	9.2	11.7
26	North Thompson	6	5.23	1.15	0.42	2.50	-	10.1	20.2	14.4	6.3
27	Cariboo-Chilcotin	41	42.75	0.96	0.69	1.30	8.8	4.8	11.3	8.6	9.7
28	Quesnel	24	42.97	0.56 **	0.36	0.83	5.9	3.0	5.4	5.6	5.7
29	Lillooet	13	13.99	0.93	0.49	1.59	10.8	20.2	8.0	3.0	5.9
30	South Cariboo	16	20.96	0.76	0.44	1.24	12.6	7.6	7.8	8.7	-
31	Merritt	22	18.30	1.20	0.75	1.82	20.8	12.6	10.5	5.1	7.6
32	Hope	13	10.15	1.28	0.68	2.19	10.1	15.2	9.2	13.8	10.8
33	Chilliwack	186	170.43	1.09	0.94	1.26	11.0	7.4	11.4	10.1	10.3
34	Abbotsford	249	264.32	0.94	0.83	1.07	9.4	6.7	8.0	8.7	10.1
35	Langley	179	178.32	1.00	0.86	1.16	10.0	9.6	8.3	7.6	10.6
36	Surrey	553	593.63	0.93	0.86	1.01	9.5	8.2	9.1	8.2	7.8
37	Delta	120	100.06	1.20	0.99	1.43	12.8	13.3	10.3	7.0	11.4
38	Richmond	187	188.64	0.99	0.85	1.14	8.5	12.7	12.4	7.3	5.6
39	Vancouver	1861	1896.49	0.98	0.94	1.03	9.8	8.2	8.7	9.3	9.0
40	New Westminster	166	163.78	1.01	0.87	1.18	10.8	6.9	11.5	9.0	8.4
41	Burnaby	514	487.98	1.05	0.96	1.15	9.2	9.5	10.3	8.8	10.4
42	Maple Ridge	124	110.86	1.12	0.93	1.33	12.5	12.9	8.1	9.6	8.6
43	Coquitlam	231	208.09	1.11	0.97	1.26	14.4	8.8	11.3	8.1	9.0
44	North Vancouver	239	196.67	1.22 **	1.07	1.38	12.3	10.6	11.4	11.2	10.4
45	West Vancouver-Bowen Is	160	169.61	0.94	0.80	1.10	8.0	5.8	9.0	9.2	10.7
46	Sechelt	70	60.30	1.16	0.90	1.47	11.5	13.5	6.9	12.3	9.6
47	Powell River	68	60.73	1.12	0.87	1.42	8.6	13.5	10.0	8.3	11.2
48	Howe Sound	11	12.88	0.85	0.43	1.53	3.6	6.7	21.1	7.2	3.2
49	Central Coast	3	2.34	1.28	0.26	3.74	♦	-	12.6	-	10.1
50	Queen Charlotte	7	10.83	0.65	0.26	1.33	12.6	-	8.4	3.6	6.3
52	Prince Rupert	33	31.53	1.05	0.72	1.47	8.4	10.1	6.8	13.3	8.9
54	Smithers	22	15.25	1.44	0.90	2.18	6.3	13.5	15.8	16.0	14.0
55	Burns Lake	12	11.70	1.03	0.53	1.79	11.9	-	5.1	23.0	6.3
56	Nechako	19	24.50	0.78	0.47	1.21	5.8	10.1	5.8	9.7	4.7
57	Prince George	83	66.20	1.25	1.00	1.55	11.9	13.5	8.4	10.0	13.7
59	Peace River South	55	49.61	1.11	0.84	1.44	9.9	6.1	15.3	8.3	11.1
60	Peace River North	41	37.86	1.08	0.78	1.47	7.0	8.8	13.2	9.0	11.0
61	Greater Victoria	1138	1117.45	1.02	0.96	1.08	10.5	8.9	8.8	9.6	8.9
62	Sooke	54	64.89	0.83	0.63	1.09	8.9	6.2	7.4	9.0	6.6
63	Saanich	136	127.46	1.07	0.90	1.26	10.0	10.9	10.8	8.1	9.4
64	Gulf Islands	42	40.91	1.03	0.74	1.39	12.0	7.6	8.4	10.3	8.9
65	Cowichan	114	116.83	0.98	0.80	1.17	9.9	8.1	9.9	9.8	7.2
66	Lake Cowichan	3	9.63	0.31 +	0.06	0.91	-	-	-	-	10.8
67	Ladysmith	48	50.40	0.95	0.70	1.26	7.9	12.1	6.7	6.3	10.4
68	Nanaimo	176	162.10	1.09	0.93	1.26	10.2	8.0	8.4	12.0	10.7
69	Qualicum	92	84.34	1.09	0.88	1.34	7.5	11.2	8.3	8.6	13.9
70	Alberni	58	43.83	1.32 *	1.00	1.71	14.4	10.1	15.4	15.2	6.9
71	Courtenay	101	107.55	0.94	0.76	1.14	7.4	10.6	8.5	8.9	7.8
72	Campbell River	48	35.51	1.35	1.00	1.79	25.3	17.3	9.3	9.4	4.4
75	Mission	79	69.43	1.14	0.90	1.42	11.0	7.4	8.4	14.1	11.1
76	Agassiz-Harrison	7	13.47	0.52	0.21	1.07	-	20.2	6.7	-	2.8
77	Summerland	68	67.82	1.00	0.78	1.27	10.5	6.5	10.9	8.4	9.6
78	Enderby	28	29.86	0.94	0.62	1.36	9.8	6.7	8.9	9.5	7.9
80	Kitimat	7	2.69	2.61 *	1.04	5.37	-	-	8.4	12.6	20.2
81	Fort Nelson	1	3.99	0.25	0.00	1.39	-	-	-	-	♦
84	Vancouver Island West	1	0.35	2.83	0.04	15.74	-	-	♦	-	-
85	Vancouver Island North	8	8.04	0.99	0.43	1.96	-	20.2	4.6	3.6	3.6
87	Stikine	0	0.54	-	-	-	-	-	-	-	-
88	Terrace	29	42.71	0.68 *	0.45	0.98	4.0	5.6	4.0	6.8	9.9
92	Nishga	3	3.50	0.86	0.17	2.50	-	-	-	25.3	33.7
94	Telegraph Creek	0	0.00	-	-	-	-	-	-	-	-
	Provincial Total	**9,090**	♦	1.00	♦	♦	9.9	8.8	9.2	9.0	8.9

Age 85 Years and Over: Female

	Local Health Area	Observed Deaths	Expected Deaths	SMR (p)	95% C.I. Lower	95% C.I. Upper	ASMR 1985	1986	1987	1988	1989
1	Fernie	31	28.43	1.09	0.74	1.55	9.6	19.8	14.9	3.8	14.2
2	Cranbrook	53	66.84	0.79	0.59	1.04	14.4	5.1	9.2	9.8	6.2
3	Kimberley	43	39.86	1.08	0.78	1.45	7.0	23.8	11.6	11.0	6.5
4	Windermere	3	7.16	0.42	0.08	1.22	-	-	6.4	12.8	-
5	Creston	63	62.16	1.01	0.78	1.30	13.4	6.7	12.5	13.2	10.2
6	Kootenay Lake	5	15.84	0.32 **	0.10	0.74	-	7.7	5.1	2.8	3.0
7	Nelson	121	106.30	1.14	0.94	1.36	14.2	14.8	7.3	14.4	11.8
9	Castlegar	34	39.66	0.86	0.59	1.20	17.7	6.2	9.4	9.0	7.6
10	Arrow Lakes	27	27.48	0.98	0.65	1.43	6.8	17.6	11.3	7.3	11.5
11	Trail	105	93.77	1.12	0.92	1.36	10.5	9.7	13.8	13.0	14.6
12	Grand Forks	39	31.48	1.24	0.88	1.69	15.4	17.3	20.6	10.0	8.0
13	Kettle Valley	1	5.44	0.18	0.00	1.02	-	-	-	♦	-
14	Southern Okanagan	99	106.27	0.93	0.76	1.13	9.1	9.3	8.1	13.1	11.4
15	Penticton	193	223.89	0.86 *	0.74	0.99	10.8	8.4	10.3	8.5	9.6
16	Keremeos	12	18.20	0.66	0.34	1.15	11.0	6.2	3.0	2.8	13.7
17	Princeton	23	21.80	1.06	0.67	1.58	7.2	5.1	19.2	12.4	14.9
18	Golden	13	11.20	1.16	0.62	1.99	-	-	33.6	16.5	19.2
19	Revelstoke	29	26.23	1.11	0.74	1.59	11.5	17.6	13.7	10.7	8.3
20	Salmon Arm	98	111.98	0.00	0.71	1.07	13.2	10.3	5.4	6.8	12.8
21	Armstrong-Spallumcheen	26	29.09	0.89	0.58	1.31	8.3	8.8	8.1	9.8	13.4
22	Vernon	218	215.54	1.01	0.88	1.15	12.8	12.5	10.0	11.4	9.7
23	Central Okanagan	483	499.44	0.97	0.88	1.06	12.1	8.0	12.3	10.6	10.4
24	Kamloops	218	212.91	1.02	0.89	1.17	11.6	10.6	13.1	11.2	10.1
26	North Thompson	2	3.84	0.52	0.06	1.88	19.2	15.4	-	-	-
27	Cariboo-Chilcotin	49	56.31	0.87	0.64	1.15	8.5	12.8	5.2	11.0	10.1
28	Quesnel	54	35.13	1.54 **	1.15	2.01	19.2	11.5	27.2	9.2	16.9
29	Lillooet	11	10.63	1.03	0.52	1.85	-	20.5	17.7	17.7	5.9
30	South Cariboo	11	14.92	0.74	0.37	1.32	3.7	11.5	11.5	3.7	10.5
31	Merritt	16	26.52	0.60 *	0.34	0.98	9.4	7.7	-	11.5	3.7
32	Hope	15	15.77	0.95	0.53	1.57	12.1	-	21.0	10.0	8.9
33	Chilliwack	249	205.91	1.21 **	1.06	1.37	15.2	15.1	16.2	10.5	10.2
34	Abbotsford	345	366.64	0.94	0.84	1.05	12.1	11.3	9.2	9.1	10.5
35	Langley	252	247.45	1.02	0.90	1.15	13.7	11.7	12.3	9.1	9.9
36	Surrey	797	821.59	0.97	0.90	1.04	10.7	12.0	11.0	10.9	9.2
37	Delta	284	249.95	1.14 *	1.01	1.28	12.5	10.8	14.7	11.6	12.9
38	Richmond	353	371.89	0.95	0.85	1.05	10.5	11.1	11.7	10.5	8.8
39	Vancouver	3476	3530.02	0.98	0.95	1.02	10.2	10.9	11.1	11.2	11.0
40	New Westminster	349	371.95	0.94	0.84	1.04	11.1	10.7	11.5	10.5	8.0
41	Burnaby	1018	1014.46	1.00	0.94	1.07	10.0	10.8	12.0	11.0	11.5
42	Maple Ridge	204	207.39	0.98	0.85	1.13	11.2	7.8	12.2	11.8	10.8
43	Coquitlam	351	321.07	1.09	0.98	1.21	16.4	11.9	12.1	9.3	11.3
44	North Vancouver	567	485.54	1.17 ***	1.07	1.27	13.3	13.0	13.8	12.1	12.2
45	West Vancouver-Bowen Is	437	412.93	1.06	0.96	1.16	10.6	10.3	12.7	13.3	11.1
46	Sechelt	84	78.42	1.07	0.85	1.33	8.0	12.4	12.6	5.4	19.5
47	Powell River	78	85.15	0.92	0.72	1.14	11.6	12.6	11.2	7.0	9.1
48	Howe Sound	21	20.76	1.01	0.63	1.55	10.0	18.5	14.2	6.6	8.8
49	Central Coast	4	2.14	1.87	0.50	4.79	♦	15.4	25.6	-	19.2
50	Queen Charlotte	7	7.01	1.00	0.40	2.06	19.2	7.7	14.0	7.7	11.0
52	Prince Rupert	32	32.15	1.00	0.68	1.41	13.5	6.2	17.3	14.6	3.6
54	Smithers	15	23.22	0.65	0.36	1.07	6.8	5.1	16.5	4.3	4.5
55	Burns Lake	14	12.92	1.08	0.59	1.82	8.9	10.3	32.9	4.3	9.0
56	Nechako	27	26.13	1.03	0.68	1.50	8.1	6.6	16.6	17.6	8.3
57	Prince George	91	93.21	0.98	0.79	1.20	10.0	10.5	11.1	9.4	12.7
59	Peace River South	48	55.97	0.86	0.63	1.14	8.8	9.6	15.6	7.2	6.0
60	Peace River North	30	32.50	0.92	0.62	1.32	7.7	9.6	4.9	11.8	14.6
61	Greater Victoria	2177	2277.67	0.96 *	0.92	1.00	10.8	9.6	10.4	11.1	10.8
62	Sooke	143	110.13	1.30 **	1.09	1.53	21.6	17.4	15.1	7.2	12.4
63	Saanich	249	233.36	1.07	0.94	1.21	11.7	10.6	13.1	12.3	11.1
64	Gulf Islands	60	55.64	1.08	0.82	1.39	15.2	7.2	9.2	15.4	12.2
65	Cowichan	175	164.72	1.06	0.91	1.23	13.1	10.3	13.2	10.8	11.4
66	Lake Cowichan	6	9.63	0.62	0.23	1.36	7.0	-	-	7.0	16.5
67	Ladysmith	49	54.32	0.90	0.67	1.19	8.3	11.9	11.1	8.8	9.6
68	Nanaimo	277	265.84	1.04	0.92	1.17	13.5	9.7	11.9	11.4	11.0
69	Qualicum	141	133.24	1.06	0.89	1.25	12.7	13.6	12.5	8.6	11.3
70	Alberni	82	78.70	1.04	0.83	1.29	12.4	9.2	11.9	13.3	10.6
71	Courtenay	156	154.56	1.01	0.86	1.18	11.0	10.8	10.9	11.6	11.3
72	Campbell River	67	69.82	0.96	0.74	1.22	11.8	10.5	11.9	11.4	7.7
75	Mission	111	104.11	1.07	0.88	1.28	10.3	8.8	15.5	9.0	14.8
76	Agassiz-Harrison	11	14.06	0.78	0.39	1.40	17.1	-	3.7	20.2	3.8
77	Summerland	104	69.31	1.50 ***	1.23	1.82	14.0	20.2	12.4	19.8	16.4
78	Enderby	29	20.39	1.42	0.95	2.04	13.6	12.3	11.4	27.5	13.7
80	Kitimat	6	13.36	0.45 *	0.16	0.98	3.1	15.4	-	3.7	7.3
81	Fort Nelson	1	2.44	0.41	0.01	2.28	-	-	-	♦	-
84	Vancouver Island West	2	2.73	0.73	0.08	2.65	-	♦	-	38.4	-
85	Vancouver Island North	6	13.20	0.45 *	0.17	0.99	-	-	12.8	12.1	-
87	Stikine	0	0.15	-	-	-	-	-	-	-	-
88	Terrace	27	25.33	1.07	0.70	1.55	14.4	8.8	12.0	20.4	2.6
92	Nishga	1	1.43	0.70	0.01	3.90	-	-	-	♦	-
94	Telegraph Creek	1	0.73	1.36	0.02	7.59	-	-	♦	-	-
	Provincial Total	**15,111**	♦	**1.00**	♦	♦	**11.2**	**10.8**	**11.5**	**10.9**	**10.7**